Competitive Advantage on the Shop Floor

Competitive Advantage on the Shop Floor

William Lazonick

Harvard University Press
Cambridge, Massachusetts
London, England
1990

Library of Congress Cataloging-in-Publication Data

Lazonick, William.
   Competitive advantage on the shop floor / William Lazonick.
      p.   cm.
   Includes bibliographical references.
   ISBN 0-674-15416-9
   1. Labor theory of value. 2. Marxian economics. 3. Cotton
textile industry—Great Britain—History—19th century.
   4. Manufactures—History—20th century. I. Title.
HB206.L39   1990   90-32203
338.4'767721'0941—dc20   rev. CIP

Acknowledgments

The research for this book began at Harvard University during the 1970s. The general impetus to study the dynamics of capitalist development came from the radical economics movement of the time. The more specific impetus to undertake the research on organization and technology in the British cotton textile industry came from Stephen Marglin's "What Do Bosses Do?". The National Science Foundation and the Merrimack Valley Textile Museum (now the Museum of American Textile History) provided major funding for the cotton textile research. The administrative efforts of Daniel Newlon of the National Science Foundation and Thomas Leavitt of the Museum of American Textile History are much appreciated. These sources of funding permitted the prolonged and indispensable collaboration of Thomas Brush and William Mass in the research project. In Lancashire, England, Alan Fowler was helpful in directing me to relevant sources and in sharing with me the insights of his own research on British labor history.

The arguments in the second half of the book have benefited from discussions with, and comments from, many people, including Maxine Berg, Amit Bhaduri, Samuel Bowles, Alfred Chandler, Ronald Dore, Bernard Elbaum, Lou Ferleger, Herbert Gintis, Howard Gospel, Bo Gustafsson, Susan Helper, Beat Hotz-Hart, Richard Hyman, David Landes, Wayne Lewchuk, Lars Magnusson, Stephen Marglin, William Mass, and Steven Tolliday. Fellowships from the Harvard Business School and the German Marshall Fund of the United States permitted time for research and writing. Additional research funds came from the Division of Research of the Harvard Business School and from Barnard College. The full development of the book's conceptual framework owes much to my regular participation in the Business History Seminar of the Harvard Business School during the last half of the 1980s as well as to my involvement in a working group sponsored by the Swedish Collegium for the Advanced Study in the Social Sciences over the same period. I am grateful to Thomas McCraw of HBS and Bo Gustafsson of SCASSS for making possible

my participation in these intellectual communities. An earlier version
of Chapter 9 was presented to the Business History Seminar of the
Harvard Business School, with Kim Clark and Takashi Hikino providing helpful comments. Chris Grandy read the Appendix carefully
enough to enable me to correct a careless error. The manuscript was
completed at the Institute for Advanced Study in Princeton in September 1989.

At Harvard University Press, Michael Aronson oversaw the evolution of the book from a collection of essays and outlines into what I
hope is a coherent and cohesive argument. His combination of pa-
tience and persistence in getting the book to press was just about
right. Jodi Simpson did a stellar job of copy editing the book, and
Jennifer Snodgrass saw the book through to publication.

I acknowledge permission to reprint substantial portions of articles
previously published elsewhere. Chapters 1 and 2 appeared originally
as "Theory and History in Marxian Economics," in Alexander J.
Field, ed., *The Future of Economic History* (Kluwer-Nijhoff, Hing-
ham, Mass., 1987). Chapter 3 appeared originally as "Industrial Relations and Technical Change: The Case of the Self-Acting Mule,"
Cambridge Journal of Economics 3 (September 1979). Chapter 4
appeared originally as "Production Relations, Labor Productivity,
and Choice of Technique: British and U.S. Cotton Spinning," *Journal
of Economic History* 41 (September 1981). Chapter 5 appeared originally, co-authored with William Mass, as "The Performance of the
British Cotton Industry, 1870–1913," *Research in Economic History*
9 (1984), a JAI Press publication.

I want to thank members of my family for the roles they played,
knowingly or not, in the writing of this book. My children, Ashley,
Leah, and Casey, constantly diverted me from studying the industrial
past and speculating on the economic future, riveting my attention
unavoidably on the things that matter most in the here and now.
Without them this book might well have appeared years ago, but in
more ways than one it would not have been the same. Kathy Cannings, with whom I have shared both family and intellectual life,
helped me to take a broader view of my subject and to keep its
importance in perspective. Finally, the book is dedicated to my parents, whose own views on life and work have encouraged me to study
how we got to where we are and how we might get to where we want
to go.

Contents

Competitive Advantage on the Shop Floor

Introduction: Organization, Technology, and Value Creation

The History and Theory of Capitalist Development

> The bourgeoisie, during its rule of scarcely one hundred years, has created more massive and more colossal productive forces than have all preceding generations together.[1]

So wrote Karl Marx and Friedrich Engels in 1848 in the *Communist Manifesto*. During the 1840s, the most powerful capitalist economy was to be found in Britain where, over the previous eighty years or so, the world's first industrial revolution had occurred.

Marx and Engels did not, of course, write the *Communist Manifesto* to render praise unto capitalism. On the contrary, their aim was to show how in the midst of plenty there was only poverty and degradation for the working masses. Capitalism had performed wonders in developing technological capabilities. But, as Marx later argued in *Capital*—his monumental contribution to economic analysis—the use of modern technologies by the capitalist bourgeoisie tended to

> distort the worker into a fragment of a man, they degrade him to the level of an appendage of a machine, they destroy the actual content of his labour by turning it into a torment; they alienate from him the intellectual potentialities of the labour process in the same proportion as science is incorporated in it as an independent power; they deform the conditions under which he works, subject him during the labour process to a despotism the more hateful for its meanness; they transform his life-time into working-time, and drag his wife and child beneath the wheels of the juggernaut of capital.[2]

The essential Marxian message was that unprecedented economic development did not guarantee widespread social development. Even when workers gained limited access to some of the material output that capitalism generated, Marx and Engels argued, their treatment as inputs into the production process stunted their development as human beings. Were the masses to rid society of the capitalist economic system, workers would have "nothing to lose but their chains."[3]

To the present day, social commentators continue to differ sharply over the extent to which different social classes bear the costs and reap the benefits of capitalist economic development. But whatever the system's current inequities, the fact is that for well over a century capitalism has survived the Marxian critique. This book is about how, through transformations in the organization of work in leading capitalist economies in different times and places, the relations between management and labor have permitted not only the survival of the economic system but also rapid economic growth.

I shall follow the transformations of work organization and attendant relations between capitalist employers and shop-floor workers from Britain, the international industrial leader of the late nineteenth century, to the United States, which assumed the position of leadership in the first half of the twentieth century. I shall then turn to Japan, a nation that has emerged as the world's foremost mass producer over the past few decades. In analyzing these shifts in international industrial leadership, I shall show how the dynamic interaction between work organization (which broadly conceived includes labor–management relations) and technological change created "value"—high quality products at low unit costs. I shall also explore how, in the cases of Britain and the United States, structures of labor–management relations that had once helped to carry these national economies to positions of industrial leadership later came to impede the value-creation process and contribute to relative economic decline.

The goal of this book is to improve our understanding of the roles of work organization and of technological change in the process of economic development. As already indicated, the empirical focus is on three national economies—those of Britain, the United States, and Japan—that have been world leaders in manufacturing for mass markets in different epochs over the past hundred years. The analytical method is historical. Only by understanding how the present evolved out of the past can we hope to delineate the realistic social alternatives and economic possibilities for the future. The historical method is the only means by which we can grasp the logic of the process of change. The ideas in this book are the result of my own attempts over two decades to use historical research to test existing economic theories and elaborate a relevant theory of capitalist development.

The starting point is the Marxian theory of shop-floor value creation. Marx used this theory to analyze the evolution and impacts of workplace organization in nineteenth-century Britain. Research on this same historical time and place permits an assessment of the strengths and limitations of the Marxian analysis. The critical evaluation of Marxian theory is an invaluable means for delving into the evolving character of the economic system. Ultimately, however, my purpose is to understand, not the strengths and weaknesses of Marxian theory, but the dynamics of capitalist development.

Economists who have an aversion to Marx's conclusions have tended to ignore the Marxian contributions to methodology and theory as well. One prominent twentieth-century economist was, however, deeply influenced by Marx's historical method. In *The Theory of Economic Development*, written almost eighty years ago, Joseph A. Schumpeter argued that "changes of technique and productive organization require special analysis," and that "non-recognition of this is the most important single reason for what appears unsatisfactory to us in [what is now called neoclassical] economic theory." Schumpeter added that his own view of the economic problem was "more nearly parallel to that of Marx" than to that of contemporary neoclassical economists (he mentions the influential American J. B. Clark).[4] By starting with Marx, this book answers Schumpeter's turn-of-the-century call for a "special analysis" of "changes of technique and productive organization"—a challenge that mainstream economists have to the present continued to eschew.

The historical argument begins with a reconsideration of the interaction of technology and work organization during the British Industrial Revolution and concludes with a broad-based comparative analysis of value creation on the shop floor in Britain, the United States, and Japan over the last few decades. The resultant analysis is by no means the whole story of shifts in international industrial leadership. A complete comprehension of the dynamics of capitalist development requires the study of many phenomena—the strategy of business organizations, the internal structure of management, the relations among firms, the impacts of family and community structures and migration patterns on the development of the labor force, the developmental and regulatory roles of the state, the relations among nation states. But without an analysis of how firms organize their production workers to transform invested resources into salable products, it is impossible to comprehend the social determinants and impacts of technological change; and without an understanding of the causes and consequences of technological change, one cannot hope to understand the dynamics of capitalist development. I should stress, however, that the shop-floor focus of these studies is necessary, but by no means sufficient, for the analysis of capitalist development.

Technology, Effort, and Shop-Floor Value Creation

What do I mean by the "creation of value," and how does the work of shop-floor labor contribute to the process? The capitalist firm creates value when it transforms investments in productive resources into useful products at competitive costs. Within the firm, the value-creation process involves a specialized division of labor that is both hierarchical and technical. The division of labor is hierarchical because some people plan and coordinate the work of others. The division of labor is technical because particular people carry out particular tasks pertaining to broader functions such as research and development, procurement of inputs, distribution of outputs, and various shop-floor production processes.

The shop-floor transformation of inputs into outputs—what may be called the *productive transformation*—is central to the value-creation process. To effect the productive transformation, the firm must have available not only physical plant, equipment, and materials but also human skills—the productive capabilities that people possess in forms such as knowledge of the physical environment as well as dexterity, quickness, endurance, and strength. People can use their skills to manipulate and transform that environment. A *shop-floor technology* combines productive capabilities embodied in plant, equipment, and materials with the human skills required to utilize the physical capital.

In the productive transformation of inputs into outputs, the human and physical resources that constitute a technology are not coequal factors of production. The production of useful products requires the agency of human beings to set in motion plant, equipment, and materials, to combine these inputs in predetermined ways, and to make adjustments to the production process when "useful" products are not forthcoming. The cognitive and physical capabilities of workers—what are generally called skills—enter into the productive transformation. But the transformation of these skills into output requires that workers also supply "effort" to the production process. If shop-floor workers on whose skills the productive transformation depends refuse to supply effort, there can be no output. Given the productive capabilities inherent in the firm's technology (which includes the workers' skills), the greater the quantity of effort workers are willing and able to supply per unit of time, the greater the quantity of output produced on the shop floor.

The limits of productivity growth under capitalism would long ago have been reached, however, if the system had to rely solely on increases in effort to yield higher levels of productivity. What has permitted capitalism to generate sustained increases in labor productivity and be such a powerful engine of economic growth is the *effort-saving* character of technological change. After the introduction of an effort-saving technological change, the same amount of effort yields a greater amount of output than was produced on the old technology.[5]

Technological change has the potential to save effort because it is *skill displacing*. Skills that were required on the old technology are no longer needed for the productive transformation. By overcoming the constraints that human skill in its varied dimensions places on the productive transformation, effort-saving technological change creates the possibility for more output to be produced with the same amount of effort.

But technological change need not be, and virtually never is, only skill displacing. In using new combinations of physical resources and human skill to produce an existing product or to create a new product, technological change is also *skill augmenting*. To develop and utilize the new technology, new skills may be required, both within the managerial hierarchy and on the shop floor. Indeed, a major issue in the structuring of work organization is the hierarchical location of particular skills—an issue that is, as I shall show, by no means independent of the social context in which the productive transformation takes place. Whatever the hierarchical structure of the technical division of labor, however, technological change is both skill augmenting and skill displacing. Some of the managerial or shop-floor labor services required to develop and utilize the new technology may increase rather than diminish the quantity of effort required per unit of output, and hence to some extent reduce the effort-saving impact of the technological change. But for technological change to have the potential to overcome the constraint that human skill places on labor productivity, it must on balance be effort-saving.

The amount of effort that workers expend on a given technology or the change in the level of effort subsequent to a change in technology are prime sources of potential conflict between management and labor. For a given wage, managers want to secure as much effort from workers as possible (consistent with the maintenance of product quality). For a given wage, workers typically want to expend as little effort as possible, particularly if they view work as lacking in intrinsic worth, and hence simply as a means to gain a livelihood. In such a situation, the amount of effort actually expended in the production process during any given pay period depends on the relative power of managers and workers to control the duration and intensity of labor.

Technological change itself can affect the balance of power between management and labor. The power of workers to control effort by maintaining their skills in scarce supply may be diminished by the skill-displacing impact of technological change. Indeed, one motivation for capitalists to invest in new technologies may be precisely to reduce the dependence of their firms on shop-floor skills. On any given technology, managers can also attempt to structure the technical division of labor in ways that minimize the range of tasks that workers perform, and hence the types and variety of skills that they must possess. In addition, managers can attempt to structure the hierarchical division of labor in ways that integrate personnel with key skills into the managerial structure, so that skills are literally taken off the shop floor. The impacts of technological change and redivisions of labor on the quantity and quality of effort that shop-floor workers supply are major issues addressed in this book.

Getting more effort from workers and producing more useful products do not, in and of themselves, create value. Even assuming that the products are useful—that, as either intermediate capital goods or final consumer goods, the products can meet needs or desires—the firm must still produce the products at a cost that other firms or households are willing and able to pay.

What determines the unit costs at which a firm can sell a product? In any production period, the firm incurs (1) fixed costs of investments in plant, equipment, and organization; (2) variable costs of the materials that enter into each unit of the product; and (3) labor costs incurred in employing the skills of, and eliciting effort from, workers. In the Appendix, I present a formal analysis of the impact of these three types of costs on the amount of value created on the shop floor during a production period.

For a given technology, the amount of effort that workers supply in a production period affects unit fixed capital costs and unit variable capital costs as well as unit labor costs. Because more effort yields more output, higher levels of effort supplied for a given wage lower unit labor costs. Higher levels of effort can also reduce wastage of material inputs per unit of output, and hence reduce unit variable costs. Moreover, as workers supply more effort and yield more output per production period—and hence as what engineers call throughput rises—unit fixed capital costs fall. The results are "economies of speed," the term that Alfred D. Chandler, Jr., the leading historian of the modern corporate enterprise, has applied to the impact of higher levels of throughput on the spreading out of fixed costs.[6]

Some might argue that higher levels of throughput cannot result in lower unit fixed costs because the underlying fixed assets have a finite quantity of productive services to render. According to this line of thinking, when throughput is higher, the fixed assets just get depleted faster, and hence will have to be replaced by new assets sooner. But the speed at which fixed assets are utilized matters, for two reasons. First, in any production period, the firm incurs carrying costs for fixed assets, irrespective of the degree to which it utilizes them.[7] Second, in a world of industrial competition, technological change can render existing fixed assets obsolete well before they have been fully depleted. In other words, it is fixed costs, not fixed assets, that are allocated over more output at higher levels of throughput, and these fixed costs of investment in productive resources must be recovered while these resources are still capable of contributing to the value-creation process.

What then determines the amount of value created on the shop floor in any given production period? In the basic model of value creation presented in the Appendix (to which those whose intellectual inclinations are more theoretical than historical may wish to refer before proceeding with the rest of the book), I define *value-created* on the shop floor as the excess of revenues generated by the sale of output over the nondirect labor costs of producing that output. By this definition, value-created represents revenues that can be shared out between workers and managers (all other claims on total revenues by suppliers and financiers having been met). Workers get their share in the form of wages, and managers get their share in the form of what I call the managerial surplus. If workers' wages are fixed at some conventional level irrespective of output, the managerial surplus represents *residual* or *net value-created* on the shop floor. *Gross value-created* is then the net value-created plus the conventional wages of workers.

In any production period, the managerial surplus may be reduced because workers are able to claim a greater share of gross value-created, and vice versa. But the sharing of value-created need not represent a zero-sum situation. By providing incentives for workers to supply more effort and for managers to invest in effort-saving technological change, the distribution of value-created can result in what I shall call value gains—an increase of the total amount of value-created on the shop floor in any given production period as well as over successive production periods. A major finding of the historical research summarized in this book is that the sharing of value-created between workers and managers is integrally related to the creation of value on the shop floor. More specifically, cooperative relations between management and workers encourage not only the greater utilization of an existing technology but also greater investments in effort-saving technological change—both of which in turn contribute to sustained economic development.

Why Marx?

The notion that capitalist development can thrive on the basis of cooperative labor–management relations contrasts with Marx's emphasis on class conflict as the dominant social characteristic of a rapidly growing capitalist economy, just as the focus on the sharing of value-created contrasts with Marx's focus on the extraction of surplus-value. Marx argued that, by investing in skill-displacing machinery that both superseded craft skills and augmented the reserve army of labor, capitalists were able to break the power of craft workers and increase the duration and intensity of labor.[8] Using technological change as a class weapon, capitalists could exploit their now unskilled and easily replaceable workers to the hilt, extracting as much unremunerated effort from them as was humanly (even if not humanely) possible. "Marxian exploitation"—increases in the labor effort supplied by workers for a given wage—and capital accumulation went hand in hand.

Many of the social ills that Marx predicted can be legitimately associated with contemporary capitalism, among them recurrent periods of high structural unemployment, the degradation of many types of work, and unseemly income inequality. But on the issue of long-run trends in the relation between effort and remuneration, capitalism would appear to escape criticism, at least in those industrial sectors in which the productive transformation is most technologically advanced—sectors in which, according to the Marxian argument, workers are supposed to be most thoroughly oppressed. Over the long run of advanced capitalist development, male blue-collar workers in technologically advanced workplaces have been able to lay claim to shares of value gains made possible by effort-saving technological change, supplying less effort per production period for greater remuneration.

Weakening as it does Marx's critique of capitalism, the distribution of some of the benefits of economic development to masses of blue-collar workers within the advanced capitalist economies makes it all too easy for defenders of the "free enterprise system" to dismiss the relevance of the Marxian theory of capitalist development for contemporary economic analysis. Modern economics is, as a result, so much the poorer. As this book demonstrates, much of Marx's conceptual framework for analyzing capitalist development is still relevant today, even though many of the conclusions that he drew from it require substantial modification, if not outright rejection.

For, in the entire history of Western economic thought, it is only from Marx's writings that one can derive a coherent framework for analyzing the dynamic interrelationships among technology, skill, effort, and value creation. If one accepts that technological change and labor–management relations are important determinants of long-run economic growth, it makes intellectual sense to make use of Marx, whatever one's ideological orientation.

In recent decades the Marxian analytical framework has provided a focal point for a considerable amount of research—some more historical, some more theoretical—into the interaction of relations and forces of production within the capitalist labor process.[9] There is by no means a consensus within the "labor process" literature on the causes and consequences of capitalist work organization. Some, such as Harry Braverman, have followed Marx in emphasizing the forces of production in the determination of the organization of work, whereas others, such as David Montgomery, have analyzed the evolu-

tion of the relations of production while neglecting the role of technological change.[10] But despite these differences, I find it difficult to
imagine a systematic approach to the relation between work organization and economic development without the Marxian framework
as an analytical point of departure.

Why History?

The importance of Marx is not only that he asked the relevant questions, generated the relevant concepts, and focused upon the relevant
variables. As an economic theorist, he also stands out in the history of
economics for adopting an explicitly historical methodology. As
Joseph Schumpeter emphasized in his book *Capitalism, Socialism,
and Democracy:* "The essential point to grasp is that in dealing with
capitalism we are dealing with an evolutionary process. It may seem
strange that anyone can fail to see so obvious a fact which moreover
was long ago emphasized by Karl Marx."[11] Earlier in the book,
Schumpeter had elaborated on a contribution by Marx that was of
"fundamental importance for the methodology of economics":

> Economists have always either themselves done work in economic
> history or else used the historical work of others. But the facts of
> economic history were assigned to a separate compartment. They
> entered theory, if at all, merely in the role of illustrations, or possi-
> bly of verifications of results. They mixed with it only mechanically.
> Now Marx's mixture is a chemical one; that is to say, he introduced
> them [the facts of economic history] into the very argument that
> produces the results. He was the first economist of top rank to see
> and to teach systematically how economic theory may be turned
> into historical analysis and how the historical narrative may be
> turned into *histoire raisonnée.*[12]

Like Marx before him, Schumpeter understood that to comprehend
the logic of an evolutionary process requires not simply historical
facts but also historical analysis that can indeed uncover the "path-
dependent" logic of those facts. In capturing the logic of the historical
process, historical analysis contributes to economic theory. Indeed, I
would argue that, compared with the deductive and static method-
ologies currently in vogue among Western economists, historical
analysis can provide much more powerful economic theory because
it derives its fundamental propositions from the historical record

and because it can comprehend the process of change—a process that continually renders static equilibrium theory irrelevant for analyzing real-world phenomena. The historical approach to economic analysis, neglected by mainstream economists even more today than it was in Schumpeter's time, remains of "fundamental importance to the methodology of economics."

In the spirit of Marx and Schumpeter, this book is part of an ongoing attempt to develop an approach to economic analysis in which the dynamics of historical reality and the theoretical abstractions constructed to comprehend that reality bear a symbiotic relation to each other. The rigorous study of economic institutions can provide an independent and informed judgment on what phenomena are fundamental to the real world, and hence what might constitute relevant economic theory. At the same time, theory focuses and organizes the study of the empirical data by generating well-specified testable hypotheses.

Such an integrated approach to economic analysis ensures the relevance of intellectual work by insisting that theory be the servant of reality rather than vice versa. At the same time, analytical rigor ceases to be defined as simply logical consistency (as economists have been wont to do) but is defined more fundamentally as empirical research of sufficient breadth and depth to give one reason to believe that one's theoretical arguments do indeed capture the essence of reality. In turn, theoretical constructs might then do what good theory is supposed to do—provide a coherent framework for further empirical exploration and for the reasoned consideration of policy alternatives. If, in the process of achieving a more profound understanding of the real world, some of the old theoretical distinctions and interpretations fall by the wayside, such is intellectual progress.

Marx's own attempt, over a century ago, to integrate theory and reality offers methodological insights and conceptual distinctions that can help economists construct a theory of capitalist development upon adequate empirical foundations. But, as already indicated, one must be careful. The Marxian approach is not an immediately applicable theory of capitalist development, only a valuable point of departure. If one accepts the methodological proposition that historical analysis can motivate and validate theoretical generalizations, it makes sense to establish the relevance of Marx's theoretical framework and conclusions for his own time—roughly the first three quarters of the nineteenth century—before one attempts to draw on Marx to analyze present-day capitalist economies. Only then can one use-fully accept, reject, modify, or elaborate the Marxian propositions as part of a much larger project—that goes beyond even the grand scope of Marx's endeavors—to develop a theory of capitalist development that makes relevant abstractions from the rigorous analysis of histor-ical experience.

What Lies Ahead

In Chapters 1 and 2 I critically assess Marx's theory of capitalist development in the light of recent research (including my own) into the historical experience on which his theory is supposedly based. These chapters focus on Marx's analysis of the evolution of capi-tal–labor relations in the rise and consolidation of British industrial capitalism through the 1860s, when Marx published Volume I of *Capital* and Britain became known as the "workshop of the world."

Chapter 1 begins by addressing a long-standing debate concerning the emergence of a wage-labor force in the British Industrial Revolu-tion. "Mainstream" (or perhaps more correctly, "anti-Marxian") economic historians have tended to argue that British workers were pulled into the factories of the Industrial Revolution by the prom-ise of higher standards of living rather than pushed into them by the erosion of their prior rights to the use of land. Marx clearly put the push before the pull, arguing that by the mid–eighteenth century the reallocation of agricultural land in Britain—a process known as the enclosure movement—had resulted in a large class of landless proletarians who were compelled to turn to wage labor to gain their sustenance.

Some economic historians have attributed to Marx the notion that, in one fell swoop, the enclosure movement drove the peasants off the soil and into the factories. Marx did not put forth such a simplistic view of the rise of a wage-labor force, although one might easily be misled by his overemphasis on the dramatic displacement of peasants as a result of enclosures in the early sixteenth and early nineteenth centuries as well as by his inadequate analysis of how a factory labor force was in fact created. Despite gaps and omissions in Marx's his-torical analysis, his basic arguments concerning the creation of a landless proletariat are both important and valid. The transformation of social relations of production and the emergence of a wage-labor force in the agricultural sector were the critical preconditions for the

Industrial Revolution characterized by the rise of the factory system. Indeed, as I shall show, Marx seems to have been quite comfortable with the view that the pull of higher wages influenced the transfer of labor resources from the agricultural to the industrial sector once the capitalist mode of production was in place.

The social transformation that separated the mass of producers from the means of production is critical for Marx's theory of capitalist development. To all outward appearances, the wage-labor relation manifests the worker's freedom to choose his or her employer, or whether to enter into a wage-labor contract at all. But Marx argued what masses of subsequent historical evidence have tended to confirm: peasant and artisanal producers give up control of their laboring capacity to others only when they no longer have direct access to their own means of production. It is force of circumstance—the lack of means of production—that compels the worker to seek out wage labor. The critical implication for the exercise of social power by the capitalist over the worker is that compulsion rather than freedom—the urgent need for the worker to find employment with a capitalist rather than the ability to choose among various alternative ways of making a living—underlies the wage-labor contract.

Marx's analytical framework contains several concepts that illuminate the relation between the development of an industrial labor force and Britain's successful industrialization. On the one hand, the Marxian focus on the importance of proletarianization and relative surplus population directs attention toward social conflicts over alternative modes of acquiring a subsistence, such as resettlement of land, poor relief, crime, emigration, and domestic industry. On the other hand, Marx's emphasis on the duration of work, the intensity of labor, and mechanization as determinants of value creation directs attention to the behavioral transformation that was required to get the proletariat to accept the work discipline that, along with automation, became a defining characteristic of the factory form of work organization.

In the Marxian account of the impact of technological change on workers under capitalism, the manifestation of the subordination of labor to capital was increased labor effort expended by workers for a given level of pay. A worker supplied a unit of labor time to the capitalist firm in exchange for a wage. But the labor exchange did not necessarily specify the amount of labor effort that the worker was to perform. For Marx, the source of this "incomplete contract"—as modern economists would call it—was not the difficulty of measuring labor effort but rather a fundamental conflict of interest between the worker and his or her capitalist employer.

The worker, for whom the act of working had been reduced to a mere means to an end, had an interest in expending as little effort as possible in return for a given wage. On the other side, the employer, as the claimant to what Marx called surplus-value, had an incentive to try to induce as much labor effort as possible from the worker in exchange for that wage. For Marx, the critical factor in the determination of the relation between effort and pay was the social power that the opposing parties to the labor exchange could exercise in the process of production. With capitalists in control of the means of production, Marx argued, the skill-displacing and labor-displacing impacts of technological change so weakened the power of workers that they could not hope to exercise sufficient control over the relation between effort and remuneration to capture the benefits of technological change.

Marx did not direct his critique of the capitalist mode of production at technological change per se. Rather he viewed the dependence of propertyless workers on the propertied capitalist for their daily bread as the actual source of the workers' oppression. Technology served the capitalist as a means of social control. Under different social relations of production, technology could be a liberating force. To support his case, Marx cited the liberal nineteenth-century economist John Stuart Mill, who argued, "It is questionable if all the mechanical inventions yet made have lightened the day's toil of any human being."[13] Eradicate the conflict of interest between the owners of the means of production and the workers who kept those means of production in motion, Marx argued, and the diffusion of technology could potentially "lighten the day's toil" of the worker even while paying him or her a higher level of remuneration.

Yet, in analyzing the evolution of the factory system in the British Industrial Revolution, Marx was overly impressed by the role of technology in shaping the structure of social power. Since Marx wrote, historians have added considerably to the knowledge of the emergence and development of a factory labor force in Britain. Empirically economists are now in a much better position to assess the weaknesses of the Marxian analysis of the interaction of the forces and relations of production in the rise of industrial capitalism, and to modify it accordingly.

Marx emphasized, and decried, the adverse social impact of industrial capitalism on the worker. But what distinguishes Marx from the well-informed muckraker or the compassionate social historian is his construction of the theory of surplus-value to analyze the economic causes and consequences of the "subsumption of labor to capital."[14] Marx's theory of surplus-value is a microeconomic theory of productivity growth and income distribution under capitalism. Despite Marx's own misuses of the theory, its focus on the interrelationships among effort, pay, and technology remains essential for analyzing the impacts of the social organization of the capitalist enterprise on the growth of productivity and the distribution of income.

Chapter 2 raises the major implications of my review of Marx's empirical work for analyzing the development of capitalism since his time. Marx predicted the rise of highly concentrated industrial structures, but for the wrong reasons. As with capital–labor relations, he overemphasized the independent impact of technology on industrial organization. Marx, as a result, not only attributed to British capitalists social power that they never had but also ended up believing quite incorrectly that future capitalist development in places such as Germany, driven by the same logic of technological change, would in all essentials imitate the nineteenth-century British experience. History shows, however, that over the past century the institutional foundations of successful capitalist development have been in a constant state of evolution, the logic of which is not adequately comprehended by Marxian theory. Nevertheless, from Marx's theory of surplus-value, economists can derive an essential, even if rudimentary, conceptual framework for analyzing the role of production relations in promoting and hindering economic growth in different historical epochs and social contexts.

Throughout this book I stress the importance of an analysis of social power for understanding the operation and performance of the capitalist economy. A fundamental conceptual contribution of Marx was to distinguish the apparent lack of social power inherent in arm's-length exchange relations from the very real social power inherent in personalized production relations. From this distinction between relations of exchange and relations of production, Marx went on to fashion a theory of the interaction of social power and technology within the production process itself.

My own research emphasizes the sources and uses of social power in determining economic outcomes. Marxian theory provided me with some initial testable hypotheses that required the study of the histor-

ical record for validation or rejection. Much of my own insight into
the dynamics of capitalist development has come from digging deeper
into the empirical reality of shop-floor value creation in nineteenth-
century Britain than Marx himself was willing or able to do. Chapter
3 represents the type of in-depth study required to shed light on the
interaction of relations and forces of production in capitalist development. The case study was not chosen at random. The "self-acting
mule," the dominant cotton-spinning technology during the nineteenth century, supplied Marx with his classic example of how British
capitalists used technology to rid themselves of troublesome skilled
workers toward the close of the Industrial Revolution.

Unfortunately Marx ignored the problem of shop-floor management even, and one might say particularly, in the presence of technological change. The case study of the self-acting mule demonstrates
that one can use the Marxian conceptual framework for the purposes
of rigorous empirical analysis, even if one ends up disagreeing with
Marx's own conclusions. Indeed, the main finding of the case study is
that the Marxian perspective underestimates, and to a large extent
ignores, the problems that competitive industrial structures and cohesive workers' organizations pose for effective shop-floor management. As a result, Marx ended up overestimating, and even miscon-
struing, technology as an instrument of capitalist power. Put another
way, Marx failed to appreciate the determining influence of social
relations of production—in this case not only the relations between
employers and employees but also, as I shall show, the relations
among different types of workers within the capitalist enterprise as
well as among capitalist firms themselves—in shaping work organization in the presence of technological change.

My decision to undertake an in-depth study of the history of work
organization in a particular production process derived only in part
from my project of reevaluating Marxian theory in the light of the
same historical experience on which Marx himself purportedly drew.
During the early 1970s, debates among left-oriented academics centered on the causal connection between the forces and relations of
production in the process of capitalist development. Of particular
importance was Stephen Marglin's well-known and controversial article, "What Do Bosses Do?," first published in 1974.[15] Marglin confronted the conventional wisdom—in part the legacy of orthodox
Marxism but shared also by many liberal and conservative social
theorists—that the imperatives of technology shape social relations

rather than vice versa. In arguing that social power rather than technology determined the organization of work, Marglin focused, moreover, on the critical dimension of the relation between effort and pay. Using the rise of the factory system in Britain, among other empirical examples, he argued, in essence, that the detailed technical division of labor which, from Adam Smith on, has been seen as the characteristic form of work organization in advanced industrial economies was not dictated by the nature of technology but was put in place by employers to enhance their ability to extract effort from their workers.

Despite my own inclination (derived from my training as an economist) to make do wherever possible with a modest number of stylized facts, I became convinced that intellectual progress in understanding the interaction of forces and relations of production required detailed empirical investigation into the process of shop-floor value creation. Chapter 3 provides some support for the Marglin thesis—it was the need to extract labor effort, rather than the imperatives of mechanization itself, that had a greater impact on the mule-spinning division of labor as the technology became more mechanized (or "self-acting"). The case study also provides a concrete illustration of the dynamic *interaction* between forces and relations of production in what was, at the time, the leading industry in the world's dominant economy.

In my own subsequent research, the study of work organization in the mule-spinning process evolved into, first, a full-blown analysis of the rise and decline of the British cotton textile industry from the Industrial Revolution to the 1980s, and then, in collaboration with others doing similar institutional research, a more sweeping analysis of the decline of the British economy.[16] Before moving on to these higher levels of aggregation and abstraction, however, Chapter 4 takes the mule-spinning case study a step further by introducing the comparative dimension. If social relations of production rather than technology shape work organization and if the critical economic dimension of work organization is the relation between effort and remuneration, then one should expect that in different social environments both work organization and the relation between effort and pay would also differ, even in the presence of the same basic technology.

The postbellum New England textile industry used British-made mule-spinning machines, and even employed experienced British mule spinners who had emigrated to the United States. The comparison of the mule-spinning processes in Britain and the United States reveals that, despite the employment of the same basic technology (machines and workers) in the two countries, labor productivity was higher in the United States even though the workers in the New England mills apparently expended less effort. What made this outcome possible were the decisions of American managers to use cotton on the mule-spinning machines that had a greater effort-saving impact than the cotton inputs used in Britain.

The most easily observable facts of the cross-national comparison—those that relate relative factor prices to choice of technique—would lead a mainstream economist to respond that for analyzing economic outcomes the institutional analysis of differences in social relations and work organization is just wasted intellectual effort. On the basis of the relative factor prices of cotton and labor in the two countries, the mainstream economist would argue, one could predict the choice of a relatively capital-intensive technique—higher quality cotton—in the United States compared with Britain. So what economic difference derives from work organization and production relations?

I argue that the response that relative factor prices provide economists with all the relevant economic information implicitly assumes that underlying the choice of technique is a "universal" production function, determined by technology, that is common to the cotton textile industries of both countries. Drawing on the institutional analysis of the impact of production relations on the relation between effort and pay, I demonstrate why a universal production function cannot be assumed. There is more than one way to spin a mule, with different economic outcomes. The structure of social power that determined the relation between effort and pay in the U.S. mills constrained American managers to make their choice of technique (cotton quality) on the basis of a relatively capital-intensive range of factor combinations that substituted effort-saving material inputs for labor effort, while the structure of social power prevailing in British mills constrained British managers to choose their technique within a relatively labor-intensive range of alternatives. As a result, if U.S. prices were to prevail in Britain and vice versa, the choices of technique would not simply be reversed, as the neoclassical economic theorist would predict. The facts might fit the conventional theory, but the conventional theory represents an incomplete explanation of the facts.

Explanatory power matters. I conclude Chapter 4 with some arguments about how the different constraints facing American and British managers help to explain the relatively slow adoption of a more advanced, effort-saving spinning technology (the ring-frame) by British firms relative to their counterparts in the United States. In particular, I argue that, because of the power of British workers to control the relation between effort and pay, the British cotton textile industry continued in the twentieth century to rely on the traditional technologies that had brought it to dominance in the nineteenth century.

Chapter 5 is based on an article coauthored with William Mass.[17] It develops further the analysis of the British cotton textile industry's technological lag and assesses its impact on the industry's international competitiveness. We show how reliance on what had by the twentieth century become *effort-using* technologies enabled the British cotton industry (the country's largest manufacturing employer in the early twentieth century) to maintain, and even extend, its advantage in international competition before World War I. In particular, we show how, by using the traditional technologies and inferior cotton inputs, British industry was able to maintain competitive advantage, despite stagnating and even declining labor productivity.

But Chapter 5 also delineates the limits to this effort-using strategy, arguing that the very methods that the British cotton textile industry used to remain competitive prior to World War I made it vulnerable to forms of economic organization with more value-creating capabilities that enabled cotton industries in other countries, particularly Japan, to gain competitive advantage in the decades after World War I. Focusing as it does on the relation between effort and pay on traditional technologies, the analysis in Chapter 5 offers insight into the shortcomings of arguments concerning the relation between economic efficiency and competitiveness that rely on conventional measures of labor productivity and total factor productivity.

In the first decades of the twentieth century and across a broad spectrum of industries, international competitive advantage shifted away from Britain, as its once-dominant economy entered into long-term relative decline. Industrial leadership passed to the United States and Germany, with the United States dominating in the mass production of manufactured goods. The rise of U.S. industry saw a shift from craft control to managerial control of the shop floor. By introducing effort-saving technologies and planning and coordinating the shop-floor division of labor, managerial control was able to achieve economies of speed that were unattainable on the basis of technologies that continued to rely on shop-floor skills.

Part II provides broad-based analyses of the organizational transformations on the shop floor that have accompanied shifts in international economic leadership in this century. Chapter 6 broadens and extends the analysis of the role of craft control in the rise and decline of the British cotton textile industry in the previous three chapters to British manufacturing in general as it evolved from the last half of the nineteenth century to the present. I argue that the exercise of craft control on the shop floor played an important part in enabling the British economy to emerge as "the workshop of the world" in the late nineteenth century, because key production workers assumed what are now viewed as managerial functions of training and supervising workers and ensuring the flow of work through the production processes.

British craft control was not, however, conducive to the utilization of the high-throughput, effort-saving, mass-production technologies that from the late nineteenth century became available, primarily from the United States. During the first decades of the twentieth century, British manufacturing could often compete on the basis of what were now labor-intensive production methods because of relatively low fixed costs and a hard-working labor force. Lacking managerial structures that could plan and coordinate the organization of work, however, British manufacturers could not imitate the American successes in developing and utilizing the new mass production technologies. British structures of work organization were, moreover, resistant to change, in large part because for long periods of time (often decades in more labor-intensive industries), British manufacturers were able on the basis of the traditional technologies to adapt to competitive pressures by eliciting more effort from immobile workers, paying these workers lower wages, accepting lower rates of profit for themselves, and neglecting to reinvest in plant and equipment.

As a result, the transition from craft control to managerial control made little progress in the first half of the twentieth century, and even beyond, in the industries that had been central to the British Industrial Revolution. British employers could not break the entrenched power of craft workers on the shop floor, in large part because the capitalists were unwilling to invest in the managerial structures required to plan and coordinate the high-throughput production processes based on effort-saving technologies. Relying on the skills and efforts of craft workers, who often continued to use traditional technologies, British capitalists were able to remain competitive for a time against their more capital-intensive international rivals. It was not entrenched unions that prompted capitalists to remain labor intensive. Even in new industries such as automobile manufacture in which during the interwar period union organization was weak, British capitalists preferred to leave considerable control over work organization with operatives on the shop floor rather than invest in managerial structures.

By the 1920s Britain could no longer lay claim to being the workshop of the world. In many industries British reliance on the skills and efforts of shop-floor workers, rather than on the interaction of managerial coordination and effort-saving technology, to create value reached its physical and social limits. Meanwhile, the value-creating capabilities of British industry fell further and further behind its international rivals, who were making more far-reaching investments in organization and technology, while the persistence of underdeveloped managerial structures and workers with vested interests in their existing positions of craft control posed severe obstacles to organizational and technological change.

In the adoption of the new high-throughput, effort-saving technologies, Britain's main rival was the United States. By contrast with Britain, where, from the late nineteenth century, control over work organization was left with workers on the shop floor, a basic objective of managerial control in the rise of U.S. industry to international dominance was *to take skills off the shop floor*—an objective achieved by investing in managerial structures and skill-displacing technological change. In the process, the American shop-floor worker tended to become, to use Marx's words, "an appendage of a machine."[18] Chapter 7 analyzes how and why U.S industrial enterprises replaced craft control with managerial control of the shop floor. I explore the strengths and limitations of managerial strategies such as those used by Frederick Taylor and Henry Ford in eliciting sufficient effort from workers to generate economies of speed on the basis of high fixed-cost technologies. I argue that the most effective way to increase effort and lower unit costs on the shop floor was through policies that held out realistic promises to workers of employment stability and shares in value gains over the long term.

These policies were most effective in the mass-production firms

that in the first decades of the twentieth century established positions
of oligopolistic market power. Chapter 8 considers some alternative
perspectives on the role of labor–management relations in generating
the phenomenal productivity growth of the 1920s. In particular, I
argue that the employment practices of dominant firms were central
to generating the high levels of labor productivity achieved in U.S.
manufacturing during the 1920s. An essential feature of managerial
capitalism that enabled it to set new standards in economic performance was that the internal organization of powerful enterprises
shaped the operation of labor markets, creating so-called market imperfections that (far from impeding the progress of capitalist development as modern neoclassical theory would have one believe) represented the institutional foundations of capitalist success.

The Great Depression destroyed the cooperative labor–management relations that had contributed to the economic success of the
1920s. As I outline in Chapter 9, to motivate workers to supply
sufficient effort to achieve high levels of throughput and low unit
costs, management erected internal job structures that, after the rise
of industrial unionism in the late 1930s, became integral to the collective bargaining process. In the postwar era, the new structure of
labor–management relations—a structure that some have called job
control unionism[19]—created incentives for management to continue
to invest in skill-displacing technologies and for workers to supply
sufficient effort to permit steady growth in real wages alongside high
corporate profit levels.

These institutional arrangements enabled U.S. mass production enterprises to maintain international competitive advantage in the post–
World War II era. British industry had already learned the lesson,
however, that structures of work organization that promote economic development in one era can later become fetters on development when challenged by a more effective mode of value creation. For
the United States, that challenge has come from Japan, and indeed in
precisely those mass-production industries in which the United States
had, through the first six decades of this century, assumed international leadership.

I continue the comparative analysis of world leaders, past and
present, by showing how Japanese business organizations have been
able to extend U.S. principles of managerial control further down the
corporate hierarchy to integrate shop-floor workers into, rather than
exclude them from, the process of planning and coordinating the

shop-floor division of labor. Like the British, Japanese managers have left considerable skill on the shop floor, but in a very different manner, for very different reasons, and with very different results. The managers of British firms left skills on the shop floor because they could take advantage of an abundant supply of skilled labor, reproduced through worker-run apprenticeship systems, while avoiding investments in managerial structures and effort-saving technological change. In the twentieth century the British managerial strategy contrasted with the U.S. managerial strategy of breaking craft unionism and taking skills off the shop floor. In contrast to both these cases, Japanese management has taken responsibility for the *development* of shop-floor skills and, through firm-specific employment policies and labor organizations, has integrated shop-floor workers into the long-term evolution of the enterprise.

Japanese management is willing to supply its shop-floor workers with skills that are relevant to the operation of new mass-production technologies because it knows that workers will tend to utilize these skills to further, rather than obstruct, the enterprise goals that management has set. The availability of workers with the requisite skills upon whom management can count to provide high levels of effort has, over the past two decades, encouraged Japanese firms to invest in a new generation of shop-floor technologies that characterize what may be termed flexible mass production. The effective use of these technologies demands that shop-floor workers ensure the high quality, as well as the high quantity, of the flow of work through the production processes. If U.S. industrial firms hope to match the recent economic successes of their Japanese competitors, then they will have to provide shop-floor workers with the skills required by advanced technological systems, and they will have to build new structures of work organization to ensure that workers use these skills to further enterprise goals.

The concluding chapter, "Organization and Technology in Capitalist Development," summarizes the cross-national comparisons of work organization, technological change, and industrial leadership and then goes on to explore the broad social and economic implications of the Japanese challenge for the transformation of work organization in Britain and the United States. My purpose in this final chapter is not to enter into a full-scale analysis of the problems and possibilities for social and economic change in the once-dominant capitalist nations—that would require a book that delves much more deeply and thoroughly into contemporary political economy. My purpose is rather to point out the need for modern policy discussions to take cognizance of an analysis of capitalist development that can comprehend the dynamic interaction of organization and technology in generating economic growth.

In particular, I focus on the need for business enterprises to make long-term organizational commitments to their shop-floor workers to elicit high levels of effort from them. I also discuss how the recent quest by conservative politicians and economists to restore labor discipline and productivity by creating reserve armies of labor—pools of unemployed—may be profitable to employers in the short run while undermining the organizational commitment that is so critical to the process of value creation over the long run. In this historical, cross-national analysis of value creation on the shop floor, I would hope to provide some of the fundamental empirical and analytical knowledge required to fashion industrial institutions that can simultaneously improve the quality of working life, the distribution of income, and the standard of living that working people experience.

PART I

Theory and History in the Nineteenth Century

1 Theory and History in Marxian Economics

Property Relations

Volume I of Marx's *Capital* examines how capital accumulation occurs in a market environment. Marx began by assuming a world characterized by commodity exchange in which equality among buyers and sellers prevails and in which the exercise of social class power appears to have no place.[1] But Marx was merely setting up the free market notions of (as he put it) "Freedom, Equality, Property and Bentham"[2] for a dialectical fall, for he went on to ask how accumulation of wealth by capitalists such as that which had taken place in the British Industrial Revolution could possibly be reconciled with a theory of equal exchange. He answered by constructing a theory in which labor-power, like all commodities, exchanges at its value, but faces social inequality when it passes from the sphere of commodity exchange to the sphere of capitalist production.

In the production process, according to Marx, capitalists exercise considerable social power over the utilization of the labor inputs that they have purchased on the market, realizing more value from the productive efforts of workers than they have to pay out to workers in wages that are determined by the laws of commodity exchange. Key to understanding both labor productivity and income distribution under capitalism are the sources of the power that capitalists and workers bring to their relation with each other in the productive enterprise.

Social power is rooted in social dependence. Marx argued that capitalist control of the means of production makes the propertyless worker much more dependent on securing employment as a wage-laborer than the capitalist is on retaining the services of that particular worker. Marx was not the first economist to argue that capitalists held the balance of power in their relations with wage-laborers. As Adam Smith wrote in 1776:

> What are the common wages of labour, depends every where upon the contract usually made between those two parties, whose inter-

ests are by no means the same. The workmen desire to get as much, the masters to give as little as possible. The former are disposed to combine in order to raise, the latter in order to lower the wages of labour. It is not, however, difficult to foresee which of the two parties must, upon all ordinary occasions, have the advantage in the dispute, and force the other into a compliance with their terms. The masters, being fewer in number, can combine much more easily; and the law, besides, authorises, or at least does not prohibit their combinations, while it prohibits those of the workmen. We have no acts of parliament against combining to lower the price of work; but many against combining to raise it. In all such disputes the masters can hold out much longer. A landlord, a farmer, a master manufacturer, or merchant, though they did not employ a single workman, could generally live a year or two upon the stocks which they have already acquired. Many workmen could not subsist a week, few could subsist a month, and scarce any a year without employment. In the long-run the workman may be as necessary to his master as his master is to him, but the necessity is not so immediate.[3]

But how did the division of society into capitalist employers and hired workers occur in the first place, and what are the implications of this class division for the development of capitalism? To these questions, Smith provided no answers. Writing on the eve of Britain's Industrial Revolution, Smith was certainly aware that a historical transformation had taken place. But his sole focus was on the accumulation of capital, without any analysis of class relations as both a cause and a consequence of prior economic growth. He contrasted the capitalist economy of his time with "that rude state of society in which there is no division of labour, in which exchanges are seldom made, and in which every man provides everything for himself."[4] In such a "rude state of society," Smith went on to say, "it is not necessary that any stock should be accumulated or stored up beforehand, in order to carry on the business of the society." But previous accumulation is a basic precondition for the emergence of a modern industrial economy with its characteristic division of labor.

The "previous accumulation" explanation did not satisfy Marx, because it failed to address the role of social power in creating the preconditions for industrial capitalism. The late fifteenth century is known as the golden age of the peasantry because the vast majority of British workers had escaped the servile status and obligations of the feudal era but were not yet compelled to seek their subsistence by selling their labor-power to others. In contrast to the feudal mode of production before and the capitalist mode of production after, Marx characterized the era stretching from the fifteenth century to the early eighteenth century as the petty proprietor mode of production. How, why, and when did the petty proprietor mode of production give way to the capitalist mode of production? For Marx, "so-called primitive accumulation . . . is nothing else than the historical process of divorcing the producer from the means of production."[5]

Marx's argument was that, whatever the stock of capital accumulated prior to the advent of industrial capitalism, this previous (or primitive or original) accumulation in and of itself would not have resulted in the emergence of a wage-labor force, the sine qua non of capitalist production and accumulation. Previous accumulation may be a necessary precondition for the emergence of industrial capitalism, but it is not sufficient to create capitalism's characteristic social relation.

An analysis of the origins of the relation between capitalists and wage-laborers is critical for understanding the conditions under which workers sought out their sustenance through wage-labor. Only when these conditions are specified can one assess the economic impacts of the social power that capitalist employers exercised over wage-laborers in the production processes of the Industrial Revolution.

Marx's historical analysis of primitive accumulation put considerable weight on the role of the redistribution of access to land in agriculture in creating a landless labor force in Britain. On the basis of relatively little empirical evidence, Marx was able to discern the main elements of the social transformation that gave rise to a critical precondition for Britain's Industrial Revolution—the existence of a large, landless population that could potentially be hired as wage-laborers.[6]

My reading of the secondary sources confirms the broad outlines of Marx's arguments.[7] The prime instruments for the redistribution of access to land were "enclosures"—the transformation of land that had provided the basis for interdependent peasant communities into private farms. Enclosures represented successful attempts by some landlords and farmers to take advantage of new market opportunities that characterized the rise of capitalism. Taking place by means of individual acts of appropriation in the early sixteenth century, enclosures were occurring through national acts of expropriation by the early nineteenth century. If not in the short run, then over the long run the massive reallocations of access to land that enclosures entailed resulted in the separation of the mass of agricultural producers from the means of production.

Beginning with a well-known article by J. D. Chambers, a number of economic historians have sought to refute the Marxian thesis that the organizational transformation of British agriculture in the sixteenth to eighteenth centuries was responsible for the emergence of a wage-labor force.[8] The critics, it turns out, have not differed substantially with Marx on the facts of agricultural transformation. But by ignoring the historical and theoretical significance of the resultant changes in the social relations of *agricultural* production, the critics have missed Marx's main point.

For example, David Landes has taken issue with the view propounded by Marx and others that "explains the accomplishment of so enormous a social change—the creation of an industrial proletariat in the face of tenacious resistance—by postulating an act of forcible expropriation: *the enclosures uprooted the cottager and small peasant and drove them into the mills.*" Citing Chambers on enclosure and labor supply, Landes went on to argue: "Recent empirical evidence has invalidated this hypothesis; the data indicate that the agricultural revolution associated with enclosures *increased the demand for farm labour,* that indeed those rural areas that saw the most enclosures saw the largest increase in resident population. From 1750 to 1830, Britain's agricultural counties doubled their inhabitants."[9]

Marx did not argue that enclosures uprooted the cottager and small peasant and drove them into the mills. Indeed, he did not dispute the argument that dispossessed landholders remained in agricultural employment after enclosures. The critical transformation that Marx identified in his analysis of primitive accumulation was not the level of agricultural employment before and after enclosure but the changes in employment relations in agriculture caused by the reorganization of landholdings and the reallocation of access to land.

If one accepts the Marxian premise that the employment of wage labor is the fundamental and distinguishing social characteristic of capitalism, then it is only of secondary importance to the analysis of the social transformation in production relations whether workers initially sold their labor-power in the agricultural or the manufacturing sector. If one wants to take on Marx's historical analysis, then the issue is the relevance of his emphasis on the separation of the mass of producers from the land as a necessary precondition for the emergence of industrial capitalism.

No one, including Chambers, has disputed the fact that those who had had the least secure ties to the land prior to enclosure were left landless. But insofar as these newly created proletarians were reemployed as wage-laborers, the social relations of production into which they entered were changed dramatically. As wage-laborers, these workers were now much more responsive to social and economic forces that might push or pull them from one sector to another. Marx argued, "As soon as capitalist production takes possession of agriculture . . . part of the agricultural population is . . . constantly on the point of passing over into an urban or manufacturing proletariat, and on the look-out for opportunities to complete this transformation."[10] As the first step in the emergence of a wage-labor force, the significance of enclosures was that these workers had become part of a landless proletariat, their sustenance dependent on securing wage employment in whatever sector of the economy such employment might be available.

Another popular anti-Marxian argument contends that there is little evidence that legal rights to land were not protected during enclosures.[11] But this argument also misses Marx's point—the importance of the transformation of property relations as a precondition for industrial capitalism. Chambers himself recognized that "of the poor without legal rights it remains true that [in Arthur Young's words] 'by nineteen enclosure bills out of twenty they are injured, in some grossly injured.' "[12] As E. P. Thompson has put it, "Enclosure (when all the sophistications are allowed for) was a plain enough case of class robbery, played according to fair rules of property and law laid down by a Parliament of property-owners and lawyers."[13]

Even if one accepts that just treatment was accorded to peasant proprietors who could show legal title to the use of land, nothing is said about the majority of the agricultural population in the eighteenth century—the masses of cottagers, squatters, and agricultural laborers—who had only customary rights. To argue that these people were not treated unfairly because they did not possess legally enforceable property rights is irrelevant to the fact that they were dispossessed by enclosures. Again, Marx's critics have failed to address the issue of the transformation of access to the means of production as a precondition for the Industrial Revolution.

Yet another argument contests Marx's statement that the yeomanry had disappeared by 1750.[14] Chambers assumed that Marx meant that the yeomanry had descended to the ranks of the proletariat; and he sought to refute Marx by showing that, after enclosures of the late eighteenth and early nineteenth centuries, the number of small farm owners increased, or at least did not greatly decline.[15]

Chambers, however, failed to comprehend Marx's analysis of the transformation of the social class structure of British agriculture that preceded the Industrial Revolution. Nowhere did Marx argue that the yeomanry disappeared because they were proletarianized. Rather, when Marx spoke of the disappearance of the yeomanry, he was referring to the demise of a social class of independent peasant proprietors who had secured decent livelihoods from their traditional landholdings and who epitomized the petty proprietor mode of production. Taking advantage of the growing commercialization of British agriculture from the fifteenth century on, some were able to climb the social ladder to become landlords or capitalist farmers, whereas others looked to improve their lot by emigrating. In each case the British yeoman ceased to be a British yeoman.

It is true that after 1750 some petty proprietors continued to occupy and work their own land. But in a world of capitalist agriculture, the yeomanry no longer played an important role in determining the course of capitalist agriculture. As a social class that could influence the evolution of British economy and society, the yeomanry had disappeared.

Even if some yeomen did become proletarians, they need not have constituted the primary source of a landless laboring class. Gregory King's statistics indicate that cottagers, paupers, and agricultural laborers along with their families made up 55–65 percent of the agricultural population and 40–45 percent of the total population of England and Wales in 1688. At this date there was already a sizable urban and migrant proletariat. There is also general agreement that smaller tenant farmers found their economic existence difficult both before and after enclosures. Even if no yeoman had lost his land during the first half of the eighteenth century, there would still have been an abundance of potential proletarians just prior to the Industrial Revolution.[16]

Finally, Marx's critics have argued that it was population growth, not enclosures, that provided the Industrial Revolution with a wage-labor supply.[17] The argument, however, ignores the dynamic between the forces and relations of production that is the essence of Marx's approach. Population growth is one form of the development of the forces of production. The Marxian approach to history leads one to ask whether the changes in the social relations of production had an impact on the observed trends toward earlier marriage and larger families after 1750. There is reason to believe that they did. As hired farm laborers ceased to be live-in servants who were treated as part of the family and became wage-laborers subject to much more short-term, impersonal contracts, social constraints on choice of spouse and early marriage may have broken down. At the same time the growth of domestic industry, probably even more than the use of child labor in the factories, created economic incentives for workers with and without land to have more children.[18]

Even if the rapid rate of growth of Britain's population after the mid–eighteenth century had been independent of the changing social relations of production, the fact remains that increasingly the off-spring of landless workers were themselves born into a landless con-dition. In other words, history matters; and unless the critics can show that the major source of the wage-labor force in the British Industrial Revolution was people who *decided* to forgo the subsist-ence that could be had on viable family farms to earn a living working for others, then Marx's thesis of forcible separation of the producers from the land has not been addressed.

Why have Marx's critics had such difficulty in coming to grips with his arguments concerning the causes and effects of proletarianization? In part, the problem may be that Marx had remarkably little to say about how the first generation of factory workers was in fact re-cruited, a deficiency that permits his critics as well as many of his followers to conflate the issues of the dissolution of the petty propri-etor mode of production and the emergence of a disciplined factory labor force. In part, the problem is Marx's provocative style of dis-course, which was undoubtedly intended to make his critics see red. Provoked, the nonsocialist camp has in turn overreacted—for ex-ample, the attribution to Marx that enclosures uprooted the peasants and drove them into the mills.

The ideological gulf is real. Over 100 years after Marx sought to dispel the notion that the capitalist economy is simply a world of free and equal exchange relations, economists have instead elaborated even more systematically the individualistic, free-market vision. Neglected has been the Marxian analysis of the role of social power in the production process. The neoclassical theory of the "capitalist" economy makes no qualitative distinction between the corporate enterprise that employs tens of thousands of people and the small family undertaking that does not employ any wage labor at all. As far as theory is concerned, it is technology and market forces, not structures of social power, that govern the activities of corporate capitalists and petty proprietors alike. Given the dominance of a theoretical vision that treats the inner workings of the production process as a "black box," it is not surprising that those economic historians who imbibe the ideology that economic activity under capitalism can be construed as a series—even a general equilibrium—of market exchanges find the Marxian focus on the evolution of relations of production difficult to comprehend.

For Marx, the analysis of the transformation of production relations in the rise of industrial capitalism provided essential historical support for the centrality of social relations of production in the further development of capitalism. Moreover, far from ignoring exchange relations, the power of Marx's approach is to show how, as far as labor is concerned, the transformation of production relations based on new property relations generated exchange relations. That exchange relations were thrust on workers who could no longer get their sustenance through their direct access to land in turn provided the basis for Marx's argument that in capitalist production it is employers rather than employees who hold the balance of social power.

Work Organization

Marx, therefore, posited a dramatic change in social relations of production as a precondition for the advent of industrial capitalism. He argued, moreover, that the forces underlying this transformation were historically and logically distinct from the rise of the factory system that was to become the characteristic organizational form of the capitalist production process. Without direct access to the means of production, the proletarianized worker could no longer be independently employed. But neither was he or she yet an industrial worker, subject to the discipline of regular work hours and direct supervision that would become the norms in the capitalist workplace. As Marx emphasized, the success of industrial capitalism depended on the extent to which capitalists could exercise control over the work time of their employees. To what extent, at what points in time, and in what ways was capitalist control imposed on the British proletariat?

To analyze these issues, Marx divided the history of industrial capitalism into two stages: the manufacturing period and the era of large-scale industry.[19] In manufacturing, the forces of production are simply the artisanal skills and tools of the preceding handicraft era. But when these forces of production are brought under the control of the capitalist, productivity growth results from two changes in work organization: cooperation and division of labor. Cooperation and division of labor in turn provide the organizational bases for the further, and most dramatic, development of the forces of production through the introduction of automated machinery, ushering in the era of large-scale industry.

In Marx's view, machinery revolutionizes the mode of production by overcoming the strength and skill constraints that human beings impose on productivity. By transforming the worker from an active force of production to an easily replaceable appendage of an automated system, machinery provides the capitalist with the ultimate weapon for imposing work discipline on workers.

In historical perspective, there are a number of serious problems with Marx's analysis, not the least of which is his notion of "manufacture" as a historical stage preceding the advent of large-scale industry. Marx asserted that "the manufacturing period . . . extends, roughly speaking, from the middle of the sixteenth century to the last third of the eighteenth century."[20] Manufacture arises either from "the assembling together in *one workshop,* under the control of a single capitalist, of workers belonging to various independent handicrafts, through whose hands a given article must pass on its way to completion" or when "one capitalist simultaneously employs in *one workshop* a number of craftsmen who all do the same work, or the same kind of work, such as making paper, type or needles."[21] In other words, Marx defined manufacture as either the vertical or the horizontal integration of crafts into one site under the direct coordination and oversight of the capitalist and his managerial agents.

Marx raised the "manufacturing period" to the status of a historical stage in the development of industrial capitalism but provided no documentation of the predominance of manufacture, as he defined it, from the mid–sixteenth century to the late eighteenth century in Britain. In the last decades of the eighteenth century and throughout the nineteenth century, nonmechanized capitalist workshops existed alongside, and at times in competition with, the mechanized factory.[22] But historical research does not support Marx's claim that "manufacture"—the gathering together of large numbers of workers in one location—constituted a significant form of work organization prior to the rise of the factory system in the last decades of the eighteenth century.

What preceded the factory system was not the manufacturing workshop but domestic industry based on the putting-out system.[23] In domestic industry (or outwork, as it came to be called once the factory system had made its impression), a small group of workers (typically a family) labored independently in their own workplace (typically a portion of the family home) under the direction of a supervising worker (typically the husband and father).

If, as was usual in the woolen industry of West Yorkshire in the mid–eighteenth century, the work group supplied its own tools, workplace, and materials and had direct access to the product market without the intervention of an outside capitalist, then domestic industry was part of the petty proprietor mode of production. When operated under the putting-out system, however, the capitalist who supplied the domestic workers with materials to be transformed had a direct interest in the quality and quantity of work performed in the labor process. The more social power the putting-out capitalist had to further this interest, the more could domestic industry be viewed as belonging to the capitalist mode of production. If, as was increasingly the case during the nineteenth century, the putting-out capitalist had access to an abundant supply of outworkers as well as a legal system that would help enforce the rapid and complete return of worked-up materials under putting-out contracts, then the control that domestic workers exercised over the actual labor process could be considerably reduced.[24]

The putting-out system existed on a large scale in the textile industries that were to lead the rise of the factory system and form the basis of the Industrial Revolution. But outwork was also widespread in diverse manufactures such as nailmaking, watchmaking, and straw-plaiting. As direct access to the land was eroded, domestic industry enabled producers to remain in the rural setting, because capital flowed to the worker rather than vice versa. Whether pursued as a by-employment to supplement income derived from agriculture or as the sole source of family earnings, domestic industry permitted the continuity of the traditional rural lifestyle, including the integration of work time and family time. In the workplace, the adult male domestic worker could continue to be his own boss and direct the work of his wife and children.

Research has shown that the "free-born Englishman" of the eighteenth century—even those who, by force of circumstances, had to submit to agricultural wage labor—tenaciously resisted entry into the capitalist workshop.[25] In his discussion of primitive accumulation, Marx correctly emphasized that "the private property of the worker in his means of production is the foundation of small-scale industry, and small-scale industry is a necessary condition for the development of social production and of the free individuality of the worker himself."[26] The historical background to the reluctance of eighteenth-century and nineteenth-century workers to enter the capitalist workplace was the independence and individualism of the "free-born Englishman" that developed during the era of widespread distribution of property under the petty proprietor mode of production from the fifteenth century through the seventeenth century.[27]

Reinforcing the tradition of independence was the common eighteenth-century equation of the workshop operated for profit with the workhouse operated for paupers. Throughout the eighteenth century, Acts of Parliament promoted the establishment of workhouses to make poor relief more punitive, to make the poor pay their own way by forced labor, and, perhaps, to train paupers to be industrious. As Marx noted, Adam Smith, writing in 1776, used the terms "manufactory" and "workhouse" interchangeably.[28] And as Sidney Pollard has argued, the popular identification of the capitalist workplace with the public workhouse could only have been strengthened by the heavy reliance of the pioneering factories of the Industrial Revolution on unfree persons—so-called parish apprentices who had been transformed from wards of local poor-law authorities to wards of factory owners.[29]

As in the workshop or factory setting, so too under the putting-out system the interests of domestic workers were to maximize earnings for a minimum of effort, whereas the interests of the putting-out capitalists ran in the opposite direction. At any point in time the social power that the capitalist and the worker could exercise over the relation between work effort and the distribution of income might be very different depending on which party controlled the physical production site. In the workshop or factory the capitalist could set the hours of work and directly monitor the pace of work. If workers were in short supply, they might ignore the factory capitalist's rules and orders. One would therefore expect that the factory would be more successful when the supply of workers was more abundant. But whatever the conditions of labor supply, a great advantage of the workshop or factory for the capitalist was that it put him formally in the position of making compliance with *his* rules and orders a condition of employment in *his* place of work.

It was not so in the privacy of the domestic worker's own home, where the direct producer could exercise considerably more control over the organization, duration, and pace of work. For capitalists, domestic industry offered the advantages of relatively low investment in fixed capital and managerial structure, but at the cost of leaving control of the labor process in the hands of the workers. In the eighteenth century domestic workers could not be counted on to work hard and steady when left to their own devices. In contrast to the time-orientation that came to characterize work behavior in the factory setting, work behavior in domestic industry tended to be task-oriented, a continuation from peasant agriculture out of which domestic industry grew.[30] In effect, task-oriented work behavior meant that during a given period of time workers would produce just enough to maintain their standards of living. As a result, domestic workers were regularly accused of working irregularly and holding onto the capitalists' materials for inordinate periods of time. In addition, aided by the privacy of their own homes, they were also known to supplement their earnings by appropriating a portion of the material put out to them, typically by adulterating or stretching the product to bring it up to the expected weight or size.[31]

The social relations of the domestic putting-out system, therefore, were qualitatively different from those of the capitalist workshop or factory. In terms of the management of the labor process, the domestic workers were subcontractors more than wage-laborers. They supplied not only their labor-power but also their place of work, assistants, tools, and even machines in some cases. Unlike the wage-laborer who contracted to work for a specific length of time within the capitalist's workplace, the domestic worker maintained his or her independent status by retaining control over the day-to-day operation of the labor process.

A flood of labor into domestic employments in the first decades of the nineteenth century, however, eroded the standards of living of the outworkers while, by the same token, maintaining the commercial viability of the putting-out system in competition with workshop or factory production.[32] Despite the use of powerlooms in textile factories from 1798, the growth of the factory system in spinning in the first four decades of the nineteenth century was accompanied by the expansion of handloom weaving carried out under the putting-out system. As late as 1830, the number of handlooms in use may have been as much as four times greater than the number of powerlooms; and the wages of handloom weavers, which had been relatively attractive at the turn of the century, had fallen to poverty levels. The 1830s and 1840s saw the large-scale introduction of powerlooms into factories and a concomitant precipitous drop in the number of handloom weavers.

It was domestic industry rather than the manufacturing workshop, therefore, that preceded the factory and that continued as its prime alternative even as the factory system became firmly implanted during the Industrial Revolution. If, as Marx posited, some two centuries of manufacture as the dominant mode of work organization had preceded the coming of the factory system, then one might expect that, on the eve of the Industrial Revolution, British workers would have long since grown accustomed to wage labor *within* the capitalist workplace.

Yet it was during Marx's period of "manufacture," when, by assumption, men were already entering the capitalist workplace, that the British proletarians were attempting to retain critical dimensions of their free-born status. "Free-born Englishmen" who found themselves without access to land sought to protect their right to work under their own direction and to determine their own hours and pace of work by turning to production within their own homes. That domestic production rather than the manufacturing workshop was the historical alternative prior to the Industrial Revolution heightened the willingness and ability of British adult males to resist entry into the factory.

From the late eighteenth century, however, the factory system did emerge as a characteristic institution of the British Industrial Revolution. Marx provided little explicit historical analysis of the conditions under which British workers came to be regularly employed in the centralized capitalist workplace. Read out of context, one well-known passage in Marx's analysis of historical changes in the length of the workday might be interpreted as referring to the resistance of the "free-born Englishman" to supervised and regulated work. Marx argued,

> Centuries are required before the "free" worker, owing to the greater development of the capitalist mode of production, makes a voluntary agreement, i.e. is compelled by social conditions to sell the whole of his active life, his very capacity for labour, in return for the price of his customary means of subsistence, to sell his birthright for a mess of pottage.[33]

Read in the context of Marx's analysis of struggles over the length of the workday, however, it is clear that he viewed the birthright that the British worker lost not as control over the labor process by entering the capitalist workplace but as the amount of his "active life" spent under the direct sway of the capitalist. For Marx, the qualitative transformation in social relations—entry into the centralized capitalist workplace—had long since taken place. If, by conflating proletarianization and the creation of a factory labor force, Marx's critics miss the point of his analysis of the transformation of production relations in the rise of capitalism, they would nevertheless be justified in arguing that Marx failed to show how a factory labor force was in fact created.

Quoting the procapitalist ideologue Andrew Ure, Marx certainly recognized the problem:

> "The main difficulty" (in the automatic factory) "lay . . . above all in training human beings to renounce their desultory habits of work, and to identify themselves with the unvarying regularity of the complex automaton. To devise and administer a successful code of factory discipline, suited to the necessities of factory diligence, was the Herculean enterprise, the noble achievement of Arkwright! Even at the present day, when the system is perfectly organized and its labor lightened to the utmost, it is found nearly impossible to convert persons past the age of puberty into useful factory hands."[34]

But if, as Marx argued, the period of manufacture, stretching from the sixteenth century to the Industrial Revolution, had preceded the coming of the factory, why had the British industrial labor force not long since renounced "their desultory habits" and become inured to capitalist work discipline?

Marx's answer was that under "manufacture" craft unions made up of skilled adult males were able to restrict the extension of division of labor and the employment of unskilled workers, at times retaining "a long period of apprenticeship . . . even where it would be superfluous."[35] "The struggle between the capitalist and the wage-labourer," Marx contended, "rages throughout the period of manufacture."[36]

> Since handicraft skill is the foundation of manufacture, and since the mechanism of manufacture as a whole possesses no objective framework which would be independent of the workers themselves, capital is constantly compelled to wrestle with the insubordination of the workers. "By the infirmity of human nature," says our friend Ure, "it happens that the more skilful the workman, the more self-willed and intractable he is apt to become, and of course the less fit a component of a mechanical system in which . . . he may do great damage to the whole." Hence the complaint that the workers lack discipline runs through the whole period of manufacture.[37]

In Marx's view, machinery solves the problem of the insubordination of the workers—hence his emphasis on the transition from manufacture based on handicraft production to large-scale industry based on machine production rather than on the transition from worker control of the place of work in domestic industry to capitalist control of the place of work in either manufacture or large-scale industry. According to Marx, machinery did away with both the skilled workers of manufacture and their unions, including restrictive rules and customs concerning the organization of work.[38] Machinery supersedes the need for human strength and skill on the shop floor, substituting the labor of docile women and children for that of the truculent craftsmen. The reserve army of labor is augmented by the greater ability of capitalists to make use of segments of the labor force that are physically weaker and less skilled as well as by technical change that makes fewer direct labor inputs necessary per unit of output. The growth of the reserve army of labor in turn forces those who remain employed "to submit to over-work and subjects them to the dictates of capital."[39] Machinery, that is, enables the capitalist to impose discipline on the workers.

Marx displayed considerable insight into the technical relation between machine technology and the laboring capacities of human beings. But, when applied to the nineteenth-century British factory, his analysis of the social impact of technology on the relative power of capitalists and workers to control the labor process was too extreme. Marx failed to see that the introduction of machinery into a labor process that has relied on skilled craft workers is only a necessary, not a sufficient, condition for the elimination of worker control.

As I shall detail in Chapter 3, Marx's source for his classic example of how factory capitalists employed machinery to dominate workers was the procapitalist ideology of Andrew Ure, not the historical experience of British industrial development. During the conflict-ridden decade of the 1830s, Ure argued that the effect of the introduction of a new, more highly mechanized technology—the self-acting spinning mule—into the cotton textile industry was "to discharge the greater part of men spinners, and to retain adolescents and children." He suggested that the self-acting mule would, among other things, "put an end . . . to the folly of trades' unions"; and he went on to proclaim: "This invention confirms the great doctrine . . . that when capital enlists science into her service, the refractory hand of labour will be taught docility."[40]

Ure's message to British workers was the futility of collective action and resistance to factory discipline in the face of inexorable technical change. Fixed in the notion that, in the era of large-scale industry, technology had become the driving force in capitalist development, Marx absorbed the Urian ideology and ignored the ongoing reality of the factory system. Far from being "taught docility," spinning operatives emerged from the long Victorian boom of the third quarter of the nineteenth century as the best-organized and best-financed union in all of Britain, a position based on very substantial control over the organization of work.[41]

Why were operatives on the mule-spinning machines able to retain control over the labor process despite substantial mechanization, and why was Marx misled about the impact of the new technology on these workers? The answer—which will be explored fully in Chapter 3—requires an understanding of how the mule spinners, almost all of whom were adult males, were recruited into cotton-spinning factories in the first place. The mule-spinning machine was invented in 1779, and in the 1780s was used as a hand-powered machine in domestic industry. In the late 1780s, mule workshops arose, and in the 1790s factory production predominated as the mule was attached to waterpower and steam power. In the mule-spinning factory, the mule spinner worked on an internal subcontract system. Transferring into the factory the essentials of the actual organization of work in domestic industry, the mule spinner was paid by the piece and out of his earnings paid time-wages to assistants whom he himself recruited and supervised.

The subcontract system shifted the burden of recruitment and supervision onto the operative spinner, an advantageous arrangement for the capitalist in the early decades of the factory system when workers other than the most destitute were reluctant to enter the mills and when those who did were as yet undisciplined to factory routine.[42] The subcontract system permitted the mule spinner to maintain a considerable degree of control over the hierarchical and technical division of mule-spinning labor within the factory. In addition, but for the fact that he could hire and supervise his own children and, in some cases, his wife, the mule spinner might not have permitted them to enter the early factories.

Indeed, the mule spinners themselves—who were the first important group of adult male operatives to participate in the factory system—would probably not have been lured into the mills had it not been for the degree of independence they could retain on the factory floor. In effect, the early mule spinners were craft workers who, even within the factory environment, were able to establish many of the conditions of independence that characterized domestic industry.

As long as mule spinners were in short supply, they could resist the time orientation that came to characterize factory life. But the very success of the workers in retaining a measure of independence within the cotton mills served to increase their numbers and reduce resistance to hard and steady work. The demonstrated ability of factory spinners to maintain substantial control over the conditions of work and pay helped to overcome the long-standing aversion of a portion of the "free-born Englishmen" to the factory setting, particularly as the flood of workers into domestic industry after the Napoleonic Wars made that alternative less and less attractive.

In combination with the negative incentive posed by a growing reserve army of labor, positive incentives also served to habituate mule spinners to factory discipline. In answer to Ure's question of "how with . . . surplus hands the wages of fine spinners can be maintained at their present high pitch," a capitalist of the 1830s replied that by maintaining wages above the going market rate, "[a] spinner reckons the charge of a pair of mules in our factory a fortune for life, [and] he will therefore do his utmost to retain his situation, and to uphold the high character of our yarn."[43] By offering them relatively high wages and secure employment (as well as possible promotion to muleroom overlooker), mule spinners could be enticed to keep regular hours and work at a hard and steady pace.

If mule spinners had employed only their own children as assistants and had as a result been able to retain the wages of these helpers as family earnings, they might have worked in the irregular manner and with the limited earnings objectives characteristic of domestic industry. But a portion of the mule spinners' gross piece-rate earnings went as time-wages to nonfamily members who typically had to be hired in addition to family members in order to constitute a complete mule-spinning team.[44] Just as capitalists had an interest in getting as much work as possible out of their workers for a given wage, so too did the mule spinners—but with the difference that, as the key operatives in the spinning team, the mule spinners themselves had to labor long and hard to exploit as fully as possible the labor-power of their assistants. The social relations of the internal subcontract system, therefore, helped to enforce factory discipline on subcontractor and assistants alike.

The most diligent of the young assistants could aspire to becoming mule spinners one day. By virtue of their early introduction to factory discipline, therefore, successive generations of mule spinners as well as many other former assistants who remained at lower-pay jobs acquired the temperament and outlook that came to characterize lifelong factory hands.

Eric Hobsbawm has argued that "somewhere around the middle of the century we see a conscious adjustment of skilled workers to the 'rules of the game.' "[45] It is critical to note, however, that mule spinners, as well as many other groups of workers who secured considerable job control within the factory setting and became part of the British "labor aristocracy," did not merely adjust to the "rules of the game." Through their collective organizations, they had a preponderant role in making the rules. By the 1830s, when a commercially viable self-acting mule finally was available, the internal subcontract system in mule spinning had evolved into a very effective mode of labor management. The adult male mule-spinning operatives who managed production on the shop floor had themselves become highly productive workers who were willing and able to work regular hours at a steady pace. At the same time, however, as skilled workers entrusted with considerable shop-floor autonomy and what in retrospect at least would be seen as managerial responsibility, the mule spinners were able to develop effective collective organizations that could seek to enforce wage agreements and lead the fight for a shorter workday.

It was this collective power of mule spinners, and not a lack of work discipline on the shop floor, that the introduction of the self-acting mule was supposed to undermine. The mule-spinning unions were momentarily weakened—and wages considerably reduced—by the depressions of the 1830s and 1840s as well as by labor-saving technological changes. Nevertheless, going into the long boom of the third quarter of the nineteenth century, the collective organizations of both mule spinners and self-acting minders remained intact. For the minders, whose social power, according to both Ure and Marx, was supposed to have been automated out of existence, what was critical for maintaining control over the conditions of work and pay was the retention of their supervisory role—the legacy of domestic industry implanted in the factory.[46]

In their virtually universal adoption of the internal subcontract system, the factory capitalists of the Industrial Revolution left considerable control of the labor process in the hands of their adult male operatives. With the coming of the self-acting mule, the factory capitalists had little incentive to undermine the shop-floor control of key operatives who had themselves become well disciplined and who were in turn disciplining the younger generation of workers. The strong inclination to continue with the established and effective methods of labor management even with the more automated machinery was further reinforced by the highly competitive conditions of the British cotton textile industry. Locked into intense competitive conditions, it was risky for an individual firm to experiment with a new mode of work organization when existing arrangements worked so well. When, in the long boom that followed the hard times of the 1830s and 1840s, prosperity enhanced the power of workers in general to control the conditions of work and pay, self-acting minders were able to use their control over the labor process as well as the competitive fragmentation of their capitalist employers to build their collective organizations and consolidate their shop-floor control.

Misunderstanding the conditions under which workers such as the mule spinners entered the factories of the Industrial Revolution, Marx vastly overrated the social power that British factory capitalists exercised in the labor process and on the labor market.[47] Mistaken in the notion that the "free-born Englishman" had labored in the capitalist workplace for some two centuries before the Industrial Revolution and convinced that the development of the forces of production in the form of automated machinery would eliminate any remaining shop-floor resistance, Marx failed to analyze the evolution of the social relations of production under industrial capitalism.

For Marx, the introduction of machinery into the factory not only resulted in the complete subjugation of labor to capital but also put to an end alternative forms of work organization—in particular, domestic industry. Although Marx did not view domestic industry as an important eighteenth-century precursor of the factory, he recognized that it coexisted with the factory system in the third quarter of the nineteenth century. He viewed the appearance of domestic industry as a passing phenomenon that could not withstand the centralizing impact of machinery. His primary empirical examples to illustrate the onward march of machinery and the factory system are the introduction of the sewing machine into the clothing industry and the use of steam power in ribbon weaving. As in the case of the self-acting mule, however, so too in the cases of the sewing machine and steam power, Marx depicted technology rather than social relations of production as the foundation for new forms of work organization under capitalism.

Like nineteenth-century manufacture, Marx characterized domestic industry by, on the one hand, the absence of labor-saving machinery, and, on the other hand, "the cheapening of labour-power, by sheer abuse of the labour of women and children, by sheer robbery of every normal condition needed for working and living, and by the sheer brutality of over-work and night-work." But such exploitation of human laboring capacities "finally comes up against certain insuperable obstacles . . . When this point at last has been reached—and this takes many years—the hour has struck for the introduction of machinery, and for a thenceforth *rapid transformation* of the scattered domestic industries, as well as the manufactures, into factory industries."[48]

Marx's prime example of the transition from domestic industry and manufacture to the factory is the introduction of the sewing machine into the apparel industries.[49] Unlike the self-acting mule, which had been in widespread use for three decades when Marx published *Capital* in 1867, the sewing machine had barely even been introduced in Britain when Marx speculated on its impact on work organization. By the end of the 1860s, there may have been as few as

500 machines in use in all of England, some in small workshops, others in workers' homes, and still others in an Army clothing factory.[50]

Marx argued correctly that, through the 1850s, domestic industry was the main form of work organization in apparel production. On the basis of an abundant labor supply set free by large-scale industry and agriculture, surplus-value was produced by a combination of "the minimum wages [sufficient] for a miserable, vegetable existence, and . . . the extension of the hours of labour to the maximum endurable by the human organism."[51]

But domestic industry as well as small workshops were just "a variegated medley of transitional forms" in the evolution of the apparel factory.[52] "At last," Marx argued, "the critical point was reached."

> The basis of the old method, sheer brutality in the exploitation of the workers, accompanied by a more or less systematic division of labour, no longer sufficed for the extending markets and for the still more rapidly extending competition of the capitalists. The hour of the machine had struck. The decisively revolutionary machine, the machine which attacks in an equal degree all the innumerable branches of [the wearing apparel] sphere of production, such as dressmaking, tailoring, shoemaking, sewing, hat-making and so on, is the sewing-machine.[53]

Marx described "the system actually prevalent in England" in 1867:

> The capitalist concentrates a large number of machines on his premises, and then distributes the product of those machines amongst the domestic workers to work it up [on sewing machines] into its finished form. The variety of these transitional forms does not, however, conceal the tendency operating to transform them into the factory system proper. This tendency is nurtured *by the very nature of the sewing-machine,* the manifold uses of which tend to compel the concentration, under one roof and one management, of previously separated branches of a trade.[54]

In addition to the "very nature of the sewing-machine," other forces promoting the concentration of production "under one roof and one management," were, according to Marx, the advantages of having vertically related production processes performed in one place, the extension of the Factory Acts even to domestic production if women and children are employed, the overproduction of machine-made goods, which forces impoverished domestic workers to sell their own machines, and the overproduction of sewing machines, which "causes their producers, who need to sell at all costs, to let them out for so much a week, thus crushing the small sewing-machine owners by their deadly competition."[55]

Marx continued:

> Constant changes in the construction of the machines, and their ever-increasing cheapness, cause the older makes to depreciate daily and compel their sale in great numbers, at absurd prices, to large capitalists, who are now the only people who can employ them at a profit. Finally, the substitution of the steam-engine for man strikes the final blow in this, as in all similar processes of transformation.[56]

Marx was wrong to assume that the inevitable outcome of the diffusion of the machine was the factory. The author of a history of the London clothing trades has argued that "the most important consequences of the invention of the sewing machine was the speedup in work and production, which, in effect, caused a proliferation of the sweating system."[57] Some large-scale factories were established in Leeds, but the future of the industry was a proliferation of subcontracting and subdivision of labor on the basis of immigrants employed in their homes and small workshops.[58] Referring to the same 1864 report of the Children's Employment Commission from which Marx culled his evidence of the rise of the apparel factory, James Schmiechen has concluded: "Early predictions that the sewing machine would encourage the centralization of production in the factory were unfounded . . . As late as 1915 there was probably no industry as untouched by factory production or in which the methods of production had been standardized so little as the manufacture of clothing."[59]

In the case of the sewing machine, Marx fell victim to his preconception that the forces of production determine the evolution of work organization under capitalism. Far from encouraging the concentration of production under one roof, as Marx argued, "the very nature of the sewing-machine"—a relatively inexpensive machine that could be used to make many different products—made it ideal for outworkers who stood ready to pick up any type of work that became available to them. The extension of the Factory Acts to workshops employing fewer than fifty persons was ineffective because of inadequate inspection and enforcement, and it did not favor centralized work organization as Marx supposed it would.[60]

No more valid is Marx's argument that price-cutting by the manufacturers of sewing machines, locked in cutthroat competition among themselves, resulted in a proliferation of sewing machines that in turn created "deadly competition" for outworkers. Far from reflecting the anarchy of market competition among machine makers, the practice of letting the sewing machines out "for so much a week" was the result of a calculated marketing effort to make sewing machines available and affordable to women working in their homes. This competitive strategy was first pursued by the Singer Manufacturing Co. and gave Singer a dominant market position that insulated it from cutthroat competition.[61] Furthermore, it is not at all clear why overproduction of machine-made goods would, as Marx argued, compel outworkers to sell their machines (or to whom they would have sold them). During slumps, domestic workers became even more dependent on the possession of their sewing machines as means of production, and held onto them all the more tenaciously.

Marx's prediction of the "final blow" to domestic production because of the attachment of the steam engine to the sewing machine never occurred on a large scale. When and where they appeared from the late nineteenth century, apparel factories based on the sewing machine tended to use, not the steam engine, but electric power, a power source that could just as well have favored decentralized production.

Even when the steam engine was the prime mover in manufacturing, it did not necessitate the factory system. In a section of his chapter on machinery and large-scale industry entitled "The Revolutionary Impact of Large-Scale Industry on Manufacture, Handicrafts and Domestic Industry," Marx allowed that a machine "may itself serve as a basis of an industry of a handicraft character." He went on to argue, however, that

> this reproduction of the handicraft system on the basis of machinery only forms a transition to the factory system which, as a rule, makes its appearance as soon as human muscles are replaced, for the purpose of driving the machines, by a mechanical motive power such as steam or water. Here and there, but in any case only for a time, an

industry may be carried on, on a small scale, by means of mechanical power . . . In the Coventry ribbon industry the experiment of "cottage factories" was a quite natural and spontaneous development. In the centre of a square surrounded by rows of cottages, an engine-house was built and the engine connected by shafts with the looms in the cottages. In all cases, the power was hired out at so much per loom. The rent was payable weekly whether the looms were working or not. Each cottage held from two to six looms; some belonged to the weaver, some were bought on credit, some were hired. The struggle between these cottage factories and the factory proper lasted over twelve years. It ended with the complete ruin of the 300 cottage factories.[62]

As far as it goes, this account of the coexistence of factories and cottage factories in the Coventry ribbon industry is accurate. But Marx did not go far enough in his analysis of the reasons for the "complete ruin" of the cottage factories, leaving the impression that, because steam-powered machines were involved, the ultimate triumph of the factory was inevitable.

From the 1840s, when the first steam-powered factories and cottage factories were built, until 1860 when the British ribbon industry was exposed to free trade under the Cobden-Chevalier Treaty, the two modes of work organization did coexist and compete with each other. The cottage factories more than held their own: between 1857 and 1860, industry expansion in Coventry took place exclusively in cottage factories, bringing the number to 383 on the eve of free trade.[63]

What determined the failure or success of the two alternative modes of production? The machine technologies used in both were identical. The two systems grew up side by side, so there was not much difference in the average vintage of plant and equipment. Total fixed costs of plant and equipment were probably about the same. It is not apparent that the weavers who entered the factories were any more or less skilled than those who worked in their homes.

What distinguished the two systems was not technology but the impacts of the different relations of production on the levels of work effort and the distribution of income. To entice workers into the factories as well as to avoid being governed by the piece-rate lists of the outworkers' union, factory capitalists paid predetermined weekly wages instead of piece-rates.[64] The earnings of factory workers, therefore, were not directly dependent on the amount of effort they expended. Moreover, with labor markets tight and workers' organizations strong during the prosperity of the late 1840s and 1850s, not only did wages rise but also factory owners had little power to use the threat of dismissal to get more effort out of their workers.

In the cottage factories, however, workers were paid by the piece. The demonstrated power of these outworkers to enforce the wage-lists and prevent rate-cutting gave them the incentive to supply high levels of effort to the production process. Moreover, cottage workers had to bear a fixed weekly charge for the rental of the workshop portion of the cottages as well as steam power, whatever the level of output they produced. Higher levels of effort and output reduced their unit power costs and effectively increased their remuneration per unit of output. In other words, because of the very different distributions of the costs and benefits of production in the two modes of work organization, the outworkers had direct incentives to work hard, whereas the factory workers did not. One can therefore infer that, with the same technology, physical productivity was higher and unit costs lower under the cottage-factory system than under the factory system. Such an inference explains the apparent competitive advantage of the cottage factories prior to 1860.

The structures of social power and work incentives changed, however, when free trade enabled French ribbons to flood the British market. In the long run, the whole of the Coventry ribbon trade, not just the cottage factories, was to meet its demise.[65] In the short run of the early 1860s, a partial adjustment to the new competition was made by a successful attack on the piece-rates paid to outworkers and the wages paid to factory workers. In the absence of a steady flow of ribbon orders, outworkers had no interest in continuing to pay steam power charges. The owners of the steam engines made some concessions to try to keep the cottage factories going. But other cottage factories either closed or reverted to handloom weaving. More important, with the workers' power of collective action and individual exit broken, the factory owners were now able to reap the main benefit that the factory setting could potentially offer: the intensification of work effort by direct supervision within the factory walls. As a result, the factories weathered the storm of free trade better than the cottage factories did.

Indeed, to create a social setting in which it would be easier to impose work discipline, some of the cottage-factory owners made the transition from domestic industry to the factory with the same workers within the same facilities. Prest has described the transformation that had occurred by 1861 at a firm that had built its cottage factories in 1857:

> A way [was] knocked through the partition walls from one shop to another, and . . . the top story of each [cottage factory block] was now run as a factory. The weavers might still be working above their own houses but they were no longer working at home. They still made their way up to their factory through their own trap doors, but soon these were to be closed, and the weavers would have to proceed to the factory by leaving their own houses, and walking through the yard to the external staircase in the corner between the two blocks.[66]

Therefore, Marx was, strictly speaking, correct to herald the ultimate success of the factory in the case of Coventry ribbon weaving. But he might have added that the factory "triumphed" only when and because the industry entered into permanent decline, wiping out the viability of the subcontracting system that permitted workers to work in the privacy of their own homes and diminishing the social power of factory workers to resist unremunerated intensification of labor. The example of post-1860 Coventry ribbon weaving supports Stephen Marglin's argument that the success of the factory system depended not on technology but on the creation of a social environment conducive to the imposition of work discipline.[67] The economic effectiveness of the factory as a mode of work organization did not occur within a social vacuum but depended on the historical evolution of conditions that determined the relative power of capitalists and workers to structure the relation between effort and pay.

Surplus-Value

In the light of the history of the nineteenth-century British economy, it is fair to conclude that Marx overemphasized the independent influence of technology as opposed to relations of production in the determination of work organization. Because machinery does change the skill content of work, it can potentially serve as an instrument of social power. How and to what extent it does so, however, depends not only on the nature of the technology but also on the nature of the social environment into which it is introduced.

If Marx did not provide all the correct answers to these questions, he did at least make the exercise of social power in the labor process central to his analysis of the capitalist economy. The main focus of his theoretical work was how capitalists use wage labor to generate and appropriate surplus-value. Marx's great insight was to recognize that capitalist production is a social process in which there can be a basic conflict of interests between capitalists and workers over the relation between effort and pay. His error was his failure to analyze closely enough the evolving sources of social power of the two sides in determining the effort–pay relation in the presence of technological change.

Despite Marx's errors of empirical application and theoretical elaboration, his theory of surplus-value remains highly relevant for empirical work because of its focus on key variables that determine the effort–pay relation: the subsistence wage, the duration of work, the intensity of work, and the skill content of work. Given technology, the higher the level of effort that the capitalist can elicit from the worker and the lower the wages he has to pay to get it, the higher the level of surplus-value that he can appropriate to himself. Unless the worker gets intrinsic satisfaction from working harder or longer for a given wage, his or her loss is the capitalist's gain. Given the inherent conflict, what has to be understood and analyzed are the sources of social power that the two sides can bring to bear in determining the relation between effort and pay.

In Marx's general theory of the capitalist economy, the theory of surplus-value must be distinguished from the labor theory of value. The theory of surplus-value, presented in Parts 3 through 6 of *Capital,* Volume I, is a microeconomic theory of the sources of productivity growth and the distribution of income within the capitalist production process. The labor theory of value, which is set forth in Parts 1 and 2 of Volume I of *Capital,* is a theory of price determination in the process of market exchange.

Unlike the labor theory of value, which takes technology, skills, and effort as given, the theory of surplus-value analyzes how productivity changes in a capitalist economy. If inputs are to be transformed into outputs, then raw materials, tools, and machines require the active participation of human beings in the production process. Active participation can involve inventing a new process, designing a new product, coordinating the transformation of inputs into outputs, handling a tool, or simply tending a machine. For Marx, the critical transformation of the production process in the development of industrial capitalism was from tool handling to machine tending. The vast majority of workers became mere appendages of the machine. Work lost any intrinsic value, so the only reward the worker got was the pay that he or she received. The alienating nature of work brought to the fore the conflict over the relation between effort and earnings.

As a microeconomic theory of a capitalist enterprise operating in a competitive environment, the theory assumes that the only way in which the individual capitalist can raise his profits is to increase the amount of work effort that is elicited from his workers. As a general rule, all market prices, including wages, are given to the individual capitalist. Moreover, in a competitive world a particular capitalist cannot retain privileged access to process or product innovations for any appreciable period of time. But the capitalist does have privileged access to, and control over, the workers that he employs. Precisely because the worker is not perfectly mobile but is dependent on the capitalist to gain a living, the capitalist is not subject to the dictates of market forces in dealing with the worker in the production process. The more dependent the worker is on his or her particular employer, the more power the capitalist has to demand longer and harder work in return for a day's pay. The resultant unremunerated increase in the productivity of the worker per unit of time is the source of surplus-value.

The measure of surplus-value is the difference between the value-added by and the value paid to the worker. As owner of the means of production, the industrial capitalist has a legal right to keep the surplus-value for himself. If the industrial capitalist has borrowed capital or rented productive resources, then he passes along some of the surplus-value to financiers or resource owners, typically on the basis of predetermined rates.

The means of production must be transformed into salable products at a cost that will yield a gross profit. Given the prices of inputs other than labor-power as well as the prices of outputs, surplus-value will depend on the levels of effort and pay of a given quality of labor. According to the labor theory of value, labor-power exchanges for a wage that is determined by the labor time socially necessary to reproduce the capacity to work. "In contrast . . . with the case of other commodities," Marx argued, "the determination of the value of labor-power contains a historical and moral element." He then asserted that "nevertheless, in a given country at a given period, the average amount of means of subsistence necessary for the worker is a known *datum*."[68]

By taking the value of labor-power as given, Marx was able to focus his attention on the extraction of surplus-value once the worker has entered the capitalist production process. Unfortunately, within Marx's general framework, what should be merely a simplifying assumption became a means of portraying the capitalist workplace as a social system unto itself. By assuming that the value of labor-power is given, Marx avoided the analysis of items such as the structure and size of the family and the resultant norms for family and supplementary wages; the role of the state in the provision of social services that may partially substitute for the market wage; the collective power of workers to obtain a permanently higher subsistence wage or to prevent the establishment of a permanently lower one, including the power of workers from one "historical and moral" background to protect their wages from erosion by the influx of workers from another "historical and moral" background; and the nature of skills, training, and education required by the historical evolution of work organization itself.

In short, the investigation of the determinants of the value of labor-power—the transformation of a subsistence wage into what can be called a conventional wage—is critical for understanding the evolving relation between economy and society. Marx's failure to analyze the wider social processes that determine the value of labor-power led him to underestimate the impact of institutions such as the family, school, and unions on the structure of social power within the capitalist enterprise.[69]

Reading Volume I of *Capital,* one gets the impression (by no means dispelled in Marx's other writings) of a working class rendered increasingly defenseless by nineteenth-century capitalist development. Even the adult male worker had no time for cultural and political activities, as capitalist domination transformed "his life-time into working-time." The working-class family was torn apart as capitalist exploitation dragged "his wife and child beneath the wheels of the juggernaut of capital."[70] Competing with the cheap labor of women and children, men could no longer earn the family wage that formed the material foundation of the working-class family. Schooling for working-class children bore no relation to the needs of production but only existed to comply with stipulations of the Factory Acts. After the achievement of the "normal" ten-hour workday through state legislation in the 1840s, trade unions no longer had an important institutional role to play in determining the generation and appropriation of surplus-value.

Such a picture of the nineteenth century is unwarranted. The working-class family was far from destroyed by capitalist development. To be sure, as Marx stressed, capitalists were able to use the structure of the patriarchal family to pay women and children wages far below those of adult males. But adult males were also able to use the same structure to support their claims to earnings to support a family. Labor movements in defense of the standard of living of the working-class family as well as state legislation such as the Factory Acts were based on patriarchal relations and attitudes—namely, that women and children were unfree persons, that a women's place was in the home, and that a man had the right to and need for a wage that would permit him to support a family. Insofar as these movements were successful, they served to consolidate the role of the family as the basic unit for the material and cultural reproduction of the labor force.[71]

Unions, moreover, did not merely fight defensive battles against a dominant capitalist class, as Marx argued in *Value, Price and Profit*.[72] Gaining power in the long boom of the third quarter of the nineteenth century, unions were able to win electoral reform that in 1867 (the same year that *Capital* was first published) extended the vote to a large proportion of the adult male workers. With this political power the working class was able to secure legislation that protected the position of the labor movement in industry and that extended the rights of workers as citizens to a decent standard of living. These legislative victories influenced both the share of the working class in the social product and the extent to which that share was dependent on the wages that were wrested from capitalist firms.[73]

Taking the value of labor-power as given, however, Marx went on to analyze the determinants of labor productivity within the capitalist enterprise. Employing labor at an externally determined wage, the capitalist faces the problem of getting effort out of the workers he has hired. At stake are not only unit labor costs but, insofar as the utilization of physical capital depends upon effort, unit capital costs as well.

Marx analyzed two dimensions of work effort: duration and intensity. Given the daily wage and the amount of labor performed per work hour, the capitalist can increase surplus-value by extending the length of the workday. Or, holding the wage and the workday constant, the capitalist can augment surplus-value by increasing the intensity of work.

For Marx, duration and intensity are two very different ways of increasing surplus-value. Like the subsistence wage, the normal length of the workday is determined by forces beyond the bounds of the enterprise, whereas the intensity of labor is determined by the exercise of social power within the capitalist enterprise itself.

Marx argued, "In the history of capitalist production, the establishment of a norm for the working day presents itself as a struggle over the limits of that day, a struggle between collective capital, i.e. the class of capitalists, and collective labour, i.e. the working class."[74] In Chapter 10 of *Capital,* Marx gave a lucid account of the struggle over the length of the workday in the rise of capitalism and its culmination in the Factory Acts of the 1830s and 1840s.

As I have noted, Marx ignored the role of domestic industry as a means by which workers maintained significant control over the length of the workday in the eighteenth and early nineteenth centuries. As a result, he in effect underrated the importance of the factories of the early Industrial Revolution as a means of extending the hours of labor.

But his account of the configuration of social forces surrounding the passage of the various Factory Acts in the first half of the nineteenth century is historically accurate. Marx described the lengthening of the hours of work in the early stages of the Industrial Revolution; the ineffectiveness of the pre-1833 factory legislation because of lack of enforcement mechanisms; the growing movement of the operatives for a shorter workday; the progression from legislation covering children to legislation covering women, and how as a result the workday of men became de facto fixed at ten hours; attempts by capitalists to prolong the workday for adults under the Factory Acts by using children in shifts; the interest of the state in ensuring the long-run reproduction of a healthy labor force; and the increasing tendency for those factory owners who could more easily adjust to a shorter workday to support the movement for effective legislation as a means of putting pressure on those competitors who were less capable of maintaining profits with the hours of labor restricted.

The result of the Factory Acts was the creation of a "normal" workday that, in Marx's view, could, like the subsistence wage, henceforth be taken as given in the analysis of the determinants of surplus-value. The formal elements of the wage contract—the wage and the hours of work—were now set, but the problem of getting effort out of the workers had just begun. The remainder of Marx's analysis of capitalist production concerns the ways in which capitalists can gain control over workers and extract surplus-value in the labor process with the wage and workday fixed.

The methods of capitalist work organization that permit the extraction of surplus-value are cooperation, division of labor, and machinery. By introducing these methods, according to Marxian theory, the owner of the means of production turns himself into an industrial capitalist. How do cooperation, division of labor, and machinery increase the physical productivity of labor and, hence, the production of surplus-value? Specifically, what was Marx assuming about the structure of social power and its impact on the relation between effort and pay when he argued that cooperation, division of labor, and machinery augment the surplus-value extracted from each worker?

According to Marx, cooperation occurs whenever the capitalist gathers a large number of workers together under his direction.[75] As a source of productivity growth under manufacture, cooperation takes the preexisting handicraft methods of production and division of labor as given.[76] As Marx said: "Manufacture can hardly be distinguished, in its earliest stages, from the handicraft trades of the guilds, except by the greater number of workers simultaneously employed by the individual capitalist. It is merely an enlargement of the workshop of the master craftsman of the guilds."[77]

Marx argued that "when the worker cooperates in a planned way with others he strips off the fetters of his individuality, and develops the capabilities of his species," thus unleashing the "productive power of social labor."[78] Marx gave four distinct reasons why cooperation unleashes this productive power. First, economies of scale in the use of fixed capital are realized.[79] Second, relatively large numbers of laborers working in concert can now perform tasks that could not be done within the strict confines of handicraft (or peasant) production because of "the physical constitution of the object of labour" relative to the laboring capacities of the individual worker.[80] Third, man is "a social animal" and "mere social contact begets in most industries a rivalry and a stimulation of the 'animal spirits,' which heightens the efficiency of each individual worker."[81] Fourth, time and motion can be saved when certain tasks are done cooperatively.[82]

As a source of productivity growth, the last reason—the saving of time and motion—really belongs under the heading of division of labor and will be discussed in that context later. As for the other three reasons, I shall consider each of them in turn to see what assumptions are being made about the nature of the underlying relations of production and the determination of the intensity of work.

To illustrate how cooperation yields economies of scale, Marx argued, "A room where twenty weavers work at twenty looms must be larger than the room of a single weaver with two assistants. But it costs less labour to build one workshop for twenty persons than to build ten to accommodate two weavers each; thus the value of the means of production concentrated for use in common on a large scale does not increase in direct proportion to their extent and useful effect."[83] If one assumes that work intensity and wages are the same in both the concentrated and decentralized work settings, then the cooperative mode will yield lower unit costs. But my earlier discussion of the coexistence of outwork and factory work in British textiles revealed that the assumption that work effort is independent of work organization does not necessarily hold. Rather, to say anything about relative work intensities, one has to make further assumptions about the structures of social power that prevail in each of the two work settings.

The second reason—that the capitalist can extract surplus-value from new tasks that can be performed cooperatively, but not individually—simply says that the capitalist can appropriate surplus-value from cooperative labor because he owns the means of production. It does not tell us why cooperative labor generates surplus-value. Only the third reason—that man is "a social animal"—speaks to the impact of cooperation on effort within the capitalist mode of production. Marx assumed that when capitalists, as the owners of the means of production, bring together large numbers of proletarianized workers under their control, they are able to appropriate the "socially productive power of labour as a free gift."[84]

But Marx was assuming what has to be proved. When proletarianized workers have entered the capitalist workplace, why should they direct their "animal spirits" to working more "efficiently" for the capitalist, with whom they supposedly have antagonistic relations? Why not direct their "animal spirits" (derived from "mere social contact") to struggle against the capitalist whose only interest is the exploitation of their labor? Why not use their collective power to restrict output and preserve their own capacities to work (and live) rather than present capital with a "free gift"?

Marx's answer appears to go beyond "mere social contact" among workers to entail direct supervision. The capitalist must not only own the cooperative production process but must also organize the appropriation of surplus-value from it. Hence capitalist production must be, as Marx put it, despotic. Supervision "is made necessary by the capitalist, and therefore antagonistic, character of [the cooperative labour] process." As the enterprise expands its scale, the capitalist "hands over the work of direct and constant supervision of the individual workers and groups of workers to a special kind of wage-labourer," namely, managers, foremen, and overseers "who command during the labour process in the name of capital."[85]

But against the resistance of workers to the exploitation of their labor-power, why does direct supervision succeed in intensifying labor to the point where it more than compensates for the costs of managers, foremen, and overlookers? Ironically, Marx posited a solution to the problem of effort that rests not on the social nature of production but on the social nature of exchange! The capitalist makes individual contracts with, say, 100 workers:

> Being independent of each other, the workers are isolated. They enter into relations with the capitalist, not with each other. Their cooperation only begins in the labour process, *but by then they have ceased to belong to themselves.* On entering the labour process they are incorporated into capital. As co-operators, as members of a working organism, *they merely form a particular mode of existence of capital.* Hence the productive power developed by the worker socially is the productive power of capital. The socially productive power of labour develops as a free gift to capital whenever the workers are placed under certain conditions, and it is capital which places them under these conditions.[86]

With cooperation as its basis, division of labor becomes, in Marx's view, the means of raising surplus-value during the period of "manufacture." Here the intensity of labor would surely seem to be important, because Marx stated that "whether complex or simple, each operation has to be done by hand, retains the character of a handicraft, and is therefore dependent on the strength, skill, *quickness and sureness* with which the individual manipulates his tools.[87]

Marx drew upon the famous analysis of Adam Smith to explain how a greater fragmentation of tasks leads to higher labor productivity. In *The Wealth of Nations* Smith argued that, by means of the division of labor, the worker (1) becomes more adept at doing one simple task; (2) saves the time of moving from task to task; and (3) becomes more inventive.[88] Smith viewed the sources of productivity growth that flow from increased division of labor as purely technical in nature; he paid no attention to the impact of the social relations of the workplace on the generation or appropriation of productivity gains.

Following Smith all too closely in explaining the impact of division of labor on the extraction of surplus-value, Marx argued that "a worker who performs the same simple operation for the whole of his life converts his body into the automatic, one-sided implement of that operation" and that as a result "in comparison with the independent handicraft, more is produced in less time" by the worker in capitalist production. Marx went on to say:

> The worker's continued repetition of the same narrowly defined act and the concentration of his attention on it teach him by experience how to attain *the desired effect with the minimum of exertion*. But since there are always several generations of workers living at one time, the technical skill, the tricks of the trade thus acquired, become established, and are accumulated and handed down.[89]

In essence, Marx was making a "learning-by-doing" argument: productivity advances result from the increasing ability of experienced workers to produce more per unit of time with the same expenditure of effort.

But the fact that workers become more adept at performing a particular task does not tell us anything about "the quickness and sureness" with which they actually apply their "strength and skill" within the capitalist labor process. Is it not likely that even when their labor has been divided, wage-laborers will use the development of their particular laboring capacities and their intimate understanding of a particular part of the production process—the "tricks of the trade" that they pass down from generation to generation—to control the pace of work and thereby reap for themselves utility gains in the form of on-the-job leisure? Alternatively, is it not likely that wage-laborers will form craft unions, the express purpose of which is to control not only the level of effort but also the relation between effort and pay?

One need only look to the history of nineteenth-century British capitalist production, summarized earlier and in Chapter 6, to answer these questions. In industry after industry, key groups of British workers did come to exercise substantial control over the relation between effort and pay within the capitalist enterprise.

Like Smith, however, Marx gave the impression that technical specialization in a cooperative labor process in and of itself—that is, quite apart from the particular social relations of production—solves the problem of getting effort out of the worker. Marx argued that "the habit of doing only one thing converts [the specialized individual worker] into an organ which operates with the certainty of a force of nature, while his connection with the whole mechanism compels him to work with the regularity of a machine."[90] The forces of production, including the worker's mindless expenditure of his or her labor-power, ensure that high levels of effort are forthcoming.

If the exercise of social power enters into Marx's analysis, it is because capitalists use division of labor to reallocate unskilled work away from men, who had made these tasks integral to their craft, to women and children. Given the patriarchal relations of the family, women and children can be employed for lower wages than men and have less social power to resist attempts to intensify their labor. Surplus-value is thereby enhanced.

It can also be argued that the real advantage of the technical division of labor that Smith and (following him once again) Marx attributed to time saved in moving from task to task is the greater ease with which supervisors can oversee workers who have no business but to stay put at a particular post throughout the workday, producing a particular component of a larger product. Conversely a worker who is permitted, say, to fetch supplies to be used in his or her primary task may use the opportunity of moving from place to place to control the pace of work.[91]

Quoting Smith, Marx stressed the detrimental effects that the extreme division of labor in the workplace can have on the intellectual development of workers.[92] One must assume that Marx was thinking of unskilled workers, for he recognized that however far the division of labor goes under manufacture, there always remain certain skills that cannot be simply divided away. Hence Marx emphasized the distinction between skilled workers (mainly men) and unskilled workers (mainly women and children) under manufacture, arguing—and this relates to Smith's controversial third reason—that the technical division of labor clarifies possible improvements and adaptations of particular tools, enabling "the specialized workers . . . themselves [to take] an active part" in the development of technology.[93]

As I have noted, Marx stressed the constraints that the social power of skilled workers place upon the extraction of surplus-value, arguing that "the complaint that the workers lack discipline runs through the whole period of manufacture."[94] In large-scale industry, however, the introduction of machinery is supposed to resolve the problem of discipline by making the skilled workers superfluous.

Marx portrayed the determination of effort in large-scale industry as simply derivative of changes in the length of the workday and mechanization, rather than as a direct outcome of capital–labor conflict. He argued that "the efficiency of labour-power is in inverse ratio to the duration of expenditure." He introduced factual evidence that, when the workday is shortened from twelve to eleven hours, output per workday actually increases "entirely as a result of steadier application to the work and a more economical use of time on the part of the workers."[95] But he did not explore changes in capital–labor relations that may have influenced this result. At best, he adopted a "human-relations" perspective on how the "animal spirits" of the workers are raised, arguing that "the moral element played an important part in the . . . experiments. The workers told the factory inspectors: 'We work with more spirit, we have the reward ever before us of getting away sooner at night, and one active and cheerful spirit pervades the whole mill, from the youngest piecer to the oldest hand, and we greatly help each other.' "[96]

Machinery, however, is a more potent means of permitting the intensification of labor because the production process is no longer reliant on the physical strength and craft skills of workers. Machinery increases surplus-value by reducing the amount of work effort required per unit of output, while at the same time making the workers needed to tend these machines easily replaceable, and hence subject to speedup and stretchout. Quite apart from the cutting of the wage bill that results from the use of cheaper segments of the labor force, Marx assumed that capitalists are able to increase surplus-value by running machines so fast that complementary labor-power is compelled to work with the maximum effort that is humanly possible. As a result, unit labor costs are lowered and fixed capital costs are spread over more output per unit of time.[97]

Marx made no mention of worker resistance to unremunerated intensification of labor. As I have shown in the case of the self-acting mule, Marx failed to see that the introduction of machinery into the capitalist labor process is only a necessary, not a sufficient, condition for the displacement of worker control over the relation between effort and pay.

Marx's assumption that mechanization enables the capitalist to intensify effort to its physical maximum has led most Marxists to ignore the relation between mechanization and the intensity of labor. Like most economists, they rarely ask why machinery results in increases in labor productivity, even though one of Marx's most important contributions to our understanding of production is to reveal the answer.[98] Simply put, mechanization overcomes the constraints on productivity inherent in human labor by embodying the strength and skill requirements of work in much more durable and precise machines. After mechanization, the same task can be performed as well as it could be before with less expenditure of work effort on the part of the operative. Such technological change should properly be called effort saving.

The introduction of effort-saving machinery does not ensure either increased physical labor productivity or surplus-value. The sufficient condition for increased labor productivity is that remaining workers be unable to reap (or eliminate, depending on one's perspective) all of the productivity gains in the form of more leisurely work. If surplus-value is to increase subsequent to the introduction of an effort-saving technology, high levels of effort will have to be restored without the inordinate use of income incentives. Furthermore, because capital costs are incurred in the process of technological change, the ability of capitalists to restore (or, in the presence of very high capital costs, augment) the level of work effort received for a given level of earnings is a precondition for the introduction of the technology in the first place.[99] Struggles over the intensity of labor and its relation to pay are, therefore, integral to the ongoing process of capitalist accumulation.

Marx avoided an analysis of how the evolving structure of capital–labor relations affects the determination of the relation between effort and pay. He viewed the intensification of labor subsequent to the introduction of machinery as nonproblematic because of two built-in mechanisms—one external to the labor process and one internal—that push the intensity of work to its maximum.

The external mechanism has already been mentioned: the introduction of machinery is assumed to create an industrial reserve army that stands ready to take the jobs of those still fortunate enough to have them, thereby forcing the employed to submit to the demands of supervisors for more intense labor. Even if one assumes the existence of an industrial reserve army, the argument is problematic for both technical and social reasons. The technical reason is that the firm has to concern itself with the costs of high levels of turnover. There are costs of hiring and training new workers (which can result not only in short-run productivity declines but also in the wastage of raw materials and damage to equipment). Such costs can be considerable, and even then the firm has no assurance that, over the long run, it will end up with more productive workers. The social reason is that, even with the introduction of "deskilling" technology, workers, as "social animals," cooperate with one another, formally in unions or informally on the shop floor, to control the relation between effort and pay, their purpose being to protect themselves from unremunerated overwork.

Marx's internal mechanism is payment by the piece—a form of wage payment that, unlike time-wages, supposedly overcomes restriction of output by workers. It was his view that by the mid–nineteenth century piece-rates had become "the general rule" in British "large-scale industry," in part because in "workshops which are subject to the Factory Act . . . capital can increase the yield of the working day only by intensifying labour."[100] Taking as given the technical productivity of workers and the piece-rate, Marx argued that "it is naturally in the personal interest of the worker that he should strain his labour-power as intensely as possible" and that "this in turn enables the capitalist to raise the normal degree of intensity of labour more easily." As he went on to argue, "the wider scope that piece-wages give to individuality tends to develop both that individuality, and with it the worker's sense of liberty, independence and self-control, and also the competition of workers with one another."[101]

This competition (now both internal to the labor process as well as external in the form of a reserve army of unemployed) in turn provides capitalists with the opportunity to lower piece-rates. Should workers in a particular craft be capable of protecting "a particular rate of piece-wage [that] has for a long time been fixed by tradition"—an "exceptional" circumstance according to Marx— capitalists may have "recourse to the forcible transformation of piece-wages into time-wages."[102]

Marx, therefore, recognized that the relation between effort and pay on a given technology is a source of capital–labor conflict. But he assumed either that workers compete with one another in blind pursuit of individual gain, the competition resulting in unremunerated intensification of labor (and hence an increase in surplus-value), or that, in "exceptional cases," capitalists are forced to scrap the piece-rate system. Yet, contrary to Marx, in virtually all cases of "large-scale industry" in nineteenth-century Britain, key groups of workers were better able to divide and conquer their capitalist employers than vice versa. Far from blindly competing with one another, as Marx assumes, these workers—the "aristocracy of labor" and even some other groups of workers who were not so highly paid—were in general far better organized than their capitalist counterparts. Through the power of their unions, they maintained considerable control in the labor process and played an active and critical role in the determination of the relation between effort and earnings.[103]

Marx ignored the substantial shop-floor control exercised by certain groups of workers in mid–nineteenth-century Britain. As a result, he was able to argue that all-powerful capitalists were intensifying labor to the physical limit for a given wage and that the piece-wage was "the form of wage most appropriate to the capitalist mode of production."[104] Marx saw the individualistic actions of workers in responding to piece-rate incentives as self-defeating. He offered no reason to believe that collective action might enable workers to control the relation between effort and earnings over the long run.

Marx also considered the more dynamic case of the use of piece-rate payment systems in the presence of technological change. When the productivity of labor rises because of the introduction of a new technology, the piece-rate is cut proportionally, leaving the worker's earnings unchanged. The result of the change in the piece-rate is, in Marx's words, "purely nominal." The implication is that the level of effort is also left unchanged—which will only be the case if changes in work effort are directly proportional to changes in output.

There is no reason to expect such proportionality. One cannot even assume that managers (or industrial engineers) know a priori the extent of the effort-saving effect of any particular technological change. Workers in a particular workplace will have a collective interest to conceal from management the true impact of a change in technology on the level of effort required to produce a given amount of output, for by so doing they lessen the extent of the piece-wage cut that management thinks is "purely nominal"—the cut that will leave the relation between effort and earnings unchanged. Because it is workers, not managers, who are actually doing the work, access to information on the effort-saving potential of a machine will be asymmetric, giving workers a distinct advantage in determining the pace of work. In addition, workers through their unions will attempt to exert industry-wide control over the relation between effort and pay on a newly diffused technology. The resultant relation between effort and earnings will depend on the exercise of social power, not on abstract "laws" of proportional change.

Marx recognized that "purely nominal" rate-cutting subsequent to technological change "leads to constant struggles between the capitalist and the worker," as capitalists, in fact, try to use the opportunity to appropriate unremunerated effort, or as workers press for a share of real productivity gains.[105] From Marx's analytical perspective, however, these battles are of little consequence to the long-run development of capitalist production for two reasons. First, deskilling and labor-displacing technology in combination with the individualism of workers is continually pushing intensification of labor to the maximum consistent with laboring capacity. Second, although conflict *within* the labor process persists, it is, like all collective actions on the part of workers, purely defensive. It does not permit particular collectivities of workers to protect themselves from the forces of the labor market or technology, nor does it permit workers in general to raise the "historical and moral" value of labor-power. The capitalists of Marxian theory, therefore, have not only an incentive to continually "revolutionize" the labor process by means of technological change but also the unfettered ability to do so.

2   From Surplus-Value to Value Creation

Relations and Forces of Production

One of the most intelligent critics of Marxist economics has said: "The difference between a scientist and a prophet does not lie in what some great man says but in how it is received. The duty of the pupils of a scientist is to test his hypotheses by looking for evidence to refute them, while the duty of the disciples of a prophet is to go on repeating his very words."[1]

In making use of Marx, my own purpose has been to treat him as a scientist rather than as a prophet. Because Marx was a "great man," the value of his work does not vanish with criticism; it can potentially be strengthened by it.

In the social sciences, "great men"—those who, in Kuhnian fashion,[2] put forth seminal and coherent worldviews within which the importance of previously ignored phenomena can be demonstrated—are few and far between. One can follow Joseph Schumpeter—another "great man" who was a critical admirer of Marx—in distinguishing between a "pre-scientific" vision of how the world works and theoretical analysis that seeks to impart scientific rigor to the broader perspective.[3] A great social scientist cannot do one or the other; he or she must do both.

Marx's greatness is his vision of economic development as the outcome of the interaction of social structure and technological change. Shaped by the unprecedented industrial development of the first half of the nineteenth century, the Marxian vision contrasted with a growing tendency of social analysts to view the new industrial world as one in which impersonal market forces predominated. Marx's focus on production in turn led him to study the works of the classical economists, whom he criticized for the sake of developing more sophisticated and relevant theory—in much the same manner that I have attempted to make use of Marx. Marx's major advance over classical economists such as Adam Smith and David Ricardo was his emphasis on the role of social power in the operation of the capitalist production process. In particular, Marx's basic criticism of Ricardian theory was its failure to distinguish between the capacity to work (labor-power) and work actually performed (labor-embodied), and hence its inability to develop a theory of surplus-value that was logically consistent with a theory of equal exchange.

The distinction between labor-power and labor-embodied brings the problem of effort and the exercise of social power to the center of the Marxian theory of production and differentiates it from both classical and neoclassical economic theory in which the relations between labor inputs and final outputs are technically determined. For Marx, the distinction between labor-power and labor-embodied lay the basis for the theory of surplus-value, which set out a fundamental theoretical framework for analyzing the relations among effort, skill, technology, wages, and profits. The greatness of Marx was not only that he constucted such a theory but also that, in keeping with his materialist conception of history, he made an attempt to generate and validate his theoretical ideas on the basis of the historical experience of the foremost capitalist nation of the time.

The strengths of Marx's work, therefore, are his overarching vision of economic development and social change, his general theoretical framework for analyzing capitalist production, and his methodological approach. The weaknesses arose when he let his theory take on a life of its own, thereby allowing theory to determine "history" rather than vice versa.

Marx was overinfluenced by the intense class conflict of the first half of the nineteenth century, a period during which rapid industrial change and frequent periods of boom and bust played havoc with the economic security and well-being of the British working class. Marx's view of the world was particularly influenced by Engels's firsthand account of the condition of the British working class in the early 1840s[4]—a time when British industrial workers were suffering from one of the worst cyclical downturns of the first half of the nineteenth century. In a largely accurate portrayal of the plight of various strata of the British working class in the "hungry forties," Engels stressed the role of labor-displacing machinery as the source of the workers' misery.[5] When combined with the testimony contained in government inquiries into work conditions—many of them undertaken before mid-century and many of the later ones dealing with occupations that were outside the factory system—Engels's depiction convinced Marx that British capitalists were exploiting British workers to the point where they had "nothing to lose but their chains." These accounts in turn undoubtedly led Marx to accept as fact the ideological pronouncements of Andrew Ure.

In the conflict-ridden 1830s, Ure's utterances reflected the world that many British capitalists hoped would come to pass rather than the world in process of evolution. Overly influenced by the intense class conflict of the first half of the century as well as by procapitalist ideology that proclaimed the unmitigated triumph of capital, Marx predicted increasing misery for the mass of British workers: their lifetimes would be transformed into work time and they would become appendages to the machine. But, during the 1850s and 1860s, when he was working out the theories that appear in *Capital*, Marx failed to recognize how profoundly the collective power of British workers would assert itself in opposition to the competitive fragmentation of British capitalists.

Throughout the first half of the nineteenth century, adult male operatives played key roles in the coordination and control of the labor process, even as they were buffeted about by periodic industrial downturns. In the long boom of the third quarter of the nineteenth century, however, these workers built their collective organizations on the foundations of shop-floor control of work organization. As they sought to regulate the relation between effort and earnings, they confronted capitalists, who, more divided by market competition than united by class interest, opted for collective accommodation with well-organized groups of workers rather than jeopardize current profits during a time of prosperity by engaging in industrial conflict.

During a period in which British industry dominated the world economy, most British capitalists came to support the industry-wide enforcement of collective bargaining agreements because it assured that all their competitors would be governed by the same basic labor-cost conditions. The Liberal–Labour alliance that brought together industrial capitalists and the "New Model" unions in the political arena enabled the labor movement to make legislative gains that greatly enhanced the ability of workers to organize unions, build up strike funds, and, when necessary, stage prolonged strikes.[6]

The result was the emergence of a "labor aristocracy" in the middle decades of the nineteenth century. These workers, whom Eric Hobsbawm has estimated made up about 10 to 20 percent of the British labor force in the late nineteenth century, labored long and hard.[7] In return for their high levels of effort, the labor aristocrats were, by the standards of the time, decently paid. Within the workplace, where they combined knowledge of production with control over work organization, the labor aristocrats cannot accurately be described as mere appendages to the machine. Outside the workplace, moreover, industrial workers had opportunities for cultural and political development even under the ten-hour day. Contrary to Marx, the lifetimes of these more privileged workers were not reduced to work time.

Gross exploitation of workers abounded in late-nineteenth-century Britain, but it was increasingly confined to domestic industry and small "sweatshops"; much less exploitation was found in large-scale factories. Where the factory system was most developed, the introduction of effort-saving machinery into the workplace meant that the conflict over the relation between effort and pay was not necessarily a zero-sum situation. Industrial-relations structures that would ensure both capitalists and workers acceptable shares of potential productivity gains through the introduction of new methods of production could promote the diffusion of those methods and actual realization of the productivity gains that could then be shared. Cooperative relations of production, that is, could create a basis for the development of the forces of production.

Opting for cooperative production relations with powerful groups of organized workers, British industrialists came to accept, and even value, significant craft control over the management of their labor processes. From the fourth quarter of the nineteenth century, when intermittent but at times prolonged recessions occurred and British industry began to feel the threat of foreign competition, many British capitalists tried to challenge the power of unions. But they were unable to replace craft control by managerial control as was being done by competitors in, among other places, the United States and Germany. Despite the continued introduction of many deskilling technologies, the power of union organization that had developed earlier had become too great. When Parliament and the judiciary sought to undermine the union movement—most notably by means of the Taff Vale decision that signaled financial ruin for any union engaged in a prolonged strike—workers turned en masse to build a political party that could protect their interests.

The persistence of structures of social power inherited from the nineteenth century made it exceedingly difficult for twentieth-century

British industry to meet the powerful international challenges based
on more coordinated managerial control over the introduction of
mass production technologies.[8] The capacity for British production
relations characterized by craft control to promote the development
of the forces of production reached its limits. Given the productivity
standards set by international competition, old arrangements for dis-
tributing the costs and benefits of productivity growth between workers and capitalists were not necessarily sufficient to give capitalists the
incentive to invest in the new technologies. Vested interests—in particular the stake that British workers had in craft control as well as
the historic underdevelopment of British management—stood in the
way of the transformation of production relations to promote the
diffusion of advanced production methods. Instead, British managers
and workers sought to adapt to international competition on the
basis of the existing structures of social power and technology, a
strategy that led to the further entrenchment rather than the transformation of the traditional relations of production.

Fixed in his views that the forces of production were securing the
domination of capitalists over workers and that, as a result, the production process was evolving into a social system unto itself, Marx
failed to analyze the ways in which relations of production were
actually evolving in his own time.[9] Instead he stressed the role of a
rising organic composition of capital—the ratio of nonhuman to human inputs per unit of output—in reproducing capitalist domination
over workers, in creating accumulation crises, and in fostering the
concentration and centralization of capital. That is, the rising organic
composition of capital permitted Marx to make technology rather
than production relations the main link between his theory of surplus-value and his theory of capital accumulation.

The argument that the rising organic composition of capital accounts for the inherent tendency for competitive capitalism to evolve
into "monopoly" capitalism is of particular importance in the history
of Marxist theory because Marx can be credited with using his theory
of capital accumulation to predict the rise of big business before its
actual appearance.

According to Marx, "two most powerful levers of centralization
[are] competition and credit. The battle of competition is fought by
the cheapening of commodities. The cheapness of commodities depends, all other circumstances remaining the same, on the productivity of labour, and this depends in turn on *the scale of production.*

Therefore *the larger capitals beat the smaller.*"[10] In the Marxian analysis, credit enables some capitalists to update their plant and equipment as well as to acquire cheaply the plant and equipment of weaker firms that can no longer meet the competition.[11]

In historical perspective, however, the Marxian argument cannot account for the tenacity of competitive forms of industrial organization in Britain. In staple industries as diverse as steel and textiles, British capitalists found themselves trapped in "competitive equilibrium," in part because the imposition of craft control across firms in an industry made it very difficult for any one firm to achieve a distinct competitive advantage through the lowering of unit costs.[12] Far from becoming "monopoly" capitalists, competition characterized the structure of these industries well into the twentieth century to the point of discouraging the constituent firms from investments in up-to-date technologies.

It is true that in the United States oligopolistic structures did emerge out of competitive conditions. But the imperative of a rising organic composition of capital provides an insufficient explanation for this transition, ignoring as it does the organizational transformation, and the structure of social power inherent in it, that characterized the rise of big business.

It is generally the case that the adoption of more advanced technology increases the firm's capital–labor ratio and requires a greater precommitment of resources. But a firm that invests in capital-intensive technology will not automatically secure lower unit costs and competitive advantage. If the investing firm does not have the organizational capabilities to utilize the fixed capital at its disposal—if it cannot create value by coordinating and controlling the efforts of its employees—then it might well find itself at a competitive disadvantage relative to a labor-intensive enterprise that is less burdened by fixed costs. To understand how large-scale precommitments of capital to advanced methods of production can be transformed from a potential competitive burden into an actual competitive advantage requires an analysis of the types of relations of production that permit the effective utilization of technology.

A relevant theory of the rise of managerial capitalism (a much better description of the nature of the new production relations than "monopoly capitalism") must begin with an intimate knowledge of the history of the place and period in question, on the basis of which generalizations that have empirical foundations and testable content can then be made. Over the past few decades, business historians have begun to acquire the relevant historical knowledge. In the *Visible Hand*, Alfred Chandler has provided a historical analysis of the emergence of corporate enterprise and oligopolistic industrial structures in the United States between 1880 and 1920.[13] He argued that the firms that came out on top were those that were able to cut costs dramatically by a strategy of vertical integration, redesign of plant layout, standardization of inputs, and mechanization of heavy and skilled work. As a result, these firms (as epitomized by Carnegie Steel, Standard Oil, Singer Sewing Machine, General Electric, and Ford Motor Company, to name a few) were able to reap enormous internal economies that were decisive in the competitive struggle.

Like most other economists, Marxists have tended to view the internal economies that permit some firms to gain a distinct competitive advantage over others as scale economies that derive from the imperatives of technology, without any analysis of the structures of social power that permit the effective utilization of "scale." Chandler's historical analysis confronts this perspective by demonstrating the importance of a distinct class of internal economies—*economies of speed*—that derive from the planned coordination of the firm's productive activities, enabling the firm to transform high fixed costs into low unit costs. At any point in time, economies of speed manifest themselves as economies of scale, but it is critical that one recognizes the role of the dynamic interaction between organization and technology that makes high fixed-cost investments worthwhile.

To use the terminology from Chandler's earlier work, *Strategy and Structure*,[14] an enterprise may embark on an investment strategy, but the more ambitious this strategy in terms of process, product, and geography, the more critical will be the development of a managerial structure that can coordinate the flows of inputs and the distribution of outputs in order to justify the large-scale commitment of capital. The speedy transformation of purchased inputs into sold outputs depends critically upon the efforts expended by employees. Indeed, the very investment in a bureaucracy to achieve high levels of throughput (the rate of flow of output) will in itself only serve to increase the precommitment of capital, making the achievement of high levels of throughput all the more critical to enterprise success. The firm, as distinct from its employees, moreover, needs to accomplish high levels of throughput while retaining some of the resultant productivity gains for itself, if it is to reap economies of speed.

As I elaborate in the following chapters, when investments in effort-saving technology form the basis for achieving high levels of throughput, it may be possible for all claimants to the firm's revenues—workers, managers, owners, the state—to secure higher returns, even while workers supply less effort than previously and consumers are able to purchase the firm's products more cheaply. Over the long run, investments in effort-saving technology are a necessary condition for the emergence of such positive-sum scenarios. Given investments in effort-saving technology, a sufficient condition for achieving economies of speed on the shop floor is the prevalence of labor–management relations that share out the costs and benefits of involvement in productive activities in ways that shop-floor workers view as fair. Only then does the value-creating capability of the firm cease to depend upon ever-increasing intensification of effort or cutting of wages—a phenomenon that I call unremunerated intensification of labor, or "Marxian exploitation."

If, over the past two centuries, capitalist development had relied primarily on "Marxian exploitation," capitalism would have long since reached its social limits, as Marx predicted. But, as I argue in later chapters, major shifts in international industrial leadership, such as the rise of the United States and the decline of Britain in the first part of this century, and the rise of Japan and the decline of the United States more recently, depend critically on institutional structures that promote investments in effort-saving technology and that ensure workers a "fair share" of the potential value gains. Basing his theory of capitalist development on the experiences of the world's first industrial nation, Marx could not garner the insights that come from cross-national historical comparisons of the rise of capitalist economies from the late nineteenth century on. Even with access to the same forces of production, relations of production will differ markedly from one political and cultural context to the next. The success or failure of capitalist enterprise will therefore differ across regions and nations because different cultural and political contexts will yield different structures of social power, which will in turn yield different relations between effort and monetary rewards.

Once one recognizes that the capitalist enterprise functions differently in various social contexts, it becomes evident that one requires a theory of capitalist development that explores the nature and impact of these social differences rather than a theory that serves as an intellectual excuse for pretending that critical differences do not exist. If it is to be and remain relevant, theory must stay in touch with the reality that it is supposed to be analyzing. One must not allow theory to take on a life of its own.

Even though Marx generated his theory of capitalist development by studying the history of the rise of capitalism, he ultimately came to regard his theory as a set of laws from which determinate solutions concerning economic and social evolution could be derived rather than as a framework for exploring further the complexities of social reality. With technology as the driving force of economic development and class conflict and social relations of production pushed into the background, Marx came to view his theory as a determinate model of capitalist development that could be applied to all times and all places where private property and wage labor could be found.

Although Marx's theory of capitalist development was based on his understanding of the British experience, when his work was done—specifically when he wrote the preface to the first edition of *Capital*, published in German—Marx sought to justify his focus on Britain by arguing that it was merely illustrative of the course of development awaiting Germany. "Until now," Marx argued,

> [the] *locus classicus* [of the capitalist mode of production] has been England. This is the reason why England is used as the main illustration of the theoretical developments I make. If, however, the German reader pharisaically shrugs his shoulders at the condition of the English industrial and agricultural workers, or optimistically comforts himself with the thought that in Germany things are not nearly so bad, I must plainly tell him: *De te fabula narratur.*[15]

Theory has detached itself from reality and taken on a life of its own. Marx continued:

> Intrinsically, it is not a question of the higher or lower degree of development of the social antagonisms that spring from the natural laws of capitalist production. It is a question of these laws themselves, of these tendencies winning their way and working themselves out with *iron necessity*. The country that is more developed industrially only shows, to the less developed, the image of its own future.[16]

There are many things to be learned about the relation between theory and history from the serious study of Marx. But the notion of "natural laws of capitalist production . . . winning their way and working themselves out with iron necessity" is not one of them. Marx supplied valuable insights into the nature of the conflict between capitalists and workers in the labor process and into the nature of technological change. In the British case that stands at the center of his analysis, however, he failed to discern the considerable power that British workers exercised over the division of labor and the utilization of technology in the nineteenth century. The serious weaknesses of Marx's analysis of the evolution of nineteenth-century industrial capitalism should make one rather wary of using his theoretical distillation of the British experience as the appropriate model for analyzing later developing capitalist economies.

The British experience demonstrates that structures of social power shape the development, diffusion, and utilization of technology. Successful capitalist development in the economies of Germany, the United States, and Japan has been based on structures of social power that, in historical and comparative perspective, reveal a serious underdevelopment of British managerial coordination and control that has persisted well into the twentieth century.[17] The nature of successful development in the twentieth century cannot merely be extrapolated from the history of the world's first industrial revolution—even, and especially, when one gets the story right. Only by comparing and contrasting the dramatic social and technological changes in the development of capitalism that have occurred in various national economies over the past hundred years can one begin to put forth, and test the empirical limits of, theoretical generalizations.

If a relevant theory of economic development is what is wanted, economists must study and compare the dynamic interaction of the forces and relations of production in widely varying cultural and political contexts. As a conceptual framework that can comprehend the dynamic interaction between forces and relations of production, the Marxian theory of surplus-value points analysts in the right direction. But only the rigorous study of comparative historical experiences of the value-creation process can ensure that one remains on a relevant theoretical path. As I demonstrate in the following chapters, the critical issue for understanding successful capitalist development is not how capitalists appropriate surplus-value from workers but how workers' skills and efforts, when combined with capital investments, create sufficient value for both capital and labor to be better off.

3 Minders, Piecers, and Self-Acting Mules

Technology and the Capital–Labor Relation

In Volume I of *Capital,* Marx portrayed a capitalist labor process in which the capitalists essentially get their way. In introducing new divisions of labor and machinery and in intensifying labor, capitalists meet with the resistance of workers. But, by turning the worker into a mere appendage of a machine and by generating a reserve army of interchangeable labor, investments in new deskilling technologies enable the capitalists who own the machines to emerge triumphant.[1]

As already indicated, Marx's classic example of a technology that permits capital to dominate labor is the self-acting mule, the foremost cotton-spinning technology of the British Industrial Revolution. In Marx's words:

> But machinery does not just act as a superior competitor to the worker, always to the point of making him superfluous. It is a power inimical to him, and capital proclaims this fact loudly and deliberately, as well as making use of it. It is the most powerful weapon for suppressing strikes, those periodic revolts of the working class against the autocracy of capital . . . It would be possible to write a whole history of the inventions made since 1830 for the sole purpose of supplying capital with weapons against working-class revolt. We would mention, above all, the self-acting mule, because it opened up a new epoch in the automatic system.[2]

Marx's authority for this statement was the "philosopher of the Factory," Andrew Ure. In asserting that the "effect of substituting the self-acting mule for the common mule, is to discharge the greater part of the men spinners, and to retain adolescents and children,"[3] Ure was repeating a marketing promise made in 1830 by the Manchester engineering firm of Sharp, Roberts & Company, the maker of the first commercially viable self-acting mule. Sharp, Roberts listed as the self-actor's first advantage, "the saving of a spinner's wages to each pair of mules, piecers only being required, one overlooker being sufficient to manage 6 or 8 pairs of mules or upwards."[4] I have already mentioned how Ure thought that the skill-displacing impact of the technological change would "put an end . . . to the folly of trades' unions." So too did another contemporary, E. C. Tufnell, a "free enterprise" Factory Commissioner:

> The introduction of this invention will eventually give a death blow to the Spinners' Union, the members of which will have to thank themselves alone, for the creation of this destined agent of their extinction. It is now rapidly coming into use; other advantages, besides the great one of the escape from the dictation of the workmen, are found to attend it; and in a few years the very name of working spinner, as well as the follies and oppression of combination, will only be found in history.[5]

The impression one gets from these accounts, as well as from Marx's recitation of these claims as fact some three decades later, is that the introduction of the invention had a devastating effect on the craft position of the adult male spinners. In 1835 Ure claimed that a pair of self-actors could be operated by two youths, aged sixteen or over. A year later he asserted that all motions on self-actors were automatic so that "attendants have nothing to do but to watch its movements, to piece the broken ends [of yarn] when the carriage begins to leave the roller-beam, and to stop it whenever the cop is completely formed, as indicated by the bell of the counter attached to the working geer [sic]."[6]

It is true that in the second half of the century a number of mills in Scotland and a few in Lancashire dispensed with adult males as mule-spinning operatives. But these were the exceptions to the rule in British cotton spinning. In virtually all of Lancashire (and its contiguous counties) adult male spinners, who became known as minders, retained their positions as the chief spinning operatives on the self-actors, one on each pair of mules, employing and supervising two or three assistants on an internal subcontract system that had characterized the employment relation in the days of the common mule. On the basis of their control over shop-floor work organization, the minders built up powerful unions during the second half of the nineteenth century. These unions in turn preserved into the second half of the twentieth century the organization of work that had emerged during the British Industrial Revolution.

In this chapter I explore the origins and persistence of worker control over the shop-floor division of labor in British cotton spinning. What was it that these diverse participants and observers—the factory machine-maker Sharp, Roberts, the factory commissioner Tufnell, the factory apologist Ure, and the factory critic Marx—failed to understand about the dynamic interaction between organization and technology in the British Industrial Revolution and its aftermath? An understanding of the incongruence between the ideology and reality of the evolution of mule spinning is of some historical significance. For it was during the second and third quarters of the nineteenth century, when the self-acting mule was replacing the common mule, that British industrial capitalism came to dominate the international economy, with cotton textiles as its leading export and the self-acting mule as its central technology.

Mule Spinning before the Self-Actor

In the mule-spinning factory, the spinner worked on a subcontract system. He was paid by the piece (that is, per pound or length of yarn produced). Out of his gross wages he paid time-wages to assistants whom he himself recruited and supervised. Ure correctly described the hierarchical and technical division of labor on the common mule—a division of labor that he incorrectly thought would be eradicated by the introduction of the self-actor.

> In working the common [mule] . . . various persons are employed to perform different portions of the work; viz., the "spinner," who directs the general operation of the machine, gives to the yarn a suitable degree of twist during the spinning, and when spun, winds the yarn in a certain form round the spindle to make what is termed a "cop," one or more "piecers" to join the threads which break during the spinning, and to remove the cops, when formed, from the spindles; a "creel-filler" to place the "rovings" from which the yarn is to be spun, in a part of the machine termed the "creel"; and a "cleaner" or "scavenger," to remove the waste cotton, termed "fly," which accumulates during the spinning, and to clean the machine generally. The "spinner" being the principal person of the set thus employed, and in most instances, an adult; the others being subordinate to him, and always young persons, or children; the set thus arranged working one pair of mules.[7]

How and when did this system of work organization emerge? In the 1780s mule spinning was done on a putting-out basis; in the late 1780s mule-shed manufactories arose; and by the 1790s factory production predominated.[8] In its domestic industry phase, mule spinning acquired the status and characteristics of a craft. Many factors served to restrict entry into the occupation: the strength required to push the mule carriage back and forth; the skills required to draw out the yarn evenly to the required fineness, to wind the yarn properly into the form of a cop on the spindle, and to maintain (and perhaps even construct) the mule; and the capital required to buy the machine. As a high-paying occupation that required concentrated physical strength and the supervision of assistants, mule spinning remained a male-dominated craft as it moved into the factory setting. Attracted by high wages in an expanding industry, many artisans—shoemakers, joiners, and hatmakers—left their trades to take up mule spinning.[9]

Difficulties in recruiting, training, and supervising factory labor during the early decades of the Industrial Revolution led to the adoption of the subcontract system as mule spinning moved into the factories.[10] Subcontracting shifted the burden of recruitment, training, and supervision onto the operative spinner, an advantageous arrangement for the capitalist in an era when most British workers resisted entry into factory employment and those who did become factory hands were as yet undisciplined to factory work. For mule spinners, who had aspirations to be independent craftsmen, the subcontract system permitted them to maintain significant control over the division of labor within the factory. But for the fact that they could hire and supervise their own children (and in some cases their wives), many mule spinners might not have permitted their family dependents to enter the factories.

By the 1790s, mule spinners had organized themselves into strong unions; and in the first decade of the nineteenth century, union activity continued, with mixed success.[11] In 1810 the mule spinners, well organized throughout Lancashire, staged a strike to bring country piece-rates to the levels paid in Manchester. After four months, the strike failed when the spinners' union ran out of funds, and in 1811 several spinners were imprisoned for "combination." Nevertheless the mule spinners remained by far the most highly organized craft union in Britain through the first half of the century, staging large-scale strikes in Lancashire in 1818, 1825, 1830, 1834, 1836–37, and 1842, as well as in Scotland in 1837.[12]

The main purpose of most of the strikes in the first half of the nineteenth century was to control the level of piece-rates in certain districts as well as to equalize rates across firms and districts spinning similar types of yarn. To enforce equal wages for equal work throughout the industry, the spinners sought to have employers adhere to printed wage-lists. Another conflictual issue of more long-term importance was the use of women as mule spinners in place of men. During the first decades of the nineteenth century, those women who were employed as mule spinners received wages that were about one-half to two-thirds of male wages for the same work.[13]

Capitalists and their spokesmen stressed not only the relative cheapness of women's labor but also women's docility; women were less prone to collective action and less likely to cause work slow-downs and stoppages.[14] Yet, despite these purported advantages, the employment of women as mule spinners never became widespread. The usual explanation is that strength and skill requirements rendered men more productive than women at mule spinning.[15] I shall argue, however, that the observed male dominance of the occupation was an outcome of the interaction of organization and technology in early mule spinning.

On the original hand mule in use during the 1780s and 1790s, the rollers, spindles, and carriage were all operated by manually turning the cranked handle of a flywheel to which the other parts were connected by bands, pulleys, and shafts. The strength required for this job varied from machine to machine, depending on the number of spindles per mule and its mode of construction. The requisite, and considerable, skill involved in operating the hand mule was to maintain the correct speed of the moving parts in order to achieve the required fineness (or count) of the yarn while imparting enough twist to it that it would not break during either the spinning process itself or the winding and weaving processes.[16]

Unlike the simultaneous spinning and winding of the yarn that characterized the water-frame and throstle technologies that had been dominant in the earlier cotton factories, the mule first spun the yarn and then wound it into a cop suitable for use in weaving processes. When the mule was attached to waterpower and, then, steam power in the 1790s, the actual spinning movements—the drawing out and twisting of the cotton to desired fineness and strength—were completely automated, superseding any strength and skill requirements of the operative for this phase of the mule's operation.[17] The power-assisted mule—called the common mule, as distinct from the hand mule that came before it and the self-acting mule that came after—quickly emerged as the dominant cotton-spinning technology as the factory system expanded. In the factory setting,. overseers were often given the responsibility of keeping the mules in repair, and most overseers were probably drawn from the ranks of mule spinners.

On the common mule, the winding (as distinct from the spinning) of the yarn was not automated. This part of the operation required coordination and attentiveness, skills that, in and of themselves, women could have learned as easily as men. The operative had to control the "faller," a wire that stretched the length of the mule and guided the strands of spun yarn onto the spindle. These manual operations also required a considerable amount of physical strength to push the mule five feet up to the roller beam to wind the spun yarn. In the 1830s a mule on which coarse counts of yarn were being spun had to be put up about three and one-half times per minute, or about 2,200 times (allowing for stoppages) for a twelve-hour day. In 1838 the weight of a mule carriage of 336 spindles for spinning course counts was 1,400 pounds and that of a carriage ("constructed on the lightest Principle") of 816 spindles for spinning fine counts was 1,755 pounds.[18] From the time that power was attached to the mule, moreover, each spinner would operate two mules, facing one another and running in and out alternately, so that the pair of mules had to be put up about seven times per minute and about 4,400 times per day. The manipulation of the faller wire also required strength, especially in spinning coarser counts of yarn. The physical capacities of an operative affected his or her ability to maintain the requisite coordination and attentiveness over this long period. A failure to do so could result in massive yarn breakages, requiring the operative to expend considerable effort just to get the machines back into operation.

Women and children were employed on smaller mules. In 1816 John Sutcliffe, a civil engineer experienced in the textile industry, claimed that manufacturers would be better off using small mules of 192 spindles rather than larger ones of 300 spindles. "It must be admitted," he said, "that wheels [that is, mules] containing 300 spindles, are unfit for any but men to work them; and the spinner will be more fatigued with working them fourteen hours; moreover, the small wheels may be worked by girls of sixteen to seventeen years of age, or by boys of fifteen, an advantage of no small importance to the master spinner."[19] Sutcliffe also argued that the smaller mules took up about the same floor space per spindle as larger mules and that they yielded better twist.

I do not possess sufficient information to determine whether circa

1816 unit costs were actually lower on smaller mules using youths. I do know, however, that an essential dimension in the improvement of mules over time was to lighten the physical load of putting up the carriage by using less weighty materials or improving the rolling parts. These improvements permitted the employment of weaker operatives on mules of given numbers of spindles and also saved on power costs per spindle. But rather than take the size of the mule as a given and the strength of the operative as a variable, spinning capitalists took advantage of such technical progress to increase the number of spindles per mule from 144 in the early 1790s to 300 in the early 1800s.[20] Rather than have women and youths operate pairs of 144-spindle machines subsequent to improvements that lightened the load, "best practice" was to have men operate pairs of the new 300-spindle machines. Similarly, when mehanical devices were developed in the 1820s that for the first time aided in the putting-up of the carriage of the common mule, men were "displaced" from pairs of 300-spindle machines to 600-spindle machines, because women could be, and to some extent were, employed on 300-spindle mules that had the new devices.[21]

The larger mules were not necessarily new mules. By the early 1830s, methods had been devised for "coupling" or "double-decking" mules—that is, attaching two 300-spindle mules together to form one 600-spindle mule, a pair of which was then operated by one mule spinner (and his assistants)—thereby throwing another mule spinner out of work.[22] As Ure remarked, in this case quite accurately, the coupling of common mules was a convenient way for capitalists to dispense with "indifferent or restive spinners."[23] By the late 1830s, there were some mules with as many as 1,200 spindles each.[24]

Although the stretching-out of the common mules by the addition of more spindles maintained the physical strength of an adult male as a job requirement, the persistence of the internal subcontract system, with its hierarchical division of labor, meant that the job of the mule spinner involved a supervisory as well as an operative function. This factor gave another productivity advantage to the adult male labor force over women and youths. The young assistants, the piecers and scavengers, had to be kept busy at their work if productivity was to be maintained, a task that often required physical coercion. There is evidence that women operatives acting in supervisory capacities were more humane than men, bribing the children with money and food to keep them at their work. But, to maintain the pace of work over a 13.5-hour workday and a 74-hour workweek, it is unlikely that such bribes were either effective or financially viable. Factory work was not an edifying experience; and, for younger workers who toiled long hours for low pay and little employment security, negative rather than positive incentives predominated during the Industrial Revolution.[25] Alongside their more threatening demeanors and more punishing physiques, adult male mule spinners brought the preparedness to exercise authority in their supervisory roles that only a patriarchal socialization and experience could provide.

Male mule spinners did not take for granted their continued dominance of mule spinning during the era of the common mule. Rather they sought to use their union organizations to discourage employers from employing women. In 1795 a small proportion of the membership of the Manchester Spinners' Society was female. But opposition to the employment of women was an issue in virtually every major spinners' strike of the first four decades of the century, as employers threatened to replace striking males with females.[26] In 1829 women were formally excluded from membership in the Grand General Union of Cotton Spinners. Male unionists agreed in principle that they should support attempts by women to gain comparable wages for comparable work. But the men were not prepared to aid the women by putting the weight of the union behind them. Instead the men told female mule spinners to form their own association.[27]

Union opposition to the employment of females as mule spinners may have deterred some employers from hiring women to work smaller mules, especially machines spinning fine counts that required less physical strength. Instead of hiring women, some employers may have opted for peaceful relations with the men, retaining the threat to hire women should the peace be broken. If so, the opportunities for women to acquire technical skills through on-the-job experience may have been diminished. But as I have already argued, technical skills alone cannot explain male dominance of the occupation. Rather it was both the physical strength requirements for operating common mules of ever-increasing size and the supervisory component of the job that secured mule spinning as a male domain and provided the basis for strong union organization.

The Self-Acting Mule

From the time when the mule was first attached to waterpower in 1790, capitalists had visions of a self-acting mule that would dispense with the labor-power of adult males completely. William Kelly, the man who introduced the waterpowered common mule, took out the first patent for a self-acting mule in 1792. "The object then," he reminisced in 1829,

> was to spin with young people . . . It will naturally be asked, why were not the self-acting mules continued in use? At first, you know, the mules were about 144 spindles in size, and when power was applied, the spinner worked two of such; but the size of the mules rapidly increased to 300 spindles and upwards, and two such wheels being considered a sufficient task for a man to manage, the idea of saving by spinning with boys and girls was thus superseded.[28]

Kelly's was in fact only the first of a number of patented attempts to develop a self-actor from the 1790s through the 1820s.[29] What challenged the inventors was the development of a self-acting mechanism for winding the yarn to form a firm and properly shaped cop.

Between 1818 and 1830, at least six types of self-actors were put into experimental operation. The one that was ultimately successful was invented by Richard Roberts of Sharp, Roberts & Co. The impetus to the inventions embodied in the company's first patented self-actor in 1825 was a request to Roberts from some Lancashire capitalists during a strike for a machine that would free them of the troublesome operative spinners. It took £12,000 and five years before Roberts secured a second patent that contained a device, called the quadrant, that could vary the speed of the spindles in inverse relation to the diameter of the cop.[30]

By 1833, about 250 to 300 Roberts self-actors, with a total of about 100,000 spindles had been put into operation. Some of these were common mules converted to self-actors. At that time, about 120,000 spindles were on order.[31] By the end of 1834, between 300,000 and 400,000 spindles had been installed for spinning twist and weft yarns in the coarse–medium range (nos. 16s–40s).[32] By the early 1850s, the self-actor dominated all counts up to 50s in Britain; by the 1860s, all counts up to 90s; and by 1885, all counts up to the very fine 150s. By the mid-1880s, the self-actor was technically capable of spinning 300s, and hardly any common mules had been manufactured for twenty-five years.[33]

During the initial transition to the self-actor in the 1830s and 1840s, the multipair system of staffing the mules—that is, an overlooker managing six to eight pairs of mules as Sharp, Roberts had promised—does not appear to have become widespread, notwithstanding the optimistic projections of Ure, Tufnell, and others.[34] There is some, rather sparse, evidence that the multipair system was tried. Testifying before the factory commissioners in 1833, an overseer of the poor in Manchester was uncertain as to the precise division of labor on the new machines but said that he knew of one mill owner who had installed fourteen pairs of self-actors under the supervision of three men, paid 33s.–34s. each. On the traditional staffing system, fourteen minders would have been paid 20s. each.[35] At prevailing wage rates for piecers, the multipair system would have saved weekly wages of 6s. on each pair of mules.[36]

In the late 1830s and early 1840s the cotton capitalist Henry Ashworth and the Manchester Chartist James Leach agreed that the self-acting mules dispensed with the services of "the spinners."[37] They were not, however, referring to the impacts of the multipair system. Rather, as indicated clearly in Leach's pamphlet on factory conditions, these observers viewed the adult male minder, who continued to operate a pair of mules, and the common mule spinner as different classes of workers. During these years the wages of minders were considerably lower than those of coarse spinners—16s.–18s. for minders and 23s. for spinners in 1839. Indeed, the minders' wages approximated those of Manchester street laborers.[38] In his Factory Inspector's Report for the second half of 1841, Leonard Horner categorized the sexes and ages of workers in common and self-acting mule-spinning rooms as follows:

Mule Spinning Department

Scavenger, is a boy or girl from 9 to 13 years of age.

Big piecer, is a young person of either sex from 15 to 20 years of age. Latterly, from the difficulty of finding better employment, adults have taken situations of this kind.

Mule spinners, are generally men from 25 years and upwards; frequently women when mules are small.

Self-Actors

Minder, is a young person of either sex from 18 and upwards.

Cipher [that is, big piecer], the same.

Horner also reported the wages on self-acting mules in 1841 as 12s.6d. to 15s. for minders, 9s. for ciphers, and 7s. for little piecers.[39]

What happened on self-actors in the 1830s and 1840s is that younger people and a higher proportion of women found employment as minders than had been the case in common-mule spinning. Nevertheless, the vast majority of minders were males entering manhood (it was also not unknown for an eighteen-year-old to take charge of a pair of common mules).[40] Moreover, the internal subcontract system remained intact, with the minder–cipher hierarchy on the self-actors replacing the spinner–big piecer hierarchy on the common mules.

What accounts for the continuity of the shop-floor division of labor in the transition from the common to the self-acting mule, particularly given the notion that the self-actor would dispense with adult male operative labor? First I shall explain why minder positions remained predominantly male. Then I shall argue that neither the technical requirements of spinning on self-actors nor the collective power of minders can account for the continuity of the hierarchical division of labor in the transition from the common mule to the self-acting mule in the 1830s and 1840s. Once the transition had been made, technology and unions were to become important for maintaining the internal subcontract system in which the adult male minder hired, supervised, and paid piecers. But the reasons for the persistence on self-actors of the relation between the operative spinner paid by the piece and the subordinate big piecer paid time-wages by the spinner are to be found in the supervisory requirements of mule spinning and more generally in the traditional management structures of the Lancashire spinning enterprise.

Persistence of Male Dominance

The prime incentive for the development of the self-actor was to displace the refractory adult male workers. But when workable self-acting mules became available to the factories, males continued to dominate as the chief spinning operatives. Although generally somewhat younger than common mule spinners, the minders were quite old enough to join unions and become troublesome to employers.

Males were retained as minders in this period for a number of reasons. First and foremost, although the minder's supervisory function distinguished him from the big piecer, much of his time was, like the big piecer, spent piecing together broken ends of yarn. Piecing work could be very arduous, the degree of difficulty increasing on larger and faster mules spinning coarser counts of yarn from cotton of inferior quality and with fewer piecers per pair of mules. To maintain the flow of output, the minder and piecers had to go back and forth from one broken yarn end to another, working in bare feet on an oil-soaked floor along a spindle carriage that at 600 spindles (a usual size in the 1840s) was about seventy feet in length. In the United States, mule spinners on self-actors, who, by the 1860s at least, had no supervisory functions, were always adult males, even though women were generally employed in throstle spinning and powerloom weaving. It was because of the physical exertion and stamina required to run to and fro in piecing for twelve hours a day that employers tended to hire fully grown males as both minders and big piecers. It should also be noted that by the 1880s mules of 1,200 spindles (2,400 per pair) had become common in Lancashire, with a team made up of a minder, big piecer, and little piecer responsible for keeping the yarn ends up.

On smaller and slower self-actors spinning higher counts of yarn, women were often employed. The employment of more piecers on longer mules permitted the use of women as well, as evidenced later in the century in parts of Europe and in Scotland.[41] It should also be noted that after the passage of the Factory Act of 1844, the employment of males over eighteen years of age offered the further advantage to employers of making it legally possible to clean the mules after engine hours, a practice that became standard until the late nineteenth century.

Second, the minder was a supervisor of labor. Like the male operatives of the common mules, men had a productivity advantage over women because they could command more "respect" from their assistants. It may well be that even male minders had difficulty exercising their authority over the big piecers in the late 1830s and early 1840s when, as I have shown, the superior and subordinate were close in age. An age differential appeared, however, with the passage of time. During the early years of the self-actor, when the position of minder was both new and relatively low paid, big piecers who had come up through the ranks of scavenger and little piecer (most likely on common mules) were undoubtedly receiving and accepting rapid promotion to minder positions. They would then tend to stay in these positions for upward of thirty years. As the occupation matured, therefore, the average age of the minder rose, whereas little piecers still became big piecers at the age of eighteen. Big piecers who showed themselves to be hard working and compliant could look forward to promotion in their twenties to mind a pair of mules, a positive incentive that was to become more attractive after the "hungry forties" when minders' wages began to rise. Female piecers, who (given the widespread adherence of both men and women to the ideology that "a woman's place is in the home")[42] were less likely to be looking forward to a career in spinning, would presumably have been less responsive to such "career" incentives. Hence, it was not only the coercive authority of the male minder but also the possibility for male big piecers to move up the hierarchy and pursue careers as mule spinners that contributed to the productivity advantages of employing males as minders.

Third, the 1830s and 1840s witnessed the mitigation of the objections—relatively high wages and a propensity to join unions—to employing men as the chief spinning operatives. During these decades the wages of minders were relatively low; but, as a distinct occupational group, they were neither numerous enough, nor geographically concentrated enough, nor experienced enough to build financially sound unions that could realistically confront employers. Many minders did join the common-mule spinners' societies, especially during the general strike of 1842, but even these unions were suffering serious defeats in these decades for lack of adequate financial resources.[43] Technological unemployment (for example, the displacement of labor because of the coupling of mules), exacerbated by long and acute stretches of cyclical unemployment, was constantly creating an ample reserve army of spinners and piecers that could be drawn on to replace troublesome minders, be they male or female.[44]

I would argue, therefore, that even with the transition to the self-acting mule in the 1830s and 1840s, the occupation of mule spinner remained male dominated primarily because of the arduous work involved in tending the longer mules with a labor complement consisting of a minder, a big piecer, and a little piecer. The physical productivity advantage in employing males was reinforced by the combination of positive and negative incentives that derived from the minder–piecer hierarchy.[45] In the 1830s and 1840s, moreover, the union power of minders was virtually nonexistent and their wages were relatively low, conditions removing the reservations that employers might have had about employing males in what was viewed as a new occupation.

In a critique of my original statement of this argument, Mary Freifeld has argued that "a breakdown in the intergenerational transmission of female craft skills" in the transition from common mules to the self-actor resulted in a discontinuity in the skill-acquisition process for women, and that this disjuncture, rather than the arguments that I posed (or at least her interpretation of these arguments), explains male dominance of the occupation. Specifically, she asserted that "skilled women were generally excluded from the 'self-actor' after they had been squeezed out of production at an earlier stage of technological development—during the shift from short to long and 'doubled' hand mules."[46]

Further on, Freifeld repeated (with my emphasis) that "it was the rupture in the female craft traditions and labour training practices that provides the key to the exclusion of women from mulespinning on the 'self-actor' *in a period when male–female physical strength differences were no longer of any actual significance.*"[47] She has agreed with me that in the 1820s and 1830s females were excluded from the occupation of mule spinner on the common mules because of the use of longer mules as a cost-cutting measure. Physical exertion gave males a productivity advantage on the common mules because the use of males permitted more spindles per worker and also contributed to an oversupply of adult male mule spinners, many of whom took work as piecers.[48] But she has ignored my argument that the stretchout and speedup of the self-acting mule also increased the physical demands of spinning, particularly on coarser counts, thereby favoring the employment of men.

Self-acting mules, which became widely used in the 1840s, should have, in Freifeld's words, "provided the opportunity for skilled women to compete equally with men in output, something their lesser muscle strength had prevented them from doing on short or long hand [that is, common] mules." But, she went on to argue,

> by the time the 'self-acting' mulespinning machine was widely introduced in the factory, a cohort of women had not been trained in the mechanical skills of mulespinning for a decade. In essence, a breakdown or discontinuity in skill transmission had occurred. A small number of skilled women remained, but the mass of factory women no longer possessed the requisite technical knowledge or eye–hand skills in their own oral and handicraft tradition. The craft of mulespinning had largely passed out of the traditional work role and cultural knowledge of women factory workers.[49]

Besides her failure to consider the physical exertion required to do piecing on stretched-out and speeded-up self-actors, there are flaws in Freifeld's argument that there was a "discontinuity in skill transmission" for women in the transition to the self-actor. Some key skills required of self-acting minders were new skills that could not have been learned on the common mules in any case. One such skill, upon which Freifeld in fact placed considerable emphasis in arguing the sources of female exclusion, was the adjustment of the quadrant nut during cop formation.[50] The quadrant mechanism was Richard Roberts's distinctive innovation in making the mule "self-acting"; adjusting this mechanism during the winding-on operation was not a skill that common mule spinners, whether male or female, could possibly have acquired.

Nor is it clear that employment of men as spinners on long common mules was sufficient to exclude females from acquiring those skills that were transferable from the old to the new technology. These skills, as Freifeld rightly indicated, involved coping with the inevitable variability in the quality of the cotton inputs and maintaining the quality of the yarn outputs.[51] In mule spinning, there was always a trade-off between causing excessive yarn breakages by running the machines too fast and reducing throughput by running them too slowly. The "proper" speed at which the machines should be run could vary dramatically, depending on the grade and staple of raw cotton that the mill purchased and the care that was taken in cleaning, carding, and roving the cotton in preparation for the actual spinning process.

The speed of the mules could be altered by simply changing the gearings, but substantial experience was required to choose the speeds that would yield optimal results from different quality rovings (the "ropes" of cotton that were placed in the creels of the mule to be stretched and twisted into yarn of the desired count). As discussed below, the muleroom overseers (typically former mule spinners or minders) had formal responsibility for setting and fixing the mules, although, in Lancashire at least, they often delegated such mechanical work to the operatives working directly on the machines. But even when (as was more uniformly the practice in New England mule spinning) the setting and fixing of the mules was left to the overseer, an experienced operative could (if he deemed it worth his while in terms of the impact on his own effort and pay) provide the overseer with advice based on "hands-on" knowledge concerning mechanical adjustments that could be made to yield superior results.

It is undoubtedly true that during the 1830s, as Freifeld has argued, fewer women were acquiring these skills on common mules. But the argument that the reduction in their numbers during the decade precluded female employment on the self-actors during the 1840s is stretched thin when, as Freifeld herself recognized (in keeping with Leonard Horner's classification of mule-spinning positions by gender cited earlier), females were widely employed as minders and big piecers on self-actors in the early 1840s, presumably on shorter self-actors or as piecers on longer machines. Freifeld argued that "women's work on 'self-actors' (or hand mules) after [the late 1840s] was almost always confined to the role of 'piecers'." She went on to explain that "piecers were unskilled attendants who worked under the supervision of the male minders, and tied together the ends of the threads that broke during the spinning process."[52] What she failed to recognize is that it was as piecers that minders gained their experience. Little piecers were "unskilled attendants" when they began their "apprenticeship," but "under the supervision of minders," some of them gained the experience that enabled them to move up the internal job ladder. From the 1840s, many Lancashire females either had the cognitive skills to operate the self-actors or, as piecers, were in a position to acquire them. Contrary to Freifeld, a "discontinuity in skill transmission" that purportedly occurred among females on the common mules in the 1830s cannot explain male dominance of the position of minder on the self-actors.

Persistence of the Minder–Piecer Hierarchy

A major part of the analytical problem, to which I shall return in the comparative analysis of work organization in Lancashire and New England mule spinning in Chapter 4, is that Freifeld ignored the role of the minder–piecer hierarchy in ensuring both the male dominance and the craft status of the operative spinner on self-actors in Britain. As a result, she not only failed to explain why female piecers were so unsuccessful in gaining promotion to minder positions but also misrepresented my own argument concerning the relation between technical skills and the evolution of the mule-spinning division of labor. She asserted that "Lazonick speaks of the mulespinners' hold on their position in production in a period in which 'any possible technical basis for such control had been undermined'."[53] Freifeld, however, pulled this statement out of context. The phrase, "any possible technical basis," refers not to the level of manual skill required for spinning on the self-actor but to the degree of craft control exercised by

the minder as an internal subcontractor. My argument was and is that
the persistence of the hierarchical division of labor provided the foundations for the union power and craft control of minders in the
second half of the nineteenth century and indeed even into the second
half of the twentieth century. I did in fact argue that

> the craft control which mule spinners had developed on the com-
> mon mule from the late 18th century was maintained well into the
> 20th century, despite the fact that any possible technical basis for
> such control had been undermined. In the transition to the self-actor
> in the 1830s and 1840s, minders were able to retain a dual role as
> both operative and supervisor, not because they collectively forced
> this hierarchical division of labour on capitalists, but because capi-
> talists had no leeway to experiment with new divisions of labour,
> particularly given the need for close supervision of younger
> workers.[54]

Besides male dominance of mule spinning, the persistence of internal subcontracting must be explained. In his history of cotton textile
unionism, H. A. Turner argued that the collective power of the minders led to the preservation of internal subcontracting with its
minder–piecer hierarchy. Turner argued that the system of one minder and two piecers on self-actors "was far from being adopted at the
employers' choice [as] is shown by the many local battles that were
fought over it."[55] Yet for the 1830s and 1840s, he referred only to the
Webbs' statement that the Oldham Spinners' Union was formed to
resist the attempt by employers to place one spinner on four to six
mules.[56] The Webbs in turn took this information from an autobio-
graphical pamphlet by William Marcroft, in which the author stated
that the resistance was to the "double-decking" and "treble-decking"
of mules.[57] As already indicated, double-decking entailed attaching
two mules together to form one machine. One spinner was then
responsible for a pair of these longer mules, while leaving the spinner–piecer hierarchy intact. It is not clear whether this case refers to
common mules or self-actors. In either case, this "local battle" was
over stretchout (more spindles per worker) and the consequent displacement of minders, and not over the preservation of internal subcontracting and the spinner–piecer hierarchy.

The only other evidence that Turner provided of "local battles"
that maintained internal subcontracting are (1) a threat to introduce a
multipair system in *1885*, and (2) the emergence of the multipair

system as the dominant mode of work organization in Scotland by the 1880s.[58] In due course, I shall comment on both of these examples, but they are irrelevant to the developments in Lancashire in the 1830s and 1840s. For this transitional period, there is no evidence that the collective power of minders can account for the persistence of the minder–piecer hierarchical division of labor on the self-acting mules. During the 1830s and 1840s, the minders simply did not possess significant collective power. Moreover, there is no evidence that the minders had to put up a struggle to maintain the minder–piecer system.

Why then did capitalist employers continue to rely on the internal subcontract system with its minder–piecer hierarchy? To explain the persistence of this substantial delegation of authority to the operatives, one must ask what tasks, manual and managerial, distinguished the minder from the big piecer.

Maintenance Tasks

Perhaps in the early years of the self-actor, but certainly by 1875, the minder was responsible for monitoring the wear and tear as well as the tightness of the straps and bands that drove the moving parts of the self-actor and for repairing any of the straps and bands that broke. Failure to do so would cause loss of production, excess waste, and damage to the machines. Minders also had primary responsibility for the periodic squaring-up of the mules, and they had to perform the weekly cleaning and oiling of the gears that regulated the movements of the machine and the regular oiling of the spindles.[59]

That the minder was responsible for these tasks was, in my view, a result rather than a cause of the minder–piecer division of labor. That is, given that this division of labor existed for other reasons, factory owners allocated responsibility for these tasks to the minder rather than to the spinning-room overlooker or the mill mechanic. On self-acting mules in the United States, where there was no minder–piecer distinction, the main mule-spinning operatives were paid by the piece but in effect performed the same tasks as Lancashire big piecers; it was assistant overseers who repaired straps and bands and made other adjustments to the mules.[60]

In Lancashire, the minder's responsibility for these tasks became institutionalized in the wage-lists that were adopted in the various spinning districts between 1850 and 1890. Nevertheless, even in the late nineteenth and early twentieth centuries, it was not always clear whether certain adjustments and repairs were the responsibility of minders or the muleroom overseer—maintenance tasks were often delegated informally on the shop floor.[61] Over time, the effect of such delegation of maintenance tasks was that, being tuned and adjusted by operatives having "little respect for the intentions of the maker or the principles of engineering" (as Harold Catling has put it), no two pairs of mules worked in precisely the same way, thus making each minder less dispensable for the successful operation of his particular pair. Catling argued that this "customizing" of the mules was an important factor in preventing the development of a multipair system in the 1870s and 1880s, by which time the perfection of the automatic motions of the self-actor made it "technically feasible for mules to be staffed like looms."[62] Although maintenance tasks do not explain the origins of the minder–piecer system, the formal and informal allocation of these tasks to minders apparently helped to maintain the hierarchical division of labor in the late nineteenth century when the privileged position of the minder came under attack.

Operative Tasks

Unlike the common-mule spinner who had his hands full with the backing-off and putting-up of a pair of mules, the minder performed a great deal of piecing. Typically, the minder and the little piecer pieced on one half of the spindles, and the big piecer on the other half. In addition, during the first few decades of the diffusion of the mules, the minder had to provide manual assistance to "nosing" and "governing" (or "strapping") motions in the winding process, despite the promises of Sharp, Roberts & Co. in 1830 that henceforth the winding process would indeed be entirely self-acting. Catling attributed the origin of the craft status of minders to these manual functions on the early self-actors, arguing that up to the 1870s or 1880s union pressure to protect this status was "entirely justified [on technical grounds], for it took almost fifty years to perfect such important accessories as the strapping and nosing motions."[63]

The purpose of the nosing motion was to compensate for the taper of the spindle so that the yarn would be wound firmly and without snarls onto the nose of the cop.[64] Firm cop noses reduced waste and downtime in the subsequent processes of winding and weaving. If (as was typically the case in Lancashire) the firm sold yarn on the market, then firm cop noses maintained its reputation as a high quality supplier. Richard Roberts had devised a motion that required a simple adjustment of a peg during the last stages of cop formation. Although completely automatic nosing motions were in use from the 1860s, in the early years of the self-actor the Roberts device was not used. On the coarsest counts, snarls did not significantly affect the quality of the yarn or the subsequent weaving processes, and could simply be ignored. But on counts above 20s, firm and unsnarled noses mattered. The noses were made firm by manually delaying the rise of the faller for the last few inches of winding on each inward run during the last stages of cop formation—a manual operation that required close attention and a degree of dexterity on the part of the minder and vested him with some control over product quality.[65]

It could be argued that the need to have an operative perform the nosing motion explains the higher wages of the minder relative to those of the big piecer. But in Lancashire the minder–piecer hierarchy was used even on the coarsest counts of yarn, on which, as mentioned above, the failure to maintain firm noses was of little if any account.

The governing or strapping motion of Roberts quadrant mechanism was the major breakthrough in the development of a practical self-actor.[66] As described in the original patent, the automatic movement of a quadrant nut varied (or "governed") the speed of the spindles in inverse proportion to the diameter of the cop of yarn. For a few decades after the introduction of the self-actor, however, the governing motion was used in a less than completely automatic form.[67] In practice, it was found that, to prevent snarls in the yarn, five small adjustments of a screw that moved the quadrant nut were required as the cop was beginning to be formed. After these five adjustments, the nut moved automatically until the full diameter of the cop was attained. But the practice on the early self-actors was to dispense with any automatic movement of the nut during about the first fifth of the cop formation period and instead have the minder, or more usually the big piecer responding to hand signals from the minder, turn the screw about 90 times during this initial stage (about 1.5 hours when spinning 40s yarn in the 1830s and 1840s).[68] Failure to perform this operation diligently could result in a sawney—a simultaneous breakage of the hundreds of strands of yarn on the mule, a disastrous occurrence for the minder, working as he was on piece-rates.

Catling's explanation for the use of the less mechanized governing motion demonstrates the importance of supervision in the choice of technique.[69] As in the case of the nosing motion, the spinning capitalist found snarls that occurred in the governing motion costly. But unlike snarls formed on the nose of the cop at the completion of cop formation, snarls formed during the initial stages of cop formation in the middle (or "chase") of the cop could usually be hidden by the minder.[70] As a result, the inferior quality of his output would often go unnoticed as it was being checked in the spinning room. The tendency was, therefore, for minders and piecers to neglect the five small adjustments when their mules were equipped with the more mechanized governing motion. With the completely manual mode of quadrant nut adjustment, however, such neglect, by causing a sawney, would lead directly to a fall in earnings and an increase in effort for the minder. Hence, it can be argued that the less mechanical method was used, not because the more mechanical method when attended to properly was technically inferior, but because, in the absence of close supervision over the minder to ensure such proper attention, the capitalist found the less mechanical technique more conducive to quality control. That is, the lack of close supervision over the minder, inherent in the minder–piecer system, determined the choice of technique, rather than vice versa.

Supervisory Tasks

There is no evidence that Lancashire cotton-spinning capitalists made any serious attempts to do away with the old spinner–piecer hierarchy when they introduced self-actors into their mills in the 1830s and 1840s. Nor is it clear that they perceived the displacement of the adult male minder as desirable. As individuals, minders were relatively easily replaceable and inexpensive in this period; and, as a group, they possessed little union power. On the shop floor, moreover, the spinner–piecer system in working the common mules (which often continued to coexist in the same factory with the minder–piecer system on self-actors) had provided capitalist employers with an effective mode of labor management.[71]

Even though some savings in money wages could have been achieved on a multipair system, it is not clear that unit labor costs would have fallen under such a radically different mode of shop-floor supervision. Indeed I would expect that, if such experiments had been attempted in Lancashire, unit labor costs would have risen considerably because of problems in maintaining the intensity of labor. The experiment would have been quickly terminated by reverting to the minder–piecer system. There is contemporary evidence in government inquiries and private investigations into factory conditions in the first half of the nineteenth century that demonstrates that the assistants who pieced, creeled, doffed, oiled, cleaned, and swept had to be closely supervised, and at times physically disciplined, if output was to be maintained. Perhaps reflecting the perceptions of capitalists themselves, Andrew Ure argued that "[common] mule spinning could not go on with any degree of prosperity if the assistants were independent of the operative."[72] Given the social relations in the spinning room, this observation applied to the utilization of self-actors as well.

The ability of any individual firm, even the most substantial, to undertake experimentation in reorganization of the hierarchical division of labor was further limited by the highly competitive conditions that prevailed in the Lancashire cotton-spinning industry.[73] The decline in productivity during the initial phase of the new arrangement might have spelled doom for the innovating firm, even though under more "protected" circumstances that permitted the development of the new management structure the multipair system might have shown itself to be economically superior to the minder–piecer system.

The impacts of different social environments on the choice of work organization are illustrated by comparing the Lancashire minder–piecer system with the modes of supervision on self-actors that prevailed in the United States and Scotland in the nineteenth century. From the late 1830s when self-actors were first introduced in New England, all the piecing on a pair of mules (of 600–800 spindles each) was done by the "mule spinner," with an overlooker supervising a spinning room of perhaps eight pairs of self-acting mules and hiring and firing assistants such as doffers, sweepers, and backboys. Later in the nineteenth century, when young lads to do creeling were scarce in the United States, the burden of hiring backboys was put on the spinners.[74] Not only was a multipair system used on self-actors in New England, but the mode of supervision that it entailed conformed to common-mule practice in the New England cotton mills, in which top-down hierarchical authority prevailed and internal subcontract systems were virtually unknown.

The transitions from the common mule to the self-actor in Lancashire and New England, therefore, saw continuity in their respective structures of shop-floor control. In contrast, the technological transition in Scotland ultimately saw the replacement of the spinner–piecer system by a multipair system. The Scottish system, moreover, unlike the multipair organization of work in the United States, employed only females as operatives. Before 1840 in Scotland, women had been used to some extent as spinners on common mules, particularly in country mills, but also on a more limited scale in Glasgow, the center of the industry. Men dominated the Glaswegian occupation, operating on the spinner–piecer internal subcontract system supported by a union that was able to maintain tight control over entry into the trade and piece-rates. In the period of general prosperity from 1825 to 1937, the Glasgow spinners controlled piece-rate adjustments by firms that installed longer common mules so completely that the workers captured most, if not virtually all, the consequent value gains. As a result, unlike their Lancashire counterparts who were better able to share in the value gains generated by increasing the number of spindles per machine, Glasgow capitalists refrained from stretching out the mules during this decade.[75]

In late 1836, however, yarn prices fell on the heels of a 16 percent wage increase for spinners earlier in the year. In the crisis, Glasgow capitalists came together to provoke a bitter strike that culminated in the breaking of the union, the introduction of longer common mules and self-actors, and the general use of women and youths as operatives on smaller common mules and self-actors. The "victory," however, inaugurated a long-run decline of the Scottish industry from which it never recovered.[76]

In the 1880s, when the Scottish cotton textile industry had been reduced to insignificant proportions, a multipair system known as the "doffing" system was generally in use. The doffing system was in fact what Sharp, Roberts & Co. had promised back in 1830, three female piecers operating pairs of 1,000-spindle mules supervised by a male overlooker, called a doffer, who was responsible for four or five pairs of self-actors. The Glasgow Spinning Co., which began operations in 1883, used this system quite successfully: in 1892, it achieved direct (doffer and piecers) wage costs per pound of 40s yarn of 0.40d. (on 1,000-spindle mules) whereas in the same year an Oldham mill using the latest machinery and the minder–piecer system to spin the same counts could only achieve direct wage costs per pound of 0.50d. (on 1,200-spindle mules).[77] As a result of the different social environments in which machines and labor were employed, there was more than one way to spin a mule.

Recruiting Tasks

With the minder–piecer system, managers and overlookers delegated to senior operatives the function of recruiting as well as supervising younger workers. The expenditure of already scarce managerial resources to recruit these workers would not have been insignificant, given that about 40 percent of all workers under eighteen years of age in the Lancashire cotton factories in the 1830s were in the direct employ of mule spinners, whose subordinates represented about 90 percent of the young people in the spinning rooms.[78] Mule spinners brought not only relatives but also children of neighbors into the mills, paying the wages of younger piecers directly to their parents. The spinners had an economic interest in seeking out the most dependable assistants, while at the same time their location in the families or communities of the supply of assistants gave them an advantage in assessing the likely qualities of new recruits. Moreover, when an assistant had to be coerced physically to work, it was the operative employer, and not the capitalist employer, who had to deal with the child's parents (that person, of course, often being the operative employer himself).

The internal subcontract system was not, however, a necessary condition for the existence of the minder–piecer hierarchy (although, as I shall show later, the preservation of internal subcontracting helped to maintain the privileged position of the minder on the shop floor). In the 1830s, for example, the capitalist employers at Birley's—the largest mill in Manchester—hired and fired piecers on both common mules and self-actors. The practice had begun in the early nineteenth century, when Birley's managers found that spinners were leaving work on the pretext of needing to find a full complement of piecers.[79] If a piecer at Birley's misbehaved, the spinner or minder referred him to the overlooker, who might fine or dismiss him. Nevertheless, even without internal subcontracts per se, at Birley's as elsewhere in Lancashire, it was the spinner or the minder who had the responsibility and authority for close supervision of piecers. In the late 1830s and 1840s, however, when the large number of unemployed spinners precluded those who had jobs from leaving work under any pretext, even Birley's began to delegate the recruitment function to operatives, and by the late 1840s the minders in this mill were hiring and firing their own assistants.[80]

Hence, with the transition from the common mule to the self-actor in the 1830s and 1840s, the spinner–piecer system was replaced by an analogous minder–piecer system—one that left minders with the responsibility for the recruitment of assistants as well as the power to exercise authority over them on the shop floor. In his book *Class Struggle and the Industrial Revolution,* John Foster argued erroneously that the survival of the adult males on self-actors was because of "the creation of a *new* pacemaker grade" whereby capitalists divided off from the rest of the operatives a group of elite workers, who "instead of enforcing discipline against the management . . . were now to do so on its behalf."[81] "Taking all the evidence together," Foster concluded, "it seems clear enough that cotton did develop a labor aristocracy and . . . it was the introduction of a new dimension of authority at work which was the key factor."[82] But, as A. E. Musson pointed out in his review of Foster's book, there was certainly nothing new in Lancashire cotton spinning about the role of operatives as supervisors of labor.[83] Indeed, as I have argued earlier, it was the very fact that capitalists had become reliant on common-mule spinners to enforce discipline on piecers and scavengers in the half-century before the introduction of the self-actor that explains the persistence of the hierarchical division of labor among shop-floor workers. The self-acting minders (later often called spinners, as common-mule spinning died out) were therefore not a new "labor aristocracy," but the legatees of the old.

Contrary to Foster, the aristocratic position of the minders was not the result of a capitalist strategy to intensify work on the new technology. That capitalists could pursue such a strategy in the mid–nineteenth century assumes that they had much more control over the structuring of the hierarchical division of labor than they in fact possessed. The minders' position derived not from the ability of British capitalists to restructure their enterprises but from the exigencies of competition that constrained individual capitalists to continue with the tried and true methods of labor management.

The industrial militancy of the common-mule spinners in the 1830s and early 1840s was fundamentally an extension of the militancy that they had exercised since the 1790s as they sought to protect their jobs, wage rates, and conditions of work. What changed was that in the 1830s and early 1840s, the spinners' quest for better work and pay gained inspiration and aid from the larger anticapitalist movements that were by then engulfing England. The rapid decline of spinners' militancy after the failure of the general strike of 1842 can be explained in the short run by the demoralizing effects of defeat, the financial bankruptcy of their unions, and the cyclical upswing in the cotton textile industry in 1843 and 1844. Over the longer run, generally prosperous conditions in the cotton textile industry from the late 1840s to the cotton famine of the early 1860s enabled the minders to pick up where the common-mule spinners had left off, as they consolidated their control over the organization of work on a technology that was supposed to have, as Marx put it in 1867, "opened up a new epoch in the automatic system."[84]

Consolidation of the Minder–Piecer System

As the dominant form of work organization on the self-acting mules during the cyclical and conflictual conditions of the 1830s and early 1840s, the minder–piecer system persisted during the long boom of the third quarter of the nineteenth century to provide a basis for the development of a highly organized craft occupation of minders. In the summer of 1842 the adult male operatives had formed the Association of Operative Cotton Spinners, Twiners and Self-Acting Minders of the United Kingdom, thus organizing the new category of minders together with the old common-mule unionists. During the next few years, the Association was active in strikes as well as in agitating for shorter working hours. But over the longer run, the union of the minders and spinners was untenable because the introduction of self-actors, or the conversion of common mules to self-acting machines, displaced the common-mule spinners. In an effort to prevent the dilution of their elite status, from the late 1840s local spinners' societies tended to expel minders from membership or refuse to organize them; as a result, separate unions of spinners and minders developed. In Bolton, where the old Association had been centered, the minders formed a Self-Actor Society in 1861. In 1870 the Amalgamated Association of Operative Cotton Spinners and Twiners was formed. This association was composed of male minders and became one of the strongest workers' organizations in Britain over the next half-century; it was still in existence a century after its formation.[85]

During this period, minders were able to raise their wages, because profitable opportunities inclined capitalists to favor conciliation rather than confrontation with their workers. One extremely important manifestation of this attitude was the emergence in the various spinning districts of Lancashire of widely recognized wage-lists, many of which endured well into the twentieth century. For example, after what was perhaps the most bitter confrontation in the history of the Lancashire cotton textile industry—the Preston strike of 1853–54—the capitalists of Preston realized that they had won the battle over wages with their workers but had lost the war over markets with their competitors in other, more tranquil, spinning districts of Lancashire. In 1859 and 1866 the "victorious" Preston employers worked out wage-lists, which brought the wages of their minders up to the levels of other districts. This list remained in effect until 1945, as did the lists of Blackburn (adopted in 1853), Ashton (1860), Burnley (1867), Oldham (1876), and Bolton (1887). The Oldham and Bolton lists were by far the most important, regulating 75 percent of minders' wages in the Lancashire and Cheshire spinning industry in 1894, and 90 percent in 1945.[86]

Originally negotiated during lengthy periods of prosperity when the Lancashire cotton textile industry dominated world markets, the terms of these long-lasting lists were generally favorable to the minders.[87] A major effect was to institutionalize the minder–piecer system as the generally recognized starting point of all collective bargaining procedures in Lancashire. Take, for example, the Oldham list—the most extensively used in Lancashire—that applied primarily to minders spinning 50s and under (broadly speaking, coarse counts). The Oldham list was the outcome of a series of strikes fought during the particularly prosperous period of 1869 to 1875, the issues being, at first, the adoption of a recognized wage-list, and, then, the modification of the list to keep down piecers' wages (on the rise because of the boom-induced scarcity of younger workers) as well as to gain compensation for more intensified work because of the speedup of self-actors, particularly by the newly established limited liability companies.[88]

The Oldham list gave the minder certain standard weekly earnings on mules of different lengths, to which was added a "quick-speed" allowance—a stated amount for each second that a particular pair of mules ran faster than three draws in fifty seconds (in 1908 renegotiated to three draws in forty-four seconds). Even though the list specified standard weekly earnings, the minders were actually paid by the piece. After deducting time for cleaning, doffing, and accidental stoppages, it was calculated how much the pair of mules should normally turn out in a week when spinning certain counts. This normal production was then divided into the standard weekly earnings to derive a piece-rate per 1,000 hanks of yarn. The actual gross earnings of the minder were this piece-rate times the number of 1,000 hanks actually spun, adjusted upward or downward by a percentage determined by collective bargaining over the business cycle.[89]

From these actual gross weekly earnings, the minder would deduct the time-wages of the big and little piecers according to fixed amounts specified in the wage-list. The minders could, therefore, capture some of the value gains from higher productivity but the piecers, who may very well have generated the extra effort that resulted in extra output, could not. The source of greater productivity was often the increased efforts of piecers who pieced broken ends more quickly, doffed the completed cops faster, cleaned and oiled the mules outside of engine hours (thus avoiding downtime during the regulation workday when the engines were running), or contributed unpaid time because of "time-cribbing"—the practice of starting and stopping the steam engines outside the limits of the workday set by the Factory Acts. The revised Oldham list that became effective in 1876 carefully specified that piecers were prohibited from sharing in payments to the minder in compensation for the extra work created by "tubing" (the placing of paper tubes on the spindles in spinning certain types of yarn), putting extra twist into the yarn, and faster carriage speeds. Again, in these tasks, the piecers performed some, and often most, of the extra work.[90]

The Oldham list, therefore, imposed what I have called Marxian exploitation—unremunerated intensification of labor— on the junior workers, to the joint benefit of minders and capitalists who shared in the consequent value gains. In Bolton and other major spinning districts, the lists only specified the method of calculating gross earnings of the minder, who was then left to strike individual bargains with his piecers. Because of the relative absence of alternative employment opportunities in the fine-spinning district of Bolton as well as the better work conditions and prospects of higher future earnings as a minder that fine spinning offered, the earnings of Bolton piecers were consistently lower than those of Oldham piecers.[91]

Cross-district variations aside, the wage-lists institutionalized internal subcontracting and the minder–piecer system in the industrial relations of Lancashire mule spinning. In the 1870s a minder earned 30s.–34s. per week (net of piecers' wages) and typically employed one big piecer (an older boy, aged fifteen to eighteen) paid 12s.–14s., and one little piecer (a younger boy, aged ten to fourteen) paid 7s.–9s.[92]

Defending the Minder–Piecer System

In the last half of the nineteenth century, capitalist employers did make attempts to weaken or circumvent the minder–piecer system when it appeared to have outlived its usefulness. To undermine the power of the minders, capitalists sought to exploit the system's tendency inherent in its very hierarchical structure to generate a perpetual oversupply of big piecers waiting to become minders. One form of attack was called the apprenticing system. A big piecer was given a pair of mules and paid less than other minders in the mill for a year or two on the grounds that he was less productive as he was learning the minder's job. Perceiving correctly that this system was an attempt to create a lower paid stratum of workers within their occupation, the minders opposed its introduction and successfully secured its elimination by the 1870s.[93]

A more dangerous and ever-present threat to the minder–piecer system was a practice called joining, or partnering, whereby the minder was downgraded and the big piecer upgraded to positions of equal pay and status, with a little piecer assisting them on a pair of mules. If, as was often the case in the 1870s, the minder was earning 33s. per week and the big piecer 13s. per week, each of two joiner–minders would earn 23s. Joining did not, therefore, lower total wages (at least in the first instance), but it did eliminate the "craft" worker—that is, a worker receiving a wage that would place him among the labor aristocracy.

If joining had been attempted before the minders had achieved craft-level wages—say, in 1840—the combined wage of a minder and big piecer would have been at most 24s., or a meager 12s. per joiner–minder, hardly enough to induce young men to make spinning their lifelong occupation. On the minder–piecer system, however, a big piecer was willing to work for very low wages, whether in 1840 or 1870, because he recognized that low pay today was a necessary prelude for promotion up the internal job ladder to the high pay of a minder's position.

But with the end of the mill-building boom of the early 1870s, and indeed into the 1930s, a big piecer was by no means assured of becoming a minder, even when he was willing to work as a big piecer (at big piecer's wages) late into his twenties. In the late nineteenth century, the oversupply of twenty-year-old big piecers waiting to become minders was on the order of three to five times the number of

minders' vacancies.[94] Moreover, from the 1880s, there was a perpetual supply of unemployed minders, the victims of layoffs and mill
closures, many of whom had accepted employment as big piecers
again in order to get another chance at a minder position.[95] By the
early 1930s the vast majority of big piecers were aged eighteen to
thirty and they received 40 percent of the weekly earnings of a
minder; little piecers were aged fourteen to eighteen and were paid 25
percent of a minder's wages. These were the same relative wages that
had prevailed in the 1860s when piecers (and particularly big piecers)
were generally much younger. By the first decades of the twentieth
century, big piecers were among the lowest paid adult male workers
in Britain.[96]

By the late nineteenth century, the joining system presented a reasonable solution to the diminished prospects for promotion facing big
piecers. But the minders' unions opposed joining, not on the grounds
that it was technically inferior to the minder–piecer system, but because it would reduce the minder from the status of a skilled worker,
capable of earning a "family" wage, to that of a laborer, receiving an
individual subsistence wage. For, by the late nineteenth century, the
minders recognized full well that their relatively high wages were
based, not on technical skills or mental abilities that were in scarce
supply, but on the power of their unions to maintain an unequal
distribution of income among shop-floor workers. The joining system
would eliminate the ability of minders to keep the wages of piecers
down, and indeed, by making it possible for many more capable
workers to compete for minders' positions, would seriously undermine their union power.[97]

Despite this opposition, in districts such as Blackburn, Burnley, and
Leigh, where weaving or coalmining offered alternative employments
to young men, the minders were forced to permit the widespread
adoption of the joining system to alleviate the difficulty of attracting
piecers into the occupation. In the main coarse-spinning center of
Oldham (but not in the fine-spinning center of Bolton), minders were
eventually compelled to agree to the limited use of joining as a form
of apprenticeship system—that is, as an intermediate rung on the job
ladder between big piecer and minder. Agreements were made in
individual mills on the proportion of mules—usually not more than
one in twelve—that could be run on the joining system. By the 1930s,
about 12 percent of Lancashire mule spinners (excluding big piecers)
were joiner–minders.[98]

Another threat to the craft position of the minder was the possibility that capitalists might use women in the occupation, displacing some of the men and creating downward pressure on the wages of the others. When the Amalgamated Association of Operative Cotton Spinners and Twiners was formed in 1870, women were expelled from membership in local minders' unions and the occupation became thoroughly male dominated.[99] Females continued to be used as piecers, however, particularly in Wigan and Manchester, where male piecers were scarce but where weaving did not offer a widespread alternative employment to females.[100] Females were also employed as piecers to some extent in the fine-spinning district of Bolton up to the 1880s. As long as minders could be sure that female piecers would not become minders, their use was sanctioned: they helped to overcome the persistent scarcity of little piecers, while at the same time they helped to reduce the oversupply of fully trained big piecers waiting to become minders.

In 1886 the Bolton minders' union prohibited the employment of female piecers. The transition to the self-actor was just being completed on the fine counts spun in Bolton, and a revision of the Bolton list was pending in 1887. At a country mill near Bolton in November 1886, three women were hired as minders on fine-spinning self-actors at about 15s. per week, probably less than half the wages of male minders on the same machines. The mill was struck, and there were debates in local newspapers and the *Cotton Factory Times* concerning the morality of females working, scantily clad, in the hot and humid mulerooms. In December 1886, after decades of turning a blind eye to such immoral conditions, the Bolton Spinners' Union voted almost unanimously "that members in the future decline to teach or cause to be taught the trade of piecing to any female child," thereby excluding females almost completely from the Bolton district mulerooms. In 1897 the *Cotton Factory Times* claimed that female minders were employed in only four mills in Lancashire (including the Bolton mill that had been struck over a decade before), and went on to say that such employment of women was contrary to trade union principles.[101]

As I have noted, by the 1880s a multipair system employing female operatives on self-actors was in use in Scotland. By its very existence, the Scottish mode of work organization questioned the legitimacy of the minder–piecer system in Lancashire. There were many cases in Lancashire and its contiguous areas of a minder being put in charge of two pairs of mules. Most cases were in weakly organized towns in Yorkshire. In the main spinning centers such as Oldham, the mere threat of a strike was usually enough to deter individual employers from adopting such a system; for, in the highly competitive structure of the industry, no individual mill could afford to be struck over this issue. It was clear that the well-financed district union (backed by the Amalgamated) would fully support the striking workers, whereas support for the firm by the local employers' association (most of whose members accepted the minder–piecer system) was by no means assured.[102]

In 1885, however, during a serious cyclical crisis in the cotton textile industry, it appeared that employers in Oldham might take a united stand to support the introduction of the multipair system. In April 1885, with a demand by employers for a 10 percent wage reduction imminent, Samuel Andrew, the secretary of the Oldham Master Cotton Spinners' Association, threatened the minders with the introduction of a three-pair or four-pair system, arguing that recent improvements on the mules had now made possible this mode of work organization.[103] In August, at the beginning of a thirteen-week strike over the wage reduction, Andrew claimed that an eight-pair to ten-pair system was even thinkable.[104] It was later claimed that one mill had established a three-pair system during the strike.[105] But employers as a collectivity were not even able to impose the full 10 percent wage reduction on the minders, let alone a multipair system. During the course of the strike, the Oldham minders were able to demonstrate the financial strength of their union, leaving an impression on employers that made them receptive, and even eager, in the coming years for the further elaboration of conciliation procedures. As I shall show in Chapter 4, the most notable conciliation procedure in the cotton textile industry would be the Brooklands Agreement of 1893.

Hence the minder–piecer system held out against alternative divisions of labor in the Lancashire spinning industry. On the one side, minders were unified by their interest in protecting their craft status—in the 1890s over 90 percent of minders in Lancashire and Cheshire were union members. On the other side, capitalists, more often than not divided by competition and still finding the minder–piecer system an effective mode of shop-floor management, never undertook a united effort to change the traditional system. As illustrated by the threat of the joining system, minders' unions recognized that their craft status was secured not by a scarcity of adequately trained and capable spinners but by their collective power to maintain big piecers in a subordinate position.

To ensure the integrity of the hierarchical division of labor, the minders' unions strenuously objected to all attempts by overlookers and managers to interfere with the shop-floor control that their members exercised over the piecers. In 1888, for example, two successive editorials in the *Cotton Factory Times,* undoubtedly authored by union leaders, made it clear that the issue was not what tasks piecers should perform but who had the right to give piecers orders. The first editorial berated an overlooker for ordering piecers not to clean the mules during meal hours. The second attacked an overlooker for discharging five piecers who refused to clean the mules during meal hours, and even admonished the other piecers in the mill for not all banding together against the overseer.[106]

At about the same time, minders were taking steps to ensure that the piecers would not band together against minders themselves, nor be used by capitalists to replace striking or sick minders.[107] Common-mule spinners and self-acting minders had always had to dispense some strike pay to piecers during stoppages to ensure that they stayed away from work. The boom of the early 1870s had greatly increased the number of piecers in the trade, many of whom were then thrown out of work by the deep depression of the late 1870s. The diminution of big piecers' prospects for becoming minders occurred just as the minders were staging large-scale strikes. Under these circumstances, the very real threat that piecers would be employed in place of striking or sick minders forced the minders' unions to begin to organize piecers into district associations. The piecers would pay contributions to the minders' union and have the right to receive strike pay.[108] Such union membership carried with it, however, no other rights or benefits—no accident or sick pay, no victim pay, no out-of-work pay, no votes, no right to attend union meetings, and no representation.[109] That is, the piecers' subordinate position in the district unions mirrored precisely their position in the workplace.

In Bolton minders were made responsible for piecers' dues. As a result, by the mid-1880s virtually all piecers in the district were members of the piecers' association.[110] In Oldham there was no such rule, but minders were encouraged to sign up their piecers, and by the 1890s almost three quarters of the piecers had joined.[111] As part of the "New Unionism" movement that had spread in Britain from 1889, some Bolton piecers formed their own Lancashire Piecers' Association in 1891–92. Tom Mann, the leader of the movement, made an attempt to organize the piecers in 1894. These efforts at organization did not proceed very far.[112] Nevertheless, during the 1890s and 1900s, the piecers independently staged many strikes against intensification of labor and the filling of minders' vacancies from outside their firms.[113]

In putting down all attempts at independent action by the piecers, the minders' unions evoked the justification of "trade union principles," arguing that one day piecers would become minders and that minders required a family wage, whereas piecers required only an individual wage. The minders thus evaded the issue of what was to become known by the beginning of the twentieth century as the "piecer problem"—the fact that only a small proportion of big piecers would ever proceed up the job ladder to become minders, the rest being thrown back on the external labor market in adulthood as unskilled laborers.[114]

Yet, despite the partial breakdown in internal promotion incentives, the minder–piecer system was to remain intact into the post–World War II decades. The minders' unions successfully opposed any alterations in work organization that would undermine their craft control. Spinning capitalists were unable even to reallocate auxiliary tasks such as cleaning, oiling, and tubing to specialized and cheaper workers as their counterparts had done in New England, because the Lancashire wage-lists stipulated that minders were to receive extra compensation for such tasks, whether or not they were the ones who actually performed them.[115] In the preface to a book on cotton mill management published in 1923, a textile industry consultant summed up the extent to which craft control had become embedded in the British cotton textile industry:

> The textile workers of the country are so thoroughly organised in trade unions that the organisation of labour is practically entirely in their hands, and the management must organise almost exactly on the lines laid down in a series of rules recognised by master and man as a basis upon which they must work. These rules have almost the force of laws, and they apply chiefly to the number of people to be employed, their duties, and their remuneration . . . Here is the place to emphasise the vast importance of good management, a recogni-

tion of a set of fixed conditions established after a long and dreary warfare between master and man, and the clear exhibition to his workmen of his intention to abide by these conditions.[116]

Minders, Piecers, and Value Creation

The manufacture of cotton textiles was central to Britain's rise to international industrial leadership in the nineteenth century. Within this industry, mule spinning was a dominant technology, and the mule spinners, first on common mules and then on self-actors, were key to the value-creation process. The case of mule spinning is important not only for understanding the institutional character of the British rise to economic power but also for assessing the validity of existing theories of capitalist development.

Observing the horrors of the factory system in the first half of the nineteenth century and the more general breakdown of social stability created by an anarchic competitive system, Marx came to the conclusion that the social basis of Britain's rise to economic power was capitalist domination of the worker. The development of the forces of production through technological change would, in Marx's view, only serve to reinforce the social relations of capitalist control. The case of British mule spinning during the Industrial Revolution and beyond shows that, for all his insights into the value-creation process, Marx misconstrued the dynamic interaction of organization and technology in capitalist development. Technological change did not, in and of itself, enable capitalists to extract surplus-value from the activities on the shop floor. What Marx missed is that value creation and surplus generation require that the skills and efforts of workers be managed—that a factory labor force with the requisite skills be developed, and that, through the supply of effort, the labor-power of this labor force be utilized.

British spinning capitalists undertook to invest in factory buildings and machine technologies. But they neglected to invest in managerial structures that could have exercised control over workers' access to skills and the amount of effort that they supplied. Instead British spinning capitalists left the development and utilization of shop-floor labor-power in the hands of shop-floor workers, and as a result gave up the power to manage the shop-floor division of labor.

While key groups of workers—in this case, the minders—were united by their common positions of craft control during the nineteenth century, their capitalist employers were divided by competition for product markets. To be sure, as I have shown, these craft workers often faced—and indeed in the late nineteenth century persistently faced—competition for their elite jobs. But far from undermining craft control, the presence of an industrial reserve army only strengthened the commitment of the minders to maintain craft unity.

Yet, if in a key occupation such as mule spinning capitalists gave up control of the shop floor, in cotton textiles, as well as in other industries (as I shall show in Chapter 6), craft control did not preclude the emergence of Britain as the "workshop of the world" during the third quarter of the nineteenth century. Craft control was consistent with, and perhaps even fundamental to, British industrial success. In cotton spinning, the minder–piecer system was an effective mode of shop-floor management until the late nineteenth century, if not beyond. Union power that fashioned and enforced the terms of the wage-lists ensured minders that they would share in value gains, whether these gains derived from improvements of the mules or from fuller utilization of the existing technology. Through the stipulations of the wage-lists, the minders were able to share in value gains derived from longer and faster mules as well as from increased effort. Backed by union power to enforce stipulated piece-rate agreements, the minders could work harder to increase their earnings without fear that rates would be reduced.

Moreover, supplying much of the effort that augmented the minders' earnings were the piecers. From a short-run perspective, a piecer was contributing unremunerated effort; he or she was being exploited in the Marxian sense of the word. But from a longer run point of view, a male piecer who showed himself capable and accommodating could look forward to promotion to a minder position, when he would in turn coerce his subordinates to supply the effort that would remunerate him for the effort he had previously supplied his minder in his youth. Females who worked as piecers were, however, less likely to adopt such a long-term time horizon; insofar as minders could coerce unremunerated effort from them, female piecers were exploited, pure and simple.

As I have indicated, by the last decades of the nineteenth century, the willingness of male piecers to cooperate in the value-creation process began to break down as the prospects for gaining access to the position of minder dimmed. In retrospect, one can see that in terms of the development of the forces of British cotton textile production, the last decades of the nineteenth century represented the beginning of long-term industrial decline. In the following two chapters, I shall analyze how and when the prevailing relations of production in the Lancashire cotton textile industry reached their limits, both technical and social, for first developing and then utilizing the industry's productive forces.

4   More Than One Way to Spin a Mule

Industrial Relations: Oldham and Fall River

In 1870 district unions of self-acting minders came together to form the Amalgamated Association of Operative Cotton Spinners and Twiners. In the decades before World War I these Lancashire unions were to become the best-organized and best-financed workers' organizations in Britain. A century after its formation, the Amalgamated was still in existence, expiring in the early 1970s as the last mules were removed from the Lancashire mills.[1]

Manifesting the bargaining power of the minders' unions were, as outlined in Chapter 3, the district wage-lists that governed the relations between "masters and men." The lists specified in detail the methods for deriving piece-rates to be paid for spinning different counts of yarn. Some lists also specified earnings adjustments for spindles per mule, the speed of the mules, and auxiliary work, as well as the division of gross earnings among the members of the mule-spinning team. Under the Brooklands Agreement of 1893, limits were placed on how much earnings could be adjusted up or down in line with cyclical changes in the demand for yarn. More significantly, the Brooklands Agreement elaborated a grievance procedure for dealing with what the operatives called "bad spinning"—the allegation that the use of inferior cotton inputs was forcing workers to supply more piecing effort to maintain the same level of earnings.[2]

Backed by union power, the minders were among the highest paid manual workers in Britain by the end of the nineteenth century.[3] The Brooklands Agreement helped to stabilize minders' wages at relatively high levels, despite a persistent pool of unemployed but experienced minders and fully apprenticed big piecers in Lancashire. In late-nineteenth-century Britain, there was little in the way of comparable alternative opportunities for a person trained as a mule spinner—all other high-paid craft occupations had their own entry requirements that involved a prolonged apprenticeship or training system. There was a tendency, therefore, for a minder who for one reason or another lost his pair of mules to remain in the British mule-spinning labor force, either augmenting the pool of unemployed minders or accepting work as a big piecer, waiting for a pair of mules to come open.[4]

One alternative opportunity for fully apprenticed big piecers and unemployed minders was to migrate to the United States where, in the 1860s and 1870s, there was a rapid expansion of mule-spinning capacity.[5] In a New England mule-spinning center such as Fall River, these émigré labor aristocrats found a system of industrial relations that differed significantly from Lancashire practice. Even though mule spinners were the best-organized group of workers in the nineteenth-century U.S. cotton textile industry, their prime source of power to influence work conditions and pay was individual exit, not collective voice. Apart from periods of widespread industrial unemployment, the generally ample opportunities for individuals to change employers and even occupations enabled mule spinners to find individual solutions to their grievances. Their ability to achieve their employment goals through exit undermined their commitment to the building of collective bargaining organizations.

In Britain, by way of contrast, the relative immobility of mule spinners weakened their abilities as individuals to seek solutions to their grievances while it simultaneously strengthened their commitment to unions as a collective force. At the same time, the British workers faced a much more fragmented class of mill owners than did the mule spinners in the United States. In Oldham, the premier Lancashire spinning center, ownership of the 200 or so cotton firms was widely distributed among small investors, whereas in Fall River, the main U.S. center for mule spinning, ownership of the 30 to 40 cotton firms was concentrated in the hands of seven closely related families.[6] As a result, Fall River capitalists were much less divided by competition among themselves than were their Oldham counterparts, particularly on industrial relations issues. Weakened by their own reliance upon individual mobility and confronted by a cohesive capitalist class, Fall River mule spinners never attained anything approaching the degree of control over effort and pay that Oldham spinners had achieved by the 1870s.

The first concentration of mules, and hence mule spinners, in New England appeared with the introduction of self-actors in Fall River in the 1840s. In 1850 a mule spinners' union, consisting almost entirely of English immigrants trained in Lancashire, staged an unsuccessful six-month strike against a wage reduction.[7] The spinners' union came into its own with the growth of the Fall River print cloth industry in the decade after the Civil War, an expansion that saw the city's spinning capacity (mostly mules) increase by 450 percent between 1865 and 1873.[8] During the 1870s, the Fall River mule spinners, almost all of whom still were migrants from the cotton factory districts of Lancashire, staged three major strikes in unsuccessful attempts to restore lost earnings or resist fresh cutbacks. Between 1873 and 1879, the mule spinners saw their weekly earnings reduced by 45 percent. The strike of 1879 lasted sixteen weeks before the depletion of their strike fund forced the spinners back to work.[9] During this last conflict, employers sought to use imported French Canadians as strikebreakers, but according to one report these inexperienced workers damaged the mules and were able to turn out only two-thirds of normal production.[10]

The Fall River capitalists certainly were not at the mercy of the mule spinners. But they did have to be cognizant of the workers' willingness to strike, as well as the difficulty of working the mule without the factory experience that the British-trained mule spinners had brought with them from Lancashire. Hence during the boom of late 1879 and early 1880, the spinners were able to raise their wages by 25 percent without going on strike, although in the name of conciliation they gave back 10 percent late in 1880.[11] In the depression of 1882–1884, however, the Fall River capitalists sought to destroy the union by blacklisting union activists, a strategy that they pursued vigorously after the defeat of the spinners in another major strike in 1884.[12]

Although greatly weakened by the onslaught, the union withstood the blacklist and remained intact. During a long period of prosperity from 1886 to 1892, Fall River employers entered into a number of agreements with the mule spinners' union.[13] One agreement issued by the executive committee of the Fall River Manufacturers' Board of Trade in August 1888 simply set out piece-rates per 100 hanks of yarn for various ranges of counts (including one broad range of nos. 22–38 that covered much of the spinning done in Fall River at the time) and for three broad ranges of spindles. Shortly thereafter the capitalists responded to workers' complaints by framing another list with finer gradations of the piece-rates according to the number of spindles per mule.[14]

Published wage-lists imparted some stability to industrial relations in Fall River. But they did not, as in Oldham, represent instruments that the mule spinners' union could use to control the relation between work conditions and pay. When Thomas Ashton, the secretary of the Oldham Operative Cotton Spinners' Provincial Association, visited Fall River and New Bedford in 1902, he found standard piece-rate lists in both centers. But he was puzzled by the simplistic manner in which the U.S. wage-lists specified the relation between work conditions and pay. "There is no person connected with the industry," Ashton observed,

> who knows anything about the principle on which the list prices have been based . . . The same piecework rates are paid for spinning whether the mules are new ones or old ones, and whether the mules run quick speeds or slow speeds; in fact the spinning overseers can put what twist they think necessary in the yarn without altering the price paid for spinning. An attempt was made a few years ago to induce the corporations to pay by the turns per inch, but they refused to adopt such a course of payment.[15]

Without realizing it, Ashton enunciated "the principle on which the list prices have been based": namely, a successful struggle on the part of Fall River mill owners against attempts by mule spinners to make the conditions of work a matter of collective bargaining. This "principle" of American industrial relations contrasted sharply with that which prevailed in Ashton's own Oldham district where the wage-lists reflected the ability of workers to exercise influence over and establish a tight link between work conditions and pay. In short, the structures of power that governed industrial relations differed significantly between Oldham and Fall River. In Oldham it was the workers whereas in Fall River it was the capitalists who held the balance of collective bargaining power in the determination of the relation between effort and pay. But, as I shall show, the more highly mobile Fall River workers wielded greater individual power to influence the conditions of work and pay than did the minders whom they had left behind in Lancashire.

Work Organization and Labor Productivity

What were the implications of the two contrasting "principles" of industrial relations for the evolution of work organization and productivity in these two important mule-spinning centers in the late nineteenth and early twentieth centuries? To answer this question, one must recognize that, unlike British spinning firms, American cotton textile capitalists did not rely on internal subcontracting in the organization of work. In the British case, the internal subcontract system survived the transition from the common mules to the self-actors in the 1830s and 1840s and involved a specific hierarchical as well as a technical division of labor.

Consider the main characteristics of the division of labor in British mule spinning. Besides overseeing the work team, the British minder himself pieced broken yarn on one-half of the mule spindles, with the help of the little piecer, a boy fourteen to eighteen years of age. The little piecer also placed rovings in the back of his pair of mules, swept up waste cotton, and carried away completed cops of yarn. The big piecer, a male aged eighteen or over and formerly a little piecer, pieced broken yarn ends on the other half of the spindles. The big piecer expected to become a minder when a pair of mules became vacant. Under the supervision of the minder, the piecers, both big and little, would oil spindles daily, doff (that is, "do off") completed cops of yarn, and help clean the gearing of the mule once a week. The minder himself was also responsible for repairing broken straps and bands connecting the various moving parts of the mule.

Both piecers were under the complete authority of the minder who, as internal subcontractor, hired and fired the piecers and paid them time-wages out of gross piece-rate earnings. The minder in turn was hired by the overlooker, who also retained the right to fire the internal subcontractor. The overlookers' right to fire was, however, severely constrained by the presence of strong local unions that could stage costly strikes against dismissal that the workers viewed as unjustified. Indeed, given the existence of the minder–piecer hierarchy, the entrenched position of individual minders (who often minded the same pair of mules for decades on end) and the elaborate and established wage-lists, the overseer's main function was not supervisory but technical. He was essentially a mule mechanic, generally recruited from the ranks of the minders, responsible for setting up the mules to spin cotton of different qualities and keeping the mules in good repair. But the long-term attachment of a minder to a particular pair of mules meant that the overseers often informally delegated some of their technical responsibilities to the minder. I have already referred to Harold Catling's observation that the delegation of maintenance tasks to the minder resulted in "customized" mules, a practice that enabled the minder in effect to make himself difficult to replace.[16]

As I have also noted, in the late nineteenth and early twentieth centuries, district organizations of spinning capitalists, supported from the early 1890s by the Federation of Master Cotton Spinners' Associations, threatened to abolish internal subcontracting—and to substitute women for men on some mules. But even when the spinning capitalists were willing to move to a new system of work organization, they were unable to contend with the power of the minders' unions. Most Lancashire capitalists simply came to accept the minder–piecer system as inherent in the nature of the process of mule spinning. As put by the author of the 1923 book on cotton mill management whom I have already quoted, the essence of good management was to abide by a "set of fixed conditions" that had "almost the force of laws."[17]

For Lancashire mule spinning, the "set of fixed conditions" was embodied mainly in the district wage-lists, which gave the minder (1) a vested interest in maintaining the existing hierarchical and technical divisions of labor on the mules, and (2) considerable protection against unremunerated intensification of labor in the form of speedup or stretchout. The lists institutionalized the minder–piecer hierarchy on terms favorable to the minder and unfavorable to the piecers. The minder could lay claim to all remuneration for productivity gains and special work while the piecers had to be content with fixed time-wages. Moreover, because the gross wage was paid to the minder as a contractor, he was able to pocket the wages of absentee piecers (a practice that would become common from the 1920s as it became difficult to attract little piecers into the industry).[18] Big piecers often had to wait until the age of thirty to get their first job as a minder, and many big piecers were former minders who had, through mill closings, lost their pairs of mules. By the late nineteenth century, many, if not most, big piecers possessed the experience and skills of a minder. Yet, at the same time, minders were among the best-paid manual workers in Britain, while big piecers were among the worst-paid males.[19]

The minders and their unions always resisted attempts by over-lookers to interfere with the hiring and supervision of piecers. The union repeatedly opposed attempts at even temporary utilization of the piecers' labor-power on other mules in the muleroom, not to mention the transformation of the little piecers into specialized teams of doffers, creelers, sweepers, and cop carriers, as was common in New England from the nineteenth century and as would be discussed (but never implemented) in Lancashire in the 1920s.[20] Such redivisions of labor would have undermined not only the absolute control of the minder over work organization on his pair of mules but also his claim for remuneration for doffing and certain special work.

Up to a point, however, the minder was willing to cooperate with management in the speeding-up and stretching-out of the mules. He was protected from arbitrary unilateral cuts in piece-rates which often follow productivity gains derived from intensified labor. The minder could, moreover, pass a good part of the burden of intensified work onto his piecers, usually at no extra cost to himself. The minder also had an incentive to cooperate with overlookers who wanted mules to be oiled and cleaned outside of "engine hours" or who were in the habit of extending engine hours beyond those prescribed by the Factory Acts. The minder's earnings were increased by the de facto lengthening of the workday, while the piecers, paid fixed time-wages, could be coerced into contributing unpaid labor time. Those piecers who were eighteen years of age or over could not even seek protection under the Factory Acts against working outside engine hours.[21]

Evidence on productivity per spindle on various counts of yarn in Lancashire indicates that the mule reached its peak of technical perfection in the 1890s. According to reports from various contemporaries, good practice productivity in pounds per spindle per week (56.5 hours) for 32s twist yarn—the standard count spun in Oldham—rose from 0.66 in the 1860s to 0.84–0.88 in the 1880s to 0.98–1.00 in the 1890s and beyond.[22] The average speed and size of mules increased throughout the last decades of the nineteenth century and into the first decade of the twentieth as new entrants into the industry adopted best-practice machines and as existing firms re-equipped or closed down. Yet, as I shall consider in detail in Chapter 5, despite the continuing increase in average speed and size of mules up to World War I, labor productivity in Oldham mule spinning stagnated from the late 1880s. Adjusting for cyclical fluctuations in wages and the shorter workweek after 1901, one finds that the gross full-time earnings of Oldham mule spinners, determined by the unchanging wage-lists and hence a direct indicator of growth in labor productivity, increased by 15 percent from 1876 to 1886, but by only 1 percent from 1886 to 1896, and only 3 percent over the following decade.[23]

The primary cause of the productivity problem was bad spinning— the inordinate number of yarn breakages per unit of time that could arise from the use of inferior cotton, an increase in mule speed, or the spinning of higher counts of yarn without increasing cotton quality or reducing the speed of the mule. The prime operative task of the minder and his piecers was to repair any of the, say, 2,000 strands of yarn whenever any of them broke. If yarn breakages per unit of time were more than usual, productivity would fall without more intensive piecing effort. Even if the machines could be kept in motion, some ends would go longer unpieced, during which time those spindles would be unproductive. If end breakages were frequent enough, the mules might actually have to be stopped to accomplish the necessary piecing. Hence, in the absence of more intense work effort, and often even despite it, bad spinning resulted in lower productivity on a pair of mules and lower earnings for the minder, paid as he was by the piece.

When yarn breakages per unit of time increased, the mule spinner would try to prevent productivity declines by driving his piecers to work harder. But hard driving had its limits. Paid fixed time-wages, piecers had no immediate interest in maintaining or increasing productivity. Although they put their long-term prospects for promotion to minder in jeopardy, they often rebelled against overbearing mule spinners by staging walkouts or going slow. The tendency to disrupt or restrict output was particularly true of little piecers, who had less invested in the industry in terms of years and who were young enough to seek other lines of work should they be fired for such actions. Increasingly from the late 1880s, whether for their own health, for the sake of maintaining good work relations with their piecers, or because all attempts at remedying bad spinning had failed, minders were prepared to stage strikes over the bad spinning issue.[24]

The cost of cotton inputs ranged from 80 percent of the total cost of no. 16 yarn to 45 percent of the cost of no. 100 yarn. A major function of the managers of spinning mills was to make weekly journeys to Liverpool to buy cotton to fill current yarn orders. The prime skill of the manager was to purchase those grades and staples of cotton that would minimize unit costs in producing a desired quality of yarn. By the 1890s, with the mule technically perfected, with foreign competition (mainly from India and Japan) in coarser product markets beginning to be felt, and with the domestic spinning industry facing cyclical instability in which periods of marked expansion in capacity gave way to periods of intensified competition, spinning capitalists came to rely increasingly on the use of inferior cotton inputs as a means of decreasing unit costs. The late 1880s appear to be the turning point. In its Annual Report of 1889, the Amalgamated observed: "Some few years ago we noticed that the great majority of disputes were due to old machinery. Last year the majority were owing to bad work."[25]

It was worthwhile for capitalists to permit productivity to fall by using inferior cotton if the reduction in unit cotton costs outweighed the increase in other unit factor costs because of more frequent yarn breakages resulting in lower throughput. If the spinning employers could get workers to supply more effort, throughput could be maintained and unit fixed capital and labor costs would not rise. Although none of the district wage-lists specified a normal rate of yarn breakage, the Oldham list did recognize the problem of bad spinning by requiring a two-step local conciliation procedure in the case of a dispute. These procedures appeared to work up to the late 1880s, almost all bad spinning disputes being settled without a strike. Managers agreed to pay compensation to the mule spinners either for the harder work involved or for wages lost as the speed of the mules was reduced to decrease yarn breakages.

In 1891–92, however, there was a major strike in Stalybridge over the issue of bad spinning that culminated in a three-week industry-wide lockout. In the process, the Lancashire spinning capitalists came together to form the Federation of Master Cotton Spinners' Associations (FMCSA) in an effort to give themselves a freer hand in cutting cotton costs. Yet, as had previously been the case in the local grievance procedures, by the industry-wide settlement reached in 1892, the FMCSA agreed to pay compensation to minders if the use of inferior cotton could be proved. The 1892 agreement was followed by an elaborate grievance and conciliation procedure to deal with bad spinning as part of the Brooklands Agreement that settled a twenty-week lockout over a wage reduction in 1893.[26]

But neither the agreement of 1892 nor that of 1893 specified standards for yarn breakages in spinning given counts of yarn at given speeds. As a result, bad spinning remained the most contentious industrial relations issue of the Lancashire spinning industry over the next twenty years. The Brooklands Agreement, however, shifted the balance of power in bad spinning disputes toward employers. With Brooklands in place, the spinners' Amalgamated and district unions could not support any group of workers in a strike over bad spinning until the remedy of a long, multilevel grievance procedure had been exhausted. Prior to the formation of the FMCSA and the Brooklands

Agreement, individual firms were constrained in their use of inferior cotton by the prospects of having to go it alone against the powerful district unions. Now these same firms knew that they would be backed fully by the FMCSA in bad spinning disputes because agreements concerning "normal" yarn breakages made in grievance settlements would henceforth set standards that could apply to all spinning firms.

It was because of the collective resistance of spinning capitalists to the institutionalization of constraints on their cotton-cost-cutting activities that the issue of bad spinning was nowhere near resolution on the eve of World War I. Minders, for their part, continually voiced discontent with the Brooklands Agreement because they were forced to put up with bad spinning for weeks and even months as each case was adjudicated. Finally in 1913 the minders withdrew from the Agreement as the number of bad spinning disputes waiting to be resolved reached unprecedented levels.[27]

The relations of production in Lancashire, therefore, came to permit, and even encourage, the use of inferior cotton in mule spinning. The spinners' union controlled their minders while grievances were being considered, and minders controlled their piecers for the sake of their own earnings. Under the Brooklands Agreement, the issue became less whether inferior cotton could be used and more the extent to which the minders would receive compensation for the intensified labor required to maintain productivity while spinning with inferior cotton.

In the United States both industrial relations and the utilization of mule-spinning technology were different. The mule spinners lacked the collective power to extract compensation from their employers for bad spinning, when and where it occurred. They also lacked the authority to intensify the labor of other workers for their own benefit. The power that American mule spinners had to influence work conditions and pay lay in "exit" rather than "voice." Macroeconomic conditions permitting, individual mule spinners who demonstrated their ability to do their work well could threaten to quit unsatisfactory conditions of work and pay. Between the Civil War and World War I, Fall River and Oldham mule-spinning firms used the same machine technologies and had access to workers of the same ethnic background with equivalent skills. Yet the very different production relations into which the U.S. and British mule spinners entered are crucial for understanding the differences in work conditions and labor productivity in the two countries.

A hierarchy of authority *among operatives* never existed on self-acting mules in New England. Instead, from the 1840s, when New England firms first put self-actors into operation, American management retained complete control over work organization in the spinning process. As a result they retained the prerogative to alter the relation between effort and pay—a prerogative that Lancashire capitalists in accepting the wage-lists had substantially ceded to workers.

As early as 1850, during a strike of mule spinners over a piece-rate reduction, Fall River capitalists argued: "Within a few years previous to the strike, many improvements had been introduced such as furnishing the mule room with spare hands to doff and clean the mules, and with sweepers to do the sweeping which had formerly been done by the backboys. These improvements enabled the spinner to run more time, and to earn about as much as usual notwithstanding reduction in wages."[28] Put differently, Fall River employers intensified the labor of mule spinners on the basis of a new technical division of labor, and then used the increased output per worker as a justification for cutting piece-rates.

It is not known how universal was the movement to such a specialized division, and intensification, of labor prior to the Civil War. It is known, however, that during the conflict-ridden period of the 1870s, a characteristic Fall River division of labor emerged. The spinner was made to do the oiling and cleaning of the mules "before work" and during mealtimes, tasks that had previously been done by the backboys whose primary task was to keep the creels of the mules supplied with roving to be spun into yarn.[29] At the same time, the Fall River employers began to give preference in hiring to spinners who could supply a backboy, whose pay was deducted from the earnings of the spinner. In Lancashire, minders used the internal subcontract system to maintain control over work organization and remuneration. But in Fall River, the system of compelling the spinner to recruit a backboy merely manifested the mule-spinning operative's weak position during the 1870s and 1880s. The practice gave him no hierarchical authority. In addition, the mule spinner was not allotted any of the technical responsibilities of the Lancashire minder who, as I have mentioned, repaired straps and bands and made minor technical adjustments on his mules. In Fall River, these tasks were performed instead by specialized and relatively high-paid mechanics.

From the 1880s on, the labor of New England mule spinners was supplemented by one backboy to two pairs of mules who creeled, swept, and assisted in cleaning. In addition, a mule room would have two or three doffers and two tubers for seven to ten pairs of mules.[30] Overseers had, as Thomas Ashton, the visting Oldham union official, put it in 1902, "full management in the [mule] spinning rooms, with power to discharge any person employed therein."[31] As the Lancashire Amalgamated reported to its minders the following year: "The spinner of America has little or no control over either his assistants or the method of working the mules. Overlookers do the changing [of the gearing of mules to spin different counts] while the piecing of straps and bands is done by a special "help." The spinner does not even doff the cops for himself. He is, in fact, reduced to a piecing-up machine."[32]

The work of the New England mule spinner, therefore, was comparable to that of a Lancashire big piecer. But the New England spinner's pay was greater than that of a Lancashire minder because of the much more abundant alternative opportunities in the United States for a strong, hard-working man. The mule spinner's job required not only a man of substantial physical strength but also a man already adapted to long, hard, and steady toil, and capable of exercising close concentration for long periods of time to ensure that ends remained pieced and productivity remained high.[33]

The Lancashire minder was noted for his "lifetime" attachment to a particular pair of mules in a particular firm, barring a mill closure beyond his control. In sharp contrast, the New England mule spinner, already a migrant from the old country, was noted for his mobility not only from mill to mill within a textile region such as Fall River–New Bedford but also from region to region, and often right out of the occupation.[34]

The power of mobility possessed by capable New England mule spinners had important consequences for the intensity of labor on the mules. The flood of mule spinners into Fall River during the seven boom years after the Civil War turned into a substantial reserve army in the relatively depressed years of 1873 through 1885, greatly reducing the power of individual mobility. It was during this period, characterized by major conflicts between the mule spinners' union and the employers of Fall River, that the workers experienced not only enforced overtime to clean and oil the mules but also substantial intensification of labor while the mules were in operation. The faster pace of work came partly from speedup, partly from stretchout as spinners lost all piecing help, and partly from bad spinning as, particularly in very depressed years such as 1882 to 1884, some mills resorted to the use of inferior cotton.[35] The mule spinners' union, fighting for its life in the midst of recurrent wage cuts and blacklisting, was powerless to oppose the intensification of labor. Nor, with an unemployment rate of 20 percent in the early 1880s, could individual spinners use the power of mobility to control the pace of work to which they were subjected.[36] Certainly, in these depressed years, the American mule spinners had no means to extract compensation from employers for bad spinning as was the case across the Atlantic.

From the mid-1880s, however, as bad spinning began to plague Lancashire, it ceased to be a serious problem in Fall River. Americans reverted to the practice of using better cotton for any given count than that used by the English, a practice resulting in higher output per spindle per hour on the New England mules.[37] Whereas production relations in Lancashire encouraged the use of inferior cotton, production relations in New England encouraged the use of superior cotton.

Inferior cotton created breakage problems not only in spinning but throughout the process of transforming raw cotton into woven cloth. Good cotton meant clean, strong yarn, which meant fewer breaks in the warping and weaving processes, which in turn meant greater potential for assigning more warping machines per warper and more looms per weaver. In the Lancashire industry, where the structure of industrial relations restricted the number of plain looms per weaver to about half the number in the New England industry, the weaving capitalists quite rationally preferred to pay less for yarn and have their workers work at a more intense pace on the restricted number of looms. In New England, where weavers had no such collective power to control the number of machines per worker, weaving capitalists (who indeed, given the extent of vertical integration in U.S. cotton textiles, tended also to be spinning capitalists) had a preference for higher quality yarn.[38]

In addition, the use of inferior cotton created special problems for New England capitalists in dealing with the highly paid and highly mobile mule spinners. In New England, piece-rates did not have, as in Lancashire, "almost the force of laws." Mule spinners in the United States had an incentive to restrict output on the expectation that higher levels of output would only serve as a prelude to piece-rate cuts. By giving the mule spinners an excuse for stopping the mules, bad spinning could provide a means of restricting output. Hence, in the context of New England industrial relations, the use of superior cotton made it easier to elicit more effort from workers. The mule spinners in the United States were, in addition, harder to supervise because they saw their stay in a particular mill as a short-term affair. If work conditions were poor in one mill, they would seek out work in another mill. Because piece-rates in Fall River were uniform across mills (testimony not to the power of labor but to the cohesiveness of the small number of families that controlled the town's factories and fixed the rates in concert), the mills that gained a reputation for the use of inferior cotton would, over time, only attract inferior workers.[39]

The very different divisions of labor in mule spinning in Britain and the United States make labor productivity comparisons difficult. The labor inputs in the two industries were composed of different combinations of skilled and unskilled labor. What can be said is that in the late 1890s, output per "direct" worker-hour (including auxiliary labor) in spinning 32s was at least 15–20 percent higher in Fall River than in Oldham. A more relevant comparison for assessing the impact of the use of different qualities of cotton is output per hour of "experienced piecer"—that is, per hour of the minder and big piecer in Lancashire and of the mule spinner in New England. On this basis, around the turn of the century, labor productivity in spinning 32s was about 40 percent higher in Fall River than in Oldham, even though the effort supplied per worker-hour was apparently lower in Fall River. The use of superior cotton in Fall River permitted about 40 percent more spindles per experienced worker than in Oldham.[40] By the same token, Fall River avoided the deterioration in work conditions that Oldham experienced from the 1890s because of the use of inferior cotton.

Explaining the Choice of Technique

A neoclassical economist would have no difficulty explaining this labor productivity difference. In the late 1880s and 1890s the cost of cotton of any given quality was slightly higher in Oldham than in Fall River because of transportation and transaction costs. During the same period, the wages per unit of time of experienced spinning labor (including big piecers in Lancashire) was 30 to 40 percent lower in Oldham.[41] Neoclassical price theory predicts that the managers in each of the two mule-spinning centers will choose factor proportions that use less of the relatively more expensive input—less labor in Fall River and "less" (that is, inferior) cotton in Oldham. As illustrated in

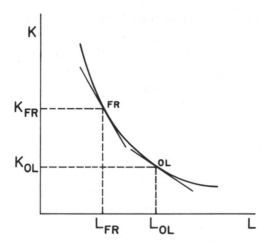

4.1 Relative factor prices and choices of technique. OL, Oldham; FR, Fall River; K, cotton inputs; L, labor inputs. See text for details.

Figure 4.1, where *K* measures cotton inputs and *L* represents labor inputs on the mule, the observed differences in the U.S. and British isocost lines lead to different observed factor-proportion outcomes—FR in Fall River and OL in Oldham—to produce the same level of output in the two countries.

Basic to neoclassical theory is the assumption that the "state of technology" determines the production function. Neoclassical economists are, however, generally willing to allow that because of different "factor endowments" and barriers to international mobility of factors of production, relative factor prices might vary across national economies. On the basis of these assumptions, economically rational managers in two different countries producing the same products using the same processes and with access to labor forces of similar quality—as indeed was the case in U.S. and British mule spinning—should face the same set of production isoquants in making their cost-minimizing decisions. But because of different relative factor prices, they will choose different production techniques. As in Figure 4.1, given a common production isoquant, the different choice of factor proportions in Oldham and Fall River can be explained in terms of the different relative factor prices that prevailed in the two spinning centers.

Neoclassical economists have long been enthralled with the purported explanatory power of readily available price information for deducing the allocative choices that economic actors would make. What then could be the significance of the preceding historical analysis of differences in production relations, work organization, and labor productivity? Does the exercise in comparative labor history that I have presented yield any insights into the impact of the combination of capital and labor on economic outcomes that cannot be found in any standard microeconomics textbook?

Fortunately for my endeavor, it does. I can begin to show why by exploring the flaws in the standard analysis of choice of technique presented in Figure 4.1. When I am finished exploring these flaws, I shall show that the entire theoretical structure that mainstream economists have long used to analyze the choice of technique caves in on itself; it cannot bear the impact that the social relations of production have on the choice of optimal economic outcomes.

The first flaw is the assumption that, at any point in time, the productivity of a technology is given to the firm, irrespective of the social context in which the firm attempts to utilize the technology. It is this assumption, typically implicit in mainstream economic analysis and derived from an ignorance of the nature of the production process as much as anything else, that would permit the neoclassical economist to depict both Oldham and Fall River spinning firms as facing the same production isoquant, as illustrated in Figure 4.1.

It is true that both Oldham and Fall River used mule-spinning machines and labor of similar quality, and both spinning centers imported their cotton supplies from the American South. Yet the historical analysis of comparative industrial relations and work organization that I have presented demonstrates the implausibility of the assumption that the British and American firms both faced the same production isoquant in making their cost-minimizing decisions. Let me use the historical analysis to sketch out plausible production isoquants applicable to each of the two spinning centers. In both cases (portrayed in Figure 4.2), I emphasize the impact of production relations on worker effort in the productive transformation of capital and labor inputs into yarn output.

In Oldham, on mules of a given size running at a given speed, the piece-rate is fixed by the wage-list, and hence so too are weekly labor costs for a given level of output. A manager can introduce superior cotton (more K). But by supplying labor with more capital, he would not be able to save on labor costs. Rather, the minder and piecers would be able to work less intensively to achieve the same level of

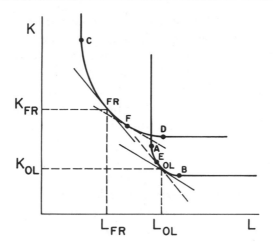

4.2 Relative factor prices, relevant production isoquants, and choice of technique. OL, Oldham; FR, Fall Fiver; K, cotton inputs; L, labor inputs. See text for details.

earnings. Indeed, if the use of superior cotton sufficiently reduced the workload, the minder might even choose not to hire a little piecer and keep that worker's time-wages for himself. In this case, the amount of actual labor hours employed on the shop floor would be reduced, but the amount of effort needed to produce a given level of output would remain the same. Hence, over the range of K above point A in Figure 4.2, the Oldham isoquant is vertical; from the point of view of the capitalist manager who is choosing the technique, the use of superior cotton does not permit a reduction in the amount of labor for which he must contract.

As the same manager attempts to introduce inferior cotton, however, work is intensified by increased yarn breakages. Assume that work intensity begins to rise above the customary norms at points below A in Figure 4.2, thereby leading Oldham minders to begin to demand compensation for bad spinning from employers. Managers might compensate the minders either by adding more piecers to the mule-spinning team at the firm's expense or by paying existing workers more to produce the same output. In practice, compensation in the form of extra payments was the rule in Lancashire, mainly because of the influence of the minder, who generally received all the extra pay but did not have to perform all of the extra work.

The very existence of ongoing compensation bargaining means

that, even in the short run, factor prices are not independent of factor productivities, as the neoclassical analysis of the choice of technique assumes. I shall take up this quite valid objection later because it represents another major flaw in the mainstream theoretical structure. But for the sake of tearing that structure apart piece by piece to better perceive its weaknesses, I assume for the moment that, up to a certain limit depicted by point B in Figure 4.2, a compensation agreement in effect fixes a certain level of payment for each extra unit of labor effort below A. The "compensation range" between A and B, therefore, entails the substitution of labor for capital, as the effort supplied by workers to produce a given level of output increases. But at B, workers are unable or unwilling to supply more effort for extra pay, and the possibility for substituting labor for capital ceases.

Note that neither point A nor point B are technically determined. Rather they are determined by the relative power of managers and workers to influence the relation between effort and pay. Point A represents a "normal" intensity of work, the product of prior social conflict and conciliation. Workers have an interest in pushing this norm upward along the production isoquant so that compensation for extra effort becomes operative at lower levels of effort made possible by the use of superior cotton. Capitalists have an interest in pushing A down the isoquant, thereby increasing the level of effort that is considered normal. In the case of British mule spinning, the position of B depends on not merely workers' preferences for supplying effort in exchange for pay but also on the power of the minders—the only mule-spinning workers actually bargaining with employers—to impose their preferences on the piecers.

Production isoquants also are shaped by the relations of production in Fall River. But here collective bargaining does not constrain capitalists in substituting cotton for labor. Starting at point FR in Figure 4.2, a Fall River manager who adds better cotton can effectively use less labor to produce a given level of output, either by actually using fewer workers or by giving existing workers less opportunity to restrict output. At some point such as C, the limits of the substitution of capital for labor are reached as yarn breaks are reduced to nil. Hence, given the power of Fall River capitalists to reap the benefits of factor substitution, it is indeed technical considerations that reduce the marginal rate of substitution of factors to zero, in sharp contrast to the collective bargaining determinants of point A in the Oldham case. But if the weakness of workers' collective organizations enables capitalists to use superior cotton, the relative power of individual workers to exit from undesirable work conditions constrains the use of inferior cotton. A Fall River manager who wants to use inferior cotton below FR has to add more workers to produce the same amount of output. At some point, D, it becomes physically impossible to crowd more workers onto the machines to compensate for bad spinning, thus setting a lower limit to the use of inferior cotton.

Rather than one "technically determined" production isoquant passing through the observed choices of technique, FR and OL, in the two spinning centers (Figure 4.1), there are two distinct isoquants, each influenced by a distinct configuration of organizational and technological forces. It should be noted that, in the case of mule spinning at least, the distinct production isoquants cannot be attributed to the availability of different technologies in the two countries; all factors of production—machines, experienced workers, and cotton—were internationally mobile. What differed across countries was the ability of capitalists to utilize mule-spinning technology because of differences in social relations of production.

It is plausible that, because of the differences in production relations that prevailed in British and American mule spinning in the late nineteenth century, there were no relative factor prices that would have made the Fall River choice of technique (FR) a viable possibility for Oldham employers, or, conversely, the Oldham choice (OL) viable for Fall River managers. To put it another way, if the observed Fall River factor prices in Figure 4.2 had prevailed in Oldham, the British managers would not have chosen the technique FR to produce the same output as at OL. Rather they would have chosen technique E, which is relatively close to the original choice. Likewise, if the Oldham factor prices had prevailed in Fall River, technique F, not OL, would have been chosen.

The second flaw in the neoclassical theoretical structure is the assumption that factor prices are independent of factor productivities. On the basis of this assumption, factor productivities arising from different combinations of capital and labor can be taken as given to the firm; hence the choice of technique depends only on variations in relative factor prices. It is, however, increasingly recognized by economists who speak of "efficiency wages" that factor prices and factor productivities may be linked, particularly for labor inputs. What the efficiency-wage literature ignores is effort-saving technological change—the possibility that changes in technology can permit workers to receive higher wages for less effort, as outlined in the Appendix.

Indeed, I would argue that, because of the interdependence of factor prices and factor productivities and the importance of effort-saving technological change in determining the technical and social limitations on the effort–pay relation, the "value-creation" approach—presented in the Appendix—provides the relevant framework for analyzing the choice of technique. In that framework, the use of superior cotton is an effort-saving technological change that raises variable capital costs but also increases the amount of yarn value that can be created with a given amount of work effort. Of course, depending on the relation between increased cotton costs and the effort-saving impact of the superior cotton, it could be that only tariffs would make the effort-saving American choice economically viable in competition with the effort-using British choice. For present purposes, the important point is that Fall River capitalists could generate and appropriate value on the basis of an effort-saving technology (superior cotton inputs) whereas their Oldham counterparts could not.

Once one recognizes that the productivity of a technology depends on the amount of effort that workers choose to supply, the whole notion of factor substitution, as depicted by the production isoquants in Figures 4.1 and 4.2, can be called into question. According to the factor substitution framework, an increase in capital inputs makes possible a reduction in labor inputs, and vice versa. Presumably the labor axis measures units of L, each unit representing the same amount of labor services irrespective of the amount of L used, and similarly for the capital axis. But as can be easily seen in the case where K represents cotton inputs, the factor substitution framework only becomes operational when one interprets *better K* as *more K*. If more *constant-quality* cotton is substituted for less labor, then the fewer units of labor can only produce the same amount of output if each unit of labor works harder—that is, if "less" L also means "better" L. In general, whether dealing with variable capital inputs such as cotton or with fixed capital inputs such as spindles or looms, giving more of the *same quality* of capital to fewer workers with given skills will not permit the same level of output unless those fewer workers supply more effort, in which case the quality of each unit of the labor services changes with movements along the L axis.

The recognition that the use of superior cotton represents effort-saving technological change has implications for understanding the longer-run technological development of the cotton textile industries in the two countries. In the 1890s the cotton-cost savings in the Lancashire spinning mills did in fact permit unit costs lower than those in New England spinning. Not only were direct unit labor costs per pound of 32s yarn on the mules about $.0030 lower in Oldham than in Fall River, but, of much greater importance, simply lowering the grade of cotton used from good middling one-inch staple to middling one-inch staple saved $.0075 per pound of yarn, whereas lowering the staple length used by ⅛ inch, holding cotton grade constant, saved $.0100.[42] At least as far as spinning costs are concerned, despite the transatlantic mobility of factors of production, the Fall River textile industry still required tariff barriers to meet British competition.

But compared with New England spinning techniques, the Lancashire method of substituting "less" cotton for "more" labor severely constrained the lowering of unit costs in Britain over the long run precisely because such cost-cutting was wholly reliant on the willingness and ability of Lancashire workers to perform ever more intensified labor. As I shall detail in the following chapter, the Lancashire mode of cost-cutting often occurred despite decreases in labor productivity because of the use of inferior cotton.

The Lancashire competitive strategy was thus the antithesis of that adopted in the U.S. cotton textile industry in which not only the use of better cotton but also the adoption of better (that is, effort-saving) machinery permitted increases in labor productivity and decreases in unit costs, without necessarily pushing workers to the limit in the supply of effort. How much effort American workers in fact supplied on new effort-saving technologies such as ring spinning frames and automatic weaving looms depended, however, on the relative power of capitalists and workers when and where these new technologies were introduced. Such an analysis of the interaction of production relations and technological change is undoubtedly key to understanding the shift of the U.S. cotton textile industry from the North to the South from the 1890s.

As for Britain the analysis of the well-known Lancashire lag in the displacement of mule spinning by ring spinning must take into account, in addition to production relations on the shop floor, the vertical and horizontal organization of the entire British cotton textile industry.[43] In the context of the present analysis, however, two important and related points can be made concerning the impact of production relations on the diffusion of the new spinning technology, the ring-frame, in Britain and the United States.

First, even though in both countries ring spinning permitted capitalists to replace adult male mule spinners with relatively low-paid female operatives, the different rates of diffusion of ring spinning in the two countries cannot be explained in terms of struggles between capitalists and mule spinners over the actual introduction of the new technology. Fall River capitalists frequently warned striking mule spinners that their obstinacy would only hasten the introduction of ring-frames. To make their point, the capitalists would even go so far as to make a show of replacing a number of old mules by rings during a dispute. But there is little if any evidence that well-functioning mules were scrapped or sold in response to labor conflicts.[44]

In the British case, one might have expected that the strong minders' union would have blocked attempts to introduce ring-frames, especially given the persistent oversupply of capable mule spinners in Lancashire from the 1870s until World War I. But there is no evidence of any local disputes over the introduction of ring-frames during this period. In seeking to use collective bargaining to consolidate and extend the control that minders exercised over work organization and pay, the minders' unions chose not to challenge the managerial prerogative to choose the machine technology. Instead, when minders in a particular mill were threatened by the displacement of their mules by ring-frames, their response was to mitigate the cost advantage of the new technology by cooperating with management in cutting unit costs on the mules—for example, by working with inferior cotton without demanding the full remuneration for the extra effort needed to maintain earnings. Such a cooperative response was made possible in Lancashire by the well-developed structure of bargaining relations between minders and their employers that permitted the working out of mutually satisfactory agreements, as well as by the control that minders exercised over piecers, who typically had to bear much of the augmented workload.[45]

Second, the very fact that production relations in Lancashire permitted minders and managers to work out agreements that favored the utilization of inferior cotton created other advantages to the retention of mules. The mule had the technical capability of spinning the same counts of yarn as the ring-frame, but with considerably inferior cotton. The spinning and winding of the yarn on the ring-frame were performed simultaneously, with the result that ring spinning put much more strain on the yarn than did mule spinning. In New England, however, the use of superior cotton to attract good mule spinners to a particular workplace and to reduce their opportunities to restrict output on the shop floor, meant that the potential for the use of inferior quality, and hence cheaper, cotton on the mules could not be exploited as it was in Lancashire. As a result, the cotton-cost saving of mules over rings for any given count was a more significant factor in Lancashire than in New England, helping to account for the widespread persistence of the mule in the British industry well into the second half of the twentieth century, by which time these relics of the First Industrial Revolution had long since disappeared from the American scene.[46]

5 Spinning and Weaving
to Industrial Decline

Expansion and Decline

The cotton textile industry was central to British economic development in the nineteenth century. It formed the core of Britain's Industrial Revolution in the first half of the century and continued to expand in the second half. Serious interruptions that occurred during the American Civil War and the depressions of the late 1870s and early 1890s proved to be short lived.[1] The expansion of the industry continued up to World War I. Indeed, in the decade prior to the war, capacity and output expanded at a rate more rapid than that of either of the two previous decades.

In the post–World War I period, however, the cotton textile industry experienced a rapid and, as it turned out, permanent decline. In 1924 the quantity of cotton piece-goods produced in Britain was only about three-quarters of that produced a decade earlier, and by 1930 production was less than half the prewar level.[2] During the interwar years the British cotton textile industry lost its lower quality markets to Japanese and Indian competition. In the decades after World War II it lost its higher quality markets to competitors in Western Europe and the United States.[3]

How can one explain the rapid and dramatic turn of events that took the British cotton textile industry from prewar expansion to postwar decline? Was the decline of the 1920s and 1930s a "trick" that history played on the managers of the British cotton textile industry, as two "new" economic historians have put it?[4] Or was it rather an explicable outcome of the very ways in which these managers had chosen to produce and sell their cotton goods in the prosperous prewar years?

There has been considerable debate on the performance of the British economy in the decades prior to World War I, with particular emphasis on alleged "entrepreneurial failure" manifested by the technological backwardness of various British industries relative to the investments in technology made by foreign competitors.[5] That the British cotton textile industry continued to rely on traditional technologies such as the mule and the powerloom is not in question. On the eve of World War I, ring spindles were only 19 percent of all British spindles and about 25 percent of British spinning capacity compared with 87 percent of U.S. spindles and over 90 percent of U.S. capacity. Automatic looms were only 1 to 2 percent of British looms but 40 percent of U.S. looms.[6]

G. T. Jones's estimates (made over a half-century ago) of productivity trends in the British cotton textile industry support the allegation that the technological lag was already undermining the competitive position of British cotton goods prior to World War I. His actual measure is an index of "real costs"—the inverse of what later came to be known as total factor productivity—derived from a weighting of cotton, wage, and other costs for the industry as a whole (that is, both spinning and weaving) at constant prices. His conclusions for the period 1870 to 1914 were: "Rising to 111 in 1870, real costs fell almost continuously from 1871 to 1882 at an average rate of ½% per annum. Thence there was a gradual rise to 108 in 1890 when efficiency began again to increase, reaching a maximum for the period in 1900. Between 1900 and 1910 real costs rose from 102 to 107, but there was a temporary improvement about 1905."[7] Jones's conclusion was that there was "little, if any, net change in the efficiency of the British cotton [industry] during the period 1885–1910 . . . [as] the real cost of manufacturing began to increase about 1900 and continued to rise until the outbreak of war in 1914."[8]

Jones's findings, however, have been challenged by Lars Sandberg in his attempt to refute the hypothesis of entrepreneurial failure as an explanation of the decline of the British cotton textile industry.[9] Sandberg's general argument is that the reliance on mule spinning and powerloom weaving reflected rational choices of technique by British managers, given the relative factor productivities and factor prices that prevailed in Britain before the war. Given the constraints that they faced, British managers were doing about the best they could. Moreover, the rapid expansion of the industry's output and capacity prior to World War I indicates that "the best they could" do was not so bad after all. How could this prewar expansion have taken place, Sandberg asked, if British industry was becoming less efficient as Jones claimed?

Jones recognized that his real cost estimates are paradoxical, indicating as they do "a progressive fall in efficiency" after 1900, accompanied by a "great expansion" in investment in plant and equipment.[10] Sandberg, however, doubted the existence of a paradox. He calculated that labor productivity increased by about 40 percent between 1885 and 1913 and that there does not appear to have been a slowdown in the rate of productivity growth after 1900. A number of adjustments to Jones's real cost index "indicate—conservatively—a reduction of real cost by 9 percent to 10 percent between 1885 and 1910 and of 11 to 12 percent between 1885 and 1914." "What is more," Sandberg went on to argue, "after my corrections have been made, this improvement is spread fairly evenly over the period. The peculiar deterioration Jones recorded for the post-1900 period has vanished. It has, roughly speaking, been replaced by a continuation of the trend he noted for the 1890s."[11]

Thus, in Sandberg's view, economic vitality, not entrepreneurial failure, characterized the British cotton textile industry before World War I. That such a healthy industry entered into a rapid and irreversible decline after the war must have been because of "forces outside the control of British management"[12]—namely, the competition of cheap labor in India and the Far East and the erection of tariff barriers around the world. Indeed, Sandberg argued: "A massive installation of automatic looms [before the war] would have greatly increased the losses experienced by the industry during the interwar period. The inevitable and painful dismantling of the British cotton textile industry would have been no less inevitable and even more painful."[13]

On the face of it, Sandberg's "economic vitality" hypothesis is persuasive. After all, how could the industry have increased its exports to open markets such as Latin America and the Far East in the decade prior to World War I if its managers were making the "wrong" technological choices or if its productivity growth had become stagnant?

The "economic vitality" hypothesis has, however, fundamental weaknesses in terms of both its theoretical conception of the process of economic development and its empirical assessment of the prewar productivity performance of the British cotton textile industry. The prewar expansion and the postwar decline were integrally related. The industry's rapid prewar expansion of capacity and output based on penetration into foreign markets occurred even with stagnating labor productivity. The methods that the industry used to capture these foreign markets were important factors in setting it up for its postwar fall. An understanding of the relation between the harvesting of competitive advantage and the onset of industrial decline sheds significant light on the institutional dynamics of the process of economic development.

The main points of the argument can be summarized. On the demand side, a large proportion of the expansion of the British cotton textile industry before the war went to the world's poorer countries, particularly to India. As peasant and worker incomes slowly grew in these countries, there was not only an increased demand for cotton goods but, more important, an increased demand for more highly finished goods. Especially in warmer climates, consumers were more interested in style than in quality—they were willing and able to pay for more highly finished, lower quality cloth rather than for less highly finished, higher quality cloth.

On the supply side, the marketing structure in the British cotton textile industry was ideally suited to meet this fashion-oriented demand. British marketing firms were highly specialized by market area and product. Upon receiving orders from their agents or other contacts abroad, Manchester marketing firms would place orders with weaving firms, which would in turn place orders for the requisite yarn with spinning firms. Upon receiving the cloth, the merchants would either ship it in the "grey" state or put it out to finishing firms to be bleached, dyed, or printed according to the marketing firm's specifications. In ordering the cloth, the merchants wanted to obtain the lowest quality (and hence cheapest) cloth that was technically compatible with the requisite finishing process as well as the lowest quality that the masses of consumers in their markets would (quite literally) bear.

The primary ways of achieving these objectives were by using inferior grade and shorter staple cotton in spinning and by heavily sizing the cloth in weaving. Prior to World War I, the British cotton textile industry was able to capture the markets of the underdeveloped world by cutting cotton costs on its traditional machinery. The continued reliance on the traditional technologies such as mule spinning and powerloom weaving combined with the structures of industrial relations that determined the relation between effort and pay on these technologies yielded total unit costs that made the strategy of degradation of cloth quality viable before the war. The use of inferior cotton and yarn on the traditional machines put strict limits on labor productivity increases. But by using inferior cotton inputs, a firm could cut unit total costs even while increasing its unit labor costs. The British supply-side strategy for capturing low income markets was consistent with stagnating, and possibly even declining, labor productivity.

Given this strategy, and particularly given its success in the prewar period, the British cotton textile industry of the postwar period was vulnerable to both import-substitution strategies by the less developed countries such as India and Brazil and open competition from "cheap-labor" countries such as Japan, producing cotton goods for lower income consumers. Moreover, given the character of its prewar development, the British cotton textile industry was unable to shift to an alternative strategy of using high-throughput technologies that required high quality cotton inputs to produce for the higher income mass markets of Europe and North America. Such a strategy would have involved far-reaching changes in the structures of industrial organization and industrial relations. The traditional structures had served the British cotton textile industry well up to World War I but now constituted institutional obstacles to both the necessary contraction and technological reorientation of the industry.

The Demand for British Cotton Goods

Until the outbreak of World War I, the Lancashire cotton textile industry was an expanding industry. As Table 5.1 shows, the industry stagnated in the 1890s after rapid growth in the late 1880s, but then recovered after 1900. Despite great fluctuations in output in the decade before World War I, the industry experienced a remarkable final burst of activity. In 1914 there were 14 percent more spinning and weaving firms in the industry than there had been a decade earlier (increasing from 1,764 firms in 1904 to 2,011 in 1914), and these firms contained 24 percent more spindles and 23 percent more looms.

This expansion was based on the growth of exports. In 1907 exports constituted 89 percent of the linear yards of cotton piece-goods produced in Britain; in 1912 they were 86 percent.[14] Data on the volume (and value) of exports exist for the whole of our period, but data on the volume of cloth production are only available from the censuses for 1907 and 1912. Table 5.2, however, shows time series of both piece-goods exports and yarn exports as percentages of the weight of cotton consumed.

Table 5.1 Growth of firms, capacity and output in the British cotton textile industry, 1870–1915

Period	Average annual growth rates (percent)			
	Firms	Spindles	Looms	Yarn produced and consumed
1870–1875	—	—	—	2.90
1875–1880	—	—	—	2.88
1880–1885	−1.03[a]	2.47[a]	4.00[a]	−0.46
1885–1890	0.50	0.06	2.18	4.52
1890–1895	−0.22	0.76	0.82	−0.02
1895–1900	0.08	−0.26	0.56	−0.30
1900–1905	−0.22	1.52	0.12	2.90
1905–1910	2.28	4.68	2.60	−2.16
1910–1915	0.32	0.74	1.74	7.32
1870–1880	—	—	—	2.89
1880–1890	−0.70[b]	0.96[b]	2.86[b]	2.03
1890–1900	−0.07	0.25	0.69	−0.16
1900–1910	1.03	3.10	1.36	0.37
1910–1914	0.43	0.68	2.10	2.32

Source: G. T. Jones, Increasing Return (Cambridge University Press, Cambridge, 1933), pp. 275–277.
a. 1882–1885.
b. 1882–1890.

Table 5.2 Exports as percentages of cotton consumption (by weight), 1870–1914

Year	Yarn (%)	Piece-goods (%)	Total exports (%)
1870	17.3	55.5	72.8
1875	17.6	52.9	70.5
1880	15.8	60.3	76.1
1885	18.9	61.5	80.4
1890	15.5	56.2	71.7
1895	15.1	55.2	70.3
1900	9.1	52.9	62.0
1905	11.3	62.4	73.7
1907	12.1	57.9	70.0
1909	11.8	57.3	69.1
1910	11.7	67.3	79.0
1911	12.0	65.2	77.2
1912	11.4	58.9	70.3
1913	9.6	59.3	68.9
1914	8.6	50.4	59.0

Source: R. Robson, The Cotton Industry in Britain (Macmillan, London, 1957), pp. 332–333.

Table 5.3 Piece-goods exports from Britain (by value), 1889–1913

Year	Piece-goods exports[a]				
	Grey	Bleached	Printed	Dyed	Total
1889	20,011 (38.9)	12,338 (24.0)	10,913 (21.2)	8,123 (15.8)	51,385
1894	17,618 (35.1)	12,996 (25.9)	10,767 (21.4)	8,835 (17.6)	50,216
1899	16,328 (32.1)	12,503 (24.6)	10,713 (21.1)	11,316 (22.2)	50,860
1904	18,880 (29.5)	16,759 (26.2)	12,557 (19.6)	15,882 (24.8)	64,078
1909	20,188 (29.6)	18,405 (27.0)	12,511 (18.3)	17,175 (25.2)	68,279
1913	27,408 (27.9)	27,054 (27.5)	17,243 (17.5)	26,570 (27.0)	98,275

Source: Annual Statements of the Trade of the U.K. with Foreign Countries and British Possessions, Parliamentary Papers, Accounts and Papers, various years.

a. Exports expressed in thousands of pounds sterling. The number in parentheses is the percentage of the total piece-goods exports for the year of each cloth type.

Piece-goods were classified according to their finished state. Unfinished cloth was classified as either "grey" or "bleached." Finished cloth was classified as "printed" or "dyed." Table 5.3 shows the proportions that each of these classifications constituted of the total value of piece-goods exports.

The largest markets for all types of British cotton goods were in the less developed countries of the world, particularly India, China, Turkey, Egypt, the Dutch East Indies (primarily Java), Brazil (especially before 1900), and Argentina (especially after 1900). Other large markets were the white-settler "colonies" of Canada, South Africa, and, especially, Australia. These areas imported more highly finished goods made from much higher quality cloth than did the markets in the poorer parts of the world. In addition, the home market took higher quality goods. The segmentation of the product market by quality was reflected in the division of the Lancashire spinning industry into two distinct branches—the "American" section of the industry, which used American cotton (as well as some Indian cotton) to spin counts of yarn mainly below 40s, and the "Egyptian" section of the industry, which used Egyptian (as well as U.S. Sea Island cotton for the finest yarn) to spin counts above 40s. Table 5.4 shows the top six markets (by value) for each of the four export classifications in 1889, 1899, 1909, and 1913.

A number of points about Table 5.4 should be noted. First, and foremost, is the importance of India in the British trade. Bombay is among the top three markets in all categories in all years but one.

Bengal is important throughout the period. India (Bombay, Bengal, and Madras) consistently accounts for more than 50 percent of grey exports and about 25 percent of bleached exports. In the 1890s it accounts for almost 20 percent of printed exports, rising to over 30 percent before the war. It was in dyed goods that Britain's markets became more diversified, but India still accounts for between 10 and 15 percent of the market in the two decades before World War I. China, an important market in unfinished (grey and bleached) goods, becomes dominant in the dyed goods market after 1900. The combined value of all piece-goods shipments to the four markets that appear most often in Table 5.4—Bombay, Bengal, Turkey, and China—is 45 percent of the total value of piece-goods shipments in 1889, 43 percent in 1899, 39 percent in 1909, and 45 percent in 1913. Britain clearly had a big stake in these markets. And, as Table 5.5 shows, it was the ability of the British cotton textile industry to expand exports to these markets as well as to Egypt, Madras, the Dutch East Indies, and Argentina that accounts for its rapid growth from the turn of the century to World War I.

Hence the markets of poorer areas of the world not only were dominant in the demand for British cotton goods but also became much more dominant in the pre–World War I expansion. From Table 5.5, it can be seen that, of the net increases in exports by the industry as a whole from 1900 to 1913, Bombay and Bengal alone account for 69 percent in grey goods, 43 percent in bleached goods, 91 percent in printed goods, and 23 percent in dyed goods. Other markets that account for over 10 percent of the net increase of a piece-goods classification are Madras in grey goods, China in bleached and dyed goods, and the Dutch East Indies in printed goods.

What is key, however, for understanding the relation between the growth of demand and the expansion of supply in the pre–World War I period is the impact of the growth of these markets on the quality of cotton yarn and cloth produced in Lancashire spinning and weaving mills. Table 5.6 shows that, with the exception of China, the growth areas were purchasing low quality cotton goods relative to the average cotton goods exported from Britain.

That the expansion of British exports prior to World War I was to markets demanding relatively low quality cotton goods at different points in time does not necessarily mean that the average quality of British exports was declining over time. For example, from the last half of the nineteenth century, Indian factories were able to compete

Table 5.4 Largest export markets (by value) for British cotton
piece-goods, 1889–1913

1889		1899	
Market	Percentage	Market	Percentage
Grey goods			
Bengal	31.0	Bengal	39.7
Bombay	16.4	China	12.3
China	12.9	Bombay	11.7
Turkey	6.4	Turkey	5.8
Madras	4.0	Egypt	2.8
Hong Kong	3.3	Madras	2.7
3 largest	60.3		63.7
6 largest	74.0		75.0
Bleached goods			
Bengal	12.7	Bombay	13.7
Bombay	12.6	Bengal	11.0
Turkey	5.9	China	7.9
D. E. I.[a]	4.8	Turkey	5.3
China	4.4	Egypt	4.2
Brazil	4.1	Hong Kong	4.0
3 largest	31.2		32.6
6 largest	44.5		46.1
Printed goods			
Turkey	11.8	Bombay	12.2
Bombay	10.7	Turkey	8.9
Brazil	9.6	Brazil	5.6
Bengal	5.8	D. E. I.	5.4
Argentina	4.2	Bengal	5.0
Australia	3.6	Australia	4.7
3 largest:	32.1		26.7
6 largest:	45.7		41.8
Dyed goods			
Bengal	11.0	Bombay	7.9
Bombay	8.0	China	7.1
Australia	5.9	Australia	6.7
Brazil	5.4	Bengal	5.6
China	3.7	Turkey	4.1
Madras	3.4	Brazil	3.5
3 largest	24.9		21.7
6 largest	37.4		34.9

Source: Same as that for Table 5.3.
a. Dutch East Indies.

1909		1913	
Market	Percentage	Market	Percentage
Bengal	38.5	Bengal	42.6
China	9.6	China	10.2
Bombay	9.3	Bombay	9.3
Madras	3.3	Madras	5.0
Turkey	3.2	Turkey	3.1
Egypt	3.0	Egypt	2.5
	57.4		62.1
	66.9		72.7
Bombay	11.7	Bombay	17.7
China	10.1	China	11.0
Bengal	8.3	Bengal	10.3
Egypt	6.0	Turkey	4.7
Turkey	5.7	Egypt	4.0
Australia	4.9	Australia	4.0
	30.1		39.0
	46.7		51.7
Bombay	13.0	Bombay	21.6
Turkey	10.7	D. E. I.	7.4
D. E. I.	6.8	Egypt	7.0
Egypt	6.7	Bengal	6.9
Australia	5.0	Turkey	6.8
Bengal	5.0	Argentina	4.2
	30.5		36.0
	47.2		53.9
China	8.9	China	12.6
Australia	6.3	Bombay	8.6
Argentina	6.2	Australia	5.1
Turkey	5.8	Argentina	4.9
Bombay	5.1	D. E. I.	4.7
Bengal	3.6	Bengal	4.5
	21.4		26.3
	35.9		40.4

Table 5.5 Growth of piece-goods exports (by volume), 1900–1913

Market[a]	Grey Increase[b]	Grey Total[c]	Bleached Increase	Bleached Total	Printed Increase	Printed Total	Dyed Increase	Dyed Total
All	22.3	100.0	56.6	100.0	31.8	100.0	71.5	100.0
Bombay	20.0	9.7	97.3	29.4	257.6	71.5	197.4	20.9
Bengal	31.4	61.1	71.5	13.8	143.4	19.8	20.5	2.4
Madras	79.1	11.3	115.6	3.4	69.0	4.9	−1.2	0.0
Turkey	−16.8	−3.7	55.5	5.6	14.9	4.3	69.7	4.5
Egypt	10.4	1.7	34.0	3.0	77.1	9.2	97.5	3.0
D. E. I.[d]	−9.5	−0.1	45.3	3.2	49.6	11.8	200.2	9.1
Hong Kong	13.6	1.0	49.5	2.8	73.1	1.3	30.6	1.3
China	13.8	6.0	174.7	16.7	−8.0	−0.7	124.6	13.1
Argentina	−11.2	−0.5	63.8	2.9	18.1	2.6	124.0	7.0
Brazil	89.7	0.4	2.4	0.1	−77.5	−11.9	84.1	4.4
Australia	−2.4	−0.1	42.5	2.2	−13.2	−1.6	18.0	1.5

Source: Same as that for Table 5.3.
a. Specified markets are those that appear at least once in Table 5.4.
b. Percentage of increase in each market.
c. Percentage of total increase.
d. Dutch East Indies.

Table 5.6 Unit values[a] of British piece-goods exports, 1899 and 1913

Market	Grey 1899	Grey 1913	Bleached 1899	Bleached 1913	Printed 1899	Printed 1913	Dyed 1899	Dyed 1913
All	7.55	11.63	9.22	13.23	10.11	13.66	13.16	18.90
Bombay	6.67	10.24	7.58	10.83	8.52	12.31	8.68	12.14
Bengal	7.07	10.59	7.89	11.39	8.88	11.62	9.06	13.90
Madras	7.91	12.46	9.66	14.88	9.83	13.77	9.92	11.68
Turkey	8.16	10.73	9.11	10.91	9.71	11.54	11.16	14.48
Egypt	7.24	8.57	9.05	12.36	10.88	15.37	11.66	14.92
D. E. I.	8.19	11.00	10.19	13.90	9.74	11.89	10.75	14.99
Hong Kong	8.95	13.05	9.99	14.61	9.68	13.20	13.30	21.70
China	7.99	13.08	9.75	15.35	10.47	14.99	14.90	23.58
Argentina	7.34	11.25	12.47	16.26	9.48	14.04	12.15	17.13
Brazil	6.56	13.65	9.40	16.08	10.36	15.81	11.76	17.96
Australia	12.72	18.04	13.74	19.15	14.40	18.75	15.86	23.49

Source: Same as that for Table 5.3.
a. Figures in the table are unit values expressed as £'s per thousand pounds of weight.

Table 5.7 Ratios of unit values of bleached, printed, and dyed cloth exports to grey cloth exports, 1889–1913

Period	Bleached:Grey	Printed:Grey	Dyed:Grey
1889–1893	1.19	1.43	1.65
1894–1898	1.22	1.40	1.79
1899–1903	1.22	1.39	1.73
1904–1908	1.17	1.27	1.70
1909–1913	1.15	1.21	1.64

Source: Same as that for Table 5.3.

effectively with Lancashire in producing the coarsest counts of yarn and the lowest grades of cloth.[15] On the other hand, the expansion of exports to these relatively low quality markets may have reduced the average quality of piece-goods that Britain was exporting around the world, even if average quality in, say, Bombay or Bengal was rising from the turn of the century to World War I.

Sandberg has constructed an index of the quality of British grey cloth exports that shows a steady and pronounced decline in quality from about 1830 until the early 1860s and a steady, but much shorter lived, rise in quality from the early 1860s until about 1880. Over the next decade there is a fall in quality, followed by a rise to the late 1890s. Most important for the arguments presented here, from about 1898 to 1913 the general trend in quality is slightly downward.[16] Over this period, moreover, there is a very high inverse correlation between expansion of output and the quality of exports.

But grey cloth exports were becoming a smaller proportion of total piece-goods exports in the decades before World War I. Table 5.7 shows the ratios of unit values of British bleached, printed, and dyed exports to grey exports for the period 1889–1913. Each ratio peaks in the mid-1890s and then declines to the immediate prewar period. From the 1899–1903 period to the 1909–1913 period, the bleached : grey ratio declines by 5.7 percent, the printed : grey ratio by 12.9 percent, and the dyed : grey ratio by 5.2 percent.

There are two possible explanations for the movements of the ratios from the late 1890s to World War I. First, structural changes or technical advances in the finishing section of the industry could have decreased the price of bleaching, printing, and dyeing at a faster rate than the price of grey goods was decreasing. There is no solid evidence with which to support or refute this explanation.[17] Second, the quality of grey cloth could have risen relative to the quality of cloth contained in the more highly finished goods. If so, then the decline in the quality of finished goods would have been even faster than the decline in the quality of grey goods indicated in Sandberg's grey cloth index.

There is evidence suggesting that the movements reflected in Table 5.7 were caused by a deterioration in the quality of the cloth content of bleached, printed, and dyed goods. From the late 1890s, a reversal in the terms of trade between industrial producers and primary producers enhanced the purchasing power of the masses of the underdeveloped world to whom the British cotton textile industry was selling the bulk of its production.[18] To some (undetermined) extent, this expansion of purchasing power resulted in an increased demand for more highly finished textile goods containing lower quality cloth. As argued in detail below, the shift to lower quality cloth was achieved by the use of inferior cotton and heavier sizing and not necessarily by a reduction in average yarn count.

This argument finds support in Marrison's account of the expansion of exports to the Latin American market in the period 1889–1913 based on the sale of heavily sized dyed goods that were both cheap and attractive.[19] Marrison argued that the highly specialized structure of British marketing was particularly adapted to the sale of such goods, because British merchants were willing to send out samples of grey cloth to local areas so that the buyers of dyed goods could select the quality and width of cloth that they desired to have finished.[20]

Before turning to an analysis of the supply-side response to international competition in the pre–World War I period, it is useful to note the qualitative difference in British exports to India and China, two of the industry's largest markets. As can be seen in Table 5.6, Bombay and Bengal (the bulk of the Indian market) took relatively low quality goods whereas China took relatively high quality goods. In India the British were supplying the masses of poor peasantry. But in China the British were supplying the wealthier classes in the towns.[21] Even though the British cotton textile industry came to rely increasingly on expansion into markets demanding relatively low quality cloth, part of its prewar expansion was to service higher quality demand.

What is of particular interest in the case of China, however, is not just that it was a higher quality mass market but also that it appears to have been supplied in large part by production from a qualitatively different type of productive enterprise in Lancashire, namely, by firms that vertically integrated spinning, weaving, and marketing. One such enterprise was Ashton Brothers, which before the war housed half of the automatic looms in all of Lancashire, taking advantage of its fully integrated structure to undertake high quality, high throughput production on the basis of advanced technologies.[22] But fully integrated firms were a rarity in Lancashire. In the much more typical specialized spinning, weaving, and marketing enterprises, the emphasis was on low-throughput, low-quality production on the basis of the traditional technologies and organization of work.[23] It was, as is argued later, industrial structure and the organizational response to foreign competition that determined the types of markets in which the Lancashire cotton textile industry was able to expand in the decades prior to World War I.

The Supply of British Cotton Goods

The British cotton textile industry was able to respond to the growing demand for low-cost cotton goods in the two decades before World War I by reducing both the quality and quantity of cotton inputs per unit of yarn and cloth. In spinning, such a strategy meant the purchase of cotton as low grade and as short staple as possible to be spun into yarn with as few processes and as little care as possible, subject to the constraint that the yarn and cloth would be acceptable to merchants and ultimately to consumers. In weaving, the strategy meant as heavy sizing of the yarn as possible prior to weaving and as much stretching of the cloth as possible after weaving, subject again to demand constraints.

Sizing had two functions, one technical and one commercial. Its technical function was to strengthen the warp yarn to withstand the tension and chafing it underwent during the weaving process, thereby reducing breakages. The stronger the unsized yarn, itself a function of cotton grade and staple as well as of processing in the spinning operations, the less sizing needed for this purpose. In Britain, the amount of sizing that served to strengthen the warp yarn (or pure sizing as it was called) was typically 15–20 percent of the weight of the unsized warp yarn, whereas in the United States it was typically only 6 percent.[24] The commercial function of sizing was simply to substitute a cheap input—typically China clay mined in Cornwall, which readily absorbed moisture and hence added substantial volume as well as weight to the cloth—for an expensive input, cotton. Other materials besides China clay were also used to make the size adhere to the yarn better, soften the feel of the sized cloth, and prevent mildew. In Britain, the addition of 50 percent of the weight of the yarn was termed "heavy sizing." Prior to World War I, however, well over 200 percent of size was often added to the weight of the yarn in producing "cotton" cloth in Lancashire. In such cases, a square yard of cloth made of uniform yarn count was, indeed, principally made of materials other than cotton.[25]

The traditional Lancashire cotton technologies—the mule and the powerloom—were well suited for the pursuit of these cost-cutting strategies. The mule with its intermittent spinning motion put much less strain on the yarn being spun than did the ring-frame with its continuous motion. As a result, for any given yarn count, it was technically possible to use inferior grades and shorter staples of cotton on mules than on rings without encountering excessive downtime in spinning because of yarn breakages. Because mule yarn was more softly twisted than ring yarn for any given count spun at any given speed, it also held size better and hence was more suitable for a strategy of heavy sizing.[26]

In the weaving process, the greater frequency of yarn breakage (and hence downtime) that occurred using inferior yarn was less costly on the powerloom than on the automatic loom, which required high throughput to justify its high fixed costs. As a result, the powerloom had a unit cost advantage over the automatic loom when inferior yarn inputs were used, and this advantage widened as the quality of the yarn inputs declined. Because the primary operative task on automatic looms was repairing yarn breakages, low quality yarn, with its high breakage frequency, severely constrained increases in the number of looms per weaver, and hence negated the labor-cost saving potential of the newer technology. On the powerloom, however, the use of high quality yarn might not have permitted any increase in looms per weaver because the most time-consuming task for operatives on this less automated technology was the changing of shuttles, a task that was not affected by yarn quality. Hence the use of low quality yarn on the automatic loom would greatly reduce both its labor-saving and capital-saving advantages over the powerloom.

In short, relative to the traditional technologies, the ring-frame and the automatic loom were high-throughput machines that required high quality cotton inputs to achieve low unit costs. But it was not simply the inherent technical attributes of its existing investments in equipment that encouraged Lancashire cotton textile firms to pursue their "cotton-saving" strategy, for in the decade prior to World War I there was ample opportunity for investment in the new technologies as the industry underwent its dramatic expansion. Rather the continued use of the low-throughput, "cotton-saving" technologies can only be understood in reference to the institutional character of the industry. For it was Lancashire's peculiar structure of industrial organization that favored the continued use of the traditional technologies, and it was its peculiar systems of industrial relations that made possible, and even encouraged, the use of inferior cotton inputs on these technologies.

The foreign demand for British yarn and cloth was serviced by a plethora of exporters and shippers centered in Manchester.[27] Exporters consigned their goods to foreign branch offices or foreign agents who then sought to find a market for the goods. Such shipments in anticipation of demand, however, made up only a small part of the total volume of cotton goods exports.[28] Most of the exports were handled by shippers to fill specific orders from foreign import houses. Shippers would have the grey yarn and cloth that they purchased from spinners and weavers finished (or "converted") according to the specifications of the order, or alternatively, they would buy the desired finished goods from other merchant converters or from finishers.

Spinning and weaving firms produced grey goods almost exclusively to order. To reap the benefits of long runs, each firm sought to attract orders for, and hence specialize in, narrow ranges of yarn counts or types of cloth. Accompanying this horizontal specialization was a high degree of vertical specialization. In 1884, 60 percent of the spindles in Lancashire were in firms that did spinning only and 43 percent of the looms were in firms that did weaving only. By 1911 these figures were 77 and 65 percent, respectively.[29]

Linking these vertical layers of the industry was a hierarchy of extremely well developed markets—Alfred Marshall referred to the Lancashire cotton textile industry as "perhaps the best present instance of concentrated organization mainly automatic."[30] A spinning manager might ride the train to Liverpool on Mondays to purchase sufficient cotton for yarn orders already in hand and visit Manchester on Tuesdays and Fridays to seek out new orders on the floor of the Royal Exchange. In many cases, spinners and weavers would transact their input purchases and output sales through cotton, yarn, and cloth agents, adding more layers to the vertical structure.

The vertically specialized structure of the cotton textile industry posed factor cost constraints on the introduction of ring spinning. Spinning and weaving were not only highly specialized in different firms but also highly localized in different areas of Lancashire.[31] As a result, yarn had to be shipped an average distance of thirty miles from the spinning mill to the weaving mill. Mule yarn was spun into packages on the bare spindle or on lightweight paper tubes, whereas ring yarn was typically wound into packages on relatively heavy wooden bobbins that were extremely expensive to ship. The alternative of rewinding ring yarn off the bobbins onto paper tubes or into larger packages saved on shipping costs but increased production costs.[32]

But the fundamental problem posed by vertical specialization was the absence of coordinated decision-making across vertically related firms—coordination that was necessary to replace traditional low-throughput technologies by modern high-throughput technologies. The vertically specialized structure of production meant that a spinning mill had a short-run incentive to produce inferior yarn, because it could try to save on cotton and processing costs by passing on breakage problems to the weaving mills. In turn, specialized weaving mills found it risky to invest in high-throughput technologies such as automatic looms because they could not be sure of a steady and adequate supply of the quality-controlled yarn that would make such investments cost effective.[33]

Even the method of buying cotton that prevailed in Britain favored the retention of the traditional technologies. In the United States, northern and southern firms bought the cotton needed for the coming year just after the harvest to ensure that, for a given staple length, the yarn would be of the high quality and consistency required for standardized, low-yarn-breakage production.[34] In effect, such advance purchasing and warehousing of cotton was a form of vertical integration—over the course of the year, a regular and consistent supply of the firm's crucial raw material was ensured.

But in Britain spinning firms rarely engaged in large-scale buying of cotton,[35] in part because yarn of high and standardized quality was not being demanded by weavers or merchants. Instead, the spinning manager would buy his cotton in Liverpool (or increasingly in Manchester) from week to week, adjusting his cotton purchases to the specifications of current yarn orders, and always keeping his eyes open for feasible mixes of cotton that would enable him to cut costs. The mule, with its intermittent motion, was much more adaptable not only to lower grades of cotton but also to a wider range of cotton quality than was the ring-frame; hence its use provided the Lancashire spinner with more week-to-week flexibility in the quality of cotton he could feasibly purchase.

Given the highly competitive horizontal structure of spinning and weaving, cost-cutting by the use of inferior cotton and heavy sizing helped mills with older, less technically efficient mules or powerlooms to remain competitive against firms that invested in newer machinery with higher throughput capabilities. Indeed, the technical improvements on the mules and powerlooms from the 1890s on that would have resulted in higher output per worker and lower unit machinery costs had the quality of cotton and yarn inputs remained constant instead simply permitted mill managers to cut costs by using inferior cotton and yarn.[36] Once the dynamic toward inferior cotton was set in motion by the growing demand for low cost, low quality cloth, it was reinforced by the highly competitive horizontal structure and highly specialized vertical structure that characterized the British cotton textile industry.

The character of the industrial relations systems that prevailed in the spinning and weaving sectors of the industry further reinforced this dynamic by creating strong incentives for management to introduce inferior cotton inputs on the traditional technologies. The wage-lists, backed by the powerful cotton textile unions, enabled spinning and weaving operatives to prevent reductions in unit labor costs even if capitalists were to use superior cotton. Unable to cut costs by lowering unit costs on the traditional technologies, Lancashire cotton capitalists were encouraged to try to circumvent the wage-list agreements by using inferior cotton inputs.

As noted in Chapter 4, the spinning wage-lists encouraged the use of inferior cotton inputs by constraining spinning managers from substituting better cotton for labor. Indeed, the quality of cotton inputs was virtually the only dimension of the spinning process for which none of the spinning lists specified a relation between effort and pay.

Weaving lists also encouraged the use of inferior yarn inputs. By 1887 there were twenty-two district lists in existence, of which the most important was that secured in the plain-cloth Blackburn district in 1853.[37] From the 1860s, the Burnley district expanded its capacity on the basis of lower wages, a practice resulting in continual conflicts as Burnley weavers sought to force employers to institute the Blackburn list. Burnley employers were by no means opposed to the principle of wage lists; as early as 1866 they had called for a uniform list. All they wanted was an agreement that, compared with other lists, favored profits more than wages.[38]

But by the late 1880s the weavers' union was gaining in strength; membership in the Amalgamated Weavers' Association increased by 143 percent between 1889 and 1895 while the number of looms in Lancashire increased by only 5 percent.[39] In 1892, at the peak of prosperity in the weaving industry, a Uniform List covering all the weaving districts was adopted on terms very favorable to wages. In late 1932 the Uniform List was modified to accommodate the "more-looms" system; but in 1935 it was altered again, this time to discourage the practice of giving weavers more than four powerlooms to tend. To ensure that all employers would adhere to the 1935 list, it was given the force of law by Act of Parliament.[40]

The stability of the lists in all their detail over, in some cases, almost a century is testimony to the strength of worker organization and the weakness of capitalist organization in Lancashire. Indeed, prior to World War I the mule spinners had by far the largest strike fund per voting member of any union in Britain.[41] The enforcement of the provisions of the lists assured the operatives that higher levels of output because of harder work would not result in the cutting of piece-rates.

Given that the lists were in place, capitalists as individuals also derived important benefits from these long-standing agreements. Individual managers recognized that in a highly competitive and labor-intensive industry, the existence of the lists meant that they would not be forced into wage-cutting competition with other capitalists and the continual conflicts with workers over the pace of work and the rate of pay that would inevitably result. By accepting the wage-lists, employers gave up the right to lower piece-rates, but they were assured that operatives would not engage in the collective slowdown—what the British called ca'canny—that characterized so many other industries.[42] Even when increases in productivity depended on more intense or prolonged work by the operatives, Lancashire spinning or weaving managers knew that their mule spinners and powerloom weavers could be motivated to work harder and longer for higher earnings.

By means of the wage-lists, a certain harmony between capital and labor had been achieved. In addition, in the "American" (coarse and medium count) section of the spinning industry, the Brooklands Agreement of 1893 helped to smooth out conflicts over adjustments to workers' earnings over the business cycle. In 1913, however, the Brooklands Agreement broke down over the issue of inferior cotton inputs—the one key aspect of the production process never successfully regulated by means of the lists.

Labor Productivity

The cost-cutting strategy of using inferior cotton is the key to understanding productivity trends in the British cotton textile industry in the decades prior to World War I. What the trends were has been an issue of debate. Sandberg claimed that labor productivity increased by 40 percent between 1885 and 1913, and that the rate of growth of labor productivity did not appear to slow after 1900.[43] There are, however, some problems with his labor productivity calculations. The Phelps Brown and Handfield-Jones labor productivity index that he used is based on overestimates of the number of operatives in the industry relative to the number reported in the censuses from which the figures were purportedly taken. These overestimates amount to 8.0 percent in 1881 but only 2.4 percent in 1911, thus resulting in an overestimate of the growth of output per worker.[44] Moreover, Sandberg made no adjustment for the decline in the proportion of half-time workers in the industry from 10 percent of all workers in 1885 to only 3 percent of all workers by 1913.[45] As indicated in Table 5.8, labor productivity calculations based on data contained in various returns of the factory inspectors on the number of operatives in the spinning and weaving industries respectively as well as on Jones's output series for yarn and cloth respectively indicate a labor productivity increase of only 15 percent for the cotton industry between 1885 and 1913.[46]

The statistics in Table 5.8, which have been adjusted for changes in the length of the workweek and employment of half-time workers, but not for changes in product quality, clearly indicate that output per worker increased rapidly in the period 1870–1890, and especially in the 1880s, but increased only slightly thereafter. They also indicate different patterns of productivity change in spinning and weaving, with weaving showing negative productivity change in the late 1880s and 1890s and spinning showing negative change in the 1900s.

Table 5.8   Growth in output per operative in the British cotton textile industry, 1870–1913

Period	Spinning		Weaving		Industry	
	Annual(%)[a]	Overall(%)	Annual(%)	Overall(%)	Annual(%)	Overall(%)
1870–1913	1.27	72.34	0.60	29.15	0.91	47.60
1885–1913	0.59	17.76	0.49	14.55	0.50	15.03
1870–1885	2.57	46.34	0.80	12.75	1.68	28.32
1885–1896	1.62	19.32	−0.24	−2.65	0.53	5.94
1896–1913	−0.08	−1.31	0.96	17.67	0.48	8.57
1870–1890	2.57	66.27	0.93	20.35	1.71	40.50
1890–1913	0.16	3.65	0.31	7.32	0.21	5.05
1870–1878	1.91	16.30	0.62	5.10	1.30	10.89
1878–1890	3.02	42.96	1.14	14.51	1.99	26.70
1890–1901	0.46	5.23	−0.03	−0.28	0.12	1.31
1901–1913	−0.13	−1.51	0.61	7.62	0.30	3.69

Sources: The output series for spinning and weaving were taken directly from the series presented in G. T. Jones, *Increasing Return* (Cambridge University Press, Cambridge, 1933), pp. 275–276. Estimates of numbers of operatives for 1870, 1874, 1878, 1885, 1890, 1895, 1896, 1898, 1901, 1904, and 1907 were taken from various Factory Inspectors' Reports. (*Parliamentary Papers* 1871, LXII; 1875, LXXI; 1878–79, LXV; 1884–85, LXXI; 1890, LXVII; 1897, XVII; 1898, XIV; 1900, XI; 1902, XII; 1909, LXXIX.)

a. The annual percentage changes presented are compounded and are based on output averages of the years preceding, including, and following the initial and terminal dates.

For these estimates to serve as indicators of productivity changes, however, requires an adjustment for any shifts to the production of finer—that is, higher yarn count—goods over all or parts of the period. Because finer count goods entail less output by weight per spindle and loom, the apparent stagnation and even decline in output per worker after 1890 may have been attributable to such a shift rather than to a real stagnation in productivity.

Drawing on his index of changes in cotton and cloth quality, Sandberg attributed 7 to 8 percent of the decrease in physical output per worker in the British cotton industry over the period 1885–1913 to a shift to finer count goods.[47] This adjustment estimate implies an overall labor productivity increase of 22 to 23 percent, still considerably less than Sandberg's 40 percent figure.

Sandberg's product quality index, it should be noted, measured the changing *value* of British cotton yarn and cloth exports, holding prices of specific types of goods constant. Changes in the index can be caused by a combination of changes in (1) the quality of cotton inputs, holding yarn count constant or (2) yarn counts spun and embodied in cloth, holding cotton input quality constant. Changes in the quality of cotton inputs do not require an adjustment to the labor productivity figures; although observed changes in labor productivity may well reflect shifts in the quality of cotton inputs. But to measure real labor productivity changes, adjustments must be made for changes in the fineness of goods produced.

Even if the value index reflects shifts in yarn counts, it is not a physical productivity index. Decreases in physical output per worker will only be directly proportional to increases in the value index if labor costs as a proportion of "real costs" increase at the same rate as product prices with the shift to finer count products. Because the cost of cotton as a proportion of total yarn costs declined at a rate of about 0.4 percent for each unit increase in yarn count, other inputs must have assumed increasingly larger shares of total costs with a shift to higher count yarns. Labor was certainly an input whose share of total costs increased faster than product prices. For example, in 1907 the decline in (good practice) output per worker in shifting from the production of no. 40 yarn to the production of no. 44 yarn was 13 percent, whereas the increase in yarn price was 10 percent. Also, because yarn cost was a declining proportion of total cost in the weaving of finer quality cloths, labor inputs undoubtedly increased at a faster rate than cloth price in shifting to higher quality goods. Hence, insofar as Sandberg's value index actually represents changes in yarn counts, it would appear to underestimate the upward adjustment to the labor productivity figures that is needed to control for shifts over time to the production of finer count goods.

Sandberg applied his adjustment evenly to the whole period 1885–1913. Indeed, he argued that over this period the industry experienced a labor productivity growth rate of about 1 percent per annum compounded and that "the rate of increase was about the same over the entire period." "Certainly," he went on to contend, "there is no evidence of an end to growth of output per unit of labor input after 1900."[48] Yet Sandberg's own cloth quality index reveals that the whole of the quality increase that he attributed to the entire period 1885–1913 had occurred by about 1896, and that there was no increase—and with the "Assumption 1" version of his index, even a decline—in cloth quality from 1896 to 1913.

Sandberg's Assumption 1 index reflects a declining quality of colored (printed and dyed) cloth relative to plain (grey and bleached) cloth between the late 1890s and the pre–World War I period as manifested by a narrowing of the relative prices of colored to plain goods over the period. The other version of the index (Assumption 2) holds the relative prices of colored to plain goods at their 1898 level over the period 1898–1913, on the speculation that the observed narrowing of the price differential was perhaps because of efficiency gains in finishing, and hence does not reflect an actual deterioration of the quality of colored cloth relative to plain cloth over this period.

As already argued, the rapid expansion of the market in low quality colored goods did lead to a decline in the relative quality of colored to plain goods. Hence it is the Assumption 1 index that is appropriate. Taking three-year averages of the Assumption 1 index around the years 1885, 1896, and 1913 yields a quality increase of 8.8 percent from 1885 to 1896, but a quality decline of 2.7 percent over the 1896–1913 period.[49] Therefore, if one were to use Sandberg's index to adjust the labor productivity figures in Table 5.8— and it would only be legitimate to do so if the index represents shifts in yarn counts rather than shifts in cotton input quality—the annual productivity growth rates become 1.3 percent for the period 1885– 1896 and 0.3 percent for the period 1896–1913. For the period 1901–1913, moreover, Sandberg's value index fell by 4.2 percent while gross productivity growth for the cotton industry rose by only 3.7 percent (see Table 5.8). The rate of productivity change for the industry as a whole becomes slightly negative when adjusted by Sandberg's index, although it remains slightly positive (on the order of 0.3 percent per annum) in the weaving sector of the industry.

It must be remembered, however, that the value index (by which the gross growth rates were adjusted to derive these figures) underestimates the fall in productivity that is attributable to a shift to higher count goods. Hence, if Sandberg's index represents a decline in average yarn count, then the change in the value index underestimates the amount of measured productivity growth that is merely attributable to a shift to lower count goods. If, for example, the decrease in physical productivity because of a shift to higher count goods in the period 1885–1896 were 10 percent (rather than 8.8 percent indicated by the change in the value index) and the increase in physical productivity because of a shift to lower count goods in the period 1896– 1913 were 3 percent (rather than the 2.7 percent indicated by the change in the value index), the real rates of labor productivity growth in the two periods would be 1.4 and 0.2 percent, respectively. And the stagnation in productivity after 1900 would be even more pronounced.

It is not clear, however, to what extent Sandberg's index actually reflects shifts in yarn counts, because changes in the fineness of goods over any given period may be augmented or even offset by changes in the cotton content of those goods. It would be helpful to have a more direct estimate of shifts in yarn counts over the various subperiods in Table 5.8. There are two sets of data that might be useful for such a project. The Worrall directories, published annually from 1882 on,[50] contain data on spindle capacity and ranges of counts spun for most of the 2,000 or so firms in Lancashire, although the broad ranges of counts given for many firms as well as a significant amount of missing data might render any estimates too imprecise for the purpose of estimating shifts in yarn counts. Gary Saxonhouse and Gavin Wright have gathered data on the cotton spinning machinery classified by yarn count purchased by British cotton spinning firms from 1878 to 1920 that indicate a shift to finer counts in terms of new machinery installed in 1901–1920 as compared with 1878–1900.[51] But it may well be that the economic viability of old machinery for spinning lower counts, for which inferior cotton inputs could be more easily used, could be maintained longer than machinery for spinning finer counts of similar vintage.

Given the rise of Indian and Japanese spinning of coarse yarns, it also seems plausible that there was an increase in the counts of yarn being exported from Britain, in which case a shift to the production of finer counts would have less of a productivity impact on weaving than on spinning within British industry. The issue of shifts in yarn counts spun and woven in the British cotton textile industry before World War I remains to be explored in more detail. For the spinning sector of the industry, if the decrease in physical productivity because of a shift to higher count goods in the period 1901–1913 was actually, for example, 5 percent, then the annual rate of productivity growth would have been slightly positive (0.3 percent) rather than slightly negative as indicated in Table 5.8.

Beyond such adjustments, what explains the stagnation of productivity in the prewar British cotton textile industry? The essential first step is to recognize that output per worker is not simply a function of technology, be it the technical attributes of capital inputs or the physicocognitive attributes of workers. Rather, it is also a function of work effort—the extent to which workers transform productive potential into actual output.

As elaborated in the Appendix, for any given technology, the determinants of labor productivity can be conceptualized as $Q = \alpha f(E)$, where Q is output per production period, α is the productive capability to transform inputs into outputs, and E is the effort supplied by the labor force. The transformation of the productive capabilities represented by α into actual output per worker, Q, depends on the supply of labor effort forthcoming from workers. Hence, to understand changes in labor productivity in the British cotton textile industry over the period 1885–1913, one must identify *how* changes in both α and E, as well as the interaction between these technical and behavioral determinants of output per worker, affected the labor productivity outcomes.

The relation between changes in technical potential and changes in work effort can be considered under four general headings: (1) changes in the utilization of the traditional technologies, including changes in the speed of machines and the number of machines per worker; (2) changes in the quality of cotton inputs; (3) the diffusion and utilization of new technologies, and (4) changes in the productive abilities of workers (an element of α) and the motivations of workers to expend more effort.

Utilization of Traditional Technologies

As mentioned earlier, the self-acting mule was first introduced in the 1830s, but it was not until the 1860s and 1870s that the last fundamental improvements in its operation were achieved, making it technically possible to replace the old hand mules on finer and finer counts as well as to build self-actors longer and run them faster.[52] These processes of stretchout and speedup were achieved utilizing the same basic work unit—the mule spinner, the big piecer, and the little piecer.

In 1885 the *Cotton Factory Times* claimed (plausibly when compared with other evidence) that between 1865 and 1885 a typical pair of mules had been stretched out by 30 percent for weft and 12 percent for twist and speeded up by 15 to 20 percent. Estimates for Oldham for each of the three decades between 1876–77 and 1906–07 show increases in the average number of spindles per mule of 11.5, 4.6, and

12.1 percent, respectively, and increases in mule speeds of 6.2, 4.4, and 4.7 percent.[53] Improvements in the working mechanisms of the mule that permitted it to run faster and carry more spindles without causing increased yarn breakages meant that higher levels of productivity could be achieved without increased effort. Such effort-saving technical progress undoubtedly was taking place up to the 1880s.

This growth in average speed and size of the mules in itself had a positive effect on labor productivity probably up until 1914, although it was mitigated somewhat by the fact that on the longest mules and on very coarse-count mules (which ran fastest), the wage-lists called for the addition of an extra piecer.[54] It should also be noted that the Oldham data presented above almost certainly overestimate the extent of stretchout and speedup in Lancashire as a whole, especially in the 1896–1906 period, because the Oldham district was the most dynamic spinning center in terms of new investment. Between 1896 and 1906 the number of spindles increased by 35 percent in the Oldham district but only by 13 percent in the whole Lancashire industry; and between 1896 and 1913, by 68 percent in Oldham and 37 percent in all of Lancashire.[55]

The experience of speedup and stretchout in powerloom weaving in the decades prior to World War I is somewhat similar. Like the mule, the fundamental technical development of the Lancashire loom occurred well before the end of the nineteenth century, technical progress in the three decades prior to the war consisting primarily in the updating of machinery through new investment, particularly in the decade after 1904 when the number of looms in Lancashire increased by 24 percent.[56]

The structure of the weaving wage-lists, however, had a different impact on the amount of equipment per worker than did the mule-spinning lists. By lowering piece-rates on larger and (in Oldham, at least) faster mules, the spinning lists encouraged the capitalists to try to maximize spindles per worker. In contrast, by setting piece-rates irrespective of the number or speed of looms tended, the weaving lists encouraged the capitalists to try to minimize the number of looms per weaver. The most time-consuming tasks of the weaver were, first, to keep the looms supplied with weft shuttles and, second, to piece together broken warp threads. Both these operations required that the machine be stopped. Moreover, if a weaver were to fail to repair a broken warp yarn immediately, there would be faults in the cloth that, depending on the quality of the product desired, might have to be repaired by hand. Hence, for a given intensity of labor, the lower the number of looms per weaver, the faster each loom could be run, the higher the output per loom, and the lower the total unit factor costs.

If there had been a perfectly elastic labor supply available at the one-loom wage, then all of the Lancashire weaving industry would have been on a one-loom system. But, in any weaving district, the one-loom wage reflected agreements on the price per piece of cloth and the number of looms per weaver that were supposed to enable local capitalists to remain competitive with other manufacturing districts and workers to earn a decent wage. The general practice was for an inexperienced weaver to start on two looms, work his or her way up to three looms after attaining an average level of proficiency, and for the best weavers ultimately to be promoted to four looms.[57] Despite his interest in minimizing looms per weaver in order to increase loom speeds and minimize downtime, a weaving capitalist was obliged to adhere to such a promotion policy if he wanted to attract and retain good workers.

Wood estimated that the number of looms per weaver increased by about 18 percent, or just over 1 percent per annum between 1870 and 1886, but only by about 4 percent, or 0.2 percent per annum, between 1886 and 1906. He noted, however, that these figures underestimate the increase in output per worker, because it had originally been the practice for three-loom and four-loom weavers to pay a tenter—a younger person—to assist them. As technical improvements to the looms reduced the frequency of yarn breakages and as the increasing minimum age requirements under the Factory Acts created a scarcity of half-timers (the main source of the tenter labor supply), first the three-loom weavers and then most of the four-loom weavers ceased to hire tenters.[58] Half-timers constituted 13 percent of all workers in the weaving industry in 1874, 10 percent in 1885, 6 percent in 1895, 4 percent in 1904, and 3 percent in 1911.[59]

Loom speeds varied widely, depending on the cloth being produced, the width of the loom, the number of looms per weaver, and the capacities of the operatives. All these sources of variability make it difficult to draw any general conclusions on the extent of speedup in the decades before World War I. On the basis of scattered information, Wood guessed that the "average" loom had been speeded up by 0.75 percent per year between 1865 and 1873, by 0.25 percent per year between 1873 and 1885, and by 0.52 percent per year between 1885 and 1906.[60]

Throughout these decades, operatives continually complained of "driving and humbugging" by the weaveroom overlookers, whose own pay was dependent on the weavers' output.[61] The overlookers— known as tacklers—were in charge of keeping the looms in working order and had complete control over the speed of the looms. One notorious method used to keep the workers in pace with the machines was the "slate-and-board" system whereby the wages and hence weekly production of individual weavers would be displayed on a board in the weaving shed with the threat of dismissal hanging over those workers who were persistently below average. Some suicides were attributed to the system, particularly just after the turn of the century. But in the years just before the war, the unions were apparently successful in having the slate-and-board system eliminated.[62]

Another factor that affects the utilization of plant and equipment is the duration of work. The productivity figures in Table 5.8 are already adjusted for changes in the statutory length of the workday. The Factory Act of 1874 restricted the employment of all women as well as all persons under eighteen to a maximum of 56.5 hours per week. Daily starting and stopping times were specified, as were mealtimes. The Factory Act of 1901 decreased the maximum workweek to 55.5 hours by ending work on Saturdays an hour earlier. The statutory workweek was also assumed to apply to males eighteen years of age and older; for example, the piece-rates on the Oldham list were calculated on the assumption of a 56.5- (and later a 55.5-) hour workweek with a time allowance for doffing, cleaning, oiling, and even accidental stoppages. Management could always choose to remain open for less than the statutory limit, a fairly usual occurrence in recessions in Lancashire. (The calculations underlying the figures presented in Table 5.8 control for cyclical variations by taking three-year productivity averages for any given year.)

But in better times management might try to exceed the statutory limit by enticing or coercing workers to work before and/or after "work" hours or during mealtimes. For those under eighteen and for women, such time-cribbing (as it was called) was not only forbidden de jure but also limited de facto by the surveillance of the factory inspectors. For males eighteen and over, such as mule spinners and their eldest assistants (big piecers) as well as for many powerloom weavers, however, there was no legal reason why tasks such as cleaning and oiling could not be performed before and after hours or during mealtimes while the factory engines were, by law, shut down. Given the nature of the wage-lists, mule spinners and weavers (but not big piecers) had a pecuniary interest in participating in such practices because it added to their earnings. By the same token, they had an interest in cooperating with employers who wanted to break the law by starting the engines a little early, running them during mealtimes, and shutting them down late. Big piecers, however, paid on fixed time rates, had no immediate interest in working overtime, but generally had little power to resist such enforced and unpaid prolongation of their workday if they wanted to remain in line for promotion to a mule-spinning position. Little piecers, who were under eighteen, might also be coerced, in this case illegally, into contributing their unpaid labor time. Such time-cribbing became especially prevalant in booms as managers sought to take maximum advantage of strong markets.[63]

In the early 1890s, however, the spinners' union began to oppose the system of time-cribbing. From the perspective of the union leaders at least, time-cribbing posed a number of dangers. In 1891–92 "New Unionism" had come to Lancashire as some Bolton piecers, who were normally compelled to become voiceless members of the mule spinners' union, had formed their own piecers' union. Even though this attempt did not go very far (and there were to be other unsuccessful ventures in this direction over the next two decades), the spinners' union woke up to the need to control the individual actions of its minders to keep the collective opposition of piecers from growing and to ensure that this subordinate occupation, which involved very hard work at very low pay and increasingly bleak prospects for upward mobility, did not become even more unattractive to new recruits.

The union also warned its senior members that the widespread practice of cleaning and oiling outside engine hours could give employers a legitimate justification for demanding a reduction in the piece-rates. Explicitly in the Oldham list and implicitly in the Bolton list, the existing rates already contained allowances for cleaning and oiling within normal working hours. In 1893 the Bolton union concluded an agreement with employers making explicit allowances for cleaning and oiling to be performed as much as possible within engine hours, and similar accords followed in other districts.[64]

The elimination of time-cribbing, a problem in all the spinning and weaving processes, also became a prime focus of the United Textile Factory Workers' Association, formed in 1890 to pressure Parliament for regulations to reduce the statutory workweek and to control unhealthy work conditions.[65] Time-cribbing did not disappear in the 1890s and 1900s, emerging as a major issue again in the boom of 1905–1907. But there is reason to believe that union pressure to eliminate it resulted in a decline of extranormal work time over the pre–World War I decades.

Quality of Cotton Inputs

If improvements to the weaving mechanisms of the mules and looms can be classed as effort-saving technical changes (permitting higher levels of output per worker, holding effort constant), then the shift to inferior cotton inputs discussed earlier can be classified as an effort-using technical change. With more yarn breaks per minute, productivity levels could only be maintained by increased labor effort. The alternatives for workers on piece-rates were either to accept lost earnings or, as increasingly became the case, to use their union power to gain compensation for bad spinning or bad weaving.

Judging from the amounts of compensation paid to mule spinners for lost wages under the Brooklands Agreement, the productivity losses attributable to the use of inferior cotton was 7 to 10 percent of normal production.[66] A reading of the sources on industrial conflict and its resolution during the period supports the hypothesis that bad spinning was becoming an increasingly serious problem up to 1913. Prior to the early 1890s, any individual firm attempting to use inferior cotton was confronted almost instantaneously by the workers backed by their powerful district unions. Not so under the Brooklands Agreement. With its drawn-out grievance procedures during which workers were forced to put up with bad material, the constraints on spinning managers in utilizing inferior cotton were loosened. It should also be noted that, although workers were sometimes able to gain compensation for wage losses caused by bad spinning, the extraction of such payment was by no means universal nor, when achieved, did it cover the full extent of lost earnings. Hence, insofar as Lancashire spinning managers were able to cut costs by the use of inferior cotton on an ever-widening and ever-increasing scale, declining labor productivity and declining unit factor costs in mule spinning were mutually consistent outcomes.

Bad yarn meant bad weaving, and the two decades before World War I were marked by conflicts over "bad material" in the Lancashire weaving industry as well. Evidence of compensation paid to weaving operatives suggests productivity losses caused by the use of inferior cotton inputs of the same order of magnitude as those in spinning— 5 to 10 percent of normal production.[67] In the light of the shift of the Lancashire industry into the production of lower quality goods from the late 1890s and the mounting industrial conflict over the issues of "bad spinning" and "bad material" from the early 1890s to World War I, it is plausible to posit this cost-cutting strategy as the prime factor in the observed stagnation in productivity in the two decades before the war.

Diffusion and Utilization of New Technologies

The Lancashire cotton textile industry was relatively slow in introducing the new technologies, such as ring spinning and automatic weaving, that were by the last decades of the nineteenth century transforming the U.S. cotton textile industry. A potentially ideal breeding ground for the proliferation of ring spinning was the Oldham district, with its standard count of no. 32 yarn and its large limited-liability companies. Oldham had 26 percent of the spindles in Lancashire in 1896 and 32 percent in 1914, yet ring spindles accounted for only 3 percent of all Oldham spindles in 1896 and 10 percent in 1914. In all of Lancashire, there were 8.3 million ring spindles and 43.7 million mule spindles in 1907 and 11.4 million ring spindles and 47.9 million mule spindles in 1913.[68] In spinning no. 32 yarn, output per worker was about 10 percent higher on rings than on mules. If no rings had been installed in Lancashire by 1913 and if the ring-frame workers actually employed at that date had all been working on mules, then there would have been just over 3 percent less yarn output in Lancashire just prior to the war. If there had been no shift to ring spinning between 1907 and 1913, then there would have been about 1 percent less yarn output in Lancashire in 1913.[69] Hence, given the relative productivities of mule spinning and ring spinning in Lancashire prior to World War I and given the slow rate of diffusion of the new technology, it is safe to conclude that the actual diffusion of ring spinning had a minimal, but positive, impact on the rate of productivity growth in the spinning industry in the two decades before the war.

On the eve of World War I, less than 2 percent of all looms in Britain were automatic, and hardly any powerlooms even used warp-stop attachments. All the automatic looms that were in place by 1913 had been introduced from 1903 on. Output per worker per year was about 2,000 yards on the automatic loom producing a standard plain cloth and only about 1,100 yards on the powerloom. The adoption of the new machines, therefore, added 10 to 14 million yards or 1.3 to 1.7 percent to 1913 cloth production.[70] Like the ring-frame, the introduction of the automatic loom had a positive, but minor, impact on labor productivity in Lancashire.

Changes in Workers' Abilities and Incentives

The real problem of productivity in Lancashire, however, was not the failure to introduce each of the new, high-throughput technologies separately but the failure to introduce them in coordinated fashion, thereby slowing separate rates of diffusion. Instead, as we have seen, managers in the British cotton textile industry opted to try to cut costs by reducing the quality of their capital inputs, and then they sought to maintain productivity by getting more effort from their workers. As a result, productivity advance came to rely increasingly on the augmented productive capabilities of workers and their motivations to work harder.

When the British cotton textile industry began to experience competitive pressures in the 1890s, defenders of the industry pointed to its skilled labor force as one of its major competitive advantages.[71] There is no doubt that, after a century of growth of the cotton textile industry in highly specialized Lancashire towns, the British labor force was both habituated to working long hours at a steady pace and extremely adept at keeping machines running and coping with minute-to-minute problems on the shop floor that would have resulted in lost production with less experienced operatives. But it also seems reasonable to conclude that, given the unchanging mechanical nature of the British production processes from the mid–nineteenth century into the twentieth, the skills of those who regularly participated in the industry had reached their peak of development by the late nineteenth century.

Under these circumstances, a decrease in the size of the cotton textile work force would increase average labor productivity because presumably the best workers would be kept on, whereas an increase

Table 5.9 Numbers of spinning and weaving operatives in the British cotton textile industry, 1870–1913

Year	Number of spinning operatives	Number of weaving operatives
1870	223,529	200,819
1874	235,823	203,005
1878	227,342	218,677
1885	218,085	252,989
1890	214,587	272,538
1895	207,955	305,608
1896	207,476	304,833
1898	205,665	297,694
1901	206,774	295,718
1904	206,609	294,710
1907	234,143	318,392
1911	257,891	325,181
1912	258,326	331,771
1913	263,235	343,748

Source: See notes to Table 5.8.

in the size of the work force would decrease average labor productivity because more inexperienced workers would be employed. Table 5.9 shows the changes in spinning and weaving employment from 1870 to 1913. In spinning, there was a decline in the number of workers from 1874 to 1898 and very little change from 1895 to 1904. But with the rapid prewar expansion of the industry, there was a big increase in spinning workers from 1904 to 1911, with a presumably negative impact on labor productivity. In weaving, there was a large increase in the labor force from 1870 to 1896, which may help to account for the negative productivity estimates for the period 1885–1896. After 1896 the weaving sector of the industry was able to draw on an experienced labor force in periods of expansion to a much greater extent than was the spinning sector.

Indeed, from the late 1890s, mule-spinning rooms experienced considerable difficulty in attracting young workers.[72] This labor shortage—which came to be known as the piecer problem—was integrally bound up with the character of production relations in mule spinning. Although big piecers received somewhat more pay than little piecers, their earnings were nevertheless low. As the pace of work became more intensified because of longer and faster mules and the use of inferior cotton, piecers were expected to bear the brunt of the harder work without necessarily receiving more immediate pay. Their ultimate reward was supposed to come when they were promoted to relatively high-paid minder positions, a transition that was expected to take place when the big piecer was in his early twenties. But an oversupply of "fully apprenticed" big piecers waiting to become minders increasingly delayed and made more uncertain promotion to the ranks of the labor aristocracy. Given the typical tenure of minders on the mules, enough new minding positions could not possibly become available to absorb big piecers by the time they had reached the age of twenty-one. With low pay and insecure job prospects for piecers, it became increasingly difficult to attract little piecers into mule spinning.

Given the labor shortage, it also became increasingly difficult for minders to keep their piecers hard at work. Little piecers, in particular, not yet definitively locked into mule spinning as a lifelong occupation, became hard to handle. In the presence of inferior cotton, good big piecers had enhanced power to resist the authority of their minders, because they could always go to work on another pair of mules. These big piecers were not beholden to any particular minder, because it was ultimately muleroom overlookers, not minders, who promoted big piecers to minding positions. From the early 1890s on, there were a number of futile attempts by piecers to form their own independent unions, as well as numerous spontaneous strikes and walkouts staged by piecers in opposition to their minders to protest hard work and low pay.[73] An important element in the stagnation of productivity in spinning from the late 1890s could well have been the reduced motivation for piecers to work hard and the reduced ability of minders to get them to do so.

The problem of motivating younger workers did not assume as much importance in weaving as in spinning, because the practice of using tenters as assistants on the looms was declining steadily in the decades before the war. Weavers, therefore, were much more reliant on their own labor effort for their incomes. Like the spinners, their union power ensured that employers would not unilaterally cut piece-rates. Hence, also like the spinners, weavers were not prone to engage in collective slowdowns on the shop floor. Nevertheless, for power-loom weavers as for minders, there were limits to how much more labor effort they were willing to trade off for more earnings.

The increased use of inferior cotton inputs undoubtedly pushed weavers as well as minders closer and closer to this limit, a notion evidenced by the rising crescendo of strikes by all workers over the issues of bad spinning and bad material in the years before the war.[74] Particularly in spinning, which was so reliant on the cooperation of low-paid time-workers, but perhaps also in weaving, stagnating labor productivity in the fifteen to twenty years before World War I can be attributed to the unwillingness of workers to work harder to produce yarn and cloth on outmoded machinery using inferior cotton inputs.

Real Costs

What are the implications of these movements in labor productivity for the estimation of trends in "real costs"? G. T. Jones, mentioned earlier, found that real costs in the Lancashire cotton industry rose from 1900 to 1914. Sandberg has criticized this conclusion on the grounds that (1) the real cost results are inconsistent with a rise in labor productivity of 1 percent per annum that purportedly occurred during this period, and (2) Jones's real cost index itself contains a number of estimation errors that, when removed, reveal increasingly efficient performance in the Lancashire cotton textile industry in the prewar period.

As shown above, Sandberg's finding of rising labor productivity in this period was itself based on a number of estimation errors, including his incorrect use of his own index of cotton cloth quality. It is also possible to dispute some of his corrections to Jones's real cost index, particularly those adjustments that are linked to Sandberg's over-inflated labor productivity figures.[75] But there are empirical and theoretical problems at issue here that go beyond Sandberg's attempt to correct Jones. The empirical problem is that both Jones and Sandberg ignored the most important element in cost-cutting in the period under consideration, namely, the use of inferior cotton inputs. The theoretical problem is that the real cost measure, which is simply the "dual" of the total factor productivity measure that economists commonly use, makes untenable assumptions concerning the distribution of income under capitalism, and particularly under competitive capitalism.

With the use of inferior cotton inputs, stagnating or even declining labor productivity is not necessarily inconsistent with declining real costs. For example, in spinning no. 32 yarn, cotton costs comprised almost 90 percent of total costs, and a shift from middling 1$^{1}/_{16}$″

cotton to fair low middling 1" cotton would have saved 5 percent of total spinning costs in 1907, and a shift from the same cotton to good ordinary 1" staple would have saved 7.5 percent. A more dramatic shift from good middling 1⅛" cotton to good ordinary 1" cotton would have saved 22.5 percent.[76] Data on the utilization of cotton inputs over this period do not exist even for one firm in the industry, let alone for the industry as a whole. But these figures (to which must be added the cost savings in weaving from heavy sizing) lend plausibility to the argument that the British cotton textile industry was able to remain competitive on world markets in the pre–World War I period by a strategy of minimizing the quality and quantity of cotton inputs.

One thing is clear. The real cost index as Jones used it is too crude to capture the changes that were taking place in yarn and cloth production in Britain in the prewar decades because it abstracts from changes in both the quality of physical inputs and the intensity of work effort utilized to produce a given output. Even when the quantity of labor and capital inputs are measured correctly in constructing the index, the problem remains of accounting for changes in the quality of these inputs—changes that are the essence of total factor productivity growth or decline.

But, in addition, there is a serious theoretical problem with the real cost index as used by Jones, and with total factor productivity indexes as they are generally used—namely, the problem of evaluating the return to capital. In constructing his index, Jones assumed that normal profits are earned at all times. But, as Sandberg noted, the construction of the index is such that high profits (because of the divergence of output prices and input costs) are associated with inefficiency whereas low profits are associated with efficiency. Sandberg noted that profits in the Lancashire cotton textile industry were generally better after 1900 than before, but he tried to rectify the problem by making a crude adjustment to Jones's index rather than by calling the whole method into question.[77]

There has been considerable debate among academic economists over what determines the return to capital.[78] American neoclassical economists have long assumed that the returns to all factors of production are determined symmetrically and simultaneously by the free operation of market forces. According to this view, normal profits are zero in equilibrium, and the return to capital is simply the return to freely mobile capital—that is, the market interest rate. In contrast,

British neo-Keynesians as well as neo-Marxists in general have followed the classical tradition of distinguishing between industrial capital, which is fixed in the form of specific types of plant and equipment, and finance capital, which may be considered to be freely
mobile. The return to finance capital is the market cost of capital, but
the return to industrial capital is a residual that reflects the real world
ease of entry and exit of capital (and capitalists) into and out of a
particular line of business as well as the ability of firms to use organization and technology to create and appropriate value.

Under competitive capitalism, where ownership and control are
typically in the hands of the same people (capitalists cum managers),
the "wages of management" cannot easily be separated from the
residual return to industrial capital. As factors of production, these
managers are tied to their relatively fixed industrial capital, the market value of which, indeed, often reflects their own personal capabilities and integrity, or, to use the accounting term, "goodwill." In
addition, even when the wages of management are properly treated as
a business expense in the firm's accounts (as, for example, they presumably were by the Oldham limited-liability spinning mills), the
return to industrial capital will depend on managerial decisions concerning the valuation of plant and equipment, and in particular the
decision whether to value it at book value or market value.

All these factors that determine the size of the residual return to
industrial capital are potentially relevant for understanding the ability
of Lancashire firms to remain competitive on world markets in the
pre–World War I period. The very existence of a residual gave firms,
and particularly older firms using the traditional technologies, the
leeway to "cut costs" by taking a lower return to industrial capital or
by living off their fixed capital. Company records for the period do
not exist to assess the importance of this method of meeting both
internal and external competition. The accounts of small companies
were typically destroyed when they went out of business or were
never kept in the first place. Evidence from the interwar period and
after, however, lends support to the notion that, in the pre–World
War I period, many capitalist-managers of British cotton textile firms
may have been ready and willing to accept a lower return on their
industrial capital or a lower return for their managerial services in
order to remain competitive, or that, alternatively, they may have
been artificially maintaining these returns by failing to put aside ade-

quate reserves to enable them to replace their plant and equipment at that future date when the viability of the traditional technologies could no longer be maintained.[79]

In sum, any attempt to understand changes in the "efficiency" of the Lancashire cotton textile industry and its resultant competitive position in world markets cannot simply abstract from changes in cotton quality, work effort, depreciation practices (or lack thereof), and the returns to industrial capital. It may well be that the technically determined and market-oriented perspective of neoclassical economics would lead one to ignore these issues—but then so much the worse for this conventional ideology. The purpose of historical analysis is to discover how input quality changes over time, how capital inputs are related to labor inputs, how enterprise managers account for costs, and how they make their investment decisions. A theory that has little to say about these issues—primarily because it is out of touch with the realities of capitalist development—should not be permitted to obstruct analytic inquiries.

The Dialectics of Development

The prewar boom in the British cotton textile industry was followed by a postwar collapse that proved to be permanent. In 1922 the volume of British piece-goods exports was only 61 percent of the 1913 level, and in 1929 only 53 percent, with the volume of grey goods at 41 percent of the 1913 level, bleached goods at 63 percent, printed goods at 45 percent, and dyed goods at 67 percent.[80] Hardest hit was the "American" section of the industry, producing coarse to medium goods for the underdeveloped areas of the world. Table 5.10 shows the relative volumes of piece-goods exports to various market areas in 1913 and 1929.

Yet, despite the decline in the demand for British cotton goods in the 1920s, spinning and weaving capacity failed to contract. In 1929 there were 3 percent more spindles and only 6 percent fewer looms in operation than in 1913. As existing firms continued to compete for declining markets, there was little incentive to undertake new investment in modern machinery. In 1927 ring spindles were only 32 percent of spinning capacity, a figure only slightly higher than the 26 percent in 1913. Even by 1936, when the number of looms in the industry had been reduced to 64 percent of the 1913 level, automatic

Table 5.10   British piece-goods exports, 1913 and 1929

Market area	Piece-goods exports in 1913[a]	Piece-goods exports in 1929[a]	1929 as percent of 1913
All	7,075	3,765	53.2
British India	3,057	1,268	41.5
China, Hong Kong, and Japan	773	221	28.6
Southeast Asia	539	310	57.5
South America	582	412	70.8
Central America and West Indies	168	86	51.2
United States and Canada	157	72	45.9
Australia and New Zealand	210	207	98.6
Europe (except Balkans)	388	340	87.6
Balkans, Near and Middle East	478	224	46.9
North Africa	357	263	73.7
West Africa	243	215	88.5
South and East Africa	121	120	99.2

Source: Freda Utley, *Lancashire and the Far East* (Allen & Unwin, London, 1931), p. 27.
a. Million linear yards.

looms made up just 3 percent of total weaving capacity—there was at most a net increase of 5,000 automatic looms in the twenty-three-year period in an industry that still had over half a million looms.[81]

With firms working short-time on the traditional technologies, labor productivity declined in the 1920s. Rostas calculated an average annual decline of 0.36 percent in output per operative between 1924 and 1930. From 1930 to 1937, however, productivity increased by an average of 5 percent per annum because of the large-scale elimination of excess capacity from the industry and the strengthening of Britain's access to Commonwealth markets by trade agreements made at the Ottawa Conference of 1932. But over the long run, the situation of the industry continued to deteriorate as labor productivity in Britain fell further and further behind that of its prime competitors. While the British industry was increasing its output per operative-hour by 35 percent between 1924 and 1937, the U.S. industry was increasing its output per operative-hour by over 50 percent and (between 1923 and 1933) the Japanese industry by 140 percent. In a productivity comparison for 1944, output per operative-hour in the U.S. was 60–65 percent greater in spinning and 160–170 percent greater in weaving than in Britain. Similar results were found in 1949 investigations by the Anglo-American Productivity Teams. In a careful study of a large number of British spinning mills, labor productivity was found to have declined by a total of 5 percent between 1939 and 1947, even after controlling for changes in average counts of yarn being spun.[82]

Elsewhere, I have shown how highly competitive and specialized structures of industrial organization stood in the way of the reorganization and reequipping of the British cotton textile industry along modern lines in the decades after World War I.[83] Underlying the failure to restructure the industry were the individualistic attitudes and the overly specialized managerial skills of Lancashire's cotton businessmen themselves—attitudes and skills that were the products of the industrial organization environment in which they were enmeshed.

In addition, any plans to reequip had to take into account the considerable power of the trade unions to control work organization, effort, and pay. On the traditional technologies, attempts to raise productivity and cuts costs by redivision of labor were stymied by the desire and power of the unions to protect their positions of craft control.[84] And firms that introduced ring spindles or automatic looms had to contend with the ring spinners' union or the weavers' union to determine the levels of piece-rates and the number of machines per worker.

In the 1920s some British travelers returned from the United States with glowing reports of the application of "scientific management" there.[85] But in Britain, cotton textile managers had long since lost the power and even the right to manage their labor processes. Rather they had to abide by the well-worked-out and deeply entrenched wage-lists that had their origins in the nineteenth century. In the 1920s and beyond, the British cotton textile industry was afflicted by a severe case of institutional rigidity: it could not adapt the organizational structures internal to its industry—structures that had developed during its period of international economic hegemony in the nineteenth century—to the new requirements of international capitalist competition.[86]

The pre–World War I expansion, if anything, reinforced the structures of industrial organization and industrial relations that blocked the contraction and restructuring of the industry after the war. During the prewar boom, it was not only industry-wide capacity that expanded but also the number of firms at each horizontal level. The larger number of competitors made the problem of the elimination of excess capacity all the more difficult in the postwar period. What is more, during the prewar expansion, the British cotton textile industry became more vertically specialized, thus peopling the industry with more and more managers who had neither the ability nor the interest to undertake the planned coordination of production and distribution activities that was necessary for the diffusion of high-throughput technologies such as high draft spinning, high speed winding, and automatic looms.[87] Finally, in the prewar decades the managers of the British cotton textile industry made no attempt to confront the power of unions to control the relation between effort and pay. Rather, they accepted the wage-lists and related structures of work organization on the traditional technologies and sought to cut costs by the use of inferior cotton inputs. This cost-cutting strategy, entailing as it did effort-using technological change, was the antithesis of the effort-saving, high-throughput methods being introduced elsewhere. The ability of British cotton textile managers to make this marginal adaptation on the traditional technologies and their ability to sell the inferior cloth to the poorer areas of the world in the pre–World War I expansion had the dual effects of cementing them to the traditional technologies and increasing their vulnerability to both competition from cheap labor and exclusion by import-substitution policies. In the postwar era, they began to pay the price.

PART II

Competitive Realities in the Twentieth Century

6   The Persistence of Craft Control

No Longer the Workshop of the World

In the early 1880s Britain could still lay claim to the status of "the workshop of the world." The nation's share of world exports of manufactured goods was 43 percent, a share significantly greater than the 6 percent of the United States and the 16 percent of Germany. By 1913 Britain's share had dropped to 32 percent, whereas that of the United States had increased to 14 percent and that of Germany to 25 percent.[1] Already in relative decline in the first decades of the twentieth century, British industry could nevertheless still compete in the world economy by relying on ample supplies of experienced factory labor to operate a vast stock of plant and equipment that had been accumulated over the previous half-century.

Underlying Britain's relative decline was a marked shift in the international productivity advantage that the nation had enjoyed in the last half of the nineteenth century. In 1870, when Britain had dominated the world economy, its labor productivity was by one estimate 14 percent greater than that of the United States. On the eve of World War I, Britain's labor productivity still remained higher than that of any other European country, but the United States outstripped Britain by 23 percent. Before World War II, the U.S.–British productivity gap had risen to 43 percent; and in the 1970s it was over 50 percent. By this time, the level of British labor productivity was among the lowest in Western Europe.[2]

As late as 1955, Britain's volume of exports stood only at the level achieved in 1913. Britain's exports tripled over the next twenty-five years as the world economy enjoyed sustained economic growth. But over the same period, Germany's volume of exports increased by almost seven times, Japan's by over nineteen times, and the United States's by more than four times. In 1973 Britain had 9 percent of world exports; the United States, 15 percent; Germany, 22 percent; and Japan (now leaving Britain behind and catching up with the others), 13 percent.[3] By any measure, Britain had fallen further and further off the pace set by the dominant industrial powers.

At the root of British decline was the persistence well into the twentieth century of the very organizational structures that had brought Britain to dominance in the nineteenth century. Fundamentally, Britain's economic problem was not its "bloody-minded workers" but its "narrow-minded managers." Major British firms continued to be controlled by proprietary interests who, for fear of losing financial and managerial control over their enterprises, failed to make the investments in managerial structures that came to characterize successful capitalist development in economies such as the United States, Germany, and Japan. With the consolidation of "managerial capitalism" in these nations in the first decades of this century, business organizations that did not build managerial structures to plan and coordinate manufacturing and marketing could not hope to compete effectively in international competition for mass markets. Of particular relevance to the story being told here, in the absence of investments in managerial structures, proprietary firms continued to rely on manual workers to coordinate the flow of work, the division of labor, and the training of young recruits on the shop floor.[4]

In the twentieth century as in the nineteenth century, the reliance of British capitalists on shop-floor labor to coordinate production activities continued to have the advantage of fixed costs that were low relative to the organizational and technological investments characterizing managerial capitalism as it was developing elsewhere. But, over the course of the twentieth century, as managerial enterprises in places such as the United States, Germany, and Japan began to transform the high fixed costs of their innovative investment strategies into low unit costs, the value-creating advantages of Britain's low fixed cost, labor-intensive strategy became increasingly difficult to sustain.

As was the case in the expansion of the British cotton textile industry before World War I, value creation came to depend increasingly on the supply of greater effort by shop-floor workers rather than on the planned coordination of effort-saving technology by managers. The British labor-intensive strategy, with its low fixed costs and reliance on worker effort, could compete for a time against high fixed cost competition. But, with the development and utilization of effort-saving technologies elsewhere, the competitive capabilities of British effort-using strategies reached their social and technical limits.

By the first decades of the twentieth century, therefore, Britain was no longer the workshop of the world. Textiles and iron and steel, along with metalworking industries producing ships, locomotives, steam engines, and textile machinery had formed the manufacturing basis of the nation's nineteenth-century economic power. Starting in the 1890s, and increasingly as the twentieth century progressed, British manufacturers in these staple industries experienced an erosion of their shares of world trade. In the more capital-intensive metal-producing and metal-using industries, the prime competitors were Germany and the United States, the emerging industrial powers. In the more labor-intensive industries such as textiles, the prime competitors were poorer nations in the process of industrialization, such as India, with its cheaper labor, and Japan, with its cheaper labor and effort-saving technological change. During the twentieth century, moreover, as even the spinning of yarn and the weaving of cloth became progressively more capital-intensive, British textile firms also began to lose out to high-wage European competitors.[5]

In some industries where highly skilled shop-floor labor remained an important asset—shipbuilding is the most clear-cut example—British firms maintained a competitive advantage through the first half of the twentieth century.[6] But eventually the failure of British business to make the requisite investments in technology and organization meant that the advantages of the nation's "early start"—in particular the advantage of an abundant supply of experienced shop-floor labor that was continually reproducing the next generation of experienced workers on the job—no longer sufficed in international competition.

A major factor in British long-run industrial decline was the failure of its manufacturing firms to take the organization of work off the shop floor. The corollary of this failure was the underdevelopment of British managerial structures in a world economy dominated by managerial capitalism. British employers left control of work on the shop floor in lieu of building the managerial structures that could have "relieved" workers of their authority and responsibility for ensuring the flow of work.

The problem of craft control in the twentieth century was not limited to the old staple industries in which union power had become entrenched in the late nineteenth century. Even in a new industry such as automobile manufacture that from the 1920s to the 1950s was largely nonunion, British firms left considerable control over work organization on the shop floor. Indeed, far from being the cause of decline (as posited by those who view "bloody-minded workers" as the cause of the "British disease"),[7] the exercise of "craft" control, even in the absence of craft skills, was the result of the historical willingness of British employers to relinquish what Americans and Germans came to define as the managerial function.

The fundamental problem of British industrial enterprise was the failure to undertake innovative investment strategies and achieve economies of speed through managerial coordination of the specialized division of labor. In the absence of managerial structures able and willing to exercise control over the shop floor, craft control—a characteristic feature of British industry in the last half of the nineteenth century when the nation was still the workshop of the world—persisted as an integral feature of a once-powerful economy that lacked the institutions to compete effectively in international competition in the twentieth century.

Origins of Craft Control

In iron and steel and the mechanical engineering industries, the reasons for the consolidation of craft control in the last half of the nineteenth century were much the same as those applying to cotton textiles.[8] As already argued in the case study of mule spinning, the foundation of nineteenth-century craft control in the British cotton textile industry was not union power. Rather, the basis of craft control was the willingness of proprietary firms, lacking managerial and financial resources and in unregulated competition with one another, to leave the organization of work on the shop floor. An abundance of labor willing and able to be trained on the job, along with the need for shop-floor skills to keep imperfect machines in motion and work in progress, induced employers to rely on more experienced workers to recruit, train, supervise, and allocate shop-floor labor. As I shall explain in Chapter 7, Britain's production strategy contrasts with that followed in the United States from the early nineteenth century, where the mobility—and hence, "scarcity"—of labor induced industrialists to invest in technologies that made them less reliant on shop-floor skills and in managerial structures that could transform the relatively high fixed costs of the capital-intensive technologies into low unit costs.

In Britain, senior workers, who came to be known collectively as the aristocracy of labor, not only provided their own skills to the building, maintenance, and operation of machinery but also recruited junior workers whom they trained and supervised on the shop floor. The reliance on experienced labor to perform these functions had the advantage of low fixed costs, not only for individual firms, but also for the British economy as a whole. The progress of British industry in the nineteenth century did not rely to any significant extent on a formal educational system, whether supported by the state or by industry. On-the-job training systems, with senior operatives training their eventual replacements, effected the reproduction of an abundant and skilled labor force at little, if any, expense for employers. Eager to gain entry to the aristocracy of labor, the promise of promotion kept younger workers hard at work.

Older workers were not adverse to long and steady labor either, provided they had some assurance of sharing in the resultant value gains. The power of their unions to bargain over the relation between effort and pay provided them with this assurance. In addition, the skilled workers' intimate practical knowledge of production methods meant that, as by-products of shop-floor experience as well as their relative autonomy on the shop floor, they were able to keep imperfect machinery running steadily and contribute to minor improvements in shop-floor technology.

As older workers trained younger workers, supplies of specialized labor expanded in certain localities during the nineteenth century. Depending on their choices of business (itself typically a function of their own specialized training in a particular locality), capitalists tended to invest where labor with the necessary specialized skills was in relatively abundant supply.

As a consequence, particular industries became increasingly concentrated in particular localities, giving employers access not only to large supplies of labor with the requisite skills but also to communications and distribution networks that supplied a regional industry with its basic inputs, facilitated the flow of work-in-progress through vertically related specialties, and marketed the industry's output. Given the localization of industry, new businesses were able to specialize in a narrow range of activities, relying on other firms to supply them with the necessary inputs and still other firms to purchase their outputs for resale downstream. As more firms set up as vertical specialists, suppliers and buyers for intermediate products became all the more readily available, reinforcing the trend toward vertical fragmentation. Given the lack of managerial organization, firms also tended to confine themselves to single-plant operations, thereby facilitating the entry of new firms into vertical specialties and hence increasing further the extent of horizontal as well as vertical fragmentation of industrial sectors.

The narrow product and process strategies of British firms reinforced both their willingness and need to rely on craft control. Their willingness to rely on craft control derived from their positions as vertically specialized producers in industries with numerous competitors. In contrast to the organization building that would characterize managerial capitalism in Germany and the United States, these relatively small, specialized firms did not invest in managerial structures with which to gain control over the supply of inputs and the sale of outputs. Hence, quite apart from the exercise of control over the flow of work on the shop floor, these British firms did not possess the organizational capabilities to achieve economies of scale and scope.[9] In the evolution of managerial capitalism in the United States, the assertion of managerial control over the shop floor was generally a final step in the development of a firm's capabilities to plan and coordinate its business activities. The underdeveloped organizational capabilities that characterized the British proprietary firms gave these enterprises no choice but to rely on craft control to coordinate the production process.

The relatively low fixed costs of generating a skilled and disciplined labor force as well as the external economies that came from spreading out more industry output over localized industry infrastructure enabled British manufacturers to gain international competitive advantage in the nineteenth century. Under the prevailing conditions of international competition, the employment of skilled shop-floor labor and reliance on craft control was an effective competitive weapon. Relative to American methods, the British use of skilled labor substituted for costly investments in effort-saving technology and managerial organization.

Moreover, because of the systems of on-the-job "apprenticeships" (whether formal or informal) that prevailed in the craft-based production processes, the very success of this system of business organization generated a growing supply of experienced workers available to proprietary firms. In the cotton textile industry, minders trained piecers who could eventually become minders, and future weavers often entered the industry as tenters. In the iron and steel industry, underhands provided a source of potential skilled workers. In some of the engineering industries, formal apprenticeship systems were widespread. Like the big piecers in mule spinning, many youths apprenticed to the engineering trades took their training and migrated abroad. But many others, motivated by the prospects of eventually joining the aristocracy of labor, remained ready and eager to take up employment in the manufacturing districts and trades in which they had been trained. The steady reproduction of a labor supply able and willing to create value on the basis of existing technologies provided employers with a viable alternative to investments in managerial structures that could plan and coordinate the redivision of shop-floor labor and effort-saving technological change.

As much as they might have been content to rely on the organizational capabilities of shop-floor workers, British employers would have preferred that craft control not be translated into union power. In the 1830s and 1840s there were major conflicts in the cotton textile industry over the right of workers to engage in collective bargaining. As late as 1854 the Preston manufacturers locked out their workers rather than recognize the union. In mechanical engineering, the newly formed Amalgamated Society of Engineers suffered a major defeat in the lockout of 1852.[10] In the iron industry, union organization was nearly obliterated in the late 1860s after a series of industrial conflicts.[11]

These confrontations between employers and their workers did not, however, usher in a nonunion era. The "great Victorian boom" that endured from the 1850s through the 1860s and into the 1870s undermined the resolve of employers to defeat unionization.[12] Eager to generate output while there were profits to be made, employers became receptive to sharing power with workers' organizations over the determination of work conditions and pay levels.

The foundations upon which collective bargains were negotiated were customary work practices and earnings norms, some of which had been embodied in wage-lists issued by employers in the nonunion era of the first half of the nineteenth century.[13] As in the case of the wage-lists in cotton textiles, with the rise of union power, preexisting hierarchical and technical divisions of labor became the starting points for formal collective bargaining as well as the bases for ongoing, and ever more entrenched, craft control. The period that proved to be the apex of British industrial dominance saw the consolidation of craft control as the basis for orderly relations between employers and experienced shop-floor workers.

Employers' acceptance of collective bargaining in turn opened the way for political transformations that served to reinforce the power of unions to preserve positions of craft control. In the eyes of the British political elite of the 1860s and 1870s, the advent of cooperative industrial relations under the aegis of business-minded union leaders transformed craft workers from uncontrollable subversives into responsible citizens. One result was the 1867 extension of the franchise to better-paid workers. To build its electoral strength, the Liberal Party entered into a political alliance with working-class leaders that would endure from the 1870s until the Taff Vale watershed at the turn of the century. With the acceptance of workers as responsible members of the political community came changes in labor law that facilitated the building of union strike funds and the staging of strikes.[14]

From the late 1860s through the late 1880s, employers and workers in various manufacturing industries sought to work out, with various degrees of success, formal systems of wage determination to ensure labor peace.[15] The cotton textile industry saw the institutionalization of wage-lists in different spinning and weaving districts; consequently, by the 1880s, the major source of conflict was the adjustment of earnings over the business cycle. In iron and steel, hosiery, and footwear, conciliation boards were set up to settle disputes, with the iron employers and workers adhering to a sliding scale of wages based on the selling prices of the industry's products.[16] In metal engineering, in which employers were continually seeking to substitute unskilled for skilled workers and in which conflict periodically surfaced, the branches of the Amalgamated Society of Engineers were able to establish and enforce standard district rates. In shipbuilding, the skilled workers—and, in particular, the boilermakers— were highly organized by the 1870s; but, because the industry was subject to severe cyclical fluctuations, they had only limited success in engaging employers in collective bargaining.[17]

The growth of union influence and the spread of collective bargaining through the 1880s enabled experienced workers to consolidate their positions of craft control on the shop floor. Even the weavers of coarse cotton goods, whose skills were much more easily replicable than those of, say, puddlers, boilermakers, or fitters, were able to maintain customary divisions of labor and manning ratios as the basis for collective bargaining.

From the late 1880s, however, foreign competition, combined with the availability of large supplies of low-paid but capable junior workers who had been trained on the job, created incentives for employers to attack the positions of craft control in an attempt to transform the industrial relations structures that had emerged over the preceding decades. In different product markets at different times, the rise of foreign competition led employers to look for ways to cut costs by abrogating prior agreements and using cheaper labor. All the while, the junior workers were looking for ways to increase their earning power, whether it be at the expense of the senior workers who lorded over them or their capitalist employers who ultimately paid the bills.

With the rise of foreign competition, some industrialists even campaigned to cease collective bargaining altogether in order to restore to themselves the "power to manage" that they had lost. As Colonel Dyer, president of the Engineering Employers' Federation (EEF) put it in a letter to *The Times* on the eve of the 1897–98 engineering lockout, the employers in his organization were determined "to obtain the freedom to manage their own affairs which had proved to be so beneficial to the American manufacturer as to enable them to compete... in what was formerly an English monopoly."[18] Dyer held up Carnegie Steel, whose victory in the Homestead conflict of 1892 had rid the company of unions, as an example of how to regain the "power to manage" that had been lost.

By contributing to a slowdown in the rate of growth of the British staple industries, the rise of foreign competition also diminished the prospects for junior workers to gain timely promotions to the ranks of the labor aristocracy. Faced by low wages well into manhood, these workers became more susceptible to employers who would try to use them as nonunion labor as well as more amenable to attempts by working-class activists to organize them into new unions that were independent of the traditional craft societies.[19] At the same time, the wave of innovation in skill-displacing mechanical technologies that occurred in the last decades of the nineteenth century, much of it emanating from the United States, expanded the possibilities for replacing more skilled with less skilled labor.

Simultaneously, therefore, the labor aristocrats began to feel pressure from above and below in the hierarchical structuring of the firms in which they worked. From above, their employers pressed them to supply more effort for lower pay; from below, the employees whom they supervised insisted on higher pay for less effort. Depending on the pressure of foreign competition and the success of the organizing efforts of junior workers, different industries saw the late–nineteenth-century attempts to transform the structure of industrial relations settled in different ways. Yet, as I shall outline briefly, the evolution of work organization in cotton textiles, iron and steel, and the mechanical engineering industries from the late nineteenth century into the twentieth reveal how resistant to change were the structures of shop-floor control that had been put in place when Britain was the workshop of the world.

The Legacy of Craft Control

In cotton textiles, the rise of Indian competition in coarser goods from the 1880s underlay the major confrontation over bad spinning in 1891–92.[20] The conflict prompted Lancashire's spinning mill owners and managers to form the Federation of Master Cotton Spinners' Associations, with a militant faction advocating that the employers use their newfound unity to renounce the wage-lists. Reminiscent of Andrew Ure's 1830s vision of mulerooms free of craft workers, the militants sensed the opportunity for defeating the minders once and for all by using the ample supply of experienced piecers as a cheaper and more pliable labor force. At a minimum, they undoubtedly thought that they could replicate the hierarchical and technical divisions of labor that existed in mulerooms of the United States.

The dominant faction in the FMCSA, however, argued that orderly relations with the skilled workers represented the industry's most valuable asset.[21] The result was the 1893 Brooklands Agreement that created formal procedures for making cyclical adjustments in earnings and resolving shop-floor grievances. In the absence of any concerted attempt by employers to transform the shop-floor division of labor, minders were able to use a combination of coercion and concessions to keep their piecers in line. All the essential features of the internal subcontract system that had characterized mule spinning throughout the nineteenth century remained intact. Indeed the minder–piecer system persisted into the post–World War II era.

In British cotton weaving as well, the late-nineteenth-century rise of international competition did little to alter the traditional division of labor on the shop floor. The Uniform List of 1892 covering all weaving districts remained in force into the second half of the twentieth century. In 1935 the List, revised to take into account the high levels of unemployment of the early 1930s, was even made statutory by an

Act of Parliament. In the 1930s cloth manufacturers made some attempts to increase the number of powerlooms per weaver above the standard four. On the whole, however, they were not overly successful in increasing "manning" ratios (about half of the weavers were women), not only because of the determination of the union to preserve jobs, but also because of the possibility of pursuing the alternative competitive strategy of using inferior cotton with the standard number of looms per weaver. As in spinning, traditional modes of work organization continued to characterize the weaving section of the cotton textile industry.[22]

In the iron and steel industry, Britain lost its dominant position in the late nineteenth and early twentieth centuries. In 1870 Britain produced 50 percent of world tonnage of pig iron and 43 percent of steel. By 1913 the United States was producing 40 percent of world tonnage of iron and steel, and Britain only 10 percent. After controlling about three quarters of world exports of iron and steel around 1870, the British industry still accounted for over one third in 1913. But by 1913 Germany had surpassed Britain as the world's leading exporter.[23] Despite this fall from hegemony, the British iron and steel industry expanded steadily in the late nineteenth and early twentieth centuries, from an average annual output of 1.8 million tons in the period 1880–1884, to 3.1 million in 1890–1894, 5.0 million in 1900–1904, and 7.0 million in 1910–1914. On the eve of World War I, British iron and steel continued to maintain international competitive advantage in higher quality sheet and tinplate markets. At home, the industry was serving the still dominant British shipbuilding industry, which alone took 30 percent of the nation's steel output in 1910–1912.[24] Like the cotton textile industry, British steel suffered from excess capacity in the 1920s. Although the industry experienced a recovery in the late 1930s, its fragmented structure of industrial organization so obstructed the rationalization and reequiping of the industry that by the 1950s nationalization had become a necessary (if by no means sufficient) condition for its technological renewal and ultimate survival.[25]

In the decades prior to World War I, steady expansion of output provided conditions conducive to harmonious relations between steel employers and unionized workers. After a series of industrial conflicts in the 1860s, the two sides joined together to set up boards of arbitration and conciliation to negotiate standard tonnage rates that formed the bases for the piece-rates of different types of skilled workers in the different manufacturing districts. Through the 1870s these skilled workers were generally contractors who employed under-hands on fixed time-wages. The boards also negotiated sliding scales for tonnage rates to adjust for cyclical variations in the selling price of manufactured iron.[26]

Over these decades, skilled iron and steel workers saw their earnings grow, because their collective bargaining power enabled them to maintain tonnage rate levels even as, largely through incremental technical change, productivity increased. Left behind at first were the underhands, paid time-wages and possessing little bargaining power to extract higher wages from the senior workers who employed them. But unlike the piecers in cotton spinning, who were never able to organize independently of their worker bosses, from the 1880s under-hands formed their own unions and were increasingly successful in putting an end to contracting. Instead, they were able to negotiate their own tonnage rates with employers.[27]

The breakdown of contracting did not spell an end to craft control, however. Even as underhands gained the right to bargain directly with the firm, work organization on the shop floor remained essentially unchanged. Indeed, with various classes of underhands now striving to control their particular occupations, craft control became even more entrenched and the collective bargaining process even more sectionalized. Such was the overall balance of power between workers and employers in the iron and steel industry, moreover, that the first national sliding-scale agreement negotiated in 1905 endured until 1940.[28] Despite conflict during the depressed conditions of the 1920s, in iron and steel, as in cotton textiles, collective agreements over work conditions and pay became "laws" of industrial relations that employers dared not challenge.

Therefore, in sharp contrast to the experiences of workers in the "nonunion era" of the U.S. iron and steel industry that lasted from the 1890s to the mid-1930s, British iron and steel workers continued to exercise substantial control over the relation between effort and pay. In particular, bargains for particular types of work that applied across all firms enabled workers to capture large shares of value gains, when and where these gains were generated. The workers' power to tie wages to productivity increases deterred the more financially solvent and potentially aggressive firms from making high-fixed-cost investments in new technologies—and hence served as an impediment to the emergence of a few dominant firms that might have enabled the British steel industry to enter the era of managerial capitalism. At the same time, the relatively low earnings of workers in low productivity plants facilitated the survival of firms that sought to rely on existing plant and equipment. Bernard Elbaum has argued that

> the prevailing industry wage structure helps account for the persistence in Britain, despite competitive pressures, of a long tail of small-scale, unmechanized open-hearth facilities. By affording such facilities relatively low labour costs, British collective bargaining arrangements protected them from competitive elimination, and added to the obstacles confronting large-scale new investment.[29]

The persistence—and, indeed, spread—of craft bargaining reinforced fragmented structures of industrial organization, also inherited from the nineteenth century, in deterring investments in best-practice steel-making technologies.

In British iron and steel, as in cotton textiles, therefore, the existence of firms too weak to exercise control over external market forces or even over their own internal organization posed obstacles to making the innovative investments that could create new foundations for sustaining the international competitive advantage that they had previously held. Confronted by the new international competition from the late nineteenth century, employers in these staple industries chose the adaptive response of cooperating with their workers on the basis of the traditional organizational structures and technologies.

A willingness to share power with workers did not, however, characterize all the manufacturing industries that had made Britain the workshop of the world. In the engineering industries that built textile machinery, steam engines, boilers, locomotives, iron ships, and agricultural implements, employers united in the late 1890s in an attempt to assert their proprietary prerogatives. In a number of dimensions, the engineering lockout of 1897–98 replicated the attack on engineering workers that had occurred almost half a century earlier in 1852. Both lockouts occurred during the upswing of the trade cycle as employers and workers sought to establish their claims to shares of value-created. Precipitating both of the lockouts, moreover, were the same workers' demands: an end to "systematic" overtime, elimination of piece-rate payments, and a ban on the use of "illegal" men. In both lockouts, the Amalgamated Society of Engineers (ASE), founded in 1850, represented the skilled workers, primarily the turners who shaped metal parts and the fitters who fitted the parts to-gether.[30]

The ASE opposed systematic overtime because it increased unem-ployment among their members during periods of slack trade. As an alternative, engineering workers could look to the cotton textile in-dustry in which workers were able to induce employers to engage in short-time working, a practice maximizing the number of workers who could share in the available wages while preventing the growth of an industrial reserve army that would pit the unemployed against the employed.[31] Like cotton textile workers, engineering workers favored short-time working during slack periods. Engineering em-ployers, however, preferred to hire fewer workers for longer hours in order to employ only those workers whom they considered the best, and in the process create divisions between the employed and unem-ployed that aided in the reduction of wages and the intensification of labor.[32] The prevalence of systematic overtime in the mechanical en-gineering industries during depressed conditions in the late 1840s and mid-1890s reflected the power of engineering employers to impose their preferences on workers—power that, relative to the cotton tex-tile industry, derived from a higher level of industrial concentration in mechanical engineering.[33]

The ASE opposed piece-rate systems, not as a matter of principle, but because in practice engineering employers had the power to use piece-rates to divide and conquer the workers in the shop-floor strug-gle over effort. In the 1852 conflict, the ASE objected in particular to the "piece-master system": the practice of subcontracting work to a skilled worker who would supervise gangs of workers paid time-wages. Unlike the mule spinners and skilled iron workers, whose unions successfully sought to preserve both internal subcontract ar-rangements and piece-rate payment systems, engineering workers found that the piece-master system enabled a small proportion of skilled workers to strike individual bargains with employers and thereby gain the right to supervise gangs of other workers, often employed on time-rates. Where possible, as in the case of the in-troduction of skill-displacing technologies, the piece-masters would employ less experienced workers, whom the displaced skilled workers deemed to be "illegal men." But even when skilled fitters and turners were employed, they found themselves in the same subordinate posi-tion as big piecers in cotton spinning, who were paid time-wages by the self-acting minders. Indeed these skilled engineering workers faced much dimmer prospects than did the big piecers of eventually becoming subcontractors themselves. Each minder generally employed one big piecer who was in line to become a minder when he entered manhood, whereas the piece-masters employed many skilled adult males, with no orderly line of promotion to piece-master status. In cotton textiles, the minder–piecer system provided the shop-floor foundation for the rise and consolidation of union power and collective bargaining after the 1840s, whereas in engineering the piece-master system served only to break down the solidarity among skilled workers.

The official reason for the 1852 lockout was to defeat workers' opposition to systematic overtime and piece-rates. But for many employers, the ultimate goal was to eliminate the ASE as an effective bargaining agent. After three months, the engineering employers emerged victorious as impecunious workers signed declarations that they would give up union membership as a condition for coming back to work. Yet, despite the apparent defeat of worker organization in mechanical engineering, during the remainder of the 1850s and the 1860s, the ASE came to epitomize "New Model" unionism that, through cooperative bargaining relations with employers, gained job security and higher wages for an emerging aristocracy of labor.[34]

During the long Victorian boom, employers found that they were reliant on the cooperation of experienced workers, particularly fitters and turners, to ensure that profitable product-market opportunities would be supplied by a large and steady flow of work on the shop floor. Keith Burgess has explained the reemergence of collective bargaining in the engineering industries:

> In the 1850s and 1860s, the district committees [of the ASE] were able to establish considerable control over 'the conditions of the trade'. This they were able to do because the fitters and turners emerged as key workers at the point of production. While careful not to question overtly employers' 'prerogatives', the ASE at branch and district level came to an *ad hoc* understanding with firms, arranging uniform rates of pay and conditions for skilled society men. Firms were willing to compromise because they recognized the bargaining strength of the fitters and turners, and as the industry's position as the 'workshop of the world' was at its zenith, they preferred in a sellers' market to get consumers to bear the cost of concessions to labour, rather than risk disputes with so indispensable a group of their employees . . . It seems that what the ASE had

failed to achieve in a direct confrontation with employers during 1851–2 it realized piecemeal in the succeeding decades. The prosperity of the industry, and the intense competition between firms, enabled the ASE to take on employers one by one and play off one against another.[35]

During these decades of strong employment and technological stability, skilled workers had little reason to complain about systematic overtime and illegal men. From the mid-1850s, the ASE made it clear that it did not object to piecework if employers and the union's district committee could settle on a mutually acceptable wage schedule.[36] In any case—perhaps because the ASE district committees gained more collective power in piece-rate bargaining—piecework and the piece-master system became less prevalent than previously. According to an 1860 survey, only 10.5 percent of ASE members in Britain were on piecework, and these primarily in Lancashire, where the standardized production of long runs of textile machines and steam engines made piece-rates potentially effective incentive mechanisms if workers could be reasonably assured that the supply of more effort would not result in piece-rate cuts.[37] Helping to provide this assurance were conditions of prosperity, technological stability, and district-wide bargaining (which standardized wage costs across firms). All these conditions reduced the pressures on employers to abrogate prior piece-rate agreements.

In 1893, with 73,000 members—most of them fitters and turners—the ASE had become the largest single union in Britain.[38] By this time, however, the cooperative relations between the ASE and employers that had evolved in the third quarter of the nineteenth century were rapidly breaking down as American and German machinery industries were mounting severe challenges to Britain's status as workshop of the world. In 1880 Britain had 63.1 percent of world exports of capital goods, but by 1899 this share had fallen to 44.2 percent. Making the greatest gains was the United States, whose share rose from 5.7 percent in 1880 to 22.5 percent in 1899, with American strengths lying in machine tools, agricultural machinery, locomotives, and sewing machines. For the British economy itself, the rise of U.S. competition in both machine tools and machinery was, by the late 1890s, being characterized as "the American invasion."[39]

Under these conditions of international competition, British engineering employers began to challenge the structures of work organization and the levels of pay that the earlier decades of prosperity and harmony had produced. As in the 1840s, so in the 1890s the introduction of skill-displacing machine tools led employers to hire less skilled and less expensive labor in place of ASE members, while the new competition prompted employers to disavow existing arrangements for the sharing of value-created. Once again in the mid-1890s, ASE opposition to systematic overtime, piece-rates, and illegal men came to the fore. Despite its size and entrenched position as a New Model union, the ASE was much more vulnerable than the Amalgamated Cotton Spinners because it organized only about half of the fitters and turners in the engineering industry. In cotton spinning, moreover, the piecers were directly dependent upon the minders for their employment and indeed aspired to become minders. But in engineering there was an ample supply of less skilled, adult male workers whose employment was independent of the fitters and turners and who had no avenues of entry into the ranks of the skilled. These semiskilled workers were willing and able to operate the new machine tools.[40]

As had typically been the case with British working-class movements of the nineteenth century, the ASE sought to unify and build its national membership by campaigning for a shorter workday (in this case, eight hours). In 1896 the engineering employers reacted by forming the Engineering Employers' Federation (EEF).[41] As the introduction of American machine tools quickened in the last half of the 1890s (particularly during the boom in bicycle manufacture that permitted the use of mass-production methods), employers renewed the assault on craft control that they had failed to carry through almost a half-century before.

Like the 1852 lockout and the defeat of the workers, the 1897–98 lockout ended with ASE members going back to work on the employers' terms. Jonathan Zeitlin has summed up the "Terms of Settlement" that the ASE executive was ultimately forced to sign:

> Employers were henceforth free to hire non-unionists; to institute piece-work systems at prices agreed with the individual worker; to demand up to forty hours overtime per man per month; to pay non-unionists at individual rates; to employ as many apprentices as they chose; and to place any suitable worker on any machine at a mutually agreed rate. In addition, the Terms of Settlement established a novel disputes procedure according to which no strike could occur without first going through a national conference between the union executive and the EEF. In this way, the Federation hoped to contain

rank and file resistance to the re-organization of the division of labour by forcing the ASE executive to discipline its members through the constant threat of a national lock-out.[42]

Yet the defeat of the ASE was only partial, particularly when compared with the eradication of collective bargaining in the metalworking industries of the United States in the early decades of this century. The very insistence by the EEF that the ASE sign the Terms of Settlement shows that British engineering employers accepted collective bargaining as a fact of industrial life. Zeitlin has argued:

> To be sure, [EEF President] Col. Dyer waxed euphoric over the regime of managerial prerogative introduced by Carnegie at the Homestead works, while the head of the London employers' association hinted that the unions might find themselves excluded from the ultimate settlement between masters and men. But even the most sanguinary expostulations of employers' spokesmen made it clear that craft regulation rather than trade unionism *per se* was their principal target, and the EEF for its part insisted throughout the dispute that it aimed not to smash the ASE, but to establish managerial prerogative once and for all.[43]

If American employers insisted on, and won, the *right* to manage, British employers had to be content merely to struggle over, as they themselves put it, the *power* to manage. Their right to manage had been irrevocably lost sometime and somewhere in the last half of the nineteenth century.

As it turned out, even the power to manage was severely circumscribed in British engineering firms after the turn of the century by the tendency to rely on experienced workers to coordinate the shop-floor division of labor. Between the end of the lockout in 1898 and World War I, British engineering employers did invest in more automatic machine tools, and they did employ less expensive labor to perform many tasks. The problem is that, unlike their American counterparts, most British firms failed to make the investments in managerial structures that, in conjunction with the mass-production technologies, were needed to take control of work off the shop floor. Like the cotton textile and steel industries, British engineering firms chose the low-cost strategy of relying on shop-floor workers to run their production processes. In 1914 some 60 percent of the labor force in firms that belonged to the EEF was classified as "skilled"—a classification that may have been more an indication of the persistence of craft control than an indication of the persistence of difficult-to-replicate craft skills.[44]

In the decade after the signing of the Terms of Settlement, EEF firms might have taken satisfaction in their enhanced "power to manage" as demonstrated by their ability to increase the proportion of workers on piecework. In 1886, 6 percent of fitters and turners and 11 percent of machinists in British engineering were on piecework; by 1906 these numbers had climbed to 33 percent and 47 percent, respectively, with most of the increase apparently coming after the defeat of the workers in 1898.[45] Yet the spread of piecework manifested the power of employers to manage wage levels, not their power to manage the labor process. In relying on "payment by results" as a means of enticing more work out of shop-floor labor, British engineering employers left responsibility for ensuring the coordination of the flow of work with workers on the shop floor.

To implement payment by results—whether straight piece-rates or premium bonus systems (which combined standard time-rates with piece-rate supplements that diminished with greater output)—employers increasingly relied on the negotiating and coordinating abilities of shop stewards, workers' representatives drawn from the ranks of shop-floor operatives. James Hinton has outlined the evolution of the shop stewards' roles:

From 1892 shop stewards were officially appointed by the union, responsible for card-checking, joining up new members, inspecting pay-lines, receiving complaints from members and reporting back to the District Committee. By 1909 shop stewards had been appointed in most major engineering centres . . . Shop stewards did not [however] confine themselves to supplying information and undertaking organizational work on behalf of the District Committees. The tradition of workshop delegates serving on deputations to their employers continued, and the workshop deputation was a recognized part of the collective bargaining procedures of the industry after 1898. To an increasing extent before 1914 the ad hoc workshop deputation crystallized into a shop stewards' committee engaged in regular negotiations. This was especially so where piece work was practised since prices, negotiated job by job, could not be brought under any centralized procedure.[46]

Hinton quoted a 1918 Ministry of Labor publication to the effect that " 'the extension of piecework and the growth of the method of collective bargaining in the shops by Works Committees of stewards, have gone side by side, and it would appear that, to a considerable degree, the one is the immediate cause of the other.' "[47]

Far from eradicating collective bargaining, the reliance of British engineering employers on "payments by results" entrenched the conflict over the relation between effort and pay on the shop floor. Making matters worse for employers was their lack of control over foremen, who were often ASE members.[48] For British engineering employers to take control of work off the shop floor, they had to invest in management structures that could plan and coordinate shop-floor activities. By and large, British engineering employers did not make these investments in organization.

From 1909, shop-floor control and plant-level bargaining became the basis for a resurgence of labor militancy that led to the replacement of the old ASE executive who had sought to help employers enforce the Terms of Settlement with a new one that dedicated itself to protecting craft control. In 1913, the same year that the cotton spinners withdrew from the Brooklands Agreement, the ASE unilaterally rejected the Terms of Settlement.[49] Craft militancy among engineering workers gained momentum during World War I, in part to ensure that "dilution" of the division of labor because of a massive influx of women into the industry would not be permanent. In 1914 the ASE had 170,000 members, up from fewer than 100,000 in 1897. By 1918 membership was close to 300,000; and by 1920, under the newly formed Amalgamated Engineering Union (AEU), about 450,000.[50]

Membership in the EEF also grew, however; from 714 firms in 1914 to 1,469 in 1918 and 2,600 in 1921.[51] In 1922 the EEF, in yet another attempt to regain the power to manage, locked out the workers, and once again the workers were forced to return to work after a few months on the employers' terms. But the very number of member firms in the EEF in the 1920s reflected a degree of industrial fragmentation born of decades of the failure of a smaller number of firms to concentrate the industry by gaining distinct competitive advantage through investments in organizational structure and technology. As in the aftermath of the signing of the 1898 Terms of Settlement, engineering employers used their 1922 victory to continue the shift from time-wages to payment by results. In 1914, 31 percent of engineering workers were paid by the piece; and in 1918, 41 percent. By 1927 pieceworkers were 49 percent of all engineering workers.[52] Engineering employers continued to rely on the manipulation of piece-rates to elicit effort from workers rather than build managerial structures that could exercise direct control.

Leaving Control on the Shop Floor

During the 1920s and 1930s, in the newer and expanding engineering industries such as motor vehicles and electrical equipment, British firms invested in mass-production machinery that permitted them to shift from skilled to semiskilled workers. The EEF victory of 1922 had rid these new industries of formal collective bargaining, thus ushering in a nonunion era of labor–management relations that would persist throughout the interwar years. Yet, quite in contrast to the development of mass production in the United States, in these new British industries that became central to the growth of the British economy, substantial control over the organization of work remained with workers on the shop floor.[53]

As I shall show in Chapters 7 and 8, by investing in managerial structures that could coordinate the flow of work and by implementing personnel policies to induce shop-floor workers to cooperate in the achievement of high levels of throughput, U.S. mass producers had, by the 1920s, taken the control of work off the shop floor. Through multinational investments in Britain, the American mode of shop-floor management was, to some extent, transported across the Atlantic. Most notably, the Ford Motor Company, which began operations in Britain in 1911, invested in management capabilities to plan and coordinate the flow of work on the shop floor. Given these investments, including reliance on close supervision of shop-floor workers by foremen who were integrated into the management structure, Ford chose to pay its workers time-wages. In Britain, as in the United States, Ford used a high-wage policy to gain the cooperation of its shop-floor workers.[54]

But as Wayne Lewchuk has demonstrated in his comparative study of the British and American motor vehicle industries, the British mass producers chose not to invest in managerial structures to plan and coordinate their shop-floor investments in mass-production machinery. Instead, they relied extensively on payment by results to elicit effort from workers on the shop floor. Stressing the critical organizational difference between the American and British systems of automobile production, Lewchuk has argued:

> The majority of British motor vehicle workers in the 1930s could not be classified as skilled workers. In fact, the production techniques used were surprisingly similar to those found in many American factories. New types of machinery and the emergence of volume production drastically reduced the skill required from individual workers. The most striking contrast between the American and British system was the limited extent to which British management had been able to exert direct control over labour effort norms and the limited extent to which management had claimed responsibility for organising the work place. Labour retained a significant say over the setting of effort norms and the organisation of work, while management controlled the process by which piece-rate prices were set allowing them to control the ratio of wages to effort.[55]

During the 1930s, when the major car producers were making large profits, motor vehicle workers received wages that were toward the high end of the earnings scale of engineering workers, with piece-workers in the automobile industry doing especially well.[56] With the level of piece-rate incentives under management control, workers had to supply enough effort to earn a decent wage but not so much as to provoke rate cuts. To avoid frequent rate-cutting that would have prompted workers to engage in restriction of output (see the Appendix), employers implemented premium bonus systems that were designed to provide workers with diminishing returns to increased output. But, without close supervision or significant managerial coordination of the flow of work between shop-floor processes, the supply of effort remained under the control of workers.

So that workers would not have the opportunity to engage in collective bargaining over the level of piece-rates, employers in nonunion engineering firms tended to avoid group incentives, preferring instead to enter into informal piece-rate bargains with individual workers for performing particular tasks.[57] In the process of demarcating tasks for purposes of rate-setting in a particular workplace, a de facto shop-floor division of labor emerged. The use of individual rates also placed pressure on shop-floor workers to ensure that the flow of work proceeded apace from one productive activity to the next—a system for sustaining throughput that, from the turn of the century, was termed "induction."[58] Particularly in the interwar era of slack labor markets during which workers were less inclined to use shop-floor control to restrict output, British managers were content to leave the coordination of throughput to the workers.

The functions of setting piece-rates and hiring and firing workers were left in the hands of rate-fixers and foremen, with little in the way of coordination of personnel policies from above. Again in contrast with U.S. practice in mass-production industries in the interwar period, personnel departments were virtually nonexistent in British firms. The first-line supervisors in turn tended to rely on workers' representatives—the shop stewards—to help create coherence out of the shop-floor anarchy. In the tighter labor markets of late 1930s, shop stewards, whose roles had been suppressed in the depressed conditions of the 1920s, reemerged as key organizational figures in the coordination of the production process and as the bargaining agents of their fellow workers.[59]

In an industry such as motor vehicles, informal bargaining based on shop stewards had generally preceded formal union recognition, precisely because management preferred bargaining with individual workers and their shop stewards to confronting the collective power that would come with union recognition.[60] In the 1940s and 1950s, as in the interwar period, workplace bargaining was left in the hands of lower level managers—rate-fixers and first-line supervisors—and within the enterprise the informal shop-floor bargaining process took place independently of whatever planning and coordination was occurring higher up the enterprise hierarchy.

During the full employment decades of the 1950s and 1960s, the mass-production metalworking industries became increasingly unionized, a situation creating the possibility of taking bargaining over wages and work conditions off the shop floor. But in the absence of managerial planning and coordination of production activities, "custom and practice" became the foundations for workplace bargaining, leaving shop stewards with considerable leverage in interpreting the customs and practices of the workplaces that they knew so well—and about which managers above the first-line supervisors knew so little.[61] As the authors of a well-known study of labor relations in the car industry in the mid-1960s argued:

> In a sense, the leading stewards are performing a managerial function, of grievance settlement, welfare arrangement and human adjustment, and the steward system's acceptance by managements

(and thus in turn, the facility with which the stewards themselves can satisfy their members' demands and needs) has developed partly because of the increasing effectiveness—and certainly economy—with which this role is fulfilled.[62]

Given the absence of personnel management structures in major British firms, the organization imposed by shop stewards was critical for maintaining labor peace and eliciting high levels of effort from shop-floor workers.

In the 1950s shop stewards were particularly predominant in the metalworking industries, but in the 1960s and 1970s the model of shop steward representation spread across all unionized manufacturing sectors.[63] Reliance on shop stewards enabled British industrialists to continue to avoid investments in personnel management, while creating a coherent, if informal, system of workplace relations.

Economically, the system of workplace bargains benefited both employers and workers as long as existing technologies and workplace practices could generate sufficient productivity to enable British firms to compete at home and abroad. But already by the early 1960s, as the Germans and Japanese, among others, joined the Americans in capturing world manufacturing markets, British mass-production industry was facing an increasingly competitive international environment. An adequate long-run response required new investments in high-throughput technologies, which in turn required significant—and, in most cases, dramatic—alterations in shop-floor "custom and practice" to make them pay. At the same time, reliance on payment by results and "informal" shop-floor bargaining were resulting in upward "wage drift"—the power of workers to capture the value gains from productivity growth by either preventing rate-cutting or negotiating favorable new rates in the presence of (often minor) technological change. The results were inflationary pressures in the British economy and an erosion of profits for British industry.[64]

The 1960s saw the public recognition of the central role of workplace bargaining in British industrial relations. The growing independence of shop-floor bargaining from the structure of industry-wide collective negotiations and agreements prompted the convening in 1965 of the Royal Commission on Trade Unions and Employers' Associations—better known as the Donovan Commission. The publication in 1968 of the *Donovan Report* focused widespread attention on the persistence of craft regulation of the shop floor in an age of mass production. The Donovan Commission recognized the existence of two systems in British industrial relations, one formal and the other informal. The formal system consisted of industry-wide collective agreements that were supposed to govern labor–management relations; the informal system consisted of workplace bargaining based on, as the *Report* put it, "the actual behaviour of trade unions and employers' associations, of managers, shop stewards and workers." The Commission argued that

> the extent to which at the moment industry-wide agreements both on pay and other issues are effective in the workplace cannot be exactly determined. What is of critical importance is that the practices of the formal system have become increasingly empty, while the practices of the informal system have come to exert an ever greater influence on the conduct of industrial relations throughout the country; that the two systems conflict and the informal system cannot be forced to comply with the formal system.[65]

Michael Terry has summed up the Donovan Commission's findings:

> All this shopfloor activity was seen to happen without the formal approval of a senior manager. The bargaining process, if indeed bargaining was involved, took place between workers and their representatives and the lowest level of management organisation— foremen and ratefixers—often without the knowledge and approval of senior management. In other words, much was attributed to the loose or inadequate nature of management control systems that enabled informal deals to go unregistered and unchecked.[66]

Even prior to the findings of the Donovan Commission, in the face of the productivity crisis of the 1960s, senior managements had begun to take notice of their lack of control over the shop floor. Their strategy was not to attack the labor movement but to incorporate it by recognizing national unions in the hope that the formal system of bargaining would be able to contain the informal. But, as the Donovan Commission concluded, the subordination of shop-floor bargaining to the "official system" was generally not the case. National agreements, negotiated between the union leadership and employer representatives, could not be implemented on the shop floor because the managerial structures were not in place within enterprises to enforce these agreements.[67]

A fundamental managerial problem was top management's failure to gain control over supervisory workers, never mind operatives. As John Child and Bruce Partridge have argued in a book on British supervisors:

> [Since] the mid-1960s, supervisors in Britain have given notice in increasing numbers that their loyalty to, and willingness to depend upon, their employer can no longer be taken for granted. The erosion of their differentials and privileges over shopfloor workers, the vulnerability of their authority to pressures from organized employees, and the threat of redundancy, have all been powerful reasons for supervisors to unionize.[68]

By the late 1970s, about 40 percent of British supervisors had become members of trade unions.[69]

Particularly in the mechanical engineering industries in which it remained possible to attain technological expertise without a higher education, lack of managerial control over line personnel extended to technical specialists in general. It is of significance in this regard that, contrary to American usage, in Britain even in the second half of the twentieth century, the term *engineer* continued to connote a skilled craft worker. But even the more highly trained technical specialists whose skills and knowledge were more comparable to the American professional engineer remained unintegrated into British management structures, in large part because even in the 1960s only a small proportion of them had undergone the university training that, as will be indicated in the next chapter, was from the beginning of the century so important in transforming professional engineers into "organization men" in the United States.

As a result, in sharp contrast to the way in which cohesive management structures were built in U.S. manufacturing enterprises, the training and promotion of lower-level "managers" in British industrial organizations kept them more closely integrated with shop-floor workers below than with general managers above.[70] A study of the occupational mobility of British managerial personnel between the mid-1960s and mid-1970s found that production and site managers were drawn mainly from supervisory positions or craft occupations. Of those employees in the study who had been classified as "managers" in 1965, 17 percent had been demoted to an operative occupation ten years later. And only 4 percent of the 2,637 employees classified as managers in the 1975 sample had begun their careers in a managerial occupation. Across all managerial categories, the first jobs of at least one fifth, and perhaps as many as half, of those in the sample were as semiskilled operatives.[71] In general, even those British industrial enterprises that employed significant numbers of managerial personnel had not fashioned the integrated lines of authority and bodies of knowledge among those personnel that were basic preconditions for exercising managerial control over work organization on the shop floor.

In the absence of integrated managerial structures, attempts in the aftermath of the *Donovan Report* to reduce the role of the "informal system" of bargaining only served to reinforce the pivotal "managerial" role of the shop steward and further entrench worker control on the shop floor. Eric Batstone argued that

> industrial relations reform rarely constituted a fundamental challenge to the way in which work was organized. By seeking marginally to change working practices, it confirmed the notions of job territory and property rights which underlay so much of British industrial organization . . . Far from removing job-based control, industrial relations reform may have led to a more explicit recognition and legitimation of job-based controls in the 1970s.[72]

Some firms sought to move from payment by results to "measured day work" to stem wage drift. Measured day work entailed the payment of fixed time-wages, combined with an increase in supervisory personnel. But, as already indicated, by the 1960s and 1970s the actions of supervisors were often more controlled by shop stewards from below than by managers from above. While the shift to measured day work did away with the ability of workers to manipulate piece-rates in their favor, it did not solve the problem of the relation between effort and pay. At Chrysler (UK) in 1968, for example, workers agreed to allow management to control the speed of the "track" (the assembly line) but retained the right to determine the number of workers per unit of capital.[73] Simply changing the mode of wage payment, and even adding supervisory personnel, did not give management the power to manage. Indeed, falling productivity in the early 1970s led many automobile manufacturers who had shifted to measured day work to revert to payment by results.

A potentially more profound mode of creating incentives for workers to provide more effort for more pay (with measured day work perhaps representing one component) was "productivity bargaining." The idea was that workers would agree to give up "restrictive prac-

tices" such as overmanning, rigid job demarcations, and explicit output limitations in return for higher earnings and greater employment
security. The assumption was that increased managerial control over
the organization and pace of work could result in positive-sum outcomes in which both sides could share.

In the first half of the 1960s, a number of firms had sought with
some success to replicate the successful experiment in productivity
bargaining at the Fawley oil refinery of ESSO in 1960. Beginning in
1966, productivity bargaining became tied to government incomes
policy; a firm could pay its workers more than the limit on annual
wage increases set by the government as part of its antiinflation policy
if the firm were to implement changes in work organization that
would yield productivity gains to warrant the extra payments. In the
period 1967–1969, there were over 4,000 productivity agreements in
Britain, covering almost 6 million workers, with over one quarter of
the agreements and workers covered in the engineering (including
vehicles) and electrical goods industries.[74]

As the popularity of productivity bargaining grew, the suspicion
arose that many deals lacked productivity substance but were merely
put in place to get around the government's income policies. More
seriously in terms of generating the value gains that were the raison
d'être of productivity bargaining, there was a tendency inherent in the
process for workers to develop restrictive work practices so that they
would have something that management could buy out, especially
under the conditions of growing unemployment in the 1970s.[75] The
attempt to use productivity bargaining to eliminate wage drift had
merely resulted in "effort drift": a progressive downward (and infla-
tion-generating) movement in the level of effort expended per worker
per workday. Far from overcoming restrictive practices inherent in
the persistence of craft control, the productivity bargaining experiments of the 1960s and 1970s often served to entrench craft control
even further.

So, too, managerial attempts to reform the workplace in the 1970s
took the critical "managerial" positions of the shop stewards as a
starting point, seeking to make the shop stewards useful to the re-
formed managerial structures. Some observers, on both the left and
the right, thought that the managements of the major firms would be
able to incorporate the shop stewards into their management structures. Such an outcome may have been possible at a company like
Ford that had spent decades building a managerial structure and

managing the labor process. But for those British companies that had for decades been content to leave the control of work on the shop floor and, the other side of the coin, to neglect the development of management structures, the result was to create shop stewards' organizations within plants and companies that, in a period of stagflation, became an even more powerful force than the "informal system" of the 1960s in constraining managerial prerogative.[76]

Despite the increased awareness and resolve that followed the *Donovan Report,* therefore, employers' attempts during the 1970s to restructure work organization and alter the relation between work and pay represented adaptations to the preexisting structures of workplace control, primarily because British employers generally failed to invest in management structures that could have taken control off the shop floor. One exception that proves the rule is that of British Leyland (BL) under Michael Edwardes from 1977 to 1982. Edwardes's mission was to invest in modern high-throughput technology and to gain the right to manage it. His regime confronted the BL shop stewards' organization and built a new managerial structure to replace it. Previously there had been 58 bargaining units at BL for workers on hourly wages; by late 1979 there was one. Certainly the high unemployment levels generated by the "Thatcher recession" of 1979–1981 aided Edwardes's tasks of enforcing labor discipline (although the strong pound sterling and the high interest rates that were key features of that recession took their toll on profits). What seems clear is that a concerted attempt to transform shop-floor organization through managerial planning and coordination did have a discernible positive impact on shop-floor value creation.[77]

Such concerted attempts at planned coordination of the labor process do not, however, appear to have been characteristic of British manufacturing industry in the 1980s—or at least what was left of it after Thatcher's policies had helped to reduce Britain's manufacturing output by over 14 percent from 1979 to 1981.[78] Rather than building up organizational structures, and complementary educational institutions, that could overcome the historical underdevelopment of management in Britain, the dominant tendency of the Thatcher era has been to create financial pressures and social conflicts that tears these structures and institutions apart. Rather than make the long-term employment commitments to workers that, as I shall show in the following chapters, have become increasingly important for the effective utilization of effort-saving technologies, during the 1980s British employers tended to rely on high levels of unemployment to shift the balance of power away from the trade union movement and enforce labor discipline on the shop floor.

Between 1979 and 1983, British manufacturing employment fell by some 22 percent, a loss of over 1.5 million jobs, with male full-time employees bearing the brunt of the job losses. Over these four years, union membership in Britain fell by almost 16 percent.[79] With these huge employment losses, the rate of productivity growth in manufacturing moved sharply upward, averaging about 6 percent per annum between 1980 and 1984, in part the result of an increase in labor effort by workers afraid that their plants might close, but probably more the result of the actual closing of the most inefficient plants. During the first three years of the Thatcher reign, real hourly earnings in manufacturing fell somewhat, although after 1982 wages recovered sharply. Workdays lost through strikes dropped dramatically from the 29 million plus figure of 1979 (the highest since 1926) to around 4 million days a year during 1981–1983. Although the days-lost figure soared in 1984 because of the miners' strike, the failure of that strike, along with antiunion legislation, certainly helped to contain labor militancy during the remainder of the 1980s.[80]

Despite the unions' defensive position in the 1980s, however, their members continued to hold their ground on the shop floor. For as I have shown, during the post–World War II decades, British manufacturing developed a "two-tier" structure of collective bargaining, in which "formal" bargaining between union leaders and companies was relatively impotent compared with "informal" shop-floor bargaining. In the attempts to reform the industrial-relations system during the 1970s, moreover, the "informal" system had become more formalized and entrenched. This system of shop-floor bargaining— the legacy of craft control—has not disappeared under Thatcher. In manufacturing between 1980 and 1984 the decline of shop stewards was slower than the decline in employment, and across all sectors of the economy the number of shop stewards actually increased. John MacInnes concluded that "these results suggest that the basic institutions of workplace trade unionism survived the economic and legal assault of Thatcherism."[81]

In a 1989 review of changes in British industrial relations during the Thatcher decade, P. K. Edwards and Keith Sisson have confirmed this assessment. They argued:

Trade unions have been on the defensive, and they have faced major challenges in coming to terms with legal and employer-led initiatives. But they have not been wiped out, and they appear to have retained a degree of influence on the pattern of change through informal processes of negotiation and compromise. British industrial relations have long been characterised by informality and the settlement of issues through unwritten agreements. This tendency remains, and in it unions retain such influence as they have.[82]

"Surveys agree," said Edwards and Sisson, "that removal of recognition rights for trade unions and efforts to reduce the numbers of shop stewards have been rare."[83]

The continuing centrality of shop-floor bargaining in British industry is less the result of what unions have done than what British employers have not done. Summarizing the studies of changes in work organization in British firms during the 1980s, Edwards and Sisson found "the absence of an integrated and coherent employment policy." They also found that the British firms gave a "low priority" to the training and development of managers—never mind shop-floor workers—viewing training as a short-run cost, not a long-term investment.[84]

The stick of unemployment, accompanied by repressive labor law, may have shifted relative power in the determination of the "effort bargain" away from workers and toward employers in Britain. But the attack on the union movement has by no means eliminated shop-floor workers from entering into and influencing the effort bargain as interested parties bent on protecting their work conditions and maintaining their jobs in a highly uncertain world. To get work done, British management must secure the cooperation of workers. If British industrial enterprises are not willing to invest in managerial structures that can take the coordination of work organization off the shop floor, as appears to have been the case during the 1980s, they will have no alternative but to continue to rely on shop-floor workers to manage their production processes for them, with all the power, however informal, that such a function implies.

Without these investments in organization, British industry will continue its long-term relative decline. As the next chapter documents, in the late nineteenth and early twentieth centuries, U.S. industrial managers took control of the shop floor by taking skills away from workers and vesting them in both effort-saving machinery and salaried personnel within managerial structures. Today's international industrial competition, as I shall show in Chapters 9 and 10, requires much more. Business organizations must develop the skills of shop-floor workers as well as those of managers and integrate both groups of people into cohesive organizational structures to ensure the effective utilization of these skills. Through the 1980s, British industrial enterprises appear to have made only a limited organizational response to the realities of the new competition, emanating primarily from Japan. Indeed, by the 1980s, British industrial enterprises had as yet failed to make an adequate organizational response to the realities of the old competition—U.S. managerial capitalism that dominated the international economy in the first half of this century and displaced Britain as the workshop of the world.

7 Managerial Capitalism and Economies of Speed

Changing Industrial Leadership

In the twentieth century the manufacture of cotton textiles would continue to provide the foundations for the economic growth of newly industrializing economies, foremost among them Japan, just as it had for Britain from the late eighteenth century and the United States from the early nineteenth century. In 1880 cotton goods represented 5.2 percent of the value of U.S. output, and in 1914 still accounted for 4.2 percent. Over this period, however, the fastest growing industries were those manufacturing metal durables (office equipment, motor vehicles, and locomotives among them) and products that required the integration of science into industrial practice (primarily rubber products, chemicals, petroleum refining, and electrical equipment).[1] Metal replaced wood as the primary industrial material; the value of iron and steel production increased from 4.1 percent of national output to 7.5 percent, and nonferrous metals from 1.5 to 4.3 percent, while the value of sawmill and planing mill products fell from 11.3 to 5.7 percent. It was in the science-based and metalworking industries that the dynamic interaction of organization and technology was to play the leading role in transforming high fixed costs into low unit costs.

The United States, along with Germany, assumed international leadership in the "second industrial revolution" of the late nineteenth and early twentieth centuries. American dominance was particularly marked in the mass production of metal durables that required both high fixed-cost capital investments and extensive use of shop-floor labor. Meanwhile the British economy entered into long-run relative decline. Since the late nineteenth century, British rates of growth of productivity and exports have consistently lagged behind the rates achieved by its major international competitors.[2] Although British industry could not match U.S. growth in the consumer durable and science-based products, nevertheless, within Britain's own economy, electrical engineering and motor vehicles were its fastest growing manufactures.[3] More than a failure to shift quickly enough into new industries, the lackluster performance of the British economy in the twentieth century stems from a failure to transform the institutions of nineteenth-century capitalism in ways that could respond to the new international competition.[4]

In the passing of industrial leadership from Britain to the United States in the early decades of this century, the institutional character of capitalism changed dramatically. Joint-stock corporations replaced proprietorships and partnerships as the predominant form of enterprise ownership, the separation of asset ownership from managerial control lifting the financial and managerial constraints on firm expansion. Those businesses that grew large through horizontal and vertical combination as well as internal growth came to depend on managerial hierarchies to plan and coordinate their multiregional and multifunctional activities.

A key feature of managerial capitalism was a shift in control over shop-floor work organization from craftsmen on the shop floor to line and staff personnel within the managerial hierarchy. As advocated and abetted by the scientific management movement, the role of managers was to organize, whereas that of workers was simply to perform. However much Marx misunderstood the relation between technology and organization in the evolution of British capitalism, his argument that, by making craft skills obsolete, capitalist investments in technology tended to "degrade [the laborer] to the level of an appendage of a machine"[5] was an appropriate depiction of U.S. shop-floor experience in the twentieth century. Unlike the British, U.S. industrialists built managerial structures designed to exercise control over work organization on the shop floor.

In combination with effort-saving technological change, managerial control carried with it the potential to effect internal economies that could permit a firm to attain and sustain competitive advantage. The greater the fixed costs inherent in a firm's investment strategy, the more important was planning and coordination of work organization to transform high fixed costs into low unit costs. Like combined investments in ring spinning and automatic weaving in cotton textiles, for example, a strategy of vertical integration of productive activities added to the firm's fixed costs but created the potential for managerial coordination of the flow of materials and work-in-progress to achieve higher levels of throughput and greater economies of speed than would have been possible on the basis of market coordination.

The Impediment of Craft Control

In both Britain and the United States in the late nineteenth century, however, craft control of shop-floor work organization obstructed the achievement of economies of speed by the utilization of effort-saving technological change. Craft unions, of course, sought to secure high wages for their members. But, as the Ford Motor Company was to demonstrate dramatically in the mid-1910s, high wages did not create problems for the capitalist firm if workers contributed sufficient effort to generate sufficient value gains. If enough economies of speed could be achieved, then management could (if need be) share some of the value gains with workers while still paying the going rate of return on finance and increasing the size of the managerial surplus.[6] In addition, the firm might even be able to lower its prices to consumers and expand its market share, a pricing strategy that in turn lowered unit costs by spreading out fixed costs. What concerned the managers of high fixed-cost production facilities much more than the ability of craft unions to bargain for high wages was the likelihood that craft control over the organization of work would impede the flow of work through the production process.

Because the power of craft unions was based on control over particular trades, craft organizations were not prepared to coordinate the specialized division of labor even within a single workplace, let alone across vertically related, and often geographically dispersed, production sites. On the contrary, in the face of managerial attempts to restructure shop-floor divisions of labor, as was generally the case after the introduction of a new technology, the strategy of craft unions was to demarcate the tasks that belonged to their particular trades. Craft organizations, therefore, had neither the ability nor the incentive to speed the flow of work through a vertically integrated structure.

Basic to the protection of the craft was the maintenance of control over the training of the next generation of workers, typically through on-the-job apprenticeship procedures. In the face of managerial attempts to develop new types of workers consistent with the cognitive and behavioral needs of the new technologies, craft unions sought to train workers who would maintain the traditions of the trade.

Finally, craft workers sought to maintain control over manning ratios, the pace of work, and wages. Their goals were to protect the quality of both their working lives and the goods that they produced, as well as, for any given level of product demand, the amount of work available to the members of their trade. Craftsmen viewed managerial attempts to stretch out and speed up their work as a prelude to either layoffs or piece-rate cuts once new norms for output per worker had been achieved. The response of craft workers to managerial attempts to alter the relation between effort and pay was to organize their crafts more thoroughly to maintain existing standards. Workers wanted what they considered to be a fair day's work for a fair day's pay. Management, however, eager to achieve high levels of through-put on the basis of their investments in process technology, viewed the craft workers' attempts to control the pace of work as restriction of output.

Faced with the existence of craft unions, managers had to decide whether to work within the constraints of existing craft control or to take steps to oust the unions and fashion a new industrial relations system more appropriate to the planned coordination of high-throughput production processes. British employers generally chose to accommodate the craft workers; U.S. employers, to confront them. British firms often continued to invest in the traditional technologies that could make use of craft skills, leaving the training of a fresh supply of workers to on-the-job apprenticeship systems. Because craft workers retained bargaining power over the relation between effort and pay, restriction of output was to some extent overcome on the traditional technologies; workers had the power to ensure that more effort would result in higher earnings. To maintain employment levels, however, British workers still resisted increases in the number of machines per worker.

American managers were unwilling to let workers have a voice in determining the relation between effort and pay on the shop floor. They wanted to maintain control over unit costs and hence the returns that the firm could reap from investments in new plant and equipment. To understand the different responses of American and British managers to the technological opportunities of the late nineteenth and early twentieth centuries, it is necessary to explore how, historically, the dynamic interaction of technology and organization in U.S. industry differed from that in British industry.

American Technological Leadership

The origins of U.S. technological (as distinct from industrial or economic) leadership go back to the early nineteenth century. Even before Britain had completed the world's first industrial revolution, the United States had already assumed the lead in the adoption of effort-saving technologies that made management less reliant on shop-floor skills.

Since the publication in the early 1960s of the provocative book by H. J. Habbakuk, *American and British Technology in the Nineteenth Century,* economic historians have both recognized the early technological lead of American industry and debated its economic rationale.[7] But, in keeping with the neoclassical methodology that I critiqued in Chapter 4, these economic historians have focused their arguments almost exclusively on the impact of relative factor prices in the two countries on the choice of technique, without considering the impact of relative factor costs—that is, the combination of prices and the physical productivities of the inputs into the production process. The implicit assumption is that physical productivity is inherent in a given technology, so only differences in relative factor prices can affect economic choices. Economic historians who argue exclusively in terms of relative factor prices lack a theory of value creation that comprehends the dynamic interaction of factor prices and physical productivity.

Because production relations affect throughput, the value-created on a given technology is not independent of the social context in which the technology is used. Because factor prices are not merely returns to the owners of factor inputs but also incentives for those owners to supply their resources—be they human, physical, or financial—to the value-creation process, the amount of value-created in a given production process depends on the expectations of different participants of their prospective shares in value gains. These expectations are, in turn, a function of the social power, either individual or collective, available to participants to capture shares in value gains.

The power that American workers had in the nineteenth century was the individual power of mobility. Compared with his British counterpart, the early American industrialist had faced a scarcity of skilled labor suitable to work the technologies, such as the common mule, that characterized the British Industrial Revolution. The problem was not an absence of skilled labor in the United States in the nineteenth century. On the contrary, throughout the century skilled labor came to the United States from Europe, and primarily from Britain and Germany, precisely because their skills were in excess supply in their native lands. The geographic mobility of skilled workers and the opportunities for self-employment in the United States meant that the locally concentrated pools of specialized labor resources that were so important to the success of the British Industrial Revolution were not available in the New World. When labor, skilled or otherwise, was hired in the United States, it came at a relatively high wage and, given alternative employment opportunities, went elsewhere when it more or less pleased. The American industrial capitalist looked, therefore, to investments in skill-displacing technology (often complemented by protected home markets) to overcome the competitive disadvantages inherent in a work force whose wages were high and whose discipline was low.

By mid-century a distinctive "American system of manufactures" had emerged in the woodworking and metalworking industries. The lead in technological innovation came in armaments where assured government orders justified high fixed-cost investments in special-purpose machinery and managerial personnel.[8] Indeed, some of the pioneering efforts occurred in government-owned armories. The focus of technological change, and the key to achieving high throughput without sacrificing product quality, was the large-scale machine production of interchangeable parts that did not require the application of skilled labor in assembly.

Analogous investments in skill-displacing technologies were also occurring in other mass-production industries, most notably in the Lowell system of cotton textile manufacture that brought the factory system to the United States. Prior to the investments by a group of wealthy Boston families—the Boston Associates as they were called—in the complex of factories at Lowell, Massachusetts during the 1820s and 1830s, the Slater system of production had been in the forefront of cotton textile manufacture in the United States. In the Slater system, operated in southern New England, only spinning was carried out on a factory basis, with the output of yarn either offered for sale on the market or put out to domestic weavers. Labor for the spinning mills was recruited from surrounding family farms, to which textile operatives gave their primary work commitments and from which they often derived their primary sources of income.[9] The Slater system experienced difficulty in imposing time discipline on such a labor force, still attuned as the workers were to the work rhythms of agricultural life.

The Lowell system overcame the dependence of American factories on rural labor in what was still in the 1820s and 1830s a predominantly rural economy.[10] Rather than rely on domestic weavers, the Lowell capitalists invested in powerlooms (developed initially by the prototypical Boston Manufacturing Company started in 1815 by some of the same Boston capitalists) to be used in factories that integrated spinning and weaving. They also invested in a system of dormitory habitation that, for periods of a few months to a few years, housed Yankee farm girls. Under this system, the girls were transferred from their New England homes to an environment where, for their parents at least, the close monitoring of their comings and goings was considered necessary to protect their femininity rather than to exploit their labor. With appropriate supervision, the Lowell labor force could now be counted on to respond to factory bells rather than to cow bells.

In the spinning process, the need for skilled labor was avoided by adopting the throstle, a continuous spinning machine (a precursor to ring spinning) that in Britain by this time had been largely superseded by the more complex, intermittent spinning motions of the mule. To ensure the attainment of high levels of throughput on these relatively capital-intensive investments in plant, equipment, and housing, the Boston Associates made further investments in a locks and canal system to generate a regular and steady source of waterpower. They also developed managerial structures to supervise the workers both in the mills and in the factories. To facilitate the distribution of the finished products, the Boston Associates completed a canal to Boston, where some members of the group engaged in marketing. In short, they incurred substantial fixed costs to create the potential for high-throughput production and distribution.[11]

Despite its high fixed costs, the Lowell system was able to outcompete less capital-intensive modes of cotton textile production within the United States. But it still required tariffs to protect them from the more labor-intensive and skill-abundant British competition. The arrival of the Irish in the 1840s and 1850s only served to enhance the competitive advantage of the Lowell system within the U.S. market by enabling the mills to dispense with the maintenance of workers' dormitories, while at the same time lowering the wages of their workers. With production already structured to make use of relatively unskilled labor, no new investments in technology were necessary to employ the immigrants. Given their relative lack of alternative opportunities, the Irish received lower wages than their Yankee predecessors had and yet could be compelled to supply more effort.[12]

The Lowell system remained the most cost-effective mode of textile production in the United States until it was challenged by the rise of the Fall River industry, with its self-acting mules, in the decade following the Civil War. Improvements in the productive potential of the ring-frame in the 1870s and 1880s, some fifty years after the spinning technology had been invented, awaited not only the impetus of the series of strikes by mule spinners in Fall River in the 1870s[13] but also innovations in machine tools that could produce the precision parts necessary to achieve high spindle speeds with a minimum of vibration. By greatly increasing the high-throughput potential of the spinning process, the adoption of the improved ring-frame encouraged a massive research and development undertaking by the Draper Company that, in the 1890s, resulted in an even more important effort-saving innovation—the automatic loom.[14] The rapid diffusion of ring spinning and then the automatic loom in the South, where relatively cheap, unskilled, and unorganized labor was available, permitted the cotton textile industry to continue to contribute to U.S. industrialization in the late nineteenth and early twentieth centuries.

For the U.S. economy as a whole, the cotton textile industry declined in relative importance with the rise of more capital-intensive industries. But the example of cotton textiles is important for understanding the evolving relation between organization and technology in economic development, for two reasons. First, even in an industry that was relatively labor intensive, the trend was toward investment in more high-throughput technologies and the development of managerial structures to coordinate the utilization of these investments. Second, even in an industry that in the 1820s was already mass producing standardized products on the basis of skill-displacing technology, the development of the basic technologies that culminated in the ring-frame and the automatic loom was to take another fifty to seventy years.

As the example of cotton textile machinery illustrates, over the course of the nineteenth century innovation in machine technologies in the United States was a vertically related process, in which developments in one firm or industry awaited and then built on developments in others.[15] The rapid growth of product markets in the last decades of the nineteenth century created the conditions for the use and improvement of machine technologies that had been introduced earlier in the century. Nathan Rosenberg has argued in his study of the development of American machine tools that

> by 1880, the proliferation of new machine tools in American industry had begun to reach torrential proportions. Although there were relatively few dramatically new machines comparable to the milling machine or turret lathe [introduced earlier], the period from 1880 to 1910 was characterized by an immense increase in the development of machine tools for highly specialized purposes, by a continuous adaptation of established techniques such as automatic operation to new uses, and by a systematic improvement in the properties of materials employed in machine tool processes.[16]

All in all, as David Hounshell has shown, the transition from the American system of manufactures, with its vision of high-throughput production based on interchangeable parts, to mass production, in which the technological vision was transformed into industrial reality, consumed the better part of the nineteenth century.[17] Indeed, it would not be until the early twentieth century, and in particular until Henry Ford's massive investments in and obsessive coordination of high-throughput technology that the early nineteenth-century vision of the mass production of metal products, unconstrained by craft skill, was fulfilled.

What is important in cross-national perspective is the fact that in a variety of industries from the early nineteenth century, American firms took up, and indeed generated, technological opportunities much more readily than did their British counterparts. In the late nineteenth century, U.S. manufacturing firms began to transform the relatively high fixed costs inherent in their innovative investment strategies into the low unit costs that enabled them to compete against the British firms, which had relatively low fixed costs.[18] To gain competitive advantage, American firms had to elicit high levels of effort from their shop-floor workers while at the same time attacking the traditional prerogatives of craft organizations that sought to maintain control over the relation between effort and pay. The dual nature of the task—the need to combine the carrot of work incentives with the stick of managerial power—was only satisfactorily completed in the 1920s. Even then the coming of the Great Depression would render short-lived the particular institutional solution to the problem of value creation on the shop floor that corporate managers had devised.

The Attack on Craft Control

In both Britain and the United States, craft control emerged in those occupations in which the slow pace of mechanization left employers reliant on craft skills. As I have shown in the case of the self-acting mule in Britain, however, even significant mechanization might not prompt employers to put in place the managerial structures to assume responsibility for the coordination of the shop-floor division of labor. Mechanization was particularly difficult and protracted in the metalworking industries because of the immalleable nature of the raw material and the need to turn out components that would fit precisely into a larger product. The rapid expansion of the metalworking industries in the decades after the Civil War created a demand for skilled workers such as machinists, pattern makers, molders, boilermakers, electricians, metal polishers, fitters, blacksmiths, and draftsmen. As David Montgomery has argued, these craft workers "exercised an impressive degree of collective control over the specific productive tasks in which they were engaged and the human relations involved in the performance of those tasks."[19] Even when a firm managed to mechanize one activity, it often only served to enhance the power of skilled workers in as yet unmechanized, vertically related activities who could, and did, create bottlenecks in the flow of work.

The relation of these craft workers to the firms that employed them was often as inside contractors,[20] an arrangement that was similar to the internal subcontracting system that prevailed in some British trades such as mule spinning. The contractor paid assistants time-wages but was himself paid on piece-rates; so he could retain whatever surplus revenues his team managed to produce. In the 1860s and 1870s inside contracting arrangements sometimes involved a relatively democratic process of sharing out the piece-rate among the shop-floor producers.[21] But more generally in the late nineteenth century inside contracting permitted a firm to delegate to a skilled worker the tasks of recruiting and driving less skilled workers. Inside contracting, as well as variants of it such as the "helper system" in which puddlers and rollers employed their own assistants in the iron industry, enabled craft workers (often of British or German origin) to exercise control over both the division of labor and the division of gross earnings.

Inside contracting, and with it craft control, was particularly prevalent in the metalworking industries of the northeastern United States. It was also these machine shops that gave birth to the scientific management movement. Frederick W. Taylor, the father of scientific management, gained his experience and worked out his ideas in the 1880s and 1890s while employed by firms such as Midvale Steel and Bethlehem Steel that had among the best equipped machine shops in the world. During these decades, Taylor's extensive experiments in "the art of cutting metals" culminated in the late 1890s in the invention (with Maunsel White) of high-speed tool steel; this invention increased dramatically the speed at which metal could be cut and stimulated a host of vertically related innovations in machine design. Taylor also made important contributions to the ongoing improvement of machine tools in the last two decades of the century, including (to quote Daniel Nelson's list), "a tool grinder, a machine tool table, a chuck, a tool-feeding device for lathes, a work-carrier for lathes, a boring-bar puppet, and two boring and turning mills."[22]

As a managerial employee, however, the development of new technologies was not Taylor's primary role. Rather his mission was to ensure high rates of utilization of existing—typically state-of-the-art—plant and equipment. Taylor's task was to elicit or, if need be, extract high levels of effort from the machine-shop workers.[23] His intimate involvement in the development of technology gave him a definite vision of *why* workers could gain by giving him their cooperation. His contention was that the effort-saving potentials of the new technologies were great enough to permit workers to expend less effort than before and receive higher pay, while keeping capitalists satisfied with the resultant returns on their financial investments. If only the workers could be convinced to cooperate in the supply of sufficient effort on the high-throughput technologies, they could reap a share in the value gains in the forms of both higher wages and less intense work. As Taylor put it, capital and labor could "together turn their attention toward increasing the size of the surplus until this surplus becomes so large that it is unnecessary to quarrel over how it shall be divided."[24]

The metalworkers of the late nineteenth century would not, however, cooperate. In *The Principles of Scientific Management,* first published in 1911, Taylor described the situation that he had confronted at the Midvale Steel Company in the 1880s:

> Almost all of the work of this shop had been done on piece work for several years. As was usual then, and in fact as is still usual in most of the shops in this country, the shop was really run by the workmen, and not by the bosses. The workmen together had carefully planned just how fast each job should be done, and they had set a pace for each machine throughout the shop, which was limited to about one-third of a good day's work. Every new workman who came into the shop was told at once by the other men exactly how much of each kind of work he was to do, and unless he obeyed these instructions he was sure before long to be driven out of the place by the men.[25]

By his own account, it took Taylor, in his role as gang boss, three years of persistent rate-busting—the cutting of piece-rates to force workers to increase output to maintain their earnings—to as much as double throughput in the Midvale machine shop. During this time the workers were (according to Taylor) continually causing their machines to break down as an indication to Taylor's own superiors that their shop-floor supervisor was running the expensive capital equipment beyond its technological capability. In proceeding with his mission to realize the high-throughput potential of the firm's capital investments in the face of the workers' complaints and sabotage, Taylor emphasized the importance of the backing that he received from his employer, Midvale president William Sellers, himself a leading machine-tool inventor and innovator.[26]

Taylor's experiences at Midvale during the 1880s led him to search for a new piece-rate incentive system to gain the cooperation of the metalworkers. His scheme, first made public in a paper presented to the American Society of Mechanical Engineers in 1895, represented both an extension and critique of earlier incentive systems presented to ASME by two entrepreneur-engineers, Henry Towne in 1889 and Frederick Halsey in 1891. All three systems had their origins in the metalworking industries, and all detailed ways to divide out value gains between management and workers on a stable, predetermined basis so as to avoid the frequent piece-rate cutting that in turn gave workers the incentive to restrict output.

Towne's system was a profit-sharing scheme that rewarded workers as a group for superior performance. Halsey and Taylor emphasized the importance of rewarding each worker according to his individual effort, and hence proposed differential piece-rate plans that would enable those who supplied more effort to receive higher wages. For Taylor, with his experience as a shop-floor supervisor, the main defect in the systems of both Halsey and Towne was that they simply recorded the quickest time in which a job had actually been performed and fixed this time as the standard. In effect, under these systems, the workers still set the pace of work. Taylor's addition to the approaches of Halsey and Towne was time study, the setting of "scientific" standards by the "planning department" as a prelude to the "scientific" determination of the shares in value-created of capital and labor.

Taylor's critical insight was that, to control the pace of work, workers had to believe that they would share in the value gains resulting from their cooperative efforts. What made this human-relations task particularly difficult, as Taylor's own description of shop-floor conflict at Midvale Steel revealed, was that management had to overcome the distrust of workers arising out of their ample experience with speedup, stretchout, and rate-busting. The workers' response was to restrict output, or "soldier," because of their quite rational fear that any increase in effort would result either in piece-rate cuts that would leave them working harder for the same pay or in higher manning ratios that would leave some of their number out of work.[27]

To make matters worse, during the same era when American industrial managers were trying to secure the cooperation of workers in realizing the high-throughput potential of the new technologies, managers were launching an all-out attack on the very institutions that could provide workers with a degree of bargaining power in the determination of the relation between effort and pay. Without their craft organizations, workers had no way of ensuring that piece-rate incentives would remain in place over time. If they were to respond to piece-rate incentives without maintaining some control over the rates, they might just be setting themselves up for a rate-cutting fall.

Confronted by the advent of deskilling technologies and redivisions of shop-floor labor that were typically a prelude to the unremunerated intensification of labor, craft workers stepped up their

unionization efforts. In 1886 a number of craft unions banded together to form the American Federation of Labor (AFL). By 1897
fifty-eight unions with over a quarter million workers had affiliated
with the AFL. Over the next seven years the number of affiliated
unions rose to 120 and membership to almost 1.7 million, representing over 80 percent of all union members in the United States.[28]
Much of this union growth was outside the burgeoning mass production industries; mining, building, and transportation workers made
up 46 percent of total union membership in 1897 and 54 percent in
1904. But in industrial manufacturing, the most significant growth in
union membership was in metalworking, with 50,000 union members (11 percent of the U.S. total) in 1897 and 213,000 members
(10 percent of the total) in 1904.[29]

Ironically, this period of rapid growth in union membership marks
the advent of a nonunion era in labor–management relations in
American industry—an era that was to last until the resurgence of
unionism in the late 1930s, this time on an industrial rather than a
craft basis. Not coincidentally, the Great Merger Movement that
concentrated the power of U.S. business interests occurred alongside
the attempt of craft unions to gain concentrated power through
affiliation with the AFL. The growth of industrial unionism in the
1930s was a response to the failure of capitalism—the mass unemployment of the Great Depression. The growth of craft unionism
around the turn of the century was a response to the success of capitalism—the coming of mass production in the 1890s and beyond that
undermined the control craft workers exercised in the production
process. In the late 1930s and early 1940s industrial unionism secured a place in U.S. mass production; in the late nineteenth and early
twentieth centuries, craft unionism could not.

In retrospect the beginning of the nonunion era can be dated to the
famous Homestead strike of 1892, when the Carnegie Steel Company, at the time the world's greatest mass producer of metal products, showed its willingness to use whatever force was necessary to
defeat the workers. Prior to Carnegie's victory in that strike, the
Homestead works had been a stronghold of the Amalgamated Association of Iron and Steel Workers, a major AFL union. In 1889 the
Amalgamated had been able to win a strike against the Carnegie Steel
Company, compelling it to pay according to the Amalgamated's sliding scale of tonnage rates for the next three years.[30]

But Carnegie Steel was in the forefront of the mechanization of the steel industry; and on the eve of the Homestead conflict, the company's chairman, Henry Frick, complained to the company's owner, Andrew Carnegie, that "the mills have never been able to turn out the product they should, owing to being held back by the Amalgamated men." One of Carnegie's partners succinctly articulated the managerial perspective on why the Homestead battle was fought: "The Amalgamated placed a tax on improvements, therefore the Amalgamated had to go."[31]

The Amalgamated was not to be the last craft union disenfranchised as an agent of collective bargaining. During the first decade of this century, employers, large and small, mounted an open-shop drive in an effort to assert their right to manage, unconstrained by the need to get the workers' collective consent.[32] With the attack on craft unionism came the definitive elimination of inside contracting and other vestiges of craft control from the workplaces of major U.S. industrial enterprises. As the turn-of-the-century growth in union membership indicates, the exclusion of craft unions from bargaining over conditions of work and rates of pay only served to heighten the resolve of skilled workers to concentrate their collective power. The growing militancy of the labor movement, in turn, only served to heighten the resolve of businessmen to keep the influence of craft unions out of their workplaces.

In the late nineteenth and early twentieth centuries, then, Taylor and his disciples faced the impossible task of convincing workers that management would treat them fairly even as managers sought to ensure that these workers would wield no influence over the determination of effort and pay standards. Taylorism, as well as the scientific management movement that it spawned, made important contributions to the rationalization of plant layout, the coordination of work flows between vertically related activities, and cost accounting.[33] But, given its vision of setting "scientific" production standards and "scientific" piece-rates that were supposed to secure the cooperation of shop-floor workers in speeding the flow of work, scientific management as such was largely unsuccessful. In the period 1901–1917, Taylor's followers redesigned work on the shop floor in some fifty firms but made little headway in using piece-rate incentives to win the workers over to their "scientific" standards.[34]

The problem in gaining the cooperation of workers was not only exploitative management. Even when managers intended to sustain the sharing of value gains promised by a wage-incentive scheme, cyclical fluctuations (such as the downturns of 1893–94 and 1908) and loss of market share to more aggressive rivals often rendered them unable to do so. Because workers possessed no formal collective voice in the determination of production standards and labor's share, cooperation between management and labor in adjusting to industrial cycles and market competition was virtually impossible. Whatever the announced intentions of employers to increase their workers' welfare by the use of the value gains generated by adherence to "scientific" standards for effort and pay, workers had little reason to believe that the promises of sustained benefits would, or could, be kept.

Taking Skills Off the Shop Floor

By spurring skilled workers to mobilize their resources and build their unions, the attack on craft control made it all the more imperative for management to take skills off the shop floor if it hoped to achieve high levels of throughput. The more intense the conflict became, the more certain could management be that workers would use their skills to restrict rather than augment the flow of work. Technological change—itself a prime impetus to the attack on craft control—helped to solve the problem by making craft skills obsolete. But existing craft unions, supported by the AFL umbrella, generally remained intact to organize the deskilled occupations along craft lines—hence the importance for managerial control of the open-shop drives of 1903–1905 and 1919–1922.

From the last decades of the nineteenth century, as the pace of mechanization quickened, the demarcations between skilled craft workers and "semiskilled" operatives in mass-production workplaces became less and less clear. Moreover, as I shall show, although deskilling technology undermined craft control by making employers less reliant on scarce skills, it was not sufficient to compel even unorganized factory workers to submit to managerial pace-setting.

Where the knowledge of how to perform work continued to remain with workers on the shop floor, deskilling technological change in one vertically related production activity only served to enhance the strategic positions of the skilled workers to obstruct the flow of work. The managerial method to gain the cooperation of these key workers was literally to take skills off the shop floor by integrating skilled workers into the managerial structure as line supervisors or staff engineers and by restructuring the technical division of labor on the shop floor accordingly. Montgomery has argued that in the first decades of this century "proliferation of white shirts and conversion of craftsmen into supervisors were universal and continuing phenomena."[35] He continued: "Skilled workers in large enterprises did not disappear, but most of them ceased to be production workers. Their tasks became ancillary—setup, troubleshooting, toolmaking, model making—while the actual production was increasingly carried out by specialized operatives."[36] Making skilled workers members of the firm helped management to divide and conquer the labor force. In 1919, for example, rollers at U.S. Steel were reluctant to join the great steel strike because the company's practice of paying them annual salaries made them "part of management."[37]

Over the long run, however, technological change rendered dispensable more and more of the craft skills on which management had been reliant in the late nineteenth century. The need for skills did not vanish from the capitalist enterprise. Technological change is skill augmenting as well as skill displacing; inherent in a new technology is the need for new types of skills, even as prior skill requirements become outmoded. Complementary to the incorporation into the managerial structure of craft workers possessing key skills that had as yet to be mechanized away, the major industrial enterprises took steps to ensure that new skills would be in the possession of those who were part of the managerial team rather than those who labored for wages on the shop floor.

The advent of management-controlled mass production required that the enterprise employ supervisors, engineers, scientists, accountants, and lawyers, among other personnel deemed to be worthy of salaried status. As the firm expanded through multiplant and multiregional operations, as it integrated production and distribution, as it diversified into new product lines, and as it committed resources to in-house research and development facilities, the managerial ranks grew.[38] In U.S. manufacturing between 1900 and 1920, there was a greater than threefold increase in the number of foremen (typically drawn from the ranks of craft workers) and a somewhat greater rate of growth in the number of engineers (typically recruited from institutions of higher education). During the 1920s, the number of engineers grew by another 60 percent to 217,000, while the number of foremen declined slightly to 293,000.[39] The total number of salaried employees in manufacturing in the United States rose from 348,000—1 for every 12.9 wage earners in manufacturing—in 1899 to 1,496,000—1 for every 5.6 wage earners—in 1929.[40]

The massive human-resource problem that industrial corporations faced was recruiting, training, retaining, and motivating hundreds and then thousands of line and staff specialists. The widespread success of U.S. industrial enterprises in planning and coordinating this highly skilled division of labor would not have been possible without a massive transformation in the system of higher education between the 1890s and the 1920s. An educational system that had been barely integrated into the manufacturing sector toward the end of the nineteenth century was supplying it with tens of thousands of graduates by the third decade of this century.[41] In 1890 U.S. higher education conferred fewer than 17,000 degrees of all kinds; in 1920 over 53,000; and in 1930 almost 140,000.[42] Between 1880 and 1920 membership in the engineering profession increased from 7,000 to 136,000, with an ever-growing proportion holding college degrees.[43] In 1870 only 100 engineering degrees were granted in the United States, mostly in civil engineering. In 1914 U.S. higher education conferred 4,300 engineering degrees, primarily in industrial, electrical, and chemical engineering. In 1898 the United States had only one business school (Wharton). In 1908 the Harvard Business School offered the first graduate program in business administration. Over the next two decades, more than 100 undergraduate and graduate business schools appeared.[44]

An irony of the evolution of class relations in the United States is that the critical transformations that brought higher education into the service of big business occurred in land-grant colleges—educational institutions endowed by an Act of Congress in the 1860s to enhance the social positions of the American artisan and farmer as the bulwarks of Jeffersonian democracy. In the 1870s and 1880s, however, aspiring farmers and artisans found little to be gained from the college courses and B.A. degrees that the land-grant institutions offered. It was only as agricultural exports became increasingly important to the prosperity of the American economy in the 1880s, and with the consequent founding of the United States Department of Agriculture, that large amounts of resources began to be devoted to the colleges to train a bureaucracy of agricultural experts who could research, develop, and diffuse agricultural innovations to the farmers. After the turn of the century, private foundations, banks, mail-order houses, and agricultural machinery manufacturers threw in their support. In addition, large sums of business money began to fund the development of engineering education, particularly at two land-grant colleges, the Massachusetts Institute of Technology and Purdue. The growing resources and relevance of these land-grant institutions in turn pressured the elite classical colleges to adapt their curricula to cater to business needs, often against the wishes of their leading educators.[45]

As David Noble has persuasively argued, in the first decades of the century leading businessmen, with the cooperation of the professional engineering societies, transformed and designed U.S. engineering education to serve corporate needs for managerial and technical personnel.[46] The transformation went beyond technical training in engineering per se and, indeed, was aimed more at creating the "organization man" than at turning out a fully trained professional. Through the liberal-arts orientation of undergraduate education, potential managers were now able to develop the social values, communicative skills, and general understanding of the social process essential for cooperative participation within a large, bureaucratic enterprise. As technical preparation for specialist roles—in which even in the 1920s virtually all recruits to the corporate bureaucracies had to begin their careers—higher education was structured to provide familiarity with basic principles of science, technology, commerce, and human relations. In addition, the professional orientation of graduate as well as some undergraduate curricula could equip the potential manager with more specialized knowledge in fields as diverse as accounting, marketing, and chemical engineering.

Once this system of higher education was in place—and it essentially had taken on its current form by the 1920s—corporate employers were able to take it for granted that recruits to the managerial bureaucracy would possess both the technical competence and the social outlook necessary for effective performance within a large and complex organizational structure. Within the corporations themselves, management development programs designed to shape social attitudes and cognitive abilities to meet firm-specific needs could build upon appropriate preemployment educational foundations.[47]

During the 1920s many, if not most, large industrial corporations began the systematic recruitment of college and university graduates. By 1930 well over 90 percent of the stock of college-trained engineers were employed in technical and managerial positions in industrial firms. The growing predominance of college graduates in U.S. business is reflected in a number of studies carried out in the 1950s on the changing educational backgrounds of top executives.[48] In both 1870 and 1900 about 30 percent had college degrees; in 1925, some 40 percent; and by the early 1950s, over 60 percent. Certainly after World War II, and in most cases well before, employers simply assumed that technical and managerial personnel would be recruited from the system of higher education.

Once recruited, these employees often had to be trained in those skills required to monitor and evaluate the performance of the firm's processes and products. Ideally, internal career ladders served as ongoing training systems that developed the capabilities of the individual at various levels of the hierarchy to contribute to the often-changing productive needs of the firm. Movements up and around the managerial hierarchy were critical to the most important and difficult type of management development: the transformation of specialists into generalists.

The multidivisional structures of managerial organization that from the 1920s on became characteristic of dominant mass producers were ideally suited to integrating valued managers into the organization over the long term. Within the multidivisional structure, most managerial employees (other than foremen recruited from the shop floor) could aspire to a career progression from the bottom to the top of the managerial hierarchy. Starting in relatively narrow technical or supervisory roles, career employees might rise to middle management positions in which a broader knowledge of the firm's products, processes, and organization formed the basis for operating decisions that involved hundreds and even thousands of people. After two or, more likely, three decades of commitment to the corporation, a career manager could even hope to capture a top management position in which acquired knowledge of the possibilities and limitations of the firm's current product lines and marketing regions provided the foundations for strategic decisions concerning investments in new products and entry into new regional markets.[49] Hence, besides providing a means for the progressive acquisition of firm-specific knowledge, the career ladder could serve as an incentive mechanism to ensure that valued employees would stay with the firm and that, for the sake of their careers, those lower down the managerial hierarchy would supply their efforts to further the goals of the firm.

Wage Incentives and Close Supervision

While hierarchical redivisions of labor and management development programs were vesting cognitive skills and coordinating authority within the managerial structure, work on the shop floor was losing much, if not all, of its intrinsic appeal. For the operative, work was becoming simply a means to make a living. As much as the factory worker was reduced to "the level of an appendage to a machine," however, he or she still could attempt to resist the intensification of labor, perhaps by deliberately sabotaging the flow of work.[50] Indeed, apart from exiting the workplace to find another job, "the conscientious withdrawal of efficiency" (as Thorstein Veblen called it),[51] was the only weapon that factory workers possessed to fight back against overbearing foremen and fast-moving machines.

As cognitive skills that could assure the quality of the product declined in importance on the shop floor, cooperative behavior that could assure high levels of throughput became increasingly important. The factory operative had to be disposed not only to take orders from above, often embodied in machine-paced production, but also to refrain from sabotaging the flow of production from below. Even if not deliberate, inattentiveness could result in considerable damage to expensive plant, equipment, and materials as well as reductions in throughput because of increases in downtime.[52]

The workers best situated to restrict output were those for whom manual dexterity as well as minute-to-minute judgment remained important on the shop floor. Writing about the automobile industry of the 1930s, Nelson Lichtenstein has argued that, in contrast to the repetitive, machine-paced work of the 15 or 20 percent of production workers who toiled on the assembly line, more skill was required of the 30 to 40 percent of production workers in subassembly and body work.[53] It was these semiskilled operatives, strategically situated to create bottlenecks in the flow of work, who offered the greatest collective resistance to managerial control.[54]

The problem that industrial managers faced in the first decades of this century was how to elicit productive contributions from factory operatives whose willingness to maintain the flow of work was critical to the firm's economic success but who performed alienating work and who were being denied any union voice that might secure the relation between effort and pay. One of Stanley Mathewson's examples in his well-known study, *Restriction of Output among Unor-*

ganized Workers, illustrates how a worker doing even the most routinized work could disrupt the flow of work:

> A Mexican in a large [U.S.] automobile factory was giving the final tightening to the nuts on automobile-engine cylinder heads. There are a dozen or more nuts around this part. The engines passed the Mexican rapidly on a conveyor. His instructions were to test all the nuts and if he found *one* or *two* loose to tighten them, but if three or more were loose he was not expected to have time to tighten that many. In such cases he marked the engine with chalk and it was later set aside from the conveyor and given special attention. The superintendent found that the number of engines so set aside reached an annoying total in the day's work. He made several unsuccessful attempts to locate the trouble. Finally, by carefully watching all the men on the conveyor line, he discovered that the Mexican was unscrewing a *third* tight nut whenever he found two already loose. It was easier to loosen one nut than to tighten *two*.[55]

If restriction of output among unorganized workers remained a managerial problem in the late 1920s, it was even worse a decade or two earlier when the radical syndicalist movement organized by the Industrial Workers of the World (IWW) was openly advocating sabotage as workers' only defense against unmitigated capitalist power on the shop floor.[56] Even for workers who did not actually join the IWW, the call for sabotage to protect jobs and earnings must have reinforced their conviction that the strategy made sense. Whether it took the more benign form of restriction of output or the deliberate infliction of damage to materials and facilities, sabotage exploited the economic vulnerability of the investment strategies of the corporate mass producers—their need to transform high fixed costs into low unit costs.

In the late nineteenth and early twentieth centuries Marx's nostrum that "the piece-wage is the form of wage most appropriate to the capitalist mode of production"[57] had resurfaced as a fundamental "principle" of scientific management, espoused by Frederick Taylor and his followers. Yet the application of wage-incentive schemes to factory operatives did not solve the problem of eliciting the supply of effort so critical to achieving economies of speed. Left to their own devices, the response of mass-production workers was sabotage. As Sumner Slichter commented in his pioneering work, *The Turnover of Factory Labor:* "The abuse of the piece work system had caused workmen to regard all merit systems simply as speeding up devices and this prejudice is frequently difficult to overcome."[58] Daniel Nelson has drawn the conclusion that "compared to other developments in the personnel area . . . the incentive wage was probably the least effective and important method by which managers increased their control over the factory labor force."[59]

Under these circumstances, management turned to closer supervision of workers on the shop floor. The ratio of foremen to operatives increased by 15 percent between 1900 and 1910 and by another 35 percent in the following decade.[60] The organization of work on the mass-production technologies aided the foreman in his supervisory task. The foreman could insist that workers keep pace with the speed of the machines—a speed over which the foreman himself increasingly had little or no control. By rendering the skill and judgment of the worker less important to value creation, U.S. mass-production methods helped the foreman to detect unauthorized "work" activities. By requiring the worker to perform a single task in a certain place, the detailed division of shop-floor labor made it easier for the foreman to monitor the effort of individual workers and coordinate their collective efforts. As Horace Arnold, perhaps the closest outside observer of Henry Ford's introduction of the assembly line in 1914, put it:

[Before the introduction of flow techniques] the straw boss could never nail, with certainty, the man who was shirking, because of the many workpiles and general confusion due to shop floor transportation. As soon as the roll-ways were placed the truckers were called off, the floor was cleared, and all the straw boss had to do to locate the shirk or operation tools at fault, was to glance along the line and see where the roll-way was filled up. As more than once before said in these stories, mechanical transit of work in progress evens up the job, and forces everybody to adopt the pace of the fastest worker in the gang.[61]

As Henry Ford had discovered in the early 1910s as his company mass produced ever-increasing volumes of the Model T, the ability of factory operatives to restrict output was greatest during precisely those periods of strong demand that held out the potential for the firm to generate the greatest value gains. In booms, tight labor markets gave workers the power to quit any particular workplace, and hence the power to resist attempts by foremen to intensify their work. The eminent labor economist, John R. Commons, noted this "curious paradox" in an address to the National Association of Employment Managers in December 1919:

> What about restriction of output? Everybody knows that in good times working people "lay down" on the job, no matter whether organized or not. People do not work as hard in good times as they do in hard times. We have the curious paradox that, in good times, when we ought to increase the output, labor restricts the output; and in hard times, when we don't want people to work so hard and increase the supply of production, then they work the hardest.[62]

Even when managers could replace obstreperous workers, the problem with high turnover rates was not that it created high transaction costs of hiring and training replacements. Rather the problem was the high production costs because of the damage that green (even if not disloyal) recruits could do to expensive raw materials and machinery.[63] As Magnus Alexander, a General Electric manager, found just before World War I, the amount and costs of turnover were much higher for semiskilled operatives than for either unskilled laborers or skilled craftsmen, because the operatives' work was more critical to achieving the effort-saving potential of mass production. Alexander estimated the turnover-cost differential between operatives and laborers to be 9 : 1.[64] During the 1910s, the managerial search for ways to reduce labor turnover became part and parcel of the more general quest to achieve economies of speed on the shop floor.

Ford's Five-Dollar Day

The most famous response to the high cost of turnover occurred in 1914 when the Ford Motor Company adopted a profit-sharing scheme that promised workers at the Highland Park plant earnings of at least five dollars a day, about double the going wage in Detroit. At the same time, Ford reduced the workday from nine to eight hours. During 1913 Ford had produced 183,572 cars, more than double the previous year's output.[65] But in speeding up throughput in 1913, the company had experienced a turnover rate among its shop-floor workers of 370 percent. Absenteeism was averaging 10.5 percent a day. What is more, the IWW was, at the time, actively organizing automobile workers in Detroit, advocating sabotage as the prime means to keep employers in line.[66] With plans underway to mechanize the assembly line, Ford management hit on the idea that, by offering the workers the possibility of earning much more than was attainable elsewhere, the company could reduce turnover, thwart union organizers, and impose work discipline on the shop floor. As Henry Ford was later to pronounce: "The payment of five dollars a day for an eight-hour day was one of the finest cost-cutting moves we ever made."[67]

When Ford announced the five-dollar day, the company had already taken a leading position as a mass producer of consumer durables. In just six years, economies of speed had permitted Ford to bring down the price of the Model T dramatically and capture 40 percent of the American automobile market. Especially with newspapers around the country providing free publicity of Ford's announcement of the five-dollar day, workers had reason to believe the company's promise that virtually every employee twenty-two years of age and older would share immediately in the company's profits. The wherewithall to pay some 15,000 operatives at least five dollars a day would, and could, come from the surplus already in hand. Of course, if the high-wage strategy could effect a sufficient lowering of unit costs and expansion of market share, Ford's financial ability to adhere to the five-dollar day could continue in the future.

Although most of the workers who took up the offer of the five-dollar day had been in Ford's employ before the plan was announced, thousands flocked to Detroit and to the gates of Highland Park, ready to fill any vacant places. To weed out the transients, Ford imposed a six-month Detroit residency requirement on all job applicants.[68] Those who got jobs found themselves under the close scrutiny of not only shop-floor supervisors but also the company's Sociological Department. Set up specifically to implement the five-dollar day, the Sociological Department evaluated the moral character of each operative, in the workplace, in the community, and in the home, to discern whether the man was worthy of a share in the company's profits (female workers were not eligible for the five-dollar day).[69]

Along with the promise of five dollars a day, Ford's personnel managers created internal job ladders that would permit the most productive and cooperative operatives to rise to shop-floor positions that could bring even higher earnings.[70] The abundant reserve army of labor attracted by such prospects of remuneration permitted Ford to select out those who would keep pace with the machines and put up with the company's rules of behavior. Workers who failed to meet

the company's standards tended to be laid off as profit sharers, remaining as regular employees until they could rehabilitate themselves.[71] After the five-dollar day had been introduced, the ratio of
resignations to discharges for terminated employees doubled.[72]

Despite the doubling of pay and a reduction of the workday from
nine to eight hours, available data indicate that unit direct labor costs
remained about the same (or perhaps rose slightly) before and after
the introduction of the five-dollar day. The same was true of unit
overhead (that is, administrative) costs. Unit materials costs fell, however. This fall may have been an accounting phenomenon: the valuation below market price of an increasing volume of internally produced inputs, generated by Ford's moves to backward integration. Or
the fall may have been a consequence of more careful, and more
supervised, workers, eager to take home their five dollars a day. It is
also probably the case that the greater fixed costs of installing the
assembling line were offset by increased throughput and the move to
round-the-clock (three-shift) operations. Even after transforming a
substantial amount of "profits" into wages, Ford's surplus rose.[73]

Ford's five-dollar day established discipline on the shop floor in the
years immediately following its introduction. Operatives were working harder than they would have without the close supervision combined with the threat of losing the right to share in profits. At the
same time, however, technological change was reducing the amount
of effort required per unit of output. Workers who were willing to
keep pace with the line and keep face with the personnel managers
received wages that were substantially above their alternative opportunities, and they got a shorter workday to boot. If the worker was
reduced to the level of an appendage of a machine, Ford was able to
make them high-paid appendages.

Ford's resolution of the labor problem did not last for long. In
January 1919, again in response to increased labor turnover and
rising labor militancy, Ford instituted a six-dollar day. But, with the
rising cost of living and the rising pay scales of its competitors, a six-
dollar day was far from the extraordinary offer that the five-dollar
day had been five years before. By the same token, the speedup of
work that accompanied the six-dollar day made employment on the
Ford shop floor all the more oppressive.

By increasing throughput and cutting prices to consumers, Ford
was able to build its market share to 56 percent in 1921. But in the
process the company exhausted the effort-saving potential of the

momentous technological changes developed in the previous decade, as supervisors demanded from operatives a faster and faster pace of work. In 1921 Ford laid off all its Highland Park operatives for a month without pay and during the rest of the year employed a labor force that was only 60 to 70 percent of the 1920 level. Yet the company doubled its output from the previous year. Keith Sward described what he called the "extraordinary 'man' speed-up of 1921":

> Men rather than machines carried the brunt of the speed-up of 1921. The upsurge of production that followed the adoption of the Five-Dollar Day was more a question of fuller utilization of a technology that had hardly started to function and that was undergoing radical change every working day. But things were different in 1921. Ford's plant was more mature; its really revolutionary days were over.[74]

Even though Ford's giant River Rouge plant was coming on-line in the early 1920s, it used the same process technologies to produce the same product. Moreover, the massive additions to capacity, along with the huge debt incurred in 1920 to finance Henry Ford's acquisition of all the shares in the company, saddled Ford with huge fixed costs at precisely the time when the market for the Model T was both becoming more cyclically volatile and entering into long-run stagnation. Clinging to the once-revolutionary Model T, now technologically surpassed, Ford lost market share to upscale competition from Chevrolet (which had adopted Ford's mass-production technologies) as well as to the used car market (including secondhand Model Ts).[75] In 1921 Ford had 56 percent of the U.S. new car market, and General Motors less than 13 percent. Four years later, with the sales of passenger vehicles up 250 percent for the industry as a whole, Ford's share had fallen to 40 percent, while GM's had risen to 20 percent.[76]

Henry Ford's response to his company's loss of market share was to demand even more unremunerated effort from his workers (just as he forced his dealers to take shipments of Model Ts, whether they could sell them or not).[77] As a result, during the 1920s Ford's name became (to quote Alfred Chandler) "synonymous with many of the most notorious labor malpractices, such as speed-up of work, the dropping of the older, higher-paid men, arbitrary discharges, and so on."[78] A decade earlier Ford Motor Company had extended its competitive advantage by taking the lead not only in technological change but also in the creation of institutional structures for sharing out value gains with labor. In the 1920s Ford sought to adapt to its loss of competitive advantage by turning to what I have earlier called "Marxian exploitation"—the unremunerated intensification of labor.

Managing the Labor Relation

Ford's fundamental problem in the 1920s was the company's failure to plan its movement into new product lines as the markets for its old product, the Model T, were eroded by both the product innovations at General Motors and the growing availability of inexpensive used cars. Ultimately, higher levels of throughput on the shop floor did not generate revenues if the output could not be sold. The success of the Model T in the 1910s had depended on the building of a managerial organization to plan and coordinate purchasing, production, and marketing activities.[79] For an already successful mass producer such as Ford to make a smooth transition from mature to new product lines—a transition that generated the revenues necessary to maintain the continuity of employment for its workers at the earnings and effort levels that they had come to expect—required managerial planning and coordination of an even more complex division of labor.

Up until 1919 Ford still had in its employ managerial personnel who could (and with other companies ultimately did) plan the movements into new products necessary to sustain the company's competitive advantage. But during the early 1920s Henry Ford effectively destroyed his managerial organization for the sake of maintaining personal managerial control over the company (a complement to the undiluted financial control already secured by the 1920 leveraged buyout). Many of Ford's key personnel found a welcome home at General Motors, a company that was taking the lead in planning new products to avoid market saturation.[80] When Ford finally ceased production of the Model T in 1927, the company had to shut down operations completely for almost a year to retool for the mass production of a car—the Model A—that was to have only short-lived success.[81]

Between 1914 and 1919 Ford had used his managerial organization to take control of work on the shop floor, creating in the process a uniquely American system of mass production. Along with the adoption of the five-dollar day, Ford pioneered in the development of personnel management (albeit of an excessively paternalistic character), even installing internal job ladders that could permit workers to improve their basic wages through promotion to jobs that purportedly demanded greater skill and perhaps offered better work conditions. But when Ford lost its distinct competitive advantage in the 1920s, it could no longer make good on its high-wage promises. With the declining company under ever-growing pressure to secure economies of speed, its ability to offer workers employment security and better work conditions also went by the board. Conflictual labor relations were the result.

But even as Ford's pioneering labor-relations strategy for securing the value-creating potential of high-throughput technology was disintegrating in the 1920s, other dominant mass producers in a variety of industries across the U.S. economy—not only in motor vehicles but also iron and steel, rubber, paper, petroleum, and food products, agricultural machinery, sewing machines, electrical equipment and supplies, and chemicals[82]—were gaining the cooperation of their shop-floor workers. Overcoming the militant unionism and labor turnover that had plagued them in the 1910s, the firms that dominated the oligopolized manufacturing sectors set in motion a dynamic interaction between managerial organization and technological change that generated rapid, and perhaps unprecedented, rates of growth in the value of manufacturing products.

According to the National Bureau of Economic Research index, manufacturing production in the United States grew by 8.0 percent per annum between 1919 and 1929, compared with 3.5 percent in the previous decade and 8.8 percent in the decade before that.[83] The basis of this rapid growth was investment in capital equipment. During the 1920s manufacturers spent (in 1958 dollars) an average of $5.3 billion per year, whereas average annual expenditures had been $3.9 billion in the 1910s, $3.2 billion in the 1900s, and $2.3 billion in the 1890s.[84] The value (in 1929 dollars) of physical capital per manufacturing employee was $5,889 in 1929, $4,307 in 1919, and $4,120 in 1909.[85]

The surge of growth in labor productivity that occurred in the 1920s suggests that the utilization of these capital expenditures was not being thwarted by an ill-disciplined labor force. In the decade 1889–1899, labor productivity in manufacturing had grown at an annual average rate of 1.5 percent; in the decade 1899–1909, at 1.3 percent, and in the decade 1909–1919, at 1.2 percent. These were decades in which, despite the ups and downs of the business cycle, the growth and spread of managerial capitalism was making the United States an international industrial power. Yet the levels of labor productivity growth before the 1920s appear almost insignificant when compared with the annual average rate of 5.6 percent achieved between 1919 and 1929, a decade during which the United States consolidated its position as the world's leading mass producer.[86]

Those who could lay claim to the returns to manufacturing capital fared well during the 1920s. A comparison of the distribution of manufacturing income in 1920 and 1929 shows that workers' wages fell by 5.7 percent, despite national unemployment rates that were higher in the earlier year. Meanwhile, managerial salaries in manufacturing rose by 21.9 percent, and the surpluses of their firms by 62.6 percent.[87] Over the post-1922 boom, the share of total manufacturing income received by workers fell from 57.5 percent in 1923–24 to 52.6 percent in 1928–29, whereas the share paid in salaries increased from 17.0 to 18.3 percent and capital's share advanced from 25.5 to 29.1 percent.[88]

The growth experience of the 1920s, and the ability of workers to share in it, varied considerably across industries. Along with the motor vehicle industry itself, among the fastest growing industries were those such as rubber, glass, and petroleum refining that supplied a substantial proportion of their output for the production and use of the automobile. High levels of concentration characterized the market structures of these mass-production industries, as well as others such as electrical equipment, chemicals, nonferrous metals, and food processing. In general, it was the oligopolized sectors of the U.S. economy that created the value gains of the 1920s. In contrast, throughout the decade, those sectors of the U.S. economy characterized by competitive industrial structures—in particular, cotton and woolen textiles, coalmining, and agriculture—stagnated.[89]

The workers who fared best during the boom of the 1920s were those who found employment with the dominant mass producers. In the automobile industry, for example, wages rose by 23.7 percent between 1920 and 1929, a trend distinctly different from the decline of almost 6 percent for all U.S. manufacturing workers. Managerial salaries in the automobile industry rose by 14.9 percent, only two thirds the rate of growth of all manufacturing salaries (in part, no doubt, because Ford was dismantling his company's managerial structure). But the wage gains of automobile workers were small when compared with the returns to capital in their industry. During the 1920s, capital surpluses in the industry rose by 192.9 percent, over three times the rate of growth of the returns to capital in all U.S. manufacturing and over eight times faster than the growth of automobile wages.[90]

Basic to corporate success in the 1920s were continual additions to the capital stock, both physical and human, in the forms of effort-saving production processes and managerial personnel to plan their development and coordinate their utilization. After the depression of the early 1920s, booming macroeconomic demand conditions, particularly for the purchase of consumer durables and the capital goods to produce them, helped to ensure a high level of utilization of corporate investments. To generate the flow of output to service this demand, however, corporate management had to gain control over the flow of work on the shop floor.

To be sure, even during the 1920s the corporate mass producers did not eliminate the restriction of output on the shop floor, as attested by Stanley Mathewson's field studies carried out in 1929.[91] But the phenomenal growth of labor productivity in the 1920s would not have been possible if corporate management had not taken substantially more control over the quality and quantity of work on the shop floor than they had in the previous decades. Given the large-scale investments in effort-saving technology, and contrary to the way in which the Ford Motor Company tried to squeeze profits out of its workers in the 1920s, there is no reason to believe that shop-floor operatives were working harder in the 1920s. Effort-saving technological change created the potential for sharing out value gains not only in the form of earnings but also in the form of better work conditions.[92] Ironically, the mass producer about which the most is known—both because of access to company archives and the self-promotion of its chief executive officer—is Ford, a company that failed to manage the labor relation in the 1920s just as most other dominant mass producers were achieving success.

For, in sharp contrast to the 1910s when restriction of output had threatened to become a creed of the labor movement and high levels of labor mobility had deprived mass producers of the disciplinary power to transform high fixed costs into low unit costs, in the 1920s most dominant mass producers were able to bring these conflicts under control. Indeed many gained a substantial degree of cooperation from their shop-floor workers. Underlying the successful man-

agement of the labor relation in mass-production enterprises of the
1920s were (1) the creation of personnel departments that could plan
and coordinate the employment and remuneration of shop-floor
workers with a view to maintaining the flow of work; (2) the elimination of the influence of workers' collective organizations in the determination of the relation between effort and pay; and (3) the attainment of levels of labor turnover that were considerably lower than
those that had plagued these companies in the previous decade.

The personnel management movement in the United States arose
during the tight labor market conditions of the late 1910s.[93] Even
before U.S. entry into World War I, net migration to the United States
had dropped precipitously from 815,000 in 1913 to 50,000 in 1915
and 19,000 in 1916. The subsequent military enlistments as well as
the spread of the eight-hour day and the move to three-shift operations exacerbated the labor shortage. By the end of the war, labor
turnover in U.S. manufacturing was double its 1914 level as the unemployment rate had dropped to 1.4 percent.[94] After years of (at
best) slow growth, union membership shot up from under 3 million
members in 1917 to over 4 million by 1919 and increased yet another
million the following year. The record 4,450 work stoppages in 1916
were not to be exceeded until 1937, and the annual average of over
3,700 work stoppages during the period 1916–1920 was not to be
exceeded until the period 1941–1945.[95]

"Under these conditions," wrote Sumner Slichter from the vantage
point of the late 1920s, "the old drive policies . . . simply drove men
to quit and strike. Consequently employers suddenly became interested in gaining labor's good will."[96] With turnover and strike activity at unprecedented levels in the late 1910s, a growing, and increasingly vocal, corps of professionals in personnel management pressed
for changes in the internal organization and operation of the enterprise that would win the loyalty and hence the cooperation of workers.[97]

Prior to the late 1910s, the most prominent means of gaining workers' loyalty had been to embellish the employment relation with (typically inexpensive) fringe benefits—a personnel policy that came to be
known as "welfare work." Some welfare programs were limited to
brightening up the work environment. But, as in the case of Ford's
Sociological Department, the more extensive programs reached into
the workers' communities and even homes, often transforming fringe

benefits such as housing and schooling support into modes of social control.

Corporate expenditures on welfare work were typically responses to labor turnover or threats of unionization. In 1919, for example, some months before the great steel strike, U.S. Steel President, Elbert Gary, warned his top executives that there was "only one way of combatting and overcoming the wave of [labor] unrest."[98]

> Above everything else, as we have been talking this morning, satisfy your men if you can that your treatment is fair and reasonable and generous. Make the Steel Corporation a good place for them to work and live. Don't let the families go hungry or cold; give them playgrounds and parks and schools and churches, pure water to drink, and recreation, treating the whole thing as a business proposition, drawing the line so that you are just and generous and yet at the same time keeping your position and permitting others to keep theirs, retaining the control and management of your affairs, keeping the whole thing in your own hands.[99]

When, by offering the basic benefits of decent wages and steady employment, a corporation had already raised the cost of job loss to its employees, the fringe benefits inherent in welfare work undoubtedly helped to augment the loyalty of the worker to the firm. The high levels of labor turnover and absenteeism that, along with restriction of output and militant unionism, prevailed in the 1910s suggest that mass-production enterprises had not yet delivered sufficient economic security to their employees to make welfare work an effective auxiliary benefit.

The primary goal of the personnel management movement that emerged in the late 1910s was to win the "good will" of workers by providing those who performed well with realistic prospects of basic economic security in the forms of employment stability and augmented wages. The initial focus of the personnel management movement was on the adverse impacts on productivity of the allegedly arbitrary actions of foremen in hiring, assigning, rewarding, fining, and dismissing workers—actions that led to quits and work stoppages rather than a committed work force. The foreman, himself typically a former shop-floor operative or craftsman, could use his authority to build his own private empire on the shop floor, extracting personal favors from dependent workers.[100] The foreman might well achieve his own personal goals while creating resentment and generating conflicts that undermined the attainment of the firm's objective of high-throughput production.

Whatever the source of shop-floor conflicts, throughput would inevitably suffer when workers' grievances had to be resolved on the shop floor. Lacking the authority or the means to implement longer run solutions to these conflicts, the foreman's stock remedy was to tell workers, "If you don't like it, get out"[101]—a response that, not surprisingly, only served to exacerbate labor turnover and restriction of output, while inviting unionization as a more effective means of grievance resolution.[102]

Even when the foreman was merely carrying out the mandate of achieving high throughput, the very nature of his job—to get repetitive effort out of alienated operatives—made it unlikely that workers would view the foreman as a legitimate arbiter of their grievances. To put an end to these adversarial shop-floor relations, ultimate managerial authority over employment decisions had to be taken out of the hands of foremen and the ultimate resolution of grievances had to be taken off the shop floor. A personnel department had to be put in place to establish employment and remuneration policies that would encourage good workers to remain with the firm, elicit the supplies of effort necessary to achieve economies of speed, and resolve workers' grievances.

The first requirement of a personnel department was a supply of trained specialists. During the war the federal government sought to augment the supply of personnel managers and assist in the rapid diffusion of modern managerial methods by setting up employment management courses around the country. Between 1915 and 1920 the proportion of industrial firms with over 250 employees that had personnel departments rose from 5 to 25 percent.[103] By 1929, 34 percent of firms with over 250 employees had personnel departments. According to Sanford Jacoby, these firms employed 20 percent of the industrial labor force, up from 14 percent in 1920. More significantly in light of the importance of giant enterprise to the U.S. economy in the 1920s, 55 percent of firms with more than 5,000 employees had personnel departments in 1929.[104]

The task facing personnel departments was to restructure the labor relation in ways that would reduce quits while increasing throughput. During the 1916–1920 era of labor shortages and union growth, reformers in the forefront of the personnel management movement had visions of personnel departments that would usurp the power of the foreman over hiring, layoffs, work allocation, and wage setting, rendering the first-line supervisor virtually superfluous.[105] In practice, however, the personnel managers who staffed these departments remained dependent on the first-line supervisors to oversee the flow of work on the shop floor and to provide the company with information on workers' conduct and performance. Effective personnel management could not dispense with the foreman or his shop-floor authority; rather, it had to make the exercise of his authority integral to a planned and coordinated personnel policy that workers would view as fair. The foreman's autonomous power in the exercise of his supervisory function had to be circumscribed without undermining his effectiveness in eliciting effort from workers. The personnel department had to create institutional relations that would resolve a classic managerial problem: the delegation of the necessary authority to the foreman to ensure high-throughput production without losing control of the shop floor to him.

Toward this end, during the 1920s the personnel department came to serve a staff function within the managerial structure, setting the firm's employment policies but endowing the foreman with sufficient line authority to oversee the implementation of these policies. By 1929 almost one quarter of industrial firms with more than 250 employees had implemented systems for centralized transfer and promotion,[106] constraining further the foreman's prerogatives. Foremen often maintained the right to determine layoffs,[107] a policy leaving them with direct disciplinary power. Many large firms, however, insulated workers with long years of service from layoffs and gave more senior workers who had been laid off preference in rehiring.

To ensure that foremen would exercise their authority in ways that were consistent with the throughput objectives of the firm, attention was devoted to their training. The goal was to transform them into "men in the middle" who would be (to quote a conference report from the YMCA, an institution that was heavily involved in foreman education) "mentally capable of representing management to the men and men to management."[108] The evolution of personnel management in the 1920s did not displace the foreman but created procedures and programs designed to integrate him more fully into the managerial structure.

Most large enterprises also set up bureaucratic channels for workers to air their grievances in order to check the arbitrary power of foremen and take the resolution of conflicts off the shop floor. A key feature in the emergence of personnel management during the labor crisis of 1916–1920 was the employee representation plan, also called the works council or, more commonly, the company union.[109] Company unions neither bestowed on workers the right to enter into collective bargaining with the firm nor provided them with funds to pursue independent union activity. But by enabling workers to make management aware of what they considered to be unjust work practices and unsatisfactory work conditions, company unions provided the personnel departments with information that was a necessary condition for fashioning the systematic employment policies that might avert the outbreak of shop-floor conflicts and induce workers to supply more of their productive effort.

In 1917 there were only twelve employee representation plans in as many companies. Two years later there were 196 company unions in 145 firms, covering an average of almost 2,800 workers per firm. By 1922 there were 726 unions in 385 firms, with union membership averaging 1,800 workers per firm. Clearly, a number of smaller firms were establishing company unions in the early 1920s, but the figures also show that many were short-lived experiments. In 1922 the number of firms that discontinued their unions was over half the number of firms that had them in 1919, and in 1924 the cancellations represented over one third of the company union firms of 1922. There were, however, enough new entrants to keep the number of company union enterprises at about 400 for the remainder of the 1920s. In 1924 close to half of the company unions were in the manufacturing sector.[110] Company unions that came into being during the last two thirds of the decade tended to be longer lived than those introduced in the late 1910s and early 1920s. Only 11 percent of the firms that had company unions in 1924 had discontinued them by 1926, and only 9 percent of those that had them in 1926 had discontinued them by 1928. During these years, it was the bigger employers that provided stability to the company union movement. The average number of workers covered per firm with at least one company union jumped from 1,800 in 1922 to over 2,900 in 1924, and continued to rise to almost 3,900 in 1928.[111]

Insofar as company unions proved effective instruments for managing the labor relation, it was because they were, as Daniel Nelson has argued, "the capstone to an advanced personnel program," creating "a system of communications that bridged, however imperfectly, the traditional chasm between blue and white collar employees."[112] Only those firms that committed considerable resources to the development of personnel management departments could hope to use company unions to constrain the independent power of the foremen as well as to acquire the information necessary to respond to the grievances of workers without losing sight of the goals of the firm.

During the 1920s the potential effectiveness of company unions was made all the greater because of a pronounced decline in the power of independent unionism as an alternative source of the workers' collective voice. In the 1910s industrial unionism had become infused with left-wing radicalism. In the 1920s militant unionism was no longer a significant force. As an element in the corporate strategy to do away with the radical workers' movement, the company union movement flourished as the power of independent unionism declined.

But social forces much more powerful than simply company personnel policy were at work in creating an industrial-relations environment more conducive to capitalist prosperity. The opposition of Socialists and Wobblies to U.S. entry into World War I combined with the specter of communism raised by the Bolshevik Revolution in late 1917 provided the pretext for political suppression of radicals on a scale unprecedented in U.S. history, and not to be surpassed until the "Red Purges" of the late 1940s that inaugurated the McCarthy era.[113]

In the process, the mainstream of the American labor movement, forever looking to maintain its role as a cooperative partner in prosperity, became disassociated from its remaining radical elements. To secure the cooperation of labor during World War I, the federal government's National War Labor Board had struck an accord with the "legitimate" labor movement—the AFL—to maintain existing output, employment, and pay standards as well as protect workers from discrimination for belonging to an AFL union.[114] Quite consistent with maintaining the existing standards specified in the accord was a simultaneous government campaign to root out those factions within the labor movement—mainly Socialists and Wobblies—who might take advantage of the emergency conditions to build their organizations and improve labor's position. After the war, the Palmer Raids of 1919–1920 and the systematic deportation of foreign-born "subversives" during the 1920s further reduced the impact of radicalism on the initiatives of the American labor movement.[115] During the early 1920s the AFL followed suit by beginning to purge radicals from its midst.[116]

In the tight labor markets of the postwar prosperity, workers had responded to state repression and the beginning of industry's open-shop drive by joining unions in record-breaking numbers. In 1921–22, however, when the national unemployment rate averaged over 9 percent—the highest level over any two-year period between the late 1890s and the early 1930s—workers who insisted on maintaining their union affiliations found themselves the victims of what came to be called "the American Plan." Workers were discharged for belonging to a union and had to sign "yellow-dog" contracts—promises not to join a union—to gain or retain employment. Reinforcing these coercive tactics were legal injunctions against work protests and a liberal use of industrial spies.[117] Supplemented by company unions, "the American Plan" all but eliminated union influence in steel, automobiles, electrical equipment, rubber, cement, textiles, chemicals, and food processing.[118]

The wartime experience of the AFL as a partner in American politics led to a shift in its philosophical orientation away from the guardianship of traditional craft demarcations and toward an acceptance of the new hierarchical and technical divisions of labor that had come to characterize mass-production enterprises. Influenced by reformers within the Taylor Society who recognized that the implementation of "scientific" standards required the cooperation of labor, the AFL sought to construct a role for itself in the 1920s as a proponent of "industrial democracy." Let management eliminate traditional craft prerogatives as a prelude to the "scientific" restructuring of work organization and the effort–pay relation. But let the workers supply their own experts to bargain with managers over the new "scientific" pay and output standards.[119]

During the 1920s the managers of mass production were undoubtedly pleased to see the mainstream of the labor movement accept the new industrial reality and relent in the battle to preserve craft control. But the most noteworthy examples of union–management cooperation in the 1920s occurred in textile and garment manufacturing as well as in the roundhouses and repair shops of the Baltimore & Ohio Railroad[120]—that is, outside the oligopolized mass-production sectors that were central to the dynamic growth of the U.S. economy. Rather than share power with unions in the determination of work standards and pay, the dominant mass producers sought to manage the labor relation through a combination of repression of union influence and the strategic application of employment policies under the control of their newly founded personnel departments.

Union influence was, therefore, banished from the mass-production industries that formed the core of the rising U.S. economy. Most successful in remaining nonunion were the mass-production firms that had gained oligopolistic power in their respective product markets. In 1920, 859,000 workers in metal, machinery, and shipbuilding had belonged to unions. Just three years later that number had declined to 257,000, and afterward slipped down toward 200,000 for the rest of the decade. During the 1920s union membership remained stable in the building and printing trades and substantial, if declining, on the railroads. In each of these three sectors craft skills remained important. In 1929 building and transportation workers together accounted for over half of the union members in the United States.[121]

Even when sustained economic prosperity returned from 1923 through 1929, the American labor movement remained enfeebled, as reflected in the slow but steady decline of union membership from 3.6 million to 3.4 million as well as by the lowest number of work stoppages for any period since the early 1880s. During the period 1916–1921, work stoppages averaged 3,500 per year; during the period 1922–1930, barely over 1,000 per year; and for the period 1927–1930, just over 700 per year.[122]

The prosperity of the 1920s revealed that it was not only the collective power of union organization that had been eliminated in the mass-production industries. Even in a booming economy, workers in manufacturing could not, or would not, avail themselves of the individual power of exit via the labor market—a strategy on which, much to the detriment and chagrin of their employers, they had relied extensively in the 1910s. The available data show that quit rates were significantly lower during the late 1920s than in earlier periods; in 1919–1923 monthly quits had averaged 5.4 per 100 employees, but during 1924–1929 that figure was cut in half, to 2.7.[123] Labor mobility—the scourge of the mass producers in the 1910s—ceased to plague high-throughput production in the 1920s. At the same time, as I have noted, labor productivity soared.

8   Perspectives on the Twenties

An explanation of why labor turnover ceased to be a problem in the 1920s is important in accounting for the dramatic increases in labor productivity during that decade. One plausible hypothesis—and the one I shall argue here—is that, by providing blue-collar operatives with stable and remunerative jobs, effective personnel management increased the incentive of workers to remain attached to firms.[1] An alternative hypothesis, put forth most recently by Sanford Jacoby, is that an excess supply of labor available to manufacturers, even in the boom years after 1922, made workers reluctant to quit their jobs in search of alternative employment.[2]

It was, according to this alternative perspective, the "push" of external labor market conditions rather than the "pull" of internal employment practices that dramatically reduced labor mobility and created discipline on the shop floor. Indeed, based on his historical study of the evolution of personnel management, Jacoby argued that the employment practices of manufacturing firms retrogressed during the 1920s. Most U.S. manufacturing firms would once again take personnel management seriously only when faced by the threat of mass unionization in the wake of the mass unemployment of the 1930s.

The existence of a reserve army of manufacturing labor even during the boom years of the 1920s appears to be real enough, at least once one digs below existing national unemployment statistics. According to Stanley Lebergott's estimates, the average annual civilian unemployment rate in the United States for the period 1923–1929 was 3.3 percent, a record (on the basis of the same statistical series) for sustained high levels of employment bettered only during World War II and the years following. But, using the same data, the nonfarm civilian unemployment rate for the period 1923–1929 averaged 5.5 percent.[3] Christine Romer has argued, moreover, that, if the size of the total labor force is procyclical, Lebergott's estimation procedures result in unemployment rates that are too high in recessions and too low in booms.[4] Using Paul Douglas's calculations, Jacoby argued that, if one excludes the depression years of 1908, 1914–15, and 1921–22, unemployment rates in manufacturing and transportation were higher in the period 1923–1927 than for any other five-year period after 1900, with annual unemployment rates averaging 5.6 percent during 1923–1927 but, for example, only 3.8 percent in 1916–1920. However imprecise the data underlying these statistics, there is general agreement that, in manufacturing at least, the last half of the 1920s was characterized by relatively high levels of unemployment.[5]

But, why would high levels of unemployment in manufacturing persist even under the boom conditions of the late 1920s?[6] Across all industries, the growth of manufacturing output did not increase the demand for labor. While manufacturing output grew approximately 50 percent between 1919 and 1929, employment of production workers in manufacturing fell by about 1 percent and employment of nonproduction workers by about 6 percent. Between 1923 and 1929 manufacturing output rose about 30 percent, whereas production workers employed increased by only 2 percent and nonproduction workers employed remained almost constant.[7]

The industrial composition of the labor force changed over the course of the twenties, an observation leading Jacoby to argue that "technological displacement contributed to unemployment because of the slow absorption of displaced workers into expanding industries."[8] By one estimate, over the course of the 1920s "technology" displaced almost 3.3 million workers in mining, railways, and manufacturing, of which 2.3 million were reabsorbed into industry.[9] The rate of absorption would have been higher toward the end of the 1920s if high rates of utilization of manufacturing capacity could have been sustained. Over the period 1923–1926, capacity utilization in manufacturing averaged almost 90 percent; over the years 1927–1929, it averaged less than 83 percent.[10]

Technologically dynamic industries tended to create jobs through rapid capital accumulation, even while they were reducing the amount of labor employed per unit of capital invested. During the boom period of 1923–1929, increases in mechanical power (as crudely measured by horsepower ratings), output, value-added, and employment varied widely across industries. For example, although both the tobacco and rubber industries had about the same rate of growth of manufacturing output over the period, employment of production workers fell by over 20 percent and horsepower rating by almost 48 percent in tobacco, whereas there were increases of 8 percent in employment and about 6 percent in horsepower rating in rubber.[11] From 1923 to 1929, value-added and the number of production workers both rose about four times faster, but horsepower rating rose over fifteen times faster in the manufacture of electrical equipment and supplies than in the rubber industry. With the exception of tobacco, those industries that experienced high rates of output growth (as well as high rates of technological change as measured by the growth in horsepower rating) sustained the demand for labor.[12]

In and of itself, therefore, technological change did not ensure that the most dynamic industries would have available the excess labor supplies that would reduce labor mobility and encourage discipline on the shop floor. To be sure, without technological change, employment might have kept pace with output, but then neither employment nor output would have grown very fast—there would not have been a boom. In Britain, for example, which experienced much less technological change than the United States in the 1920s, output stagnated and the unemployment rate averaged 10 percent during the decade.[13]

The real problem for technologically displaced workers in the United States was not the slow growth of the demand for labor but the unprecedented number of workers seeking industrial jobs. In the period 1920–1924 immigration from abroad was almost 2.4 times the level of the previous five years, even though it was just over half the level of the record-breaking 1910–1914 period. Restrictive legislation, which in particular limited the entry of unskilled laborers from southern and eastern Europe, reduced dramatically the inflow of labor from an annual average of 555,000 in the period 1920–1924 to an annual average of 304,000 in the period 1925–1929. But the number of immigrants in this latter period was still 30 percent greater than for the period 1916–1920.[14] In addition, in the late 1920s fewer of the immigrants returned to their homelands because of the difficulty of being readmitted to the United States.[15]

The greatest source of an expanded industrial labor supply in the 1920s was not from abroad but from the American farm. From 1921 through 1929, the gross out-migration from American farms was 17.4 million, and the net out-migration was 5.8 million. The annual averages for the years 1923–1929 were almost 2.2 million gross and 0.7 million net. During the 1920s the net out-migration of blacks from the South was 903,000, up from 555,000 in the 1910s; and the net out-migration of Southern whites was 704,000, up from 663,000 in the previous decade.[16]

Large supplies of labor, both black and white, streamed into the industrial centers in search of substantially higher wages than could be found in the rural sector. The most rapidly growing industries such as chemicals, electrical manufactures, motor vehicles, tire manufacture, glassmaking, and food processing—industries that a few firms had come to dominate—not only were providing more jobs but also were offering higher pay and more stable employment prospects. As I have noted, in the automobile industry, the managerial surplus grew about eight times faster than wages during the 1920s. Yet the remuneration of automobile workers was greater than that of most other blue-collar workers. As had been the case when Ford offered the five-dollar day in 1914, the demand for industrial workers by dominant firms was creating excess supplies of workers clamoring for the "elite" jobs.

I do not have data on job tenure by industry for the 1920s, and indeed most of the information available on the nature of the employment relation for the decade is fragmentary.[17] Nevertheless, the existing evidence supports the argument that it was the ability of the dominant mass producers to provide higher wages and more stable employment conditions during the 1920s as well as their willingness to share some of the growing managerial surplus that attracted labor from the more stagnant (primarily agricultural) sectors of the economy.

Just after the turn of the century, Frederick Taylor had put forth the vision that the scientific management would permit capital and labor "together [to] turn their attention toward increasing the size of the surplus until this surplus becomes so large that it is unnecessary to quarrel over how it shall be divided."[18] Taylor's own particular methods may not have been responsible for the burgeoning surpluses generated in the 1920s. United States industrial history would show, moreover, that the "quarrel" over how these surpluses would be divided was far from over. Yet during the 1920s managers of dominant firms did use a portion (even if only a small one) of the surpluses at their disposal as a carrot to entice workers into their employ. In the process they created the excess demand for these "elite" blue-collar jobs that made those who held these jobs all the more eager to keep them. Relative to existing alternatives, these employers provided what Jacoby defined as "a good job": "one that pays well, offers stability and promotion opportunities, and protects against arbitrary discipline and dismissal."[19] Contrary to Jacoby, I would argue that the primary cause of the decline of interfirm labor mobility in manufacturing in the 1920s was the "pull" of employment practices that provided "good jobs," which in turn generated the "push" of excess laborers, attracted from rural areas, striving to get these jobs.

The firms that were in a position to offer these "good jobs" were not giving away the managerial surplus. On the contrary, when product-market demand was strong, the progressive firms were managing the labor relation in ways that were augmenting the managerial surplus. In return for relatively high wages and stable employment, corporate managers got relatively low labor turnover and high levels of effort on the shop floor. Even if the dominant mass producers of the 1920s were not offering their workers wage premiums as dramatic as Ford's five-dollar day had been in 1914, nevertheless, in an environment in which union influence was virtually nil, these firms were using their dominant positions strategically to gain the cooperation of their shop-floor workers. All other things equal, that cooperation, once secured, generated even greater surpluses that made the renewal of cooperative relations all the more possible and effective.

This perspective on the dynamic interaction of the forces and relations of production resolves a puzzle that Sumner Slichter posed in a well-known article written in 1929. Looking back to the conditions of labor shortage and militant unionism under which the personnel management movement had arisen in the late 1910s, Slichter argued that, on the face of it, there was no reason to expect that corporate management would maintain its new-found interest in personnel management during the 1920s. "The severe depression of 1920–21," he noted,

> changed the labor market from a sellers' to a buyers' market. Except for a few months in 1923, the market has remained continuously favorable to employers. The net immigration, it is true, has been less than before the war, but this has been more than counteracted by the enlarged flow of labor from farm to city; labor turnover has been low except for a short time in 1923; and, from 1920 to 1926, the total union membership in the United States dropped about 30 percent. *In short, every aspect of the post-war labor situation might be expected to cause employers to abandon their newly acquired interest in labor's good will and to revert to pre-war labor policies.*[20]

"And yet," Slichter went on to argue,

> except in a few cases, this has not happened. On the contrary, the efforts to gain labor's good will have steadily grown . . . The outstanding task of one who essays to account for the present labor policies of American industry is to explain why this interest in industrial good will has continued to grow, despite the shift in power in favor of the employers.[21]

Slichter's explanation of the persistence of employers' "efforts to gain labor's good will" in the 1920s involved the interaction of (1) a fear of a resurgence in militant unionism in the early 1920s, (2) a consequent reluctance to cut money wages as fast as prices in the depression of 1920–21, and (3) the search for ways to increase the "efficiency of labor" in the face of rising real wages.[22] Slichter then went on to outline the ways in which management sought to increase labor efficiency. The least important method was to encourage workers to save and invest their earnings in ways that made them "stakeholders" in their communities (via homeownership) and firms (via stockownership).[23] A more important method was the training of foremen in order to diminish their tendency to wield supervisory power in an arbitrary fashion. Along with foreman training, company unions also increased labor efficiency by protecting workers against the arbitrary treatment that continued to occur.[24]

But to gain the cooperation of workers, nothing could match the provision of continuous employment. "Of the most recent developments in personnel practice," he asserted, "by far the most important is the endeavor to make the jobs of their men more secure."[25] Fearing the disruptive power of militant unionism that they had experienced in the late 1910s, employers not only permitted real wages to rise in the depression of 1921 but also, once prosperity returned, looked for ways to provide their workers with more regular employment and prospects of steady increases in remuneration. "Managers readily appreciated," Slichter argued, "that nothing is more likely to make a workman radical than uncertainty of employment, and nothing more likely to keep him conservative than the prospect of steady work."[26]

Recently, Jacoby challenged Slichter's argument that corporate employers maintained and even increased their interest in personnel management during the 1920s. On the basis of the most thorough research to date on the rise of personnel management, Jacoby has argued that, although the proportion of firms with over 250 employees that had personnel departments increased from 25 to 34 percent between 1920 and 1929, this increase was slow compared with the meteoric growth of these departments during World War I and its aftermath. Moreover, Jacoby alleged, within the firms that maintained or established personnel departments in the 1920s,

> more conservative policies prevailed. Personnel departments usually continued to have responsibility for selecting employees and administering welfare programs, but they lost much of their independent authority and their effective control over foremen. Allocative decisions were decentralized and once again left to the foreman's discretion. Although the companies did not completely revert to prewar drive policies, very few of them were committed to expanding the liberal policies of the war period. As a result, personnel management lost most of its zeal for reform.[27]

"This picture," Jacoby contended, "conflicts with the conventional view of the decade" put forth by Slichter in 1929. "Slichter's optimistic meliorism," argued Jacoby,

> applies only to those few highly visible firms—employing at most 10–15 percent of the industrial labor force—that expanded their personnel programs during the 1920s. Here memories of the war period kept personnel programs in place long after the union threat was gone. But elsewhere, even in firms with personnel departments, there was a retrogression.[28]

Jacoby, therefore, did allow that a "few highly visible firms"— enterprises that he collectively labeled "the progressive minority"— did establish and maintain some of the personnel practices that created more stable employment:

> By tying the worker more closely to his employer, these companies had begun to realize some of the incentive effects of an internal labor market. Policies such as seniority rules, internal promotion, and the new welfare work encouraged workers to remain with the firm and be loyal to it. As observers like Sumner Slichter realized, these policies—by improving morale at the same time as they raised the cost of dismissal—could stabilize effort norms and enhance the employer's control in a gently coercive fashion.

Yet, Jacoby went on to conclude, "even companies in the progressive minority adopted [these personnel policies] in a halfhearted and contradictory fashion."[29]

After presenting the evidence for a "retrogression" in employment practices during the 1920s, Jacoby reiterated these arguments:

> In most manufacturing firms in 1929, even those that had personnel departments, employment continued to be somewhat transitory. Layoffs came without notice, seniority was often ignored, dismissals were unregulated, and rehires were haphazard, if they occurred at all. Although companies in the progressive minority were more likely to provide stability and security to their workers, this was done only within very narrow limits.[30]

As I have already indicated, Jacoby's explanation for the decline of labor mobility in the boom years of the 1920s is simply that the supply of labor became more abundant during the decade, thus making it unnecessary for employers to concern themselves with shop-floor management. "As we have seen," said Jacoby in concluding his chapter on the 1920s,

> the weak labor market and the decline of manufacturing unionism sharply reduced the pressure to adopt new policies. But change was also inhibited by management's own reluctance to make labor a fixed factor, or to do anything that might interfere with the foreman's prerogatives. It was cheaper and less disruptive to control worker effort by a combination of close supervision, traditional allocative practices, and a plethora of wage incentives.[31]

Jacoby's book represents a prodigious effort to synthesize the literature on the evolution of personnel management in manufacturing in the first half of this century. Yet he failed to recognize the role of firm-level employment policies in the 1920s in enabling dominant mass producers to achieve phenomenal economies of speed—economies that both created the incentive for firms to make further investments in effort-saving technology and enabled the most successful firms to gain dominant market positions that made possible the continuation of progressive personnel practices. The very success of these dominant enterprises shaped the labor market environment—the conditions of labor supply and interfirm mobility—in which they did their business. In short, Jacoby made virtually no attempt to integrate his analysis of "managers, unions, and the transformation of work in American industry" (to quote from the subtitle of his book) into a more general analysis of the dynamics of managerial capitalism and its consolidation in the 1920s.

As a result, Jacoby's basic arguments concerning the evolution and impact of manufacturing personnel policies in the 1920s are mislead-ing. His most general contention was that during the 1920s there was a "retrogression" in the implementation of personnel policies that provided employment stability and opportunities for upward mobil-ity. He even argued that this backward movement can be detected among the "progressive minority" of firms that were in the forefront of personnel practice in the 1920s. Jacoby asserted that the decade saw the resurgence of aspects of traditional shop-floor manage-ment—particularly the autonomous power of the foreman and re-liance on piece-rate incentives—replacing the "liberal model" of em-ployment practices advocated by the personnel management movement that emerged during the labor shortages of the late 1910s.

The case for a retrogression in shop-floor management practices assumes that (1) the "liberal model" was not only widely advocated but also widely implemented in the late 1910s, and (2) the employ-ment practices implemented in the 1920s were indeed a reversion back to the traditional drive system. On the first point, the labor crisis during the war and its immediate aftermath and the government-sponsored rise of the personnel management profession made the late 1910s a period of profound intellectual change on the management of the labor relation. Jacoby claimed that in this period "a substantial minority had, through personnel management, introduced a more equitable employment relationship, one that encouraged workers to remain with the firm and be loyal to it. Line managers lost their exclusive right to determine corporate labor policies, and foremen gave up some of the power they wielded in their balkanized fiefdoms."[32] He also argued, however, that the implementation of the "liberal model" was limited during these years:

> Yet despite the efforts of personnel managers to persuade employers and line officials of the virtues of the new approach, old attitudes and practices persisted, limiting the scope of pre-1921 employment reforms: Internal labor market arrangements affected only a minor-ity of the work force and were unevenly applied for this minority. That these arrangements were either restricted to particular groups or ineffectually practiced suggests that most employers had a less-than-wholehearted commitment to an enduring employment re-lationship.[33]

To what extent and in what ways did the experience of the 1920s deviate from this limited introduction of the "liberal model" in the late 1910s? The number of personnel departments continued to expand in the 1920s. By Jacoby's own account, the proportion of the industrial labor force in firms with personnel departments rose from 14 percent in 1920 to 20 percent in 1929.[34]

Jacoby argued that the existence of a personnel department did not mean that progressive personnel policies were being maintained. But, by the same token, the absence of a personnel department did not necessarily mean the absence of personnel management or even the absence of new employment practices that provided workers with higher and more stable wages. For example, the National Industrial Conference Board referred to a number of manufacturing enterprises with more than 10,000 employees that did not have industrial relations departments or directors of industrial relations but that nevertheless had "highly developed industrial relations programs administered through an executive of the company, in combination with elaborate employee representation systems."[35]

General Motors was a case in point. Here was a company that in the 1920s developed a well-articulated managerial structure.[36] Yet, according to GM President Alfred Sloan, personnel administration only became a regular staff function at GM in 1931 and only centralized its operations in 1937 (in the wake of the sit-down strikes and the recognition of the United Auto Workers).[37] Not until 1934 did foremen become salaried. But given the success of GM in the 1920s and its pioneering efforts during the decade in enterprise rationalization and the use of statistical controls, it is difficult to accept that its management was simply relying upon traditional methods to manage the labor relation. Certainly, in contrast to British automobile firms in the 1920s, a company like GM had the managerial capability—and particularly the lines of authority—to take control of the shop floor in the 1920s, even though it did not clearly demarcate personnel administration as a staff function.

As evidence of a reversion toward the drive system in the 1920s, Jacoby argued that "during the 1920s, only a handful of companies introduced classification and evaluation techniques to rationalize their rate structures. In fact, industry moved in the opposite direction by converting a growing number of jobs to incentive pay. By 1928, 53 percent of all manufacturing workers were on piecework, and 39 percent on some kind of incentive pay."[38] But reliance on piecerates did not necessarily mean a reversion to the drive system. One contemporary observer cited a case in the automobile industry of a scheme for

guaranteeing the [piece] rates for a period of 12 months, the prevailing rates to stand for that period unless there was a mechanical
change. At the same time the foreman of each department was
furnished with the "cost per piece" for the day before and with
other information concerning the efficiency of his department. At
the end of 12 months if there was no perceptible change in the cost
of living as evidenced by State and Federal figures the rates were
again guaranteed for 12 months, and if a change had occurred the
rates were revised. The result was that the wage earner in this factory could see no limit to his earning capacity as long as there was
work to be done.

As a result, the author concluded, the worker could devise ways "by
which he could do his work easier and faster without the fear of
having the rates lowered."[39] The use of incentive pay, that is, need not
necessarily have been a prelude to rate-cutting, restriction of output,
and labor unrest. Rather, by giving workers reason to believe that
they would share in the value gains generated through economies of
speed, such an incentive pay scheme could have been integral to
rational, progressive management.

In the absence of unions that could ensure workers that "incentive
pay" would not mean unremunerated effort or loss of jobs, what was
important to workers was that those managers who controlled the
incentive schemes had an interest in generating and sharing out value
gains. Merely pointing to the spread of piecework and other forms of
incentive pay says nothing about whether the administration of the
payment systems promoted or discouraged the cooperation of labor
on the shop floor. Beyond scattered accounts, such as the one just
cited (which may or may not be entirely accurate), little is known
about the impact of pay incentives on labor effort in the 1920s. But it
would seem that the consolidation of oligopolistic industry structures
and rationalized managerial structures during the decade created an
environment more conducive to the implementation of stable incentive pay systems than had existed in the 1910s.

A key element of the rationalized managerial structures was the
increased control that higher level management exercised over the
activities of the foreman.[40] Jacoby talked of "the foreman's return to
power" in the 1920s as manifested by his continued involvement in
layoff decisions. He used the example of Ford to illustrate arbitrary
layoffs and rehiring—as if this company were representative of the
"progressive minority."[41] Among dominant firms in the 1920s, how-

ever, Ford was in the "regressive minority," and indeed was almost unique in the extent to which its labor relations retrogressed.

As for mass producers (like GM) that were building up their managerial structures rather than tearing them down, the quest for economies of speed and the alienating character of shop-floor employment meant that they could not dispense with the exercise of authority by a first-line supervisor, notwithstanding the fantasies of the "liberal reformers" of the wartime personnel management movement. What higher level management had to do was delegate authority to the foreman without losing control over the flow of work on the shop floor, and it is plausible to argue that the industrial conditions of the 1920s enhanced the ability of higher level management to do so. First, as illustrated by the "guaranteed piece-rate" example, by the 1920s corporate managers had more sophisticated cost control systems in place that they could use to monitor the foreman's activities. Second, through more systematic selection and training, efforts were being made to ensure that the foreman identified with the goals of the firm. Third, the work of the foreman was undoubtedly easier in the 1920s, not only because management had created a more defined institutional framework within which he had to function but also because of the absence of radical labor movements.

Fourth, and perhaps most important, as an employee of the firm, the foreman himself was in a much more vulnerable position in the 1920s than in the 1910s. To retain his own job, the foreman had a much greater incentive to identify with the goals of the firm than had been the case in the 1910s. The ratio of foremen to operatives had increased by 15 percent in the first decade of the century and by 35 percent in the 1910s. Between 1910 and 1920, the demand for foremen in manufacturing had increased by over 80 percent.[42] Yet during the 1920s, the demand for foremen stagnated. At the same time, the growth in the stock of experienced workmen habituated to mass-production methods and no longer influenced by radical labor movements increased the labor pool from which foremen could be drawn. During the 1920s, that is, movement into a first-line supervisory position became more difficult for workers, a situation making it easier for management to dispense with any foreman who sought to use his authority in ways that frustrated the quest for economies of speed. Less dependent on any particular foreman, management was in a stronger position to delegate authority to the first-line supervisor without losing control.

Jacoby ended his chapter on the 1920s with the observation that "the quasi-permanent employment relationship with which we are familiar was largely a post-1929 development."[43] But this viewpoint is teleological, a mode of argumentation against which Jacoby himself warns.[44] Mass producers in the United States were far more able and willing to provide workers with "good jobs" in the 1920s than in previous decades.

Yet, one can agree with Jacoby that even the most well-placed firms were tentative in the extension of "good jobs" to their blue-collar workers in the 1920s. Whether in the 1910s, 1920s, or beyond, business enterprises invested in personnel management and made commitments to workers strategically. These firms wanted to maintain managerial power over the shop floor, including flexibility in the utilization of shop-floor personnel. Even in the most dominant firms, shop-floor workers had the formal status of "hourly" workers, ostensibly easily replaceable by the firm. In reality, however, good shop-floor operatives—ones who were hardworking and loyal—were not easily replaceable. The "progressive minority" certainly could have gone much further in the 1920s in sharing out gains with workers. But compared with firms in the rest of the economy, the progressive minority did maintain wage premiums and provide more rational employment procedures. Given the weakness of the labor movement, just to maintain wages above a market-clearing level represented a progressive employment practice. Moreover, firms that could afford to pay higher wages tended to be firms that could offer more employment stability.

How important were these dominant firms in shaping the labor markets of the 1920s? Jacoby argued that the progressive minority only employed 10–15 percent of the industrial labor force, by which he apparently meant the goods-producing sector of the economy—manufacturing, mining, and contract construction.[45] Therefore the progressive minority would have employed 15–20 percent of the manufacturing labor force and a somewhat larger percentage of manufacturing workers not covered by collective bargains, and hence dependent upon the personnel practices of their employers. There is reason to believe that the employment policies of the "progressive minority" had impacts throughout the economy. As argued earlier, it was the "few highly visible firms" that were attracting the flow of workers from rural areas, in effect producing the pools of available industrial workers that made those who landed "good jobs" all the more eager to hold onto them.

There is evidence, moreover, that the employment policies in the dynamic oligopolized sector of the economy helped to improve the employment conditions of workers in the more competitive sectors of the economy in which firms were less able to "afford" to pay higher wages and provide stable employment. For example, Gavin Wright has shown that in the 1920s southern textile wages increased markedly relative to southern farm wages after decades of only a small and steady wage differential.[46] In the 1920s southern textile mills were competing for workers on what had become a national labor market. As Wright put it, "The southern labor market was isolated before the war; afterward, as a result of the flows initiated during the war, a truly *national* labor market was established, or at least in the process of being established."[47] Whether or not these southern firms were producing the surpluses that would allow them to pay higher wages, their wage bills were influenced by the ways in which dominant firms in the Northeast and Midwest were sharing out value gains with workers. Indeed, the need to pay relatively high wages to attract workers contributed to the crisis of profitability in the cotton textile industry in the 1920s. From 1921 through 1929, the manufacturers' margin in cotton textiles averaged 77 percent higher than in 1913, whereas wages averaged 130 percent higher.[48]

I would argue, therefore, that dominant industrial firms did maintain relatively progressive employment policies in the 1920s, and that by virtue of the high visibility of these firms in the national economy these firms influenced the operation of national labor markets. In particular, the very attempts by dominant firms to gain "labor's good will," as Slichter put it, generated the reserve armies of industrial labor that helped ensure that workers who landed the good jobs these firms had to offer would be cooperative on the shop floor.

It should be noted that Slichter did not make the argument that the progressive employment practices of dominant firms helped to create the excess supplies of labor, which in turn helped to reduce labor turnover. Although Jacoby took issue with Slichter on the persistence of progressive personnel policies in the 1920s, Slichter's ultimate conclusion to his 1929 article is quite compatible with Jacoby's argument that it was labor market conditions that determined the productivity outcomes of the 1920s, independently of the employment practices of firms. Slichter allowed that, during the 1920s, "the new labor policies have played an important part" in generating increases in labor productivity, decreases in union membership and strikes, and low rates of labor turnover. "But," he went on to argue, "it seems reasonably clear that a far more important part has been played by general economic conditions."[49] Indeed, Slichter concluded that relative to the impacts of these "general economic conditions" on labor productivity, labor militance, and labor turnover, "the new personnel policies have thus far produced only limited effects on the labor situation in the United States."[50] What were these "general economic conditions" that, quite apart from the management of the labor relation, enabled American business to solve the labor problem in the 1920s? Slichter's rather inadequate discussion of the decline of union membership ignored the repressive role of the state, focusing instead on the severe depression of the early 1920s as well as, after 1923, the decrease in the number of manufacturing workers and the disruptive influence of communists in the International Ladies Garment Workers' Union. As for high levels of productivity and low labor mobility, all the "general economic conditions" that Slichter cited were either results of the ways in which firms were managing the labor relation or else conditions that, to be fulfilled, required that shop-floor management raise productivity or reduce turnover. A consideration of the relation between Slichter's "general economic conditions" and shop-floor value creation illustrates how a leading institutional labor economist failed to integrate his knowledge of the evolution of labor–management relations into a dynamic analysis of capitalist development.

"Undoubtedly," Slichter argued, "the greatest cause of [increased labor productivity] has been the elimination of inefficiencies which grew up during the war and post-war boom, when speed was all important, and less attention was paid to costs."[51] Slichter did not elaborate on this point. But insofar as these "inefficiencies" occurred in the production process, their elimination cannot be separated from the ability of management to control labor effort. The creation of value on the shop floor requires the generation of high quality products at low unit costs. Inattentive or disloyal labor not only results in high unit labor costs but also high unit capital (both fixed and variable) costs, in part because mishandled machinery means downtime and repair costs and defective products mean less throughput and more wasted materials. The increased costs attendant on such waste are especially great in capital-intensive production processes in which value creation is dependent on achieving high rates of throughput while maintaining the quality of the product.

The other important cause of increased labor productivity that

Slichter cited is the change in relative factor prices over the course of the decade:

> The pronounced downward trend of long-time interest rates since 1921, the rise in wages between 1922 and 1924, and the stability of wages since 1923 have made it profitable for employers to replace methods of production which require *less waiting* and more labor with methods which require *more waiting* and less labor.[52]

For those uninitiated in the history of neoclassical economic thought, Slichter's use of the term *waiting* reflects the influence of Alfred Marshall, who introduced the concept into the academic jargon as an "explanation" for the return to portfolio investment in the forms of interest or dividends.[53] Prior to Marshall, mainstream economists had invoked the notion of "abstinence" to account for interest, but Marshall opted for *waiting* because it had a less apologetic ring to it (there were just too many wealthy people around who clipped their coupons or received their dividends without ever having abstained from anything).[54]

To say that those who hold financial instruments can lay claim to a portion of the social product by abstaining or waiting provides no explanation of what makes the production process profitable, and hence to what extent interest claims or dividends can be paid. Reliance on a waiting theory of the return to capital represented nothing less than a reluctance of economists to confront the sources of value creation and analyze the process of economic development.

By invoking waiting, Slichter avoided an analysis of why interest rates were low in the 1920s (at least until the speculative boom in stocks toward the end of the decade pushed them up), and why real wages remained high. The prime reason for low interest rates in the decade was the ability of the mass-production firms that made up the oligopolistic sector of the economy to generate such huge surpluses that they became net providers of loanable funds to other businesses as well as consumers. Indeed, the mass producers used a portion of their surpluses to draw down their prior indebtedness.[55]

The surpluses that enabled these dominant firms to keep their own indebtedness low, and indeed to make cheap financing available to others, derived not from waiting but, on the contrary, from *reducing the time* required to transform purchased inputs into sold outputs. Key to the achievement of high throughput was management of the labor relation. And a key ingredient of successful labor relations in the 1920s was the sharing-out of a portion of the surplus with workers in the forms of higher wages and more stable employment. In return, employers received the cooperation of workers in the supply of effort on the shop floor. The persistence of high wages was to a large extent a result of corporate employment practices, and not an independent "general economic condition" as Slichter contended.

As for the diminished rates of labor turnover, Slichter conceded that the new personnel policies had an impact:

> The protection of workers against arbitrary treatment, rewards for continuous service, and stability of employment have all, of course, tended to diminish turnover. Stabilization of employment has been doubly important. It has reduced turnover directly by decreasing the number of lay-offs, and indirectly by diminishing the necessity of hiring new men, among whom resignations and discharges are greatest.

In a footnote, Slichter pointed out that "the decrease in turnover tends to be cumulative, because as resignations and discharges decrease, hirings also decrease; consequently new jobs become more difficult to obtain and men become more reluctant to resign."[56]

"But," Slichter asserted, "the outstanding causes for lower turnover rates have not been personnel policies."

> The most important single influence has probably been the condition of the labor market—the relative abundance of men and scarcity of jobs which have existed (outside the building trades) almost continuously since 1920. This is indicated by the fact that for several months early in 1923, when there was a shortage of men, resignations underwent a spectacular increase. A second important influence has been the increasing efficiency of wage earners. Labor turnover is largely a function of hirings. It is greatest when forces are being expanded. The rising output per worker has made possible a gradual decrease in the number of men employed in manufacturing. This has greatly diminished the number of hirings and consequently the turnover rate. A third reason for the small turnover has been the relative stability of wages since 1923. Resignations increase during periods of rising wages because men leave the plants which are slow in advancing wages to seek positions in plants which have increased their scales. This is well illustrated by the sudden jump in the resignation rate during the late winter and the early spring of 1923. In this time occurred nearly half of the entire increase in hourly earnings which marked the business recovery of 1922–1923

. . . Since the end of 1923, however, factory wages have been stable and labor turnover has been low.[57]

I have already made the argument that the employment practices of the dominant firms—their willingness and ability to offer relatively high wages and prospects of employment stability—was a major factor in creating the "relative abundance of men and the scarcity of jobs" during the prosperity of the 1923–1929 period. In sharp contrast to the high labor mobility and restriction of output that had prevailed in the 1910s, these employment practices were also, as Slichter himself recognized, essential to securing "the rising output per worker [that] made possible a gradual decrease in the number of men employed in manufacturing." In short, the personnel policies of dominant mass producers (whose experiences are preponderant in the turnover figures that Slichter and others cited) underlay the so-called general economic conditions—an abundant labor supply, high labor productivity, and stable real wages—that Slichter cited as "the outstanding causes for lower turnover rates" in the 1920s.

To this day economists view the "well-functioning" capitalist enterprise as a passive player in the "market economy," responding to exogenous technology and the dictates of market forces. Even institutional economists who have explored the history of capitalist enterprise in the United States have failed to challenge this market-oriented perspective. Yet the essence of the rise and consolidation of managerial capitalism in the United States was the ability of a relatively small number of capitalist firms to shape and exert control over market forces—product markets, labor markets, capital markets. These dominant firms used this market control, not to raise prices and restrict output and not to increase effort and reduce earnings, but to realize economies of speed that became the basis for simultaneously increasing wages, lowering product prices, and increasing the returns to management and finance. The phenomenal success of American capitalism in the 1920s cannot be understood without an analysis of the development and utilization of this value-creating capability— nor can the debacle of the 1930s. For, the problem that the American economy faced in the 1930s was not that its productive capabilities were too weak but that they were too strong. Renewed value creation in the United States would require even more far-reaching institutional changes to realign the relations of production to support the development of the forces of production.

9   The Challenge of Flexible Mass Production

Mass-Production Unionism in the United States

With a phenomenal rate of productivity growth during the 1920s, U.S. industry definitively surpassed its once-powerful British rival as the world's premier producer for mass markets. Indeed, during the 1920s the technological dynamism and productivity growth of U.S. manufacturing contrasted sharply with depressed conditions in Britain, relying as its staple industries did on traditional technologies and divisions of labor. Between 1913 and 1929, Britain's share of world exports of manufactures declined from 32 to 24 percent while the share of the United States (whose economy, moreover, was much more reliant on domestic sales and whose manufacturing corporations were increasingly making direct foreign investments in production facilities) increased from 14 to 22 percent.[1] While the U.S. economy boomed during the 1920s, the British economy stagnated, its national unemployment rate averaging about 10 percent, or more than double the American average.

Yet in the Great Depression of the 1930s (or the "Great Slump" as it was called in Britain), it was the dynamic U.S. industry, not the stagnating British industry, that suffered the more severe collapse. The central economic problem in the United States in the 1930s was the industrial dominance of powerful corporate enterprises that were setting world productivity standards but *would not* produce because of a lack of effective demand. The American problem was not, as was the case in Britain, the presence of weak proprietary enterprises that, technologically and organizationally backward, could not, quite apart from macroeconomic conditions, produce up to international standards. In the United States, dominant manufacturing enterprises, unburdened by debt and hence under no compulsion from creditors to continue producing to avoid bankruptcy, cut back production, laid off workers, and stopped ordering from suppliers. From 1929 to

1933, output declined by 59 percent in iron and steel, 62 percent in machinery, and 65 percent in automobile production.[2]

During the 1920s it had been these very same dominant firms that, by holding out the realistic promise of employment security to their blue-collar workers, had apparently solved the problem of value creation on the shop floor. The Great Depression revealed to the American blue-collar worker, however, that under adverse macroeconomic conditions, when employment security became all the more critical, even the most powerful of the mass producers would not guarantee their well-being. Despite initial attempts at work-sharing, the deepening depression of economic activity demonstrated to more and more blue-collar workers (and a large but lesser proportion of white-collar workers) that, whatever the promises of employment security implicit during the prosperity of the 1920s, they did not count as permanent members of the firm. In 1929 Detroit firms employed 475,000 autoworkers; by the end of 1931 almost half of this number had been laid off.[3] In 1933 wages and salaries in U.S. manufacturing were less than half their 1929 levels and, in automobiles and steel, were well under 40 percent of the 1929 levels.[4]

The inability of the mass producers to provide stable employment led workers to look once again to independent collective organization. New Deal labor legislation—in particular, the Wagner Act— provided critical legal and political support to the quest for union recognition. But it was the threat of disruption of the flow of work, particularly in the upturn of early 1937, that led management to take cognizance of organized labor. By February 1937 the General Motors' sit-down strikes led that company to begin to bargain with the United Auto Workers. In March 1937 U.S. Steel announced that it would recognize the Steel Workers Organizing Committee as a bargaining agent of its members.[5]

As David Brody has argued, the permanence of the new industrial unions in the mass-production industries was not secured until the outbreak of World War II and subsequent U.S. entry into the war, as tight labor markets and urgent product demand compelled management to build cooperative relations.[6] Union recognition did not, however, necessarily mean amicable industrial relations. The managers of most of the mass-producing corporations remained hostile to unions during the 1940s, perceiving them as a threat to management's "right to manage."[7] Writing in 1947, for example, Frederick Harbison and Robert Dubin described the ideological stance of one top executive:

"On several occasions [in the 1940s], C. E. Wilson, president of [General Motors] has indicated that the UAW has had three guiding principles: first, to get more pay for less work; second, to free workers from the discipline and authority of management; third, to conduct a hate campaign designed to undermine the loyalty of the workers to the corporation."[8] Nevertheless, once it was clear that industrial unionism had come to stay, managerial ideology had to adjust to the need to secure the cooperation of the workers in creating value on the shop floor. Even though corporate executives still insisted on the "right to manage," they struggled with the unions over the definition of the scope of collective bargaining.

For management, the right to manage the shop floor meant unilateral decision-making power in the determination of the firm's investments in machines and skills as well as the organization and allocation of work. The "right to manage" clause in the 1945 UAW–GM contract laid down a clear statement of managerial prerogative:

> The right to hire, promote, discharge or discipline for cause, and to maintain discipline and efficiency of employees, is the sole responsibility of the Corporation except that union members shall not be discriminated against as such. In addition, the products to be manufactured, the location of plants, the schedules of production, the methods, processes and means of manufacturing are solely and exclusively the responsibility of the Corporation.[9]

In general, during the post–World War II decades, management maintained control over the investment and scheduling decisions listed after "In addition" in the right-to-manage clause quoted above. General Motors, for example, rebuffed Walter Reuther's demand that the company "open its books" to union representatives so that workers might influence the firm's investment strategy.[10] Instead, beginning in 1948, GM committed itself to the payment of general wage increases that would bestow on workers some of the expected value gains as well as protect them against the inflationary erosion of real wages.[11] By getting the union to accept systematic wage escalators that were not tied to actual increases in productivity or profitability, GM management obviated the need to "open the books" to the union and thus maintained its unilateral control over strategic decision-making and the disposition of the managerial surplus.

Blue-collar workers, however, wanted more than general wage increases. More fundamentally, they wanted employment stability—

something that the economic system had denied them during the 1930s. Rising out of the devastation of the Great Depression to defend the interests of workers, the mission of the new industrial unions was, as two officials of the Steel Workers Organizing Committee put it in 1941, the "Quest for Security."[12] Workers would have security when, through an enforceable collective bargain, they had acquired "a qualified property interest in their jobs"—a property right that the unions hoped "to make as inviolate as the most sacred interests of real-estate property."[13]

Workers acquired a property right to employment, it was argued, through years of continuous service with the company—that is, "seniority."

> As each seniority rule is agreed upon by unions and management, and every new interpretation becomes a precedent for similar cases to follow, a body of common law in industry is being built up that guarantees to each worker a property interest in his job. Union membership assures job protection, and only those individuals who claim seniority or property rights in a job as their sole asset—with children, a wife, sickly mother-in-law, doctor bills, etc. ad infinitum, as liabilities—can fully appreciate how precious and valuable— dearer, in many ways, than life itself—is this asset of seniority.[14]

It was the ability of the CIO unions to make seniority fundamental to the employment contract that won them the loyalty and financial support of shop-floor workers in the mass-production industries. In the 1920s the corporations had tried to provide employment stability to a portion of their shop-floor workers, but in the 1930s, as Brody has put it, "the guarantee had not been honored."[15] The failure of the corporations to deliver jobs created the opportunity for the unions to recruit workers. By the late 1930s seniority provisions had become basic elements of collective agreements in mass-production industries such as automobiles, aluminum, flat glass, steel, rubber, oil refining, and electrical manufacturing.[16]

American workers never established a legal right to remain employed by their current firms.[17] But, by protecting workers from layoffs, seniority reduced the power of employers to use the threat of job loss to extract more effort per unit of labor-time. Seniority also deprived antiunion employers of a union-busting weapon. Union members could not be fired indiscriminately. The establishment of seniority rights both manifested and sustained a fundamental shift in social power on the shop floor; and during the postwar decades, the application of seniority rights was to have important impacts on the creation and distribution of value.

Under seniority provisions, any worker could still be dismissed for failure to perform his or her work "sufficiently" or "satisfactorily." But the discharged worker, supported by the union, had the right to file a grievance to determine whether "sufficient" or "satisfactory" standards had been met. Hence, by gaining seniority rights, the union (typically through local bargaining) became a party to the setting and institutionalization of standards for skill and effort on the shop floor. Whatever the contractual rhetoric, management found its "right to manage" on the shop floor considerably constrained.

If, with the advent of industrial unionism, management could no longer hire or fire at will, it might still have been able to maintain control over the organization of work and the allocation of labor on the shop floor. Through the design of internal job structures it could develop workers' skills and, more important given the deskilling of the blue-collar worker that had been going on since the late nineteenth century, create incentive systems that, by offering promotions to jobs with better pay and work conditions, would elicit more effort from workers. Yet here too the unions sharply curtailed management's "right to manage."

In contrast to the experiments of the 1920s when a "progressive minority" of corporate employers had unilaterally extended job security to key production workers, from the late 1930s management had to contend with union attempts to influence how workers would be allocated to jobs and rewarded with pay increases. The unions wanted internal wage increases to be based on seniority, thus making the prize of long-term employment security all the more valuable to its members, while weakening the power of management to use wage incentives as a means of eliciting more effort from individual workers. Management wanted internal wage structures to be based on merit, thus giving them a free hand to choose which workers to reward.

To implement effective internal job and wage structures, management had first to divide and classify jobs into a hierarchical structure—an administrative task that became known as "job evaluation." In the 1920s some companies had begun systematic job evaluation in order to design shop-floor structures that developed skills and elicited effort—with the latter of paramount importance in the mass-production jobs. But the unions' demands for control over internal wage structures during this period and their willingness to support workers' grievances over what they considered to be wage inequities compelled management to devote more attention to its promotion policies for shop-floor workers. According to Slichter, Healy, and Livernash, the "earliest applications of job evaluation on a significant scale were in the years 1935 to 1940, when they were stimulated by the growth of the union movement, particularly of industrial unions."[18]

Unions were invariably opposed to job evaluation because they saw it as a managerial strategy to control the pace of work on the shop floor by setting new effort standards for particular tasks in the process of job evaluation, and then using those standards to determine which workers had sufficient "ability" to be promoted.[19] Often, in the manner of the path-breaking agreement between U.S. Steel and the United Steelworkers of America in 1945, the cooperation of the union was only secured by setting up a joint union–management committee to undertake the evaluation.[20]

Even if management had succeeded in installing merit-based internal promotion systems, the unions might still have succeeded in securing the right to bargain over job structures and wage structures and to define what was meant by "merit" and hence shop-floor production standards, thus limiting managerial ability to restructure the shop-floor division of labor. In other words, whatever the official statements of management's "right to manage," union participation in the bargaining process was bound to influence the organization of work. In fact, the unions had considerable success in introducing seniority as a criterion for internal wage increases, in part because of the problems management had in determining "merit" among groups of workers who were not highly skilled and in part because of the number of grievances and disputes the application of the merit systems generated. As Harbison wrote in 1940:

> Seniority is nearly always applied with some reference, either stated or implied, to skill and ability. The more rigid systems make length of service the governing factor in layoffs and promotions if skill and ability are *sufficient* for the work to be performed. On the whole, employers would prefer to make seniority the determining factor only among employees of *equal* merit or competence.[21]

"Within the past twenty years," Slichter, Healy, and Livernash wrote in their 1960 opus, *The Impact of Collective Bargaining on Management*,

> seniority has come to play an increasingly more important part in deciding who among several competing employees is entitled to fill a promotional vacancy. Unions have succeeded in establishing as a minimum the principle that where ability is relatively equal, seniority shall govern. In many cases they have been able to assign even greater weight to the seniority criterion.[22]

Insofar as seniority prevailed, management had lost the use of promotion incentives as a means of motivating workers. As internal job structures evolved, moreover, workers developed vested interests in the exclusion of "outsiders" (including workers from other occupations, departments, or plants in the company) from access to the jobs in their "seniority districts." Management became increasingly constrained in the intrafirm reallocation of shop-floor labor.

As technological changes occurred and as union–management bargaining sought (typically at the local level) to resolve conflicting pressures concerning layoffs, rehires, transfers, and promotions, ever more complex internal job structures appeared along with bureaucratic rules that determined the movement of workers up and around these job structures. The resultant focus of local-level bargaining on the redivision of labor and reallocation of workers on the shop floor has recently been described as "job-control unionism"; control over access to better paying positions within the internal job structure became central to the attempts by managers and workers to control the relation between effort and pay.[23]

The consolidation of mass-production unionism that took place in the 1940s dramatically changed the balance of power between management and labor on the shop floor. Before the Great Depression, many of the dominant mass producers had, in the absence of unions, undertaken to provide shop-floor workers with employment stability and even systematic pay increases in order to elicit effort and maintain the flow of work. But after the debacle of the 1930s, it is unlikely that American blue-collar workers would have placed their trust in these companies to provide "good jobs." Assurance that corporate promises of stable employment and rising incomes would be kept required the presence of powerful unions. Particularly during World War II, many nonunion employers found that, without a union to support workers claims to a share of the firm's value gains, the shop floor became unmanageable.[24]

As much as corporate executives may have detested the loss of managerial control that union recognition entailed, they nevertheless found that, with the tight labor markets of the 1940s following on the heels of the turbulent political conditions of the 1930s, they needed the unions if they were to manage at all. In the postwar decades, collective bargaining served management by keeping conflicts off the shop floor, as union officials sought to uphold their contractual obligations by policing illegal work stoppages among the rank and file. By institutionalizing orderly procedures for hiring, firing, transfer, and promotion, the structure of collective bargaining helped to eliminate many sources of shop-floor grievances, while at the same time enabling those disputes that did arise to be resolved through bureaucratic procedures so that they would not disrupt the flow of work on the shop floor. When technological change required that the shop-floor division of labor be restructured and workers reallocated to jobs, the local union could work out with management new job structures and assignments that took a multitude of vested interests into account, thereby minimizing rank-and-file resistance to the changes. With the industrial-relations emphasis on employment stability and rising incomes in the postwar decades, large numbers of blue-collar workers found that they were indeed sharing in the growing value that their labor was helping to create.

At the same time, however, management remained adamant that unionization not advance too far up the organizational hierarchy. Especially now that shop-floor workers had acquired effective means to struggle over the conditions of work and levels of pay, management had to ensure that the foremen on whom it relied to maintain the pace of work and monitor the supply of effort would identify with the goals of the firm, and not with the goals of the union movement and shop-floor workers. As I have noted in Chapter 6, in British industrial enterprises with their underdeveloped managerial structures, employers tended to lose control over the first-line supervisors, many of whom joined their own unions to bargain with management over work conditions and pay. In the United States, where by the 1940s major industrial firms had well-developed managerial structures with which to work, steps were taken to ensure that foremen pursued the goals of the firm.

In the 1920s, as I have indicated in Chapter 7, U.S. manufacturers took some initial steps to train their foremen to perform as first-line supervisors—that is, as lower level managers in a well-defined managerial hierarchy. But, as I have also indicated, during the 1920s managerial attempts to make the foreman perform as a part of the managerial structure were aided by an excess supply of shop-floor workers with the requisite company experience who were competing for a stable number of first-line supervisory jobs. Conditions were different in the 1940s. Management faced a shortage of experienced and loyal shop-floor workers who could qualify as competent foremen. The depression of the 1930s and then the removal of men from the factories to the front during World War II created a discontinuity in the employment of shop-floor workers. Of those experienced workers who stayed in the factories, many were union militants, and hence unsuitable candidates for the job of enforcing work discipline on the shop floor.

While the supply of qualified foremen dwindled, the very success of union organization (including the disruption of informal subforemen hierarchies of "pushers" and "straw bosses" that had previously helped the foremen maintain the pace of work) compelled management to increase the ratio of foremen to workers in order to exercise control on the shop floor. In 1930 the number of foremen per 100 workers in U.S. manufacturing had stood at 3.1, but by 1940 it had declined to 2.8. By 1950, however, the ratio was up again to 3.4, with a 69 percent increase in the number of foremen employed from 1940. From 1941, moreover, foremen organized themselves into their own union, the Foreman's Association of America (FAA), winning early recognition at Ford's River Rouge plant. By 1945 the FAA had 33,000 members in 152 chapters; and by 1947, 50,000 in 300 chapters, primarily in the automobile, steel, and rubber industries and virtually always in plants in which shop-floor workers had been organized by the new mass-production unions. The AFL and CIO also sought to organize first-line supervisors; consequently, in the immediate postwar years collective bargaining covered approximately 100,000 foremen—perhaps 25 percent of the foremen in U.S. manufacturing.[25]

The managerial response to this movement of mass-production unionism up the organizational hierarchy was both economic and political. On the economic front, corporate management upgraded the pay and status of foremen, putting them on salaries and having them dress in white shirts and ties. Upper-level management tried to make the foremen feel like managers, even though new foremen continued to be recruited from the shop floor and could not expect promotion further up the managerial hierarchy. On the political front, and of more immediate consequence for union organization, the 1947 Taft-Hartley Act—a piece of legislation that generally weakened the power of organized labor, both supervisory and operative—determined that first-line supervisors were not "employees," and hence deprived the foremen's unions of the right to collective bargaining that the Wagner Act still afforded to shop-floor workers. With first-line supervisors now legally deemed to be part of management, the mass-production corporations no longer were under legal obligation to enter into collective bargaining with foremen. For all intents and purposes, by the end of 1947, the unionization of foremen in American industry was history.[26]

As management's man on the shop floor, the foreman's job of gaining the cooperation of shop-floor workers in the supply of effort was made easier by the availability in the postwar decades of ample value gains to be shared out between the companies and the unionized workers. The international economy was expanding, with the value of manufacturing output of the major capitalist economies (Germany, France, Italy, Britain, the United States, Canada, and Japan) growing at over 4 percent a year in the 1950s and over 6 percent a year in the 1960s.[27] United States manufacturers entered the postwar decades, moreover, with enormous competitive advantages over their international rivals—advantages that had been cumulating since the late nineteenth century when these same firms had taken the lead in the development and utilization of mass-production technologies. Among U.S. firms, the greatest competitive advantages were held by the dominant mass-production firms, most of which where highly unionized. For decades, these firms had been making investments in product innovation, high-throughput machine technologies, and managerial structures to plan and coordinate the value-creation process. Although the 1930s had wreaked havoc with shop-floor employment, these firms had maintained their organizational continuity by keeping their managerial structures intact. With the return of international prosperity in the 1940s, the U.S. mass producers had the organizational and technological capabilities to generate high quality products at low unit costs. Given these competitive advantages in the postwar prosperity, these firms could amply afford cooperative shop-floor relations.[28]

In 1951 the value of manufacturing output in the United States was about 40 percent greater than that of Germany, France, Italy, Britain, Canada, and Japan combined; and even as late as 1967 the U.S. share among this group of nations was still 80 percent. In 1951 labor productivity in U.S. manufacturing was over 250 percent greater than labor productivity in the manufacturing sectors of these other capitalist economies, with Canada and Britain as the United States' closest competitors. Labor productivity in U.S. manufacturing was over six times that of Japan and almost three times that of Germany. By the late 1960s, the U.S. productivity advantage over Japan had been reduced to a factor of about two. It was not until the early 1980s that Japanese manufacturing recorded labor productivity that was slightly higher than that of the United States.[29]

The Collapse of Cooperation

From the late 1960s the cooperative relations between management and labor in the United States began to show signs of strain.[30] The first symptom was a reaction of younger workers—less integrated into the seniority system and many of them black—to the bureaucratic rules and detailed division of labor in the factories.[31] These workers used both "voice" and "exit" in their attempts to exercise control over effort and pay.[32] Fueled by the social unrest of the 1960s, voice took the form of rising shop-floor militancy, often manifested in acts of sabotage that one observer described as "counter-planning on the shop floor."[33] Supported by the tightening labor markets during the Vietnam mobilization, exit took the form of increased rates of turnover and absenteeism.

Wage gains, built into union contracts by cost-of-living allowances as well as annual improvement factors, began to outstrip the growth of labor productivity. Manufacturing productivity in the United States grew at an annual average rate of 5.1 percent from 1960 to 1965 and 0.6 percent over the following five years, whereas manufacturing wages grew at an average annual rate of 3.6 percent in the first period and 5.9 percent in the second period.[34] A primary purpose of the short recession engineered by the Nixon Administration in 1969–70 was to restore order in the labor market. But to complete the job in the early 1970s, Nixon (who helped to nail the lid on the Keynesian coffin by declaring that "we are all Keynesians now") had to turn to wage–price controls, with a heavy emphasis on freezing wages.[35] In

1974 Arnold Weber, a labor economist who as director of the Cost of Living Council had administered the wage–price controls, expressed the intent of the policy quite clearly: "Business had been leaning on [Nixon's economic advisors] Schultz and McCracken to do something about the economy, especially wages. The idea of the [wage] freeze and Phase II [of Nixon's New Economic Policy] was to zap labor, and we did."[36]

The lifting of wage–price controls, however, saw the resurgence of inflationary pressures, reinforced by the OPEC-induced oil shortages. Real wages in U.S. manufacturing continued their secular climb in the late 1970s, while sporadic but generally slow productivity growth combined with high finance and energy costs led manufacturers to seek to maintain profitability by increasing prices and demanding more effort from workers.

To increase the supply of effort, management adopted two strategies, one potentially innovative and the other merely an adaptation to existing conditions. The potentially innovative strategy sought to reshape the "quality of worklife," whereas the adaptive strategy sought to escape the high wages and shop-floor restrictions of union labor. The innovative strategy was to restructure jobs and reallocate labor in ways that "enriched" and "enlarged" work experiences on the shop floor. Building on the "human relations" approach to shop-floor management that originated with the work of Elton Mayo, the objective of the job enrichment and job enlargement experiments was to overcome worker alienation on the shop floor by making work more satisfying.[37] Management hoped that by changing the nature of workers' involvement in the production process it would be able to reshape workers' preferences concerning the relation between effort and pay.

During the 1970s one of the more far-seeing and persistent proponents of union–management cooperation in improving the "quality of worklife" (QWL) was Irving Bluestone, a vice-president of the United Auto Workers. Bluestone recognized that to secure the cooperation of workers they must be convinced that the restructuring of work and the reallocation of tasks inherent in QWL projects were not merely managerial strategies to reduce employment and speed up production.[38] Drawing on the experiences of the 50 or so QWL programs established at GM plants under the auspices of the National Joint Committee to Improve the Quality of Worklife in the last half of the 1970s, Bluestone argued: "Studies at locations where a quality-of-worklife program has existed long enough to be meaningful indicate a more constructive collective bargaining relationship; a more satisfied workforce; improved product quality; a reduction in grievance handling, absenteeism, labor turnover, and disciplinary layoffs and discharges."[39]

Many attempts at job enrichment and job enlargement in the first half of the 1970s resulted in the supply of more and better effort by workers. Yet many "successful" experiments were cut short when the workers whose work had been enriched and enlarged began questioning traditional management prerogatives inherent in the existing hierarchical structure of the enterprise. "It was not until the late 1970s and early 1980s," wrote Kochan, Katz, and McKersie, "that [QWL] programs caught the attention of many line managers, when pressures to increase productivity, improve product quality, and lower costs intensified as a result of the deteriorating American economy and the growing popularity of Japanese managerial techniques."[40]

But, as Richard Walton argued, the success of these work innovations required that managers abandon the "control" model of shop-floor relations for the sake of a "commitment" model. Walton highlighted first-line supervision as "one of the most problematic aspects of the commitment model."

> The commitment model implies a new set of role requirements for first-line supervisors: they should facilitate rather than direct the work force, impart rather than merely practice their technical and administrative expertise, and promote the development of self-managing capabilities of individual workers or work teams. In short, supervisors should delegate themselves out of their traditional functions—if not completely, then almost.[41]

Yet during the 1970s one way in which management had dealt with the lack of work discipline on the shop floor was to increase dramatically the number of foremen whose job it was to exercise control. Throughout the postwar decades the number of foremen per 100 workers had been rising in U.S. manufacturing—from 3.4 in 1950 to 4.5 in 1960, reaching 4.8 in 1970. Yet during the 1970s, as reformers spoke of job enrichment and enlargement and as the manufacturing labor force increased by 13 percent, the number of foremen (now classified as "blue-collar worker supervisors" because of the presence of a small proportion of women among their ranks) increased by 87 percent. Over the decade, the ratio of foremen to 100 workers in manufacturing shot up from 4.8 to 8.0.[42]

The "commitment" model advocated by the shop-floor reformers required that foremen (or forewomen) train workers and coordinate work teams concerned with the quality of the product and the very nature of work, and not that they merely enforce the pace of work. Some firms began the practice of starting college-educated managerial recruits in first-line supervisory positions, but the vast majority of foremen continued to be recruited from the shop floor. The college-educated supervisors, with their sights set on moving up the managerial hierarchy, were generally too socially distant from the blue-collar workers to take the lead in "the development of the self-managing capabilities" of shop-floor workers required by the "commitment" model. The traditional "blue-collar" supervisors, with their career-long involvement in the "control" model, first as operatives and then as enforcers of work discipline, generally lacked the knowledge and social skills required to implement the "commitment" model. Without massive social and technical retraining, there was no reason why they should willingly "delegate themselves out of their traditional functions," as Walton recommended.

What was required was a massive retraining of labor—both workers and managers—and a dramatic restructuring of work organization. For work innovations such as QWL to be successful over the long run, they had to be more than "experiments" that could be ended whenever management found that they were generating more trouble within the managerial structure than they were worth on the shop floor. Rather, the restructuring of jobs and reallocation of work had to be embedded in a new structure of industrial relations that could ensure various groups of workers and managers that they would benefit from the programs. It was not just the vested interests and limited capabilities of first-line supervisors that stood in the way. The structure of "job control" that had regulated the allocation of workers to jobs posed an institutional barrier to the "enrichment" and "enlargement" of work. For example, in a report on the impact of QWL at the GM assembly plant at Tarrytown, New York, Robert Guest described how plant-level industrial relations had markedly improved during the 1970s. But he also indicated how the progress of the QWL program could be disrupted by adherence to preexisting structures of job control, particularly during downturns when layoffs led to massive "bumping"—the reallocation of workers to jobs throughout the plant—according to seniority rules.[43]

In any case, because of the deeply rooted segmentation between management and workers, work innovation was not the predominant response of the U.S. mass producers to the productivity problems of the 1970s and early 1980s. To deal with reluctant workers, management relied much less on the redesign and reallocation of work and much more on the termination and relocation of employment. During the 1970s, plant closings became endemic. In their book, *The Deindustrialization of America*, Barry Bluestone and Bennett Harrison estimated that "over the whole decade of the 1970s, a minimum of 32 million jobs were probably eliminated in the United States as a direct result of private disinvestment in plant and equipment."[44] Much of this disinvestment represented the search for cheaper and more compliant sources of labor, both within the borders of the United States, particularly in the South, and increasingly in less developed countries such as Mexico, the Philippines, and Singapore.[45] The very threat of movement of investment capital to new locations put pressure on remaining high-wage, unionized workers to make wage and work-rule concessions while supplying more effort.[46] American manufacturing enterprises tended to use the stick of unemployment rather than the carrot of improvements in the quality of worklife in attempting to control the relation between effort and pay on the shop floor.

The Japanese Challenge

During the 1980s, however, the search for new structures of cooperative industrial relations took on a new urgency in the United States as formerly dominant mass producers realized that they were rapidly, and perhaps irreversibly, losing their market shares to foreign competitors, and in particular to the Japanese. The U.S. trade balance became the media's favorite "leading indicator" of future economic prospects. The improvements in the monthly trade balances that occurred, however, did not so much predict how well U.S. industry would do in international competition in the future, but merely reflected how very badly the United States had done in the recent past. Although much of the interest in the trade balance came from those who tried to guess which way the stock market would go, for many Americans any improvement, even from one month to the next, provided a sign of hope.

Since the 1970s the low technology and medium technology industries that rely more on shop-floor value creation (as distinct from product innovation and marketing) have been hardest hit by the rise of international competition.[47] As Stephen Cohen and John Zysman stressed, however, the value-creating capabilities of Japanese as well as German manufacturing derive in large part from the ability of their firms to apply advances in high technology industries to the production of "lower technology" goods. The United States, they argued, "has a 'comparative' advantage in high-technology goods because we have a trade deficit in everything else."[48]

> What our "comparative advantage" in high technology may suggest is not an easy superiority over our competitors in new, knowledge-based goods, but rather a radical inability, relative to them, to apply high technology to the production of traditional goods and to maintain our competitive position by diffusing technology and know-how widely throughout the manufacturing economy.[49]

"The primary cause of our deteriorating competitive position," Cohen and Zysman suspect, is "to be found in production; we are being beaten on the shop floor."[50]

At the beginning of the 1980s—after a decade in which the Japanese share of the U.S. automobile market had increased from 4.2 percent (less than half the European share) to 22.8 percent (well over five times the European share)[51]—prominent U.S. government and corporate officials took the position that lower wages accounted for Japanese competitive advantage.[52] Remuneration to Japanese automobile workers at the beginning of the 1980s was only approximately half that paid to their American counterparts.[53]

It was not, however, only lower wages that were driving Japanese competitive advantage. Productivity estimates showed the Japanese advantage in terms of small cars produced per unit of labor time to be anywhere from $1.2:1$ to $2.4:1$. According to the estimates of Abernathy, Clark, and Kantrow (rounded off for ease of exposition), the total Japanese labor-cost advantage per car was about $1,100, of which about $470 was attributable to higher productivity and about $630 attributable to lower wages. But they also showed that the Japanese firms had a unit cost advantage of about $670 in purchased components and materials (which constituted about 55 percent of total unit costs in the United States and about 57 percent in Japan), and another $340 in other manufacturing costs. That is, lower wages only represented about 30 percent of Japan's unit manufacturing cost advantages. Of the $2,110 in higher unit manufacturing costs, U.S. firms recouped about $810 because of lower shipping, sales, and administration costs.[54] But the salient point is that, whatever the wage advantages of the Japanese automobile producers, they were clearly superior to their U.S. competitors in the creation of value on the shop floor.

The argument that Japan's prime competitive advantage was lower wages justified the adaptive response of U.S. producers to the competitive challenge by relocating in areas where they would have access to cheaper, nonunion labor. But, as the Japanese continued to make inroads into the U.S. market, despite "voluntary export restraints" that began in 1981—and as more and more observers from U.S. industry and academia trooped over to Japan to see just what the "miracle" was all about—Americans began to recognize Japanese manufacturing superiority, not only in automobiles, but also in consumer electronics, electrical machinery, semiconductors, and steel. It became clear, moreover, that Japanese value-creating capabilities derived not only from the possession of superior product design and process technology but also, and perhaps even more fundamentally, from the way in which the Japanese manufacturing enterprise *organized* its productive activities.[55]

In particular, Japanese manufacturers surpassed their U.S. competitors by developing the skills of their shop-floor workers. But skills mean nothing unless effort is forthcoming. Whereas, since the late nineteenth century, American managers have had an obsession with taking skills off the shop floor for fear that workers would use these skills to "restrict output," Japanese managers have been able both to put skills on the shop floor and to elicit high levels of effort from the workers possessing these skills.

Visitors to Japanese factories observed, and began to write about, Japan's use of just-in-time inventory systems, statistical quality controls, shop-floor quality circles, and flexible manufacturing systems. In these workplaces, the creation of value requires not only that shop-floor workers have more and better skills than has been traditional in the United States but also that they have degrees of authority and responsibility to plan and coordinate the flow of work that, since the late nineteenth century, have been denied to most American workers.[56] Japanese shop-floor workers have responsibility, and the necessary skills, for ensuring the quality as well as the quantity of the manufactured goods they produce.

Flexible manufacturing systems (FMS) permit frequent variations in the characteristics of products manufactured in a given workplace.

In contrast to the traditional mode of transforming high fixed costs into low units costs by manufacturing large volumes of a standardized product, with FMS, high levels of capacity utilization can be achieved by serving various smaller segments of product markets during a given period of time. Critical to the success of FMS are rapid setup times in changing equipment from one relatively short production run to the next. In Japan, the term *single setup* means making the necessary changes in under ten minutes; setups that in other countries take several hours.[57] Dramatically reduced setup times have been achieved in Japan in part through mechanization but also by training workers to coordinate the setup process, including the performance of preparatory tasks, while machines are still producing the previous production run.

The success of FMS requires that workers possess the skills necessary to coordinate the changes and that they supply their effort to set up the new run as quickly as possible. The more skills workers possess and the more effort they supply, the greater the reduction in unit costs as the fixed costs of plant and equipment are spread over the output produced for a variety of market segments. In effect, such "flexible mass production" lowers unit costs by means of "shop-floor economies of scope."[58] The use of the just-in-time (JIT) inventory system is particularly cost effective in flexible mass production. With input requirements changing from one product run to the next, long runs of "product-specific" intermediate inputs cannot be transformed into final output as quickly, and hence JIT avoids the stockpiling of many different types of supplies.

The just-in-time inventory system originated at Toyota in 1948 not only as a cost-cutting measure but also because, facing a total market demand for all types of transportation vehicles that was a tiny fraction of the U.S. market (one and one-half days' production in 1950), a large variety of short runs was required to spread out fixed costs.[59] Developed at Toyota in the 1950s and 1960s and then diffused to other Japanese mass producers in the 1970s and 1980s, JIT requires workers to coordinate the flow of work across vertically related activities, using the kanban system of worker-generated orders and withdrawals to "pull" the necessary intermediate products where and when they are needed.

The involvement of shop-floor workers in coordinating JIT gives them significant power to control the pace of work. The failure to order and deliver inventories "just in time" can bring the whole set of downstream activities to a halt. As practiced in Japan, therefore, the success of JIT assumes that management can rely on workers to cooperate in supplying their effort to facilitate the smooth and speedy flow of work. In addition, the success of JIT requires that Japanese shop-floor workers possess broad-based skills, developed through systematic job rotation, that enable them to participate in the prevention of machine breakdowns, the minimization of downtime, and the repair of defective work-in-progress whenever and wherever they are needed. Japanese workers involved in JIT also have the authority to stop the flow of work if and when bottlenecks arise.[60]

The use of JIT creates a greater need for quality control on the shop floor. When defective inputs appear using JIT, throughput cannot be maintained by drawing replacements from a buffer stock; there is none. But the very involvement of shop-floor workers in the coordination of JIT puts them in the position to engage in quality control. They can inspect work-in-progress while they coordinate the flow of work. Quality control (QC) can be made a line rather than a staff function. As operated in Japan, QC does not require a large quality control bureaucracy within the managerial structure.[61] For QC to occur on the shop floor requires, however, that workers have the skills to determine when an intermediate product is defective. The Japanese have developed relatively simple statistical control techniques that can be used and applied by shop-floor workers in contrast to the much more complicated techniques generally used in the United States that can only be understood and applied by highly trained engineers.[62] In 1962 Japanese mass producers began to establish QC circles—groups of workers meeting together to discuss quality control problems—to promote, in Michael Cusumano's words, "the shift of QC and inspection responsibilities to the shop floor and the improvement of company methods for personnel administration and worker training."[63]

The Sources of Japanese Shop-Floor Advantage

Like FMS and JIT, therefore, QC as applied in Japan both requires considerable skills on the part of shop-floor workers and puts them in positions of considerable authority and responsibility to coordinate the flow of work. Why have Japanese manufacturers been more successful in developing and utilizing these work innovations than have their American competitors? It may well be that Japanese workers have different "utility functions" than their American counterparts have, and hence are willing to supply more effort for a given amount of pay, even though their skill endowments provide them with more power than workers in the United States have to control the pace of work. If so, I would argue that these effort–pay preferences are not simply or even primarily the products of a distinctive Japanese culture (whatever happened to the Protestant work ethic?) but have been greatly influenced by the social relations of the workplace that have evolved in Japan over the past century. In participating in the value-creation process, Japanese workers are involved in a structure of social relations that provides them with incentives to cooperate in achieving high rates of throughput. It is indeed the expectation of such cooperation that gives Japanese management the incentive to invest in both human skills and effort-saving machines as well as to delegate considerable authority and responsibility for the coordination of work to employees on the shop floor.

Once one recognizes how institutional structures can influence economic behavior, the "secrets" of Japanese success need not remain buried in the mysteries of culture. Although there are undoubtedly profound cultural differences between U.S. and Japanese workers, it is possible to explore the origins of these differences by comparing and contrasting the institutional histories of the two national economies and, in particular for present purposes, by considering the comparative historical evolution of shop-floor relations.

Since the late nineteenth century, as I have already outlined, management in U.S. mass-production firms has been concerned with taking skills and authority off the shop floor to deprive workers of the power to control the pace of work. It would require a dramatic restructuring of labor relations in U.S. mass production to give managers the confidence that shop-floor workers would use the skills and authority inherent in Japanese practices to augment the managerial surplus rather than restrict output. Hence the shop-floor roots of the "productivity–technology dilemma" that American mass producers have faced.[64]

Shop-floor skills and worker attitudes required to create value using flexible mass production do not appear just because a firm has invested in flexible machine technologies.[65] United States firms that invest in FMS do not take advantage of the potential complementarity between programmable technology and shop-floor skills. On the contrary, management tries to use the new technologies in ways that increase its control over the flow of work.[66] The transformation of labor–management relations to give shop-floor workers an interest in using their skills to enhance productivity rather than restrict output constitutes a precondition for the effective utilization of these technologies in today's international competition.

The history of manufacturing at Toyota, for example, indicates that in Japan flexible mass production originated before the advent of numerically controlled machine tools, computers, and other high technology components of modern FMS. The prior development of shop-floor skills and the delegation of authority to workers created the human-resource base for the introduction of flexible technologies, which in turn have enabled Japanese manufacturing firms to transform the high fixed costs of these investments in flexible mass production into low unit costs.

It should also be noted that, although the new flexible technologies have created the possibility for many small-scale firms in various places around the world to engage in what Michael Piore and Charles Sabel have called "flexible specialization,"[67] the dynamic interaction of organization and technology that underlies Japanese manufacturing success has permitted flexible mass production. In a sense, U.S. mass producers are not strangers to flexible mass production, or at least to an earlier form of it that, indeed, enabled them to generate the "economies of scope" that helped them to dominate international markets after World War II. Pioneering in the use of the multidivisional structure, American firms that had secured a dominant position in one product market used their organizational capabilities to move into new, technologically related, markets.[68]

But the development of human resources and the delegation of authority that was critical for the success of this strategy of product diversification only extended down the managerial hierarchy. Unlike the more recent Japanese success with flexible mass production, the development of human resources and delegation of authority did not extend to workers on the shop floor.[69] Whereas the dominant Japanese mass producers have integrated a portion of their blue-collar work force into the organizational structures of their firms, dominant U.S. mass producers have pursued a strategy of segmenting shop-floor workers from participation in the planning and coordination that forms the essence of firm-specific organizational capability.

Given this institutional legacy, it is not surprising that, from the perspective of American management, the skilled shop-floor worker has represented a threat to the managerial surplus rather than a source of enhanced value creation. In his account of the development of JIT at Toyota in the 1950s, Michael Cusumano related how the "workers checked for mistakes as they took the parts they needed, eliminating large numbers of inspectors, and corrected defectives in process, eliminating large rework or reject piles."[70] The unorganized worker on the American assembly line who, as Stanley Mathewson told it on the basis of his field work in the late 1920s, loosened one nut rather than tighten two may not have been typical of the American shop-floor worker from the late 1930s on.[71] But struggling as they were with unionized workers over "the right to manage" in the postwar decades, U.S. management had little reason to believe that, if the necessary skill and authority were vested in shop-floor workers, the rejects would not pile up. In any case, the detailed internal job structures and promotion policies that had become basic to plant-level collective bargaining would have made it impossible for workers to develop the broad-based skills necessary to contribute to JIT.

Yet many of the ideas that the Japanese put into practice originated in the United States. In 1956 Armand V. Feigenbaum, who, like his fellow Americans William Deming and J. M. Juran, introduced Japan to QC concepts, wrote in a *Harvard Business Review* article entitled "Total Quality Control" that "in organizing a modern quality control function, the first principle to recognize is *that quality control is everybody's job*."[72] From his perspective as head of quality control at General Electric, Feigenbaum went on to say:

> The simple fact of the matter is that the marketing man is in the best position to evaluate adequately customer's quality preferences; the design engineer is the only man who can effectively establish specification quality levels; *the shop supervisor is the individual who can best concentrate on the building of quality* [my emphasis]. Total quality control programs therefore require as a first step, top management's re-emphasis on the responsibility and accountability of *all* [his emphasis] company employees in new design control, incoming material control, product control, and special process studies.[73]

For Feigenbaum, as for most other managers of U.S. mass-production enterprises in the postwar decades, "*all* company employees" did not include shop-floor workers. Whatever the seniority rights that the unions had foisted on management, U.S. managers did not consider hourly rated shop-floor workers to be members of the firm. Hence for purposes of making "quality control everybody's job" (as well as for virtually all other activities requiring the integration of conception and execution), "everybody" went no further down the organizational hierarchy than the first-line supervisor—that is, those employees who were part of the managerial structure. As in the case of JIT, so too with QC: U.S. management was not about to grant workers skills and authority that they might use to exercise control over the flow of work.

In 1981 Ishikawa Kaoru, a leader of the QC movement in Japan, explained why firms in his country had been successful in introducing quality control on the shop floor whereas U.S. firms had made quality control a managerial function. As described by Cusumano, every reason that Ishikawa gave pointed to the organizational segmentation between management and labor in the United States.

> Most important, he believed, was Japan's weak tradition of speciali-
> zation in industry. Japanese companies never felt comfortable with
> the Taylor system of creating a rigid set of rules for job routines to
> distinguish responsibilities among workers and between labor and
> management. The absence in Japan, after the mid-1950s, of power-
> ful industrial unions, which enforced job classifications in the
> United States, also allowed managers to rotate employees freely and
> to assign them multiple tasks. Furthermore, the "vertical" character
> of personal relationships in Japanese society, reproduced in com-
> panies, made it seem natural for managers to make QC primarily a
> "line" rather than a "staff" function, and to extend the responsibil-
> ity to maintain quality to the factory level while reducing the roles
> of staff specialists.

Ishikawa went on to add that Japan's superior education system made it possible to teach statistical control methods to workers and that the practice of lifetime employment gave the firm an interest in investing in the worker, while secure employment and the Japanese seniority-based pay system made it easier for the worker to identify with the goals of the enterprise.[74]

But why have the Japanese been blessed with institutional structures and cultural traits so conducive to integrating shop-floor workers into the industrial enterprise? A brief comparison of the evolution
of Japanese labor–management relations with the U.S. experience
that I have already outlined can provide some insight into how and

why Japanese mass producers avoided the organizational segmentation between management and labor that became characteristic of their U.S. competitors.[75]

In many respects, the evolution of organizational structure in dominant Japanese industrial enterprises from the late nineteenth century into the 1930s resembles the "managerial revolution" in the United States. As successful firms expanded, there was increased separation of asset ownership from managerial control and the replacement of owner-entrepreneurs by professional managers promoted from the ranks. Just as the first two decades of the twentieth century saw a radical transformation of the U.S. system of higher education to serve the technical and organizational requirements of big business, so too in Japan, the larger firms in industries such as textiles, shipbuilding, machine making, electrical manufacture, and oil refining were recruiting large numbers of college graduates by offering them careers within their organizations.[76] During the 1920s in both the United States and Japan, dominant industrial enterprises established systematic internal career structures for the purpose of developing managerial skills and forming the next generation of top executives.[77]

As the managerial hierarchies evolved during the interwar period, foremen became the lowest ranking salaried employees. In both countries, foremen tended to be promoted from the shop floor and occupied the highest position to which blue-collar workers could normally aspire.[78] In both countries, male blue-collar employees of dominant firms had by the 1920s received implicit promises of employment security that were broken in periods of depressed trade. In both countries, through the interwar period, shop-floor workers failed to get formal employment security, and the organized labor movements, although often militant, remained weak.[79]

In the late nineteenth century, Japan, like the United States, had skilled workers, often employed as internal subcontractors, who exercised considerable control over hiring, firing, and the organization of work on the shop floor. But there was one critical difference between U.S. and Japanese shop-floor relations in this era. Japan's skilled workers did not form collective organizations that sought to enforce craft control on the shop floor. In the United States, the American Federation of Labor (AFL) was formed in 1886 to increase the bargaining power of craft workers as industrial firms themselves expanded in size and became more powerful and as the combination of mechanization and the influx of immigrant labor threatened the craft workers' jobs. A victory such as that of the Amalgamated Association of Iron and Steel Workers over Carnegie Steel in 1889 revealed the considerable power that an AFL union could wield, although stunning and irreparable defeats such as the very same Amalgamated suffered at Homestead in 1892 showed how powerful mass producers could, and did, get the upper hand.

As I have suggested in my outline of the American experience, the struggle over the "right to manage" that U.S. management took up when it confronted the craft unions and created the nonunion era profoundly influenced the evolution of U.S. labor–management relations during the first half of the twentieth century and beyond. First U.S. management determined that skills had to be taken off the shop floor, in the hopes of making any particular worker easily replaceable and of depriving current workers of the power to control the flow of work. Then, when the crisis of the Great Depression precipitated the rise of mass-production unionism, U.S. management insisted on its "right to manage" even as the union members were establishing seniority rights to employment, and indeed often to particular jobs.

Rather than recognize that, de facto, these shop-floor workers had become "permanent employees" of the firm who, as in the case of salaried personnel in the United States and all male regular workers in Japan, should be rewarded as such, U.S. management continued to tie rewards to a structure of hourly rated jobs as if it made no difference which "hourly" workers flowed in and out of them. The unions then, quite naturally, linked seniority to these job structures; so, ironically, U.S. management ended up making the long-term commitments to specific workers that, in their insistence on "the right to manage," they had been so eager to avoid. At the same time, U.S. management gave up considerable control over the organization of work and the allocation of workers. Rather than maintaining flexible control over the development and utilization of the human resources that had become attached to the firm, U.S. management became entrapped in the elaboration of a structure of job classifications and work rules that became increasingly difficult to change.

The craft traditions that engendered these managerial strategies and responses in the United States did not exist in Japan in the late nineteenth century.[80] Much of the U.S. craft traditions as well as skills had been imported to the United States during the nineteenth century by skilled Western European workers (primarily British and German). Japan had no such influx of skills and traditions. Although the Japanese labor force was highly literate at the onset of industrialization, it lacked industrial skills, never mind well-defined craft skills. Without the possibility of a highly specialized division of craft labor, workers with a broad array of skills were most useful to Japanese employers, particularly in the as yet unmechanized metalworking and shipbuilding industries. The institutional means for developing such workers was reliance on the *oyakata,* skilled workers who, as internal subcontractors, took on from 60 to 300 apprentices and trained them on the job.

The trainees did not necessarily remain committed to one *oyakata,* but would often change "masters" in order to develop their skills and enjoy better pay and work conditions. The absence of craft unions meant that there were no institutional barriers to the movement of workers or the development of broad-based skills. Because of the slow mechanization of Japanese industry as well as the absence of masses of immigrants competing for existing jobs, skilled Japanese workers felt much less pressure than Americans to create craft organizations. Rather, both the *oyakata* and their trainees relied on the power of exit. In the words of Andrew Gordon, "They set the tone of worker behavior in heavy industry with frequent job changes, movement from small shop to large factory and back, disregard for effective craft restrictions, and the desire for independence."[81]

Nevertheless, in 1897 unions arose throughout heavy industry under the leadership of some workers who, while in the United States, had developed connections with the American Federation of Labor and had brought back Samuel Gompers's philosophy of cooperation with employers. But these unions were soon repressed out of existence by the Public Peace Police Act of 1900, transforming the ideology of the union leadership from Gompersism to Socialism.[82] Although the union movement reemerged in Japan in 1912, again influenced by AFL-inspired notions of labor–management cooperation, by the 1920s a variety of ideological orientations, most of them leftist, sought to exert their influence.[83]

Meanwhile, in the first two decades of this century, the larger employers, particularly in heavy industry, were pursuing policies to integrate skilled or "key" workers into their organizations, in part to reduce labor mobility and in part to fend off the union organizers. From 1900 (when independent trade unionism was repressed), the larger firms replaced the *oyakata* with or transformed existing oyakata into first-line supervisors who, through the offer of salaries and regular employment, were integrated into the emerging managerial hierarchies.[84] These "key" workers did not necessarily enjoy "lifetime employment"— they could be, and were, laid off during periods of depressed trade.[85]

The transition from labor contractor to salaried supervisor did not put an end to one of the prime functions of the oyakata—the training (as well as the recruiting) of unskilled labor. Severe shortages of skilled labor plagued employers during periods of prosperity throughout the first four decades of this century. But labor shortage did not lead Japanese management to pursue strategies to take skills off the shop floor as was the case in the United States. Rather they set up in-house training schools, admitting boys between the ages of fourteen and seventeen.[86] The role of the first-line supervisor was not simply to drive workers in the manner of the American foreman but also to transform unskilled workers into skilled workers. However much the Japanese foreman sought to extract more effort from his subordinates, his task was made easier by the fact that he was the one who provided these workers with the skills that would enable them to earn a living.

"There was no real shortage of recruits into industry," Ronald Dore has argued. "The problem was to train them, and having trained them, to keep them."[87] To do so, Japanese management applied, in a piecemeal, selective, but still reversible fashion, the inducements that have become identified with the "Japanese employment system," and in particular the promise of employment security and pay increases based on seniority.[88] Again, on the surface, these attempts to reduce labor mobility were not very different from the employment strategies pursued by the most progressive American mass producers in the 1910s and 1920s. But because Japanese employers were not engaged in a battle to obliterate craft control and, what is the other side of the same coin, because they were willing to develop the skills of their shop-floor workers in whatever manner could best serve the needs of production, they tied pay increases directly to length of service with the company as well as life-cycle needs and individual merit. Japanese management did not insist, as was the case in the United States both during and after the nonunion era, on paying for the job rather than for the worker.

In the aftermath of World War II, with the aid of prounion legislation promoted by the Supreme Commander of the Allied Powers (SCAP), Gordon has argued that "Japanese workers very nearly established a labor version of the Japanese employment system: guaranteed job security, an explicitly need-based seniority wage, and a significant labor voice in the management of factory affairs."[89] The most radical shop-floor action of the new unions was not to control the allocation and demarcation of jobs, as did both the AFL and CIO unions in the United States, but to exercise "production control": the taking over of idle factories by the workers so that they could be put into operation, create value, and enable the workers to earn a living.[90] As far as workers were concerned, it was management that was guilty of the "restriction of output" that was keeping them unemployed.

Through SCAP containment of the union movement, including a Red Purge of 12,000 union activists in 1950 (that mimicked the ouster of 900,000 alleged communists from the American CIO in 1949) and the promotion by the companies of enterprise unions that organized blue-collar workers with white-collar workers, the "labor version" of the Japanese employment system was defeated.[91] Although Japanese management moved forward under the slogan "recovery of management authority," yet, unlike the "right to manage" movement in the United States in the 1940s, the Japanese managerial movement never questioned the importance of creating a structure of labor relations that permitted the skills of the Japanese worker to be developed and utilized.

Indeed, by forcing reluctant Japanese management to recognize enterprise unions as an alternative to independent industrial unions, Japanese workers helped to create a system that would ensure them a share in value gains. Although only an estimated 30 percent of the Japanese labor force are "regular" workers with "lifetime" employment, virtually all the male employees of the dominant mass producers—the companies primarily responsible for Japan's penetration of world markets—have this status. Since the late 1950s the enterprise unions that represent these workers in bargaining with their particular employers have been able to capture shares of the value gains that, by adjusting to variations in the firms' economic performances, reflect the abilities of their companies to pay.[92] Although the union may take up any particular worker's grievance concerning promotion or transfer, the bargaining process has not imposed the rigid work-rules and job classifications that in the United States have created barriers to the development of workers' skills by means of job rotation and the retraining of workers to meet the labor requirements of technological change.

Although disciplined by the presence of the enterprise union (as well as by evolving labor law) to keep their promises of employment security, Japanese management remains both willing and able to place skills and authority on the shop floor.[93] With the cooperation of the enterprise union and the complementary skills of its shop-floor labor, Japanese management has also been both willing and able to remain in the forefront of changes in process technology.

Can U.S. mass producers extend organizational integration further down the hierarchy in the manner of the Japanese as a precondition for implementing flexible mass production? Wickham Skinner has argued that "we have a management problem in American manufacturing today which is due to a 'mind set' of mistaken premises and implicit objectives which are rooted in the history of production management and are now inappropriate and dysfunctional."[94]

Altering the "mind set" will require significant institutional change on the shop floor. Because the resolution of the relation between effort and pay entails conflict and cooperation—because it depends on the social relations between managers and workers—simply convincing managers to update or even shed their outmoded "mind sets" will not suffice.

In the face of the Japanese challenge, the 1980s saw a search for new structures of labor–management cooperation and new models of workplace relations that stressed commitment rather than control.[95] In many cases it has been Japanese employers in the United States who have undertaken innovations in the organization of the American workplace.[96] Among the dominant U.S. mass producers that have been on the scene since the rise of managerial capitalism, a century of managerial obsession with taking skills, and initiative, off the shop floor is not easily overcome.[97]

During the 1990s, new ventures in the institutional transformation of the shop floor must confront outmoded labor–management relations and work practices as well as conflicting ideologies of the "rights" of management and labor that are deeply embedded in the American past. At the same time movements toward cooperation and commitment must confront the value-creating power of the new competition. The need for institutional and ideological change has not arisen in the United States simply because, like a rusty old machine, traditional ways of conducting business have broken down. Rather it is the emergence of international rivals with superior value-creating capabilities that has rendered the institutions and attitudes that worked yesterday obsolete today.

10 Organization and Technology in Capitalist Development

The Creation and Distribution of Value

Over the past two centuries capitalism has proved to be a powerful engine of industrial development. Driving the engine have been not only effort-saving machine technologies but also the complementary skills and efforts of human beings doing various types of work in various types of workplaces. In this book, I have focused on the "classical" capitalist workplace—the shop floor of the manufacturing establishment—a production site that even in the late twentieth century remains of critical importance to the process of value creation. Drawing on the historical record of capitalist development, my purpose has been to discover how shop-floor workers have been organized in relation to their work, other workers, and their employers in the most technologically dynamic capitalist economies since the British Industrial Revolution.

The prime finding of the historical analysis is the importance for industrial leadership of cooperative relations between manufacturing employers and shop-floor workers. Cooperative shop-floor relations permit high levels of utilization of investments in machine technologies. As a result, the high fixed costs inherent in capital-intensive investments can be transformed into low unit costs and large market shares. Cooperative relations can also lead employers to invest in the skills of workers themselves—skills that enable shop-floor workers to influence the quality as well as the quantity of production.

To build cooperative shop-floor relations, leading employers have been willing—and ultimately able—to pay workers higher wages than they could have secured elsewhere in the economy. More important, in keeping with the long-term planning horizons of enterprises that undertake innovative investment strategies, leading employers have been willing to offer shop-floor workers long-term employment security. In addition, in recent decades technologically advanced employers have made substantial investments in the skills of shop-floor workers to complement investments in machine technologies. As has been the case for the past century with managerial employees, these investments in the capabilities of shop-floor workers have in turn reinforced the willingness of employers to adopt personnel policies that ensure the long-term relation of the employee to the firm.

Whether as investments or remuneration, the willingness of leading capitalist employers to distribute value to their shop-floor workers has not come at the expense of profits but rather has been a precondition for making profits. Through their impacts on workers' supply of effort and capitalists' direct investments, expectations concerning shares in value-created have a dynamic impact on how much value is in fact created. Employers who can be confident of securing high levels of effort from their workers and who are willing and able to ensure that their workers possess technologically relevant skills have a powerful incentive to make high fixed-cost investments in advanced machine technologies. Moreover, insofar as the investments in these machine technologies are effort saving—and saving on effort is precisely what characterizes "more advanced" machine technologies— the "high" levels of effort that the employers secure from their shop-floor workers need not necessarily be high relative to the effort supplied by workers who toil in workplaces that rely on less advanced—less effort-saving—technologies.

In making investments in effort-saving technology and sharing out value gains with shop-floor workers, therefore, leading capitalist enterprises have set in motion a dynamic process of value creation. More than that, by generating relatively high-paying, stable jobs for a stratum of nonelite male workers, these employers have helped to ensure the political survival of capitalism as an economic system. Had it not been for this integration of a substantial section of the male blue-collar labor force into the mainstream of economic life in nations such as Britain, the United States, and Japan, the capitalist system would most probably have long since fulfilled the revolutionary predictions of Marx.

As I have shown, across national economies and over time, manufacturing employers in the major capitalist economies have depended on markedly different structures of work organization to secure the cooperation of shop-floor workers in the value-creation process. Although work organization occurs at the level of the manufacturing establishment, the national character of these institutional arrangements reflects broad-based and distinctive political and cultural contexts with deep historical roots, and the most marked changes in the organization of work have occurred with the rise of national econo-mies as new leaders in international economic competition. I have outlined these changes in the cases of Britain, the United States, and Japan, although a more comprehensive comparison of international leaders would certainly include Germany and perhaps some other West European countries as well.

Historical Transformations

I shall review the main findings of the comparative analysis as a prelude to a discussion of the ideological and institutional problems that British and U.S. manufacturing face in responding to the Japa-nese challenge. In the British rise to industrial power in the nineteenth century, manufacturing firms had available an ample supply of labor skilled in keeping (what in retrospect were) rudimentary machine technologies in motion. Employers ceded to senior workers consider-able control over the shop-floor division of labor as well as the opera-tion and maintenance of machinery. On the basis of their positions of shop-floor control, these senior workers built strong unions to protect the conditions of work and the levels of pay, and in return, given the technological possibilities of the time, they ensured high levels of throughput on the shop floor.

British manufacturers benefited as well from the low fixed costs that reliance on craft control entailed. The reproduction of an abun-dant and skilled labor force, effected as it was by worker-run, on-the-job training, required neither business firms nor the public sector to finance investments in human capabilities. The localization of indus-try that arose as industrialists sought to tap regional pools of experi-enced labor also permitted what Alfred Marshall called external economies of scale as the fixed costs of infrastructural investments located in a region were spread over a larger industry output. Even though individual firms tended to be vertically specialized and indus-trial organization was characterized by horizontal fragmentation, yet each firm could benefit from the growth of the regional industry, and consequent external economies of scale.[1]

With firms increasingly specialized in a narrow range of productive activities and with experienced labor readily available to organize work on the shop floor, British manufacturing firms of the nineteenth century had little need to invest in the development of managerial structures. As a result, craft control on the shop floor persisted into the twentieth century in the staple industries where trade union power and the underdevelopment of managerial structures had left craft control entrenched. But the legacy of craft control also shaped work organization in new mechanical industries such as automobiles where, despite investments in mass-production plant and equipment, the unwillingness of employers to invest in American-style management structures and the inadequacy of the national educational system for training managerial labor meant that British firms had to leave considerable control on the shop floor.

For a time, Britain's accumulated resources and labor-intensive investment strategies permitted its manufacturers to remain competitive in international markets. Over the course of the twentieth century, however, the low fixed costs inherent in reliance on skilled labor and craft control ceased to yield international competitive advantage. The development and diffusion of effort-saving technologies as well as investments in managerial structures to ensure high levels of utilization of these technologies generated internal economies of scale abroad, particularly in the United States, that pushed unit costs far lower than British enterprises could achieve.

The rise to international dominance of U.S. industry was itself a century-long process that had begun in the early nineteenth century in the midst of the British Industrial Revolution. During the first half of the nineteenth century, a scarcity of skilled labor available to capitalist firms induced the development of skill-displacing technologies in the United States. Capitalists found that highly mobile skilled labor could demand wages that were, from the point of view of profitability, too high in exchange for effort that was too low. To overcome this problem, firms that wanted to produce for mass markets invested in technologies that displaced skilled labor. To ensure the development and utilization of these effort-saving technologies, American capitalists also had to build managerial structures. The result was the rise of a characteristic "American system of manufactures."

Nevertheless, during the rapid postbellum expansion of American industry, U.S. manufacturing enterprises, and particularly those that sought to compete on growing national markets, found that they had to rely extensively on skilled labor to coordinate, and even in many cases plan, production activities. By comparison with the embeddedness of craft control in Britain, however, American reliance on skilled shop-floor labor to coordinate production activities was generally short-lived as industrialists developed technological and organizational alternatives to leaving skills, and the control of work, on the shop floor. By employing unskilled immigrants from eastern and southern Europe, investing in deskilling technological change, and elaborating their managerial structures to plan and coordinate the productive transformation, U.S. industrial capitalists attacked the craft control that workers—typically of British and German origin—had staked out during the 1870s and 1880s.

The initial response of shop-floor workers to the exercise of capitalist power was to form craft unions to protect their prior positions of control. When capitalists refused to bargain with these unions, shop-floor workers turned to the restriction of output to exercise direct control over the relation between effort and pay. Both of these responses—craft demarcations and restriction of output—were antithetical to the transformation of high fixed costs into low unit costs on the basis of investments in effort-saving technologies.

During the first three decades of this century, American capitalists used both political and economic power to eradicate and diffuse workers' attempts to assert shop-floor control. They relied on repression, instigated and financed both privately and publicly, to eliminate radical elements in the American labor movement. But, having deprived the American workers of militant alternatives, leading industrial employers also gained the cooperation of their shop-floor workers by sharing some of the managerial surplus with them and by holding out (what during the 1920s at least appeared to be) plausible promises of employment security.

As I have argued in Chapter 7, the phenomenal productivity growth in U.S. manufacturing in the 1920s could not have been achieved without managerial success in gaining control of the shop floor. At the same time, however, the decades-long capitalist offensive against craft control, combined with the evolution of a highly stratified educational system that effectively separated out future managers from future workers even before they entered the workplace, left a deep social gulf between managers and workers within U.S. industrial enterprises. Even as the "progressive minority" of dominant firms shared out some of the surplus with workers in the forms of higher wages and more employment security, American managers continued with their quest to take, and keep, skills off the shop floor, for fear of a reassertion of craft control.

The Great Depression only deepened the social separation of management and the shop-floor labor force, because not even the "progressive minority" could continue to make good on the promise of employment security. In response, the U.S. labor movement reorganized, but this time on an industrial rather than on a craft basis, and used the crisis of the 1930s to wring from the state a measure of economic security for workers that private enterprise had shown itself incapable of providing. When, in the renewed prosperity of the 1940s, dominant mass producers once again sought to gain the cooperation of workers by offering them high wages and prospects of employment security, they had to deal with the mass-production unions that had come to stay.

These unions did not challenge the principle of management's right to plan and coordinate the shop-floor division of labor. In practice, however, the quid pro quo for union cooperation was that seniority be a prime criterion for promotion along well-defined, and ever more elaborate, job structures, giving older workers best access to a hierarchical succession of jobs paying gradually rising hourly wage rates. In return, union leadership sought to ensure orderly collective bargaining, including the suppression of illegal work stoppages.

From the 1940s into the mid-1960s, union–management cooperation in the coordination of shop-floor relations permitted high enough levels of throughput to sustain competitive advantage, despite the failure of the dominant mass producers to address the issue of deskilled, monotonous, and hence alienating work. By sharing out some of the value gains that came with international dominance, U.S. mass producers exercised a degree of control over—even if they did not gain the loyalty of—their blue-collar workers. But, just as the structures of cooperative labor–management relations that served British employers well in the nineteenth century were to become barriers to organizational transformation in the twentieth, so too would the labor–management relations that prevailed in the U.S. era of economic dominance prove problematic when a more powerful mode of developing and utilizing technology came on the scene.

Over the past two decades, Japanese manufacturing has outperformed its U.S. competitors in the mass production of consumer durables, and particularly in automobiles and electronic equipment. These are the industries in which the United States had its greatest international competitive advantages in the first six decades of this century. Japanese manufacturing has also made great progress in vertically related capital goods industries—steel, machine tools, computers, and semiconductors—in large part, it would appear, because of the secure and extensive product markets as well as the advantages for product development that the nation's already successful consumer goods industries provide.

As was the case historically in the rise of the United States to industrial leadership, protection of home markets has played an important role in permitting Japanese business organizations to develop and utilize their productive resources to the point where they could attain competitive advantage in international competition. But the Japanese state has gone further in its developmental role. It has maintained a stable macroeconomic environment, including high levels of employment and a relatively equal distribution of family income, thus enlarging the extent of the Japanese market for manufactured goods. It has created incentives for consumers and businesses to purchase goods (for example, televisions and computers) that embody state-of-the-art technologies. It has helped to limit the number of firms competing in major manufacturing industries, thus creating incentives for these firms to undertake the high fixed-cost investments necessary to attain international competitive advantage. It has promoted cooperative research and development among major Japanese competitors. It has ensured manufacturing corporations access to inexpensive long-term finance, the sine qua non of innovative investment strategies. And, by planning and financing a sophisticated system of mass education, the Japanese state has ensured that industry has access to supplies of blue-collar, white-collar, and managerial labor with the behavioral traits and cognitive skills required to function within highly collective, technologically advanced, business organizations.[2]

But however important the role of the Japanese state in shaping an environment conducive to industrial development, the formulation of investment strategies and the building of organizational structures to carry them out has been left to private-sector enterprises that must remain profitable over the long run to survive. These organizations have outperformed their U.S. counterparts because of more thoroughgoing *organizational integration*: the planned coordination of the skills and efforts of individual participants in the business organization toward the achievement of organizational goals.

In major Japanese businesses, organizational integration extends beyond the limits of the planned coordination of the specialized division of labor as practiced under U.S. managerial capitalism. First, organizational integration extends across vertically related firms to a much greater extent in Japan than in the United States, so planned coordination spans units of financial control; the business organization comprises a number of financially distinct business firms. Second, within dominant firms, organizational integration in Japan extends further down the organizational hierarchy to include male blue-collar workers who, like male white-collar and all managerial employees of the firm, have permanent employee status, and hence can consider themselves to be "members" of the business organization. By ensuring that key participants in other firms and on the shop floor are willing and able to work toward organizational goals, these two extensions of organizational integration beyond the once-dominant American model of business organization significantly enhance the value-creating capabilities of Japanese manufacturing.

The combination of far-reaching organizational integration within private-sector manufacturing and the developmental role of the state in creating an economic and social environment conducive to the emergence of innovative capitalist enterprises represents a qualitatively new model in the evolution of capitalist business organization. The high degree of planned coordination of specialized divisions of labor under Japanese capitalism represents a dramatic advance in collective organization when compared with the already considerable planned coordination within managerial firms that arose in the United States in the first half of this century, and even more so when compared with the generally anemic attempts of British industry to enter the age of managerial capitalism.

As I have shown, the ability of Japanese enterprises to include shop-floor workers in the process of planned coordination without losing control over the pursuit of organizational goals has as its basis the historical willingness of Japanese employers to develop skills on the shop floor. In contrast, since the late nineteenth century, U.S. industrial employers have been obsessed with taking skills off the shop floor in an attempt to make any individual worker dispensable and thereby deprive workers of a means of controlling the relation between effort and pay. By doing so, however, American firms have failed to develop the capabilities among shop-floor workers that can enable them to utilize flexible machine technologies—technologies that, when combined with appropriate organizational structures, are transforming the possibilities for value creation in the late twentieth century.

Indeed, by deskilling work on the shop floor, U.S. managers have not only diminished the capabilities of shop-floor workers to contribute to the value-creation process but they have also given these workers, alienated by their deskilled jobs and lack of organizational citizenship, reason to work against rather than for the achievement of enterprise goals. Moreover, by failing to grant "membership" in the business organization to "hourly" workers on a par with "salaried" employees, U.S. managers have made it necessary for shop-floor workers to build independent collective organizations that are not constituted to identify with the goals of the firm, and at times may be utterly opposed to these goals.

Whereas Japanese managers have sought to put skills on the shop floor and American managers to take skills off the shop floor, British industrial employers, for lack of developed managerial structures, have simply left skills on the shop floor, thereby giving workers effective control over the flow of work, and hence over the utilization of the firm's investments. Even in the absence of unions, British employers came to rely on shop stewards to ensure the utilization of shop-floor technologies—a dependence that resulted in the rise of an informal system of collective bargaining within the workplace that tended to dominate the formal bargaining processes between union leadership and company management. The attempts to reform the informal system in the aftermath of the *Donovan Report* only served to enhance the role of shop-floor bargaining on the basis of shop-steward organization. The result was the persistence of the legacy of craft control as a characteristic feature of labor–management relations and a prime determinant of the relation between effort and pay.

The Thatcherite attack on the trade union movement in the 1970s succeeded in diminishing the ranks of union membership in manufacturing and the ability of unions to stage effective strikes. But, in the absence of positive measures to encourage the building of managerial structures to plan and coordinate the productive transformation on the shop floor, British firms have tended to continue their reliance on shop-steward organization. Indeed, the very means adopted by the Thatcher government for attacking the unions—particularly the massive unemployment generated by the policies of high interest rates and exchange rates in the early 1980s—also decimated much of British manufacturing and left what remained financially weak. At the same time, the financial strangulation of higher education under Thatcher in the 1980s reversed the progress that had been made in the 1970s in enabling British universities to turn out "organization men and women" capable of planning and coordinating modern industrial enterprises.

Thatcher's attack on the British union movement has weakened the political power of British labor. But, committed as it is to the ideology of letting markets do their work, Thatcherism has not built the business and educational institutions that industrial leadership in the late twentieth century requires. In an industrial age that calls for greater organizational capabilities to plan and coordinate specialized divisions of labor, laissez-faire policies will not overcome the legacy of underdeveloped managerial structures and shop-floor craft control.

Integration, Commitment, and Value Creation

The historical transformations of work organization in successful capitalist development demonstrate the growing importance of organizational integration as a key structural element in international industrial leadership. The behavioral foundation of organizational integration is *organizational commitment:* the inclusion of individuals as members of an organization with the rights to enjoy its benefits and the consequent willingness of those individuals to contribute to the organization's success.[3] Organizational commitment entails long-term commitments by the business enterprise to the interests of the individual as well as by the individual to supply his or her skill and effort to the pursuit of the organization's goals. A prime proposition that derives from my comparative analysis of organization and technology in the capitalist workplace is that, over the course of the twentieth century, organizational commitment has become increasingly important for value creation on the shop floor.

The basic principle of successful economic performance is the transformation of the fixed costs of investments in plant, equipment, and personnel into low unit costs by achieving a high degree of utilization of these investments. Organizational commitment is a fundamental determinant of the development and utilization of invested resources. It follows that, for any particular industry, what has rendered organizational commitment increasingly important in international competition over the course of this century is the growing importance of investments in plant, equipment, and personnel required to give the business corporation access to superior productive capabilities.

Increasingly, business organizations do not merely buy inputs—whether of a "fixed" or "variable" nature—on the market (as standard microeconomics textbooks have long taught students to believe).[4] Instead, value-creating business organizations increasingly invest in the development of the productive capabilities of the resources—both physical and human—that they have purchased. They develop these resources, moreover, not as separable inputs but rather as integral and interconnected elements of an investment strategy. Having developed these resources, the business organization must then manage their utilization if it hopes to create, rather than waste, value. Increased reliance on the development of productive resources (as opposed to purchasing them "ready-made" on the market) increases the importance of investments over market purchases—and hence of fixed costs over variable costs—because of (1) the greater time lag between the investment expenditures and the realization of returns and (2) the resultant greater uncertainty that the resources in which the organization has invested will actually constitute value-creating inputs at a future point in time.[5]

By eliciting high levels of effort from individuals in the pursuit of organizational goals, organizational commitment reduces both the time lag and uncertainty—and hence the fixed costs—inherent in a given developmental investment strategy. That is, organizational commitment enables the superior utilization of the resources required for the development of the organization's productive capabilities. But to create value, the developed resources still remain to be utilized. By eliciting high levels of effort and hence resource utilization, organizational commitment transforms the high fixed costs of the developmental investments into low unit costs.

As applied to shop-floor labor, organizational commitment ensures that the worker will expend effort to develop the skills that the organization requires and that the worker will give the organization privileged access to those skills once they are developed. Organizational commitment also ensures that the worker will supply high levels of effort in the actual utilization of these skills. The amount of effort supplied by the individual worker determines not only the utilization of his or her skills but also the utilization of interconnected investments in plant and equipment as well as the skills of others in the organization's specialized division of labor. What has changed during the twentieth century in the historical transformations of organization and technology on the shop floor that I have outlined is *the extent to which industrial leadership requires that the enterprise extend organizational commitment to the shop-floor worker.*

When Britain was still the workshop of the world, the investments of individual firms were primarily in already developed plant and equipment. In addition, workers developed their skills under the tutelage of other workers on the job and in their communities, at little cost to their employers. Because firms tended to purchase productive resources in general—plant and equipment as well as personnel—ready-made on the market, fixed costs were relatively low. An abundance of skilled labor in particular industrial regions made organizational commitment less important because of the ready availability of ready-to-use replacement labor.

Even then, in any production period, once the workers had been hired, the supply of effort still affected the utilization of the firm's productive resources. Indeed, in the absence of developmental investments that could differentiate one firm from another, the supply of effort by shop-floor labor (and by the firm's personnel in general) was a prime source of the competitive edge that any single firm could attain. The willingness of a firm to bargain over conditions of work and levels of pay, and the enforcement of these bargains by powerful craft unions, provided the degree of organizational commitment that workers required to induce them to deliver high levels of effort on the shop floor.

Organizational commitment played a major role in the rise of the United States to industrial leadership. Unlike British industry in which firms relied on other firms to supply them with ready-made inputs and to sell their finished products, U.S. firms tended to vertically integrate in order to pursue developmental investment strategies that could, if successful, give them distinct competitive advantages over rivals. To plan and coordinate these high fixed-cost investment strategies, U.S. firms had to build managerial structures; they had to train, and then retain, large numbers of technical specialists who could plan and coordinate the firm's productive activities. To retain the services of these managerial resources and to elicit high levels of effort from these specialists, the firm promised to share with them some of the value gains that the very development and utilization of the firm's productive resources would, it was expected, make possible. These gains were not to be distributed at one point in time, but gradually, and increasingly, over the course of the managerial employee's career with the firm. The organizational commitment among managers thus engendered was critical to the long-run success of the enterprise.

With their integrated managerial structures in place, dominant U.S. firms also used their competitive advantage to buy the cooperation of shop-floor workers in the supply of effort. Given the quest by U.S. managers to take skills off the shop floor, dominant firms devoted few resources to develop the skills of shop-floor workers. Nevertheless, the high fixed costs of vertically integrated investment strategies, including the costs of building managerial structures to plan and coordinate the development and utilization of investments in capital-intensive technology, made it all the more necessary for dominant U.S. manufacturers to gain the cooperation of their workers in the supply of effort. Their dominant market positions enabled these firms to pay their workers wages above the market rate and hold out realistic promises of employment security in exchange for their hard work.

At the same time, however, as the Great Depression demonstrated, and as, over the following decades, both the "hourly" status of workers and their membership in independent industrial unions continued to attest, U.S. shop-floor workers neither enjoyed a generally recognized organizational commitment from their employers nor did they offer such commitment to their firms. Even though many of those who achieved seniority would spend their working lives in the employ of the same firm, they were never admitted as members of the business organization with long-term rights to participate in the value-creation process and share in the value-created.

Not so in the case of Japanese men who have been able to gain entry to blue-collar positions in dominant Japanese firms. In Chapter 9 I argue that, whatever the reinforcing role of a uniquely Japanese culture may have been, the Japanese system of permanent employment arose historically out of the need for Japanese firms to develop skills of key employees—an institutional response not so different from the building of managerial structures by American mass producers from the late nineteenth century. Indeed, like firms in the United States, in the decades prior to World War II Japanese firms generally made explicit promises of permanent employment to managerial personnel. At the same time, however, in contrast to the U.S. experience, an irreparable social gulf did not develop between managers and workers in Japan—a social gulf that, as U.S. experience shows, would have made Japanese employers reluctant to place skills in the hands and heads of shop-floor workers.

I have shown how, despite the existence of militant unionism in Japan at various points in the first half of the twentieth century, there was never any attempt by Japanese workers or their organizations to establish craft control on the shop floor. Historically, the problem facing Japanese capitalists was not to rid themselves of workers who might use their scarce skills to control the organization of work on the shop floor. Rather, their problem was to transform unskilled workers into skilled workers and then retain them by integrating them into the organization. Under these conditions, the Japanese foreman was not merely an enforcer of effort norms, as was the case in the United States, but also a developer of the skills of his subordinates—skills that, combined with hard work, would make the blue-collar worker a valuable asset to the enterprise.

As a result, after World War II, when, in the face of a capital strike by their employers, Japanese blue-collar workers formed independent industrial unions and used their skills to keep their factories running, major firms showed themselves willing and able to regain the commitment of their shop-floor workers by extending permanent employment—explicit membership in the organization—down the hierarchy. Over the past four decades the enterprise unions that were put in place to coopt the industrial unions have safeguarded that membership for blue-collar and white-collar workers of dominant firms. These enterprise unions also exert an influence over their members' contributions to and shares in the value-creation process.[6]

For male blue-collar workers as for male white-collar workers (most of whom eventually enter the managerial ranks), Japanese permanent employment functions both as a training system that develops the skills of employees in a planned and coordinated way and as an incentive system that elicits high levels of effort from individuals. During the first decade of an employee's career, promotion and pay increases occur by gradual steps and by seniority—"fast tracks" have been rare in the Japanese enterprise. During this initial period, the firm invests in considerable specialist training of its permanently employed personnel. In contrast to the American practice of applying the terms *unskilled, semiskilled,* and *skilled* to different types of jobs to be filled by different types of workers, the Japanese have used these terms to apply to the stages through which a particular male worker passes during the first ten years of employment. The firm also provides more general training by the rotation of employees to different departments within the organization. When qualitatively new investment strategies require qualitatively new skills, the permanent employment system gives Japanese firms the incentive to invest in the retraining of mid-career personnel.[7]

The existence of permanent employment and the emphasis on seniority in promotion and rewards, particularly in the early years of an employee's career, encourages workers to cooperate with one another in pursuit of the goals of the firm. It is only in midcareer that promotion on the basis of individual performance becomes important, although even then seniority continues to have some influence on promotion decisions, and remains the predominant determinant of salary increases. But individual incentives are not the only, or necessarily even the best, means of motivating employees. In a technologically complex environment, economic success depends not only on individual initiative but also on cooperative effort among those who participate in the specialized division of labor. Collective rewards may, therefore, provide the appropriate incentive mechanism. Backed by the bargaining power of enterprise unions, all permanent employees receive semiannual bonuses, which typically constitute one third of an individual's annual earnings but are adjusted according to the profitability of the firm, and hence its ability to pay.[8]

As I have shown in Chapter 9, through the organizational commitments inherent in permanent employment, the skills and efforts of male blue-collar workers have been made integral to the organizational capabilities of their firms, an employment practice enabling the Japanese to take the lead in innovative production systems such as just-in-time inventory control, quality circles, and flexible manufacturing. Critical to the functioning of these production systems is the willingness of Japanese managers to develop skills and leave initiative with workers on the shop floor. The recent success of Japanese mass producers in introducing flexible manufacturing systems owes much to the fact that, for decades before the introduction of the new automated technologies, blue-collar workers were granted considerable discretion to monitor and adjust the flow and quality of work on the shop floor.

In Japan, organizational commitment extends beyond the dominant firm itself. The growth of dominant enterprises has fostered the spread of subcontracting arrangements for the supply of inputs, at times as an explicit strategy of a dominant firm to avoid making long-term commitments to more permanent employees. Employment in smaller enterprises provides opportunities to workers who fail to secure a permanent employment position and also caters to the preferences of those Japanese males who choose not to spend their working lives in a large bureaucratic organization. One might be tempted to identify the proliferation of small firms with a move away from organizational coordination to market coordination of the Japanese economy. However, a closer examination of the relations between dominant firms and subcontractors reveals tight organizational integration of the investment strategies and administrative structures of these groups of firms.[9]

In the presence of organizational commitments within and across enterprises, Japan's employers have retained a degree of market flexibility in their utilization of the labor force by reserving permanent employment to men and treating women as a "secondary" labor force to whom organizational commitments need not be made. In this treatment of women, the Japanese are by no means either unique or original. Throughout the history of industrial capitalist development in the West, women have served as a source of cheap labor that can be hired and fired as the short-term needs for more or less labor inputs ebb and flow. The patriarchal structure of both Western and Japanese families leads employers to assume (even though it need not actually be the case) that any given woman has an "organizational commitment" from a male head of household who will bring home a "family wage" from the world of paid work, and hence that women in general do not need to be supplied with either a living wage or employment security when they participate in the paid labor force. Women have therefore been offered, and in the absence of countervailing political power, have historically been prone to accept, "supplementary" wages for their "supplementary" work.[10]

The offer of high wages to men—that is, wages sufficient to support a family at a decent standard of living—typically entails as well a degree of organizational commitment from the employer to the male worker. To quote once again Andrew Ure's statement from the 1830s that "one of the best informed manufacturers" had told him that his firm kept the wages of mule spinners "as high as we can possibly afford" so that the "spinner would reckon the charge of a pair of mules in our factory a fortune for life," and hence would "do his utmost to retain his situation, and to uphold the high character of our yarn."[11] During the 1920s in the United States, firms that could af-

ford to do so also paid male operatives in high-throughput production processes wages above the market rate in order to secure the
long-term commitment of these workers to the firm, and with it the
cooperation in supplying higher levels of effort.

The patriarchal structure of capitalist societies, East and West,
ensures that men, not women, get these "good jobs." Recent studies
of the sex-based division of labor in U.S. manufacturing in the first
half of the twentieth century suggest that women tended to be employed on piece-rates in more labor-intensive production processes in
which extra output, but not necessarily lower unit costs, could be
secured by employing more workers. In running these production
processes, employers were concerned more with low labor costs and
less with the generation of a committed work force that would supply
high levels of effort. In contrast, men tended to be employed on time-
wages, with earnings higher than those women received, in more
capital-intensive processes in which extra output could be secured by
eliciting more effort from the committed workers. Even with the
higher wages, managers expected a sufficiently high utilization of the
high fixed-cost capital equipment to generate lower unit costs.[12]

Because the technologies operated by men in U.S manufacturing
were more effort saving than those operated by women, the effort
expended by men in their so-called heavy work was not necessarily
greater than that expended by women in their so-called light work.
Moreover, because the "male" technologies also tended to be more
skill displacing in their application on the shop floor, the skills that
men (with their relatively high pay) brought to their jobs were not
necessarily of a higher quality than the skills that women brought to
theirs. As Ruth Milkman's study of the U.S. automobile and electrical
manufacturing industries in the 1930s and 1940s reveals, the critical
difference between the employment of men and women was that
firms were willing to extend a degree of organizational commitment
to men but not to women; and as a consequence, managers allocated
men to work on high-throughput production processes in which the
worker's cooperation in maintaining high throughput was essential to
transform high fixed costs into low unit costs.[13]

What is different about the Japanese labor force is the lesser importance than in the West of ethnic minorities from impoverished backgrounds (such as many blacks and Hispanics in the United States)
who, whether male or female, can be allocated along with women in
general to labor-intensive, low-commitment jobs. Hence, Japanese

women have borne much more of the brunt of supplying the second-ary labor force in Japan.[14] The allocation of Japanese women to jobs that do not involve permanent employment reinforces (and perhaps even to some extent causes) the tendency of married Japanese women to drop out of the labor force, particularly during the prime child-bearing and child-rearing years. Even though the labor force partici-pation and attachment of Japanese women has been rising steadily over the past two decades, the prevailing ideology has been that women should not, and indeed because of family commitments can-not, remain committed to a business organization.

In recent years, however, in the face of an acute labor shortage for technically trained personnel, Japanese employers have begun to grant permanent-employment status to college-educated women, al-though in doing so, employers have largely confined them to employ-ment tracks that offer limited, if any, career access to the managerial ranks.[15] As for most Japanese women employed in the paid labor force, it would appear that their cooperation in the supply of effort is secured, as is the case in the West, more by their lack of social power and means of protest in a highly patriarchal society than by their ability to secure organizational commitment and lay claim to a sub-stantial share of the value that their skills and efforts help to create.

Organizational Commitment versus Market Flexibility

One clear manifestation of the organizational commitment of Japa-nese workers is the ability of Japanese manufacturing to maintain high rates of productivity growth in the presence of low rates of unemployment. The business-oriented Liberal Democratic Party, in power since the 1950s, has maintained high rice prices to make small farms viable and has passed legislation to limit the size of firms in the distribution sector.[16] It is these policies, combined with the rapid growth of the Japanese economy (including consumer and financial services), that keep Japanese unemployment rates low. Yet, despite the relative ease with which Japanese workers can find alternative (although not necessarily as attractive) employment opportunities elsewhere in the economy, the organizational commitment that char-acterizes labor—management relations in the major Japanese enter-prises induces shop-floor workers to supply high levels of effort. In effect, to use Albert Hirschman's apt terms, despite the ease of "exit" to alternative employment in Japan, the strong "loyalty" of Japanese workers to their firms as manifested by high levels of effort derives from the "voice" that Japanese firms extend to shop-floor workers in the organization of work and the allocation of rewards.[17]

In sharp contrast to Japan, the Western capitalist economies, with the highly individualistic British and U.S. economies foremost among them, have found that low unemployment rates result in low levels of labor effort as workers use the threat of "exit"—the difficulty that management will have in finding replacements in a boom period—to control the pace and duration of work. Indeed, as I have shown in Chapters 6 and 9, in response to sagging productivity and rising wages during prolonged periods of prosperity, a basic thrust of conservative economic policy in both Britain and the United States in the 1970s and 1980s was to "slow down" the "overheated" economy in order to create a reserve army of labor that could, in Marxian fashion, discipline the labor force.

Reliance on the stick of unemployment rather than on the carrot of prospective value gains to boost labor productivity and restrain current wage increases serves to erode, if not destroy, organizational commitment rather than build it up. Employers who look to employment insecurity rather than employment security to control unit costs are sacrificing the development of long-term value-creating capabilities for the prospect of short-term gains. For, as Frederick W. Taylor understood about 100 years ago, once workers' expectations of sharing in the gains of the enterprise are shattered, it may take years to regain their trust in managerial promises of employment security and higher remuneration in exchange for the supply of high levels of effort. As I have shown in Chapter 7, Taylor's own efforts at convincing workers to trust in "scientific management" failed. Even in the late nineteenth century, the Taylorist incentive system that tied today's earnings to today's output was much too short run to build the organizational commitment that the development and utilization of high-throughput technology required. Because of the high fixed costs inherent in the investment strategies of the more technologically advanced firms, to build organizational commitment required as its basis the granting of employment security so that the contribution of effort to the firm today would be rewarded not only today, but even more so tomorrow and the day after and for years beyond.

In the early decades of the twentieth century, the stick of unemployment still worked to enforce labor discipline in the United States, although even then the insufficiency of this mode of labor management is well reflected in John Commons's apt observation that "in hard times, when we don't want people to work so hard and increase the supply of production, they work the hardest."[18] In the post– World War II decades, however, collective organization among American workers significantly lessened the impact of the threat of unemployment on the supply of effort in the workplace. Seniority provisions and bureaucratic grievance procedures protected union- ized workers from indiscriminate layoffs or terminations, depriv- ing first-line supervisors of their prime weapon for increasing the pace of work. In addition, the social security legislation that was the political response to the massive unemployment of the 1930s, com- bined with the continuing political pressure of the labor movement as well as specific union–management agreements in the era of mass- production unionism, provided American workers with a safety net of unemployment insurance, welfare payments, and supplemental un- employment benefits. The safety net significantly decreased what some economists have called the "cost of job loss."[19] As the cost of job loss declines, so too does the effort that the threat of job loss can coerce from reluctant shop-floor workers. Hence the reliance of busi- ness organizations on the market mechanism to discipline labor may not be very effective in lowering unit costs even in the short run, and it surely destroys the organizational commitment required in a tech- nologically dynamic and complex industrial era over the longer run.

Yet there are those who, evidently ignorant of the role of collective organizations in successful capitalist development, insist on the efficacy of the unimpeded market mechanism for solving economic ills. Indeed, with the engine of managerial capitalism stalling in both the British and U.S. economies by the 1970s, free-market ideology attained political hegemony and sought to rid itself of the allegedly debilitating rigidities created by the allegedly misguided interventions of the Keynesian welfare state. The overriding mission of both the Reagan and Thatcher administrations in the 1980s was to reduce social benefits, along with union power, in order to restore the disci- plinary powers of a "flexible" labor market. For example, Michael Edwardes, then running BL (formerly British Leyland), related how, at a meeting with BL senior executives in 1981, Alan Walters, an economic advisor to Thatcher,

> launched into the theory that the closure of BL, whether as a result
> of a strike or in cold blood, could have a positive effect on the

British economy within six months. The short-term impact on regions such as the West Midlands and on the balance of payments might soon be offset, according to Alan Walters, by the beneficial effect of the shock of closures on trades union and employee attitudes across the country. Restrictive practices would be swept away, pay increases would be held down and a more rapid improvement in Britain's competitiveness would thus be achieved through the closure of BL than by any other means available to the Government![20]

The ideological support for such free-market economic policies has come not only from political conservatives within the economics profession—the "monetarists" and "supply-siders"—but also, often unwittingly, from some more liberal economists who have sought to explain the relatively poor macroeconomic performances of the British and American economies in the 1970s and 1980s by reference to rigidities in the labor market that prevented full employment. These economists argue that, for some reason, going wages remain above their market-clearing level, thereby rendering involuntarily unemployed those workers who demand the going wage but can find no employer who is willing to supply it. The policy implication is that if we could reduce the causes of wage stickiness, market flexibility would restore the economy to full employment.

Prominent among wage-stickiness explanations are the efficiency-wage models of the labor market.[21] These models generally locate the origins of involuntary unemployment in the propensity of workers to restrict output or, as the efficiency-wage economists typically put it, "shirk"—that is, supply less effort per unit of time than the employer thinks they should.[22] Full employment gives workers the power of exit that makes it difficult for employers to impose their effort norms. As a result, individual employers offer their workers higher wages to make employment in their particular firms more attractive than alternative opportunities, and thereby elicit more effort. But when all employers (operating subject to the same conditions of cost, price, and technology) offer the higher efficiency wages, workers begin to shirk again. Employers then lay off workers at the higher wage, a response resulting in unemployment and less shirking. If the unemployment leads employers to lower wages, however, shirking will reappear. The efficiency-wage models then seek to determine the equilibrium relation between effort and pay within each firm and the equilibrium level of involuntary unemployment in the economy as a whole by making assumptions concerning the costs that the firm incurs in monitoring shirking and the costs that the worker incurs if he or she is detected.[23]

Efficiency-wage models represent a significant advance in mainstream economic thinking. They bring the "effort bargain" into economic analysis and, indeed, make it a central microeconomic phenomenon in the determination of macroeconomic outcomes. These models also recognize Marx's century-old insight that the reserve army of labor affects not only the level of wages but also the supply of effort. By the same token, from my perspective, the most valuable theoretical and empirical contributions to the efficiency-wage literature are those of radical economists who, by integrating efficiency-wage arguments into a Marxian analytical framework, explore the role of social power, within the workplace and through the agency of the state, in the determination of the relation between effort and pay.[24]

For understanding the dynamics of capitalist development, however, what is missing in the efficiency-wage models—radical and mainstream—is the analysis of the causes and consequences of effort-saving technological change. Mainstream economists simply ignore the role of technological change in the determination of the relation between effort and pay, primarily because their idealization of the market-coordinated economy leaves them without a theory of the firm as an agent of technological change. Radical economists working in the Marxist tradition do not generally suffer from such a handicap. They tend to follow Marx in viewing technology as a capitalist weapon that, by displacing the skills of workers, augments the coercive power of capitalists to lower pay and increase effort on the shop floor. Nevertheless, with their focus on class conflict as the driving force in capitalist development, Marxists tend to ignore the possibilities that investments in effort-saving technology create for cooperative relations between workers and managers.[25]

Technology may be and has been, as Marxists argue, used to give employers the upper hand over their workers. But, whatever the short-run gains in extracting effort from workers, the use of technology as a class weapon creates problems for the development and utilization of technology. It removes the possibilities for developing complementary skills on the part of workers, and hence, as I have noted in the case of U.S. mass production, limits the firm's flexibility in the use of shop-floor technology. Moreover, even when the technological change deskills shop-floor workers, the attempt by capitalists to press home their new-found social power can result in costly sabotage, as the American historical experience of mass production also shows. But once the capital cost of an investment in effort-saving technology has been sufficiently reduced and its effort-saving impact has been sufficiently increased (both the results of the development and utilization of resources in the production of the technology itself), effort-saving technological change creates the positive-sum possibility for managers to share out value gains with shop-floor workers in the forms of reduced effort and higher pay, while still increasing the managerial surplus.

The historical record of advanced capitalist development that I have reviewed strongly suggests that capitalist enterprises that have been willing and able to make use of effort-saving technological change to fashion cooperative labor–management relations have been the ones that, through the consequent development and utilization of their organization's productive resources, have been able to gain sustained competitive advantage. This perspective can explain not only the stability of labor–management relations in dominant enterprises for significant periods of time but also a firm-specific basis on which these enterprises differentiate themselves from their competitors and indeed emerge as dominant.[26] The perspective can explain, moreover, why cooperative labor–management relations turn conflictual once a firm has been surpassed in its ability to develop and utilize effort-saving technology and finds that the distribution of value-created has become a zero-sum situation.

I have also argued that the foundation for cooperative labor–management relations is not merely the sharing-out of value gains at a point in time but also the long-term commitment of the enterprise to do so—a commitment that is manifested by employment security, rising incomes, and better work conditions. In return for this commitment from the enterprise, workers supply sufficiently high levels of effort to the value-creation process to enable the firm to secure and maintain its dominant competitive position, and hence enable it to afford to live up to its commitments to them.

Contrary to the policy implication of efficiency-wage models, then, effort-saving technological change means that capitalist firms do not have to rely on the flexibility of the labor market to enforce discipline on their workers. Organizational commitment manifests an alternative labor-relations strategy with far more powerful value-creating potential. In the conventional economic models, in which effort-saving technological change in particular and economic development in general play no role, *labor-market inflexibility is the source of the economic problem;* the firm looks to unemployment as the way to get reluctant workers to supply effort. In my model, with its central focus on effort-saving technology in the process of economic development, *labor-market inflexibility is the solution to the economic problem;* the firm builds organizational commitment that makes possible the development and utilization of effort-saving technological change.

In my model, when a firm has not been able to gain distinct competitive advantage and when workers shirk because they know that they can easily find alternative employment elsewhere, it is because the firm has not gone far enough in building an organizational structure that, on the basis of the positive-sum benefits of effort-saving technological change, can make the relation between management and workers immune from market influences. Conversely, managers who view the existence of unemployment as a means of gaining the upper hand in the effort bargain—that is, managers who favor market flexibility over organizational commitment—will destroy what organizational commitment they may have built up in the past. Based as it is on workers' expectations for employment security, once destroyed, organizational commitment is difficult to rebuild.

In a technologically dynamic industry, therefore, to rely on market flexibility may increase productivity and profitability in the short run but place the firm at a competitive disadvantage over the long run. But what about the impact of organizational commitment versus market flexibility on the economy as a whole? The history of capitalist development and shifts in international industrial leadership suggests that national economies populated by firms that make organizational commitments to their key employees, and that consequently lead in the development and utilization of technology, are economies that have the capability of creating high levels of employment for their labor forces.

The growth of employment within technologically dynamic firms during their rise to dominance within their industries suggests that the labor-displacing impact of effort-saving technology per unit of output is more than offset, and usually overwhelmed, by the labor-using impact of the growth of market share. Although the process of "creative destruction" may mean that the rise to dominance of one firm reduces employment in other firms, these other firms may be foreign competitors, in which case the growth in market share will expand domestic employment. The growth of dominant firms also engenders employment-creating opportunities for smaller enterprises to supply goods and services. In addition, the higher incomes produced by dynamic enterprises create more product demand in the economy, an outcome that in turn creates more demand for domestic labor in industries in which national firms have competitive advantage. Also, some of the value gains generated by the development and utilization of effort-saving technology can be used to pay taxes that finance public-sector expenditures that increase the demand for labor. Insofar as firms have augmented their surpluses by the superior development and utilization of technology, the corporate taxes that pay for the increases in employment-generating public-sector spending need not reduce the returns to labor or capital and need not absorb so much of the managerial surplus that tax-paying firms must reduce their levels of expenditures on investments in plant, equipment, and personnel.

The economy just described is a prosperous one, driven by the dynamic interaction of organization and technology within dominant business organizations. Yet mainstream economists have a rather negative name for the product-market power and organizational commitments that characterize dominant enterprises: "market imperfections." Neoclassical economic theory says that "market imperfections" lead to less than "optimal" outcomes. Its theorists fail to note, however, that, driven as "optimal" outcomes are by exogenously determined household preferences, they need not have anything to do with rapid and sustained economic development. The history of capitalist development, and the theory based on that history that I have outlined, predicts that if one were to put a *perfectly* competitive economy with the same initial resource endowments in direct competition with an imperfectly competitive economy of, say, the Japanese (or even the American) variety, the perfectly competitive economy would soon fall far behind, its productive potential dissipated by market flexibility—or, put differently, its lack of organizational commitment.

Almost a half-century ago, Joseph Schumpeter, one of the twentieth century's foremost students of capitalist development, chastised economists for clinging to the perfectly competitive ideal:

What we have got to accept is that [the large-scale enterprise] has come to be the most powerful engine of [economic] progress and in particular of the long-run expansion of total output not only in spite of, but to a considerable extent through, this strategy that looks so restrictive when viewed in the individual case and from the individual point in time. In this respect, perfect competition is not only impossible but inferior, and has no title to being set up as a model of ideal efficiency.[27]

Schumpeter sought an historically relevant theory of economic development, a task that conventional economists have all but ignored. Like mainstream efficiency-wage theorists, modern macroeconomic theorists in general extoll the virtues of labor market flexibility. One example during the 1980s was Martin Weitzman's call for a "share economy" to replace the prevailing "wage economy" which was, it was alleged, the prime cause of stagflation—high rates of unemployment in the presence of high rates of inflation—in countries like Britain and the United States.[28] By making the remuneration of the labor force in any particular company a predetermined share of revenues rather than a fixed wage bill, wages could become flexible enough to ensure full employment. Employers would have an incentive to hire any unemployed workers because the expanded labor force would only get a share of the marginal revenue of labor.[29] Something approximating a flexible labor market would as a result be restored as firms would find it profitable to employ any available labor. Weitzman concluded his book with this statement:

> Those who clamor for an "industrial policy" to improve capitalism need look no further than a change in the way workers of large industrial corporations are compensated. Just let labor be paid on a share system—and turn loose the dogs of competition. That simple change will unleash more powerful forces for economic prosperity and social progress than are to be found in the wildest visions of national planners or cultural revolutionaries.[30]

As I have argued throughout this book, the sharing of the gains of the value-creation process between management and labor is critical for the prosperity of the enterprise and the national economy as a whole. But there any semblance between Weitzman's arguments and mine end. For, as in the mainstream efficiency-wage arguments, technology and economic development play no role in the "share economy" solution. Witness Weitzman's notions of the firm's "three major economic decisions: (1) how much output to produce; (2) how much labor to hire; (3) what price to charge."[31] Left out are what I consider to be the three major decisions of the firm: how much to invest, in what type of technology, and with what type of organizational structure.

Weitzman recognized that "a relatively small number of large-scale firms . . . set the tone for the entire system. I have in mind such companies as the Fortune 500, a group that accounts for over 80 percent of sales in the industrial sector. If these big corporations are doing well, so is the economy, and vice versa."[32] Agreed. But for any one of these dominant firms to do well, the critical decisions (as the work of Alfred D. Chandler, Jr., the most assiduous student of the collective histories of these companies, has shown) have to do with its investment strategy and organizational structure. Compared with these decisions—ones that involve long-term financial and organizational commitments—Weitzman's three major decisions (the standard ones of textbook microeconomic theory, it might be noted) represent but marginal adjustments.[33]

Lacking a theory of enterprise organization, Weitzman was vague about how "the share economy" will affect labor effort, investments in human capabilities, and unit costs. Weitzman argued that the full employment that results from the share economy will lead employers "to create in the labor market a rich panoply of nonprice competition for workers," including "innovative recruitment and training procedures," while increasing "the security of workers knowing their present job can be kept because a share firm de facto offers lifetime employment; and even if a job should be lost or a worker wishes to transfer, another job can be found relatively easily in a share economy."[34] Weitzman made no mention of the possible costs of these "innovative recruitment and training procedures," giving the reader the impression that he thought that these costs are trivial. Nor did he raise the possibility that, absent substantial organizational commitments to workers in the form of items such as training, seniority pay (which Weitzman argued will have to go in a share economy),[35] and the realistic promise of (and not just, as Weitzman put it, "de facto") lifetime employment, workers will use the ease of exit via the labor market to reduce their supply of effort.

Indeed, despite his insistence that "the share economy" will "turn loose the dogs of competition," Weitzman made no reference to the efficiency-wage literature (mainstream or otherwise), which stresses the inverse relation between full employment and effort under competitive market conditions. With his focus on the form of remuneration in the labor exchange, and little if any thought devoted to the social relations of production (and absolutely no mention of the problem of technological change), it is not surprising that Weitzman did not recognize that, in the late twentieth century, organizational commitment, not market flexibility, would be required for a "share economy" to create sufficient value to generate full employment. Nor is it surprising that, in his brief discussion of the Japanese labor system, Weitzman focused on the twice yearly enterprise bonuses as the essence of the system, with barely a mention of permanent employment, which in fact provides the institutional foundation for workers to lay claim to, and bargain over, the sharing-out of the firm's surplus revenues.[36]

Absent from both the efficiency-wage explanation of inferior macroeconomic performance and the share-economy proposal to resolve the problem is, therefore, the role of organizational commitment in fostering the development and utilization of effort-saving technological change. Both approaches start from the conception that a modern capitalist economy is basically a market economy, and that any remuneration to labor that does not equilibrate the market for labor must have a negative impact on macroeconomic performance. In contrast, the study of the history of twentieth-century capitalist development shows that increasingly, far from representing movements toward the perfectly competitive ideal of the neoclassical economist, the basis of international competitive advantage and superior national economic performance has been the ability of business enterprises *to take control of market forces by building organizational commitment*—by extending to its key participants full and enduring membership in their organizations, with all the potential costs and benefits that membership entails.

During the 1980s there was a growing recognition in the United States and Britain of the need for institutional transformations that could enhance the role of labor in the economy as a means of creating the conditions for rapid technological change.[37] A key buzzword of the 1980s was *flexibility,* and although it was not always clear what flexibility meant or implied, it would appear that those who called for policies that would elevate the role of shop-floor labor meant what I would call organizational flexibility as distinct from the market flexibility advocated by the mainstream of the economics profession.[38]

The distinction between organizational flexibility and market flexibility is inherent in the work of Ronald Dore, a leading scholar of Japanese economy and society who has articulated the implications of Japanese economic success for Western capitalist societies.[39] Referring to the role of industrial policy in permitting Japan to respond to inflationary pressures and international competition in the 1970s, Dore noted the importance of "flexible rigidities"—in effect, organizational flexibility at the level of the state. Dore argued that

> With Mrs Thatcher and Mr Reagan showing the way, it has become orthodoxy in OECD circles that only by restoring to markets their competitive vigour can the dynamism of the world's leading economies be restored. 'Monetarist' may be what the new orthodoxy is usually called, but 'marketist' better describes its inspiration.

But Dore then asked,

> Why on earth . . . should Japan, an economy which almost flaunts its rigidities as a matter of principle, be the most successful among the OECD countries at dynamically adjusting to the three challenges [of the 1970s]—absorbing the oil-price rises, controlling inflation at a low figure, and shifting the weight of its industrial structure decisively away from declining to competitive industries?[40]

Whether used as a tool of business policy or government policy, organizational flexibility may appear to be an oxymoron. Just as the term *mass production* implies the commitment of resources to specific machines to produce specific outputs, so the word *organization* implies the commitment of resources to specific people to do specific tasks. In either case, investments, whether in machines or people, represent *commitments,* which by definition impart rigidity to future decisions and actions.

Yet, in an economic world where the interaction of organization and technology has become increasingly important for the successful development and utilization of productive resources, the rigidities inherent in these organizational and technological commitments represent increasingly essential foundations for flexible investment responses to new economic opportunities and new competitive challenges. The source of flexibility is the higher level of economic development that the prior interaction of organization and technology has generated. Successful economic development creates financial and organizational foundations for making the high fixed-cost investments that can renew and sustain the development process. The flexibility to make these innovative investment decisions may not be available to firms, industries, and societies that have yet to experience successful development.

The issue, therefore, is not whether or not an advanced capitalist economy will have organizational and technological rigidities; such rigidities are inherent in the very process of economic development, relying as it does upon collective organization and complex technology. Rather the question is whether, when an economy is faced with the need for change, these "rigidities" promote or impede the development process—whether the organizational commitment and technological capabilities that constitute these rigidities are sufficiently well developed to make participants in the value-creation process able and willing to make the investments that renewed innovation and economic development require.

Organizational and technological rigidities impede economic development when those who exercise control over the process of planned coordination are unable, and hence unwilling, to lead in the process of change. Although I have by no means analyzed the impacts of all aspects of business organization on economic performance, I have made the case that the failure to integrate shop-floor workers into the structure of business organization is impeding the ability and incentive of British and American industrial managers to respond to the Japanese challenge. The legacies of British craft control and American job control remain deeply embedded in the structure of work organization in the late twentieth century precisely because these institutional arrangements gained legitimacy and power as elements of the prior successes of these two once-dominant economies. The rise of more powerful modes of combining organization and technology transformed the older institutions of shop-floor control from agents to impediments of industrial progress because of the continued presence of groups of individuals with vested interests in preserving the bargaining power, and perhaps even the way of life, that these older institutions had offered.

Indeed, as one can see quite clearly in the long history of British decline, business enterprises, national industries, and a national economy as a whole can adapt to current conditions on the basis of institutions that can no longer contribute to a process of industrial innovation, making existing institutions all the harder to change. Following William Abernathy, some have called the phenomenon the productivity–technology dilemma:[41] the ability of a business organization to generate value by utilizing the productivity potential of past investments in organization and technology as an alternative to undertaking costly investments required to develop the productive potential of new effort-saving technologies. As I have shown in the case of the British cotton textile industry, sooner or later the economic and social limits of such an adaptive strategy will be reached, as participants in the value-creation process find themselves struggling over slices of a shrinking pie. In the absence of a strategy for technological innovation, those who (by birth or by training, or both) believe in the efficacy of the free market will be able to point to the vested interests that now manifest themselves as the cause of the productivity problem and will attack their positions of control without building new value-creating organizations to take their place. Industrial renewal may well require the destruction of outmoded economic institutions, but business and government policies that are merely destructive will not cure the problem of technological stagnation and industrial decline.

Rather, what will happen—as indeed I believe has already happened in Britain and the United States over the past two decades—is that the vast majority of the working population will find themselves working harder to acquire the same standard of living, or, alternatively, borrowing against the future without gaining access to the value-creating assets (both human and physical) that will ultimately be required to pay back the debts. Various modes of adaptation may enable these countries to prolong the day of reckoning—but as a result it will be all the more harsh when it finally comes.

In both Britain and the United States, there is growing recognition of the need to retrain the labor force and create long-term organizational commitments as basic conditions for getting these national economies back on track. The history of successful capitalist development in the twentieth century shows that the institutions that must take the lead in making the necessary investments in and commitments to the labor force are well-financed business organizations that, through innovative investment strategies, can attain the industrial dominance that can make the organizational commitments real. Yet in both Britain and the United States in the 1980s, the trend was in the opposite direction. Highly mobile finance, that was anything but committed to the process of economic development, tore once-powerful business organizations apart when what was needed was to build them up. Just as mobile labor increases wages and undermines the utilization of resources on the shop floor, so too mobile finance increases the cost of capital while undermining the development of the business organization's productive resources. Whether from financiers or workers, value creation requires commitment to the organization, not mobility via the market.[42]

The development of a labor force capable of implementing the technologies of flexible mass production requires that not only business organizations but also the state make investments in human resources. Public education is nothing new to either Britain or the United States. But the mass educational systems that prevail in these countries today are inherited from eras when, as was more the case in Britain, relatively uneducated youths learned industrial skills through on-the-job experience, or, as was more the case in the United States, somewhat older youths with more years of education entered de-skilled jobs that required little in the way of cognition or intellect. There was a time in the history of these national economies when a mass education system that offered only the rudiments of human knowledge while stressing conformity and social discipline prepared its students well for the work roles that lay ahead.[43] But a mode of mass education that was consistent with the development and utilization of productive resources in a bygone era has become dysfunctional now.

Because managerial capitalism developed so vigorously in the United States, the American economy is far ahead of Britain in investments in higher education that can potentially (if they do not just produce hordes of financial manipulators) serve the needs of technologically dynamic business organizations. In mass public education, however, the United States may well be worse off than Britain (which is in any case no model of comparison) because of the drastic deterioration of inner cities over the past two decades, and with it the drastic deterioration of the productive capabilities of the youth that had supplied the blue-collar labor force. Indeed, the very deterioration of the inner cities is in part a result of U.S. industrial decline. For prior to industrial decline, inner-city youths could aspire to "good jobs"— jobs that paid living wages and offered employment security. Hence they could see the point of acquiring a high-school diploma as an aid to gaining entry to these jobs.[44]

To reverse the social as well as the economic decline that has beset the United States, there is therefore a need for simultaneous investments in the creation of "good jobs" and in an education system that can prepare the masses of American youth to participate in a "high-technology" world. But just as private-sector financial mobility, and the massive levels of corporate indebtedness that it has created, militate against the huge investments in job creation that are required, so too the massive public-sector borrowing spree of the 1980s, and the consequent drain of government revenues abroad (and particularly to Japan) that will continue into the very distant future, militate against the huge commitments of public resources to mass education that are required.[45]

In the face of such needs for institutional restructuring in Britain and the United States, the prevailing faith that market flexibility will set the economy back on track reflects at best an extreme ignorance of the dynamics of capitalist development and at worst a means for those with economic and political power to open up more avenues for the "free marketeering" that permits them to extract value from the economic system without contributing to the value-creation process. The history of capitalist development in the twentieth century demonstrates the need for organizational commitment to generate enduring economic prosperity. A first step toward building the organizational commitment in—and rebuilding the organizational capabilities of—the economies of Britain and the United States is to shed the ideology of a long outmoded market capitalism which views accumulation without commitment as a virtue rather than a vice. Value creation in the late twentieth century requires a social system that rewards those who commit their resources to the value-creation process—particularly the masses of workers who, given sufficient training and incentives, stand ready to exercise skill and supply effort on the shop floor.

Appendix

The Basic Analytics of Shop-Floor Value Creation

Value-Created

The most basic conception of the employment relation is the exchange of labor-time for a wage. The profit-seeking firm employs an income-seeking worker when the value-created per unit of labor-time is equal to or greater than the wage paid. For a given amount of labor-time, value-created on the shop floor can be derived from the following formula:

$$V = R - F - M,$$

where V is value-created, R is revenues, F is the firm's fixed costs of organization and technology, and M is the firm's nonlabor variable costs.

In the determination of revenues, $R = pQ$, where p is product price and Q is the quantity of product sold. In the determination of fixed costs, $F = rS$, where r is the return to financial capital and S is the total cost of the fixed investments in technology and organization employed alongside wage labor to manufacture and market the product. These costs are fixed because, in a given production period, they are incurred irrespective of the amount of output produced on the shop floor. In the determination of nonlabor variable (or materials) costs, $M = gHQ$, where g is the market price per unit of materials and H is the quantity of materials required to produce a unit of output. As in the revenues term, Q represents the quantity of output sold during the production period. Hence the value-created equation can be rewritten as

$$V = pQ - rS - gHQ.$$

The total quantity of value-created in a production period depends on the levels of prices, p, r, and g, and quantities, Q, S, and H.

The distribution of value-created between management and labor depends on the size of the wage bill required to produce V. The wage bill is equal to wL, where w is the wage per unit of labor-time and L is the number of units of labor-time employed. Because value-created, revenues, and costs are monetary flows per unit of time (the production period) for which the wage bill is paid, the generation of profits in excess of the cost of capital requires that value-created be greater than the wage bill. I shall call these excess profits the "managerial surplus."

The size of the managerial surplus relative to the wage bill can be calculated by deriving a unit cost equation:

$$n = \frac{rS}{Q} + \frac{wL}{Q} + gH,$$

where n equals unit costs and the rest of the terms have already been defined. Solving for rS and substituting into the second value-created equation presented earlier yields

$$V = (p - n)Q + wL = X + Y.$$

$X = (p - n)Q$ is the managerial surplus, and $Y = wL$ is the wage bill. Therefore, this form of the value-created equation expresses the distribution of value-created between management and labor. Algebraically, the managerial surplus can be expressed simply as revenues (pQ) minus costs (nQ). But substantively, an analysis of the size, sources, and uses of the managerial surplus is central to understanding the process of value creation because it enables one to comprehend the economic impacts of investments in organization and technology on the application of skill and effort on the shop floor.

Strategy and Structure

What determines the prices and quantities that enter into the value-created equation? In the conventional theory of the firm (found in virtually any standard economics textbook), p, r, g, and w are market-determined prices that the firm takes as given. The firm then chooses the level of output, Q, that maximizes profits, as well as that combination of capital and labor inputs from a given array of technological alternatives that minimizes the costs of producing the profit-maximizing level of output. The choice of technology determines the amount of physical capital, K, inherent in S and H combined, as well as the amount of L required to complement K.

The acceptance of this orthodox theory of the firm renders one ill equipped to analyze the process of shop-floor value creation. The theory assumes that p, r, g, and w are given by the market and that Q, K, and L are given by technology. Technology also determines the division of K into fixed and variable inputs. Market forces and technological alternatives, both determined external to the firm, combine to determine economic outcomes. In this conception of the firm, there is no apparent role for either enterprise strategy or organizational structure in the creation of value.

The analysis of the process of value creation requires a conception of the nature of the firm that recognizes that the levels of any or all of the prices and quantities that determine the amount of value that a firm creates may depend on firm-specific investment strategies and organizational structures, as well as on the nation-specific and industry-specific competitive environments in which the firm attempts to create value. A theory of value creation that has historical applicability must at least contemplate the possibility that the relevant prices and quantities are determined by the strategy and structure of the firm in response to its competitive environment.

The contribution to a historically relevant theory of value creation that I shall present focuses on enterprise strategy and structure in determining the organization of work on the shop floor. Work organization can play a critical role in generating the expansion of output per unit of time that results in value creation. The firm's management provides physical resources (buildings, machines, materials) required to produce the product as well as organizational resources (engineers and administrators) required to plan and coordinate the specialized division of shop-floor labor. To finance these investments in technology and organization, management pays financiers returns on their capital in the forms of dividends and interest. In the value-created function, this return to financial capital is represented by r.

Workers provide skill and effort. The combination of machines, materials, and workers' skills constitute the shop-floor technology. A given shop-floor technology is characterized by the productive capability to transform inputs into outputs—a capability that I shall signify by the production coefficient, α. At any point in time, productive capability as captured by α only represents *potential* output. The extent to which the productive capability inherent in α is realized depends on the amount of productive effort (E) that workers expend on the job. For a given technology using L units of labor-time, the firm's production function can be described as

$$Q = \alpha f(E),$$

where increases in E result in increases in Q, but at a diminishing rate up to some maximum physically and mentally sustainable level (E_M in Figure A.1). An increase in the productive capability of a technology from α_1 to α_2, as depicted in Figure A.1, can be termed *effort-saving* because the same level of output can be produced with less expenditure of human effort. The value-creating potential of technological change inheres in its effort-saving impact on the process of transforming inputs into outputs.

Substituting this production function into the value-created equation renders value-created a function of technology (which includes the productive capabilities of skill as well as those of machines and materials), effort, product price, and fixed and variable capital costs:

$$V = (p - gH)\alpha f(E) - F.$$

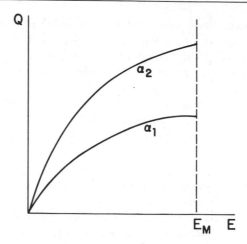

A.*1* Effort-saving technological change. E, productive effort; Q, firm's output; α, technological coefficient.

The relation between value-created and effort expended on the shop floor described by this equation is graphed on the right-hand side of Figure A.2. The horizontal axis on the left-hand side of the figure measures the firm's wage bill (Y) that distributes a portion of the value-created to the firm's workers.

Assume that the wage bill is Y_1. As shown in Figure A.2, if workers provide an amount of effort equal to E_A, the value of output produced just covers fixed and variable capital costs, and value-created is zero. If effort rises to E_B, value-created increases to V_1, which equals Y_1. The firm is generating enough value to replace the cost of the fixed capital stock, but workers are capturing all the value-created. Only when value-created on the shop floor is greater than V_1 will there be a managerial surplus—value-created under the control of management over and above the return to financiers, r, and prevailing managerial salaries, which, for the sake of analyzing value creation *on the shop floor,* are included as elements of the fixed capital stock, S. For a managerial surplus to exist, effort must be greater than E_B.

The managerial surplus is central to the achievement of managerial goals over a series of production periods. The managerial surplus can be used for new investments in technology and organization that permit the firm to remain competitive or gain competitive advantage. It can provide management with resources to increase their own compensation, as well as a justification for doing so. It also furnishes management with resources that can be used in economic downturns to pay financiers their expected rate of return and avoid challenges to management control. It can be passed on to

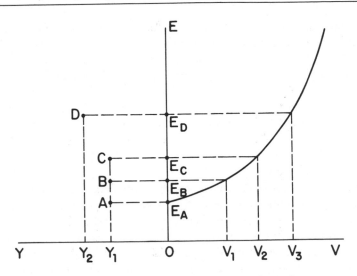

A.2 Effort, value-created, and the managerial surplus. E, productive effort; V, value-created; Y, firm's wage bill.

consumers in the form of price reductions, thus increasing the firm's market share. Or, by providing management with the internal resources to provide employment stability and increased earnings and benefits to their workers, the managerial surplus may form the foundations for cooperative shop-floor relations.

Augmenting the Managerial Surplus

How might the managerial surplus be increased? Recall that the managerial surplus is $(p - n)Q$. Assume that the firm can sell more output without lowering the product price. The most general condition for an increase in the managerial surplus is that an expansion of output, say from Q_1 to Q_2, results in revenues that more than offset the increased costs, $n_2Q_2 - n_1Q_1$, necessary to achieve the output expansion, where n_1 and n_2 are, respectively, unit costs before and after the increase in output.

The challenge facing management is to expand output without an untoward increase in costs. Obviously, if management can increase Q without incurring any additional costs, then more value is created and the managerial surplus expands. Indeed, the managerial surplus increases not only because (assuming that p remains unchanged) the output expansion provides more revenues but also because of the decline in unit costs as fixed costs and the wage bill are spread over more output.

Such costless output expansion can be achieved by eliciting *unremunerated* effort from workers. If workers who are supplying less effort than the maximum that they could physically and mentally sustain would only work up to their productive potential without demanding more wages, more output would be produced without any increase in the firm's costs. The influence of effort on output for a given productive capability is captured in the firm's production function, $Q = \alpha f(E)$. If $\alpha f(E)$ is substituted for Q in the unit cost function above, then it can be seen that the lowering of unit costs, and hence the increase of the managerial surplus, depend on decreases in not only unit labor costs but also unit fixed capital costs. If fixed costs are greater than the wage bill, then an increase in effort lowers unit fixed costs more than it lowers unit labor costs.

For any given wage bill, management may complain that their workers are "shirking," "not pulling their weight," "lying down on the job," and so on. But unless there is an exogenous change in the firm's socioeconomic environment that increases the social power of managers to extract effort from their workers, the level of effort and the managerial surplus will remain unchanged. Two important examples of such changes are increased unemployment that makes workers more fearful of losing their jobs or labor legislation that decreases the bargaining power of unions. In the absence of an exogenous restructuring of social power, management must incur extra costs to elicit more effort from its workers.

A managerial strategy to elicit more effort from workers is closer shop-floor supervision. Supervision costs must then be added to the shop-floor labor costs incurred in the value-creation process. In Figure A.2, supervision costs increase the total wage bill (operative and supervisory) from Y_1 to Y_2. Assume, as shown in Figure A.2, that the resultant closer supervision increases effort from E_C to E_D. The managerial surplus increases if the extra effort achieved through increased supervision results in sufficient value-created to offset the higher shop-floor labor costs. In Figure A.2, the managerial surplus increases because $V_3 - V_2$ is greater than $Y_2 - Y_1$.

The amount of extra effort, and hence value-created per supervisory dollar, depends on the relative social power of management and labor to control the pace of work on the shop floor. Social power in turn depends in part on the technological requirements of production—specifically the dependence of management on the skills of its workers. It also depends in part on the socioeconomic environment in which the firm operates, particularly the opportunities for individual workers to quit undesirable work conditions and the degree of collective organization of shop-floor workers.

Consider the implications for value creation of some of these determinants of social power. Periods of economic boom create opportunities for management to expand output. To take advantage of these demand conditions, the firm must exercise control over the supply of effort. But in periods of economic boom, tight labor markets diminish the costs of job loss to workers because they can easily secure alternative employment, a situation enabling even less skilled workers to resist coercive attempts by supervisors to induce more effort from them. The returns to increased supervision are, therefore, relatively low at precisely those times when, if more effort were forthcoming from workers, the opportunities for increased value-created—for generating value gains—are greatest.

The supervisor *may* (in the absence of workers' organizations that exercise control over hiring, firing, promotion, and remuneration) have the right to dismiss or otherwise penalize workers who do not perform as expected. If, in the attempt to discipline a reluctant labor force, highly skilled workers are replaced with less skilled workers, the decline in α means that more effort will be required to generate a given value-created. If both wages and value-created are directly proportional to skill level, then the managerial surplus will be unaffected by the shift from fewer highly skilled to more less skilled workers. Any increase in value-created and the managerial surplus must come from management's ability to use the hiring (or the threat of hiring) of less skilled workers to depress wages per unit of skill or increase effort per unit of wages.

If workers of different skill levels are not, however, easily substitutable—if the lack of relevant skills results in defective products or damage to plant, equipment, and materials—a deterioration in skill level can both lower revenues and increase costs substantially. Unless management is willing and able to invest in an alternative machine technology that will make the highly skilled workers dispensable (a case that I take up below in the analysis of effort and technological change), it cannot use the availability of less skilled workers to discipline highly skilled workers.

The power inherent in the right to penalize is diminished, therefore, if workers with relevant skills are costly to replace, either because market competition for labor of a given skill level is intense or because the skills that enter into the production coefficient, α, must be developed within the firm. As skill levels rise, labor market conditions have less impact on the supply of effort because the skills of the firm's workers tend to be more "firm specific"—their skills must be developed within the particular firm on the basis of its particular combination of organization and technology. The underdevelopment of these firm-specific skills will result in defective products and damage to the firm's capital stock.

When skills are firm specific, the only way in which the firm can replace reluctant workers is by training new ones, a process that not only requires increased organizational investments (raising F) but also takes time; so there is a lag before the managerial surplus is increased. Moreover, given the firm-specific nature of the skills, the training of newer workers may depend on the cooperation of older workers—a task to which the veterans are not likely to supply much effort if the managerial objective is to generate replacements for them. Furthermore, the firm has no assurance that the new workers will supply any more effort than the old ones.

The effectiveness of supervision and the threat of dismissal as means of

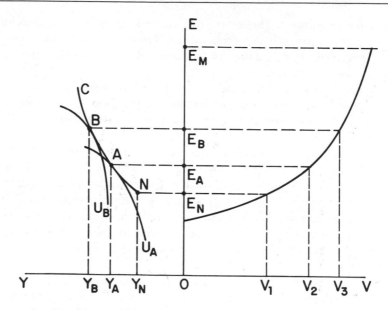

A.3 Workers' preferences, wage incentives, and value-created.
E, productive effort; V, value-created; Y, firm's wage bill.

increasing effort and the managerial surplus may, therefore, be limited by the external economic environment and the internal structure of production. Instead of the stick of job loss, the alternative approach to the problem of effort is the carrot of wage incentives. The amounts of extra effort and output elicited for a given wage incentive depend on the elasticity of the supply of effort in response to wages—an elasticity inherent in workers' utility or preference functions. As illustrated in the left-hand side of Figure A.3, point N connotes the wage bill, Y_N, and effort, E_N, that prevail prior to the introduction of a wage-incentive scheme. The increase in effort and hence output in response to a piece-rate bonus, d, is less for workers with utility functions U_A (which shows the combinations of effort and wages that result in the same level of utility) than for workers with utility functions U_B. The curve CN represents premium earnings as a function of extra effort—in this case, earnings greater than Y_N for effort greater than E_N. The premium earnings function is, therefore,

$$B = d(Q - Q_N) = d\alpha[f(E) - f(E_N)],$$

where B is premium earnings, d is the piece-rate incentive, and Q_N and E_N are the output and effort levels with basic wages, Y_N.

The more willing workers are to supply effort for extra pay, the greater is the augmented output and value-created that can be derived from a wage-incentive scheme. Because fixed costs (F) are held constant as value-created increases in response to a wage-incentive scheme, the additional amount of value-created (or what can more generally be called the value gains) is $(p - gH)(Q - Q_N)$. For any given amount of extra output, the greater the gap between product price and nonwage unit variable costs, the greater are the value gains.

What determines the distribution of the value gains between wages and managerial surplus as workers supply more effort and increase output? The cost to the firm of the wage-incentive scheme is $d(Q - Q_N)$, which represents the workers' share of the value gains. Management's share of the value gains is $(p - gH - d)(Q - Q_N)$. The managerial surplus increases, therefore, if $p - gH$ is greater than d—that is, if the piece-rate incentive is set at less than the excess of price over nonwage variable costs. If this condition is met, then the greater the effort that workers supply in response to the incentive scheme, the greater the output and the greater the managerial surplus.

If, for example, output rises to Q_S, then the wage bill becomes $Y_N + d(Q_S - Q_N)$. The managerial surplus is $(p - n_S)Q_S$, where n_S represents unit costs at Q_S. By using a wage-incentive scheme, management may be able to increase its share of value-created not only because of an increase in revenues as output expands but also by a decrease in unit costs as fixed costs as well as the fixed portion of the wage-bill are spread over more output. With the wage-incentive scheme, the unit cost function is

$$n_S = [F + Y_N + d(Q_S - Q_N)]/Q_S + gH.$$

As output increases, unit costs fall unless the wage incentive, d, is large enough to outweigh the combined cost-reducing effects of the spreading out of the nonincentive wage bill and fixed costs over the greater amount of output. Even if unit costs do rise, however, total managerial surplus will increase as output expands from Q_S to Q_N as long as d is less than $p - gH$.

Limits of Wage Incentives

But what will determine how much extra effort and hence output workers supply in response to a given wage-incentive scheme? Workers will supply more effort up to the point where the marginal disutility of increased effort equals the marginal utility of increased income. Figure A.3 illustrates two such effort-earnings outcomes, A and B, depending on whether workers have U_A or U_B, respectively. If d (inherent in the curve CN) is less than $p - gH$, management would prefer that workers have utility functions U_B rather than U_A. Management, therefore, has an interest in the effort–pay preferences of the workers that it hires, and indeed in the implementation of shop-floor relations that might shape these preferences over time.

Workers may quite rationally refuse to supply any additional effort in response to wage-incentive schemes. Workers may view management's use of wage incentives as simply a speedup or stretchout strategy to reduce the number of workers employed to produce the current level of output (in this case, Q_N) rather than as a market expansion strategy that, by increasing the firm's output, will protect existing jobs. Rather than risk the loss of some of their jobs, workers may attempt to band together, often through informal shop-floor organization and the application of peer pressure, to maintain existing levels of output per worker. Insofar as this collective (even if informal) organization succeeds, the attempt to use wage incentives to increase the managerial surplus is undermined.

When product demand is strong, the supply of more effort may not threaten a reduction in employment because managers can market the expanded output. Nevertheless, workers may believe that a positive response to a wage-incentive scheme might, by increasing generally accepted effort norms, create the conditions for management to extract unremunerated effort. Moreover, with product demand supporting the demand for labor, workers are in a strong position to resist managerial strategies that they believe will eventually result in unremunerated intensification of their labor. Hence, even though their jobs are not at risk, workers may attempt to limit their supply of effort and restrict output.

The earnings and effort levels per unit of time that prevail prior to the introduction of a wage-incentive scheme represent norms that, through shop-floor practice, supervisors had come to expect and workers had come to accept. Compared with effort norms, however, it is easier for shop-floor workers to reach a consensus on what constitutes a normal wage because earnings levels, changes, and variations across workers are easily observable. But because the supply of effort is more difficult to measure than earnings received, workers have more difficulty in exercising a collective voice in the determination and maintenance of effort norms. It is always possible for managers to insist that workers who produce more output per unit of time are doing so because they are more skilled, not because they are exerting more effort. Although one can distinguish between skill and effort conceptually, to do so in practice can be problematic.

Hence the villain in the shop-floor drama is the rate-buster, the worker who demonstrates that it is possible to produce more output per unit of time and thereby justifies management's contention that the other workers are shirking—producing below their productive potential (which, of course, is always the case when E is less than E_M, the maximum effort level physically and mentally sustainable). The manifestation of the rate-busting strategy is a cut in piece-rates that compels workers to supply more effort than E_N to achieve normal earnings, Y_N. If workers view a wage-incentive scheme as a managerial strategy for extracting unremunerated effort rather than as a longer term commitment for sharing value gains, then they will quite rationally refuse the lure of the short-term earnings increases that the scheme offers. In general, if workers view management as engaged in a speedup or stretchout strategy to extract unremunerated effort, they will themselves adopt a "workers' control" strategy (often organized informally on the shop floor) of collective restriction of effort and output in order to influence the determination of effort norms.

To secure the cooperation of workers in the creation of value, therefore, management must manifest its willingness to share out the value-created in terms of both employment stability and wages that workers view as fair (the slogan "a fair day's wage for a fair day's work" extends far back in time). If management manifests both its willingness and ability to provide employment stability and higher wages to workers over a sustained period of time, the aversion of workers to responding to incentive schemes will tend to dissipate. The foundations for cooperative shop-floor relations will have been put in place.

The increase in effort that workers will provide in response to wage incentives has limits, however. Even before workers reach the physical and mental limits of effort expenditure (E_M in Figure A.3), their supply response of effort to wage increases may fall to zero; given workers' preferences, no amount of monetary incentive will induce more effort. Indeed, the effort-supply curve may be backward bending as higher pay per unit of effort induces workers to work less.

Cooperative Shop-Floor Relations

Nevertheless, over time the demonstrated willingness of management to share out value gains not only may induce workers to supply more effort on the basis of given preferences but may even transform workers' underlying utility functions in ways that increase the elasticity of effort in response to wage incentives. Long-term attachment to the firm and cooperative management–labor relations may encourage workers to identify with the goals of the firm, while employment stability and higher wages may induce workers to adopt lifestyles (families, homes, cars, travel, and so on) or aspirations (eventual self-employment, more and better education for their children) that increase the amount of effort they are willing to supply for a given wage.

Cooperative shop-floor relations can affect not only the quantity but also the quality of effort that workers provide for a given wage. Workers may be willing not only to work harder but also to be more careful in the work that they do; they supply not only more effort but also better effort. Even though they were capable of doing more careful work—a capability or skill captured in α—their carelessness, inattentiveness, or even intended destructiveness (commonly termed sabotage) led them to supply a lower quality of effort than their skills would allow. One result of better effort is to reduce the amount of wasted materials or defective products that are considered normal, so fewer materials, H, are required per unit of sold (that is, nondefective) output. As the quality of effort increases, unit costs fall, and value-created rises. Another result of better effort is to reduce machine downtime and repair costs, so less fixed capital, S, is required to maintain a given productive capability, α, in any given time period. In effect, H and S, both of which enter into the value-created function, are themselves functions of the quality of effort.

Over time, the practice of supplying more and better effort results in workers who have more and better skills. Put differently, when shop-floor value creation is considered as an evolutionary process, the assumption implied in the simple production function, $Q = \alpha f(E)$, that the level of effort, E, and the contribution of shop-floor workers to the level of productive capability, α, are independent of one another cannot be sustained. Since Adam Smith it has been a commonplace that repetitive work results in workers who are more skilled in doing that particular work—essentially "learning by doing" on the shop floor. It follows that the greater the quantity of effort workers expend per unit of time, the faster they develop their specialized skills to the peak of their capability. Likewise, it can be argued, the better the quality of effort workers expend per unit of time, the better the quality of the skills they develop over time. In effect, workers who make persistent efforts to do better work learn how to do the work better.

Hence, by encouraging workers to supply more and better effort, cooperative shop-floor relations enable workers to develop more and better skills over a given time period. Moreover, because the development of shop-floor skills occurs by means of learning by doing, the increase in shop-floor productive capability does not require investments that add to the fixed costs of the firm. As both E and α increase over time, and as the growth in one reinforces the growth of the other, value-created on the shop floor will rise *if the firm can retain these specific workers in its employ.* The essence of cooperative shop-floor relations is the willingness and ability of the firm to provide employment stability, higher earnings, and better working conditions to its workers, all of which will help to secure their attachment to the firm, which in turn increases the firm-specific value-created available for managers and workers to share. A dynamic interaction between cooperative shop-floor relations and shop-floor value creation has been set in motion.

Cooperative relations enhance not only management's ability to develop and utilize the skills of shop-floor workers but also its willingness to do so. In the presence of conflictual relations, it cannot be taken for granted that management will want its workers to have more rather than fewer skills, because they may use these skills to exercise control over their jobs and defend themselves against unremunerated intensification of their labor. Indeed, the fear that workers will use their skills to limit rather than increase value-created may induce management to introduce skill-displacing technologies to rid themselves of truculent workers. In contrast, cooperative relations render management willing to rely on the skills of workers and indeed to encourage the development of shop-floor skills in ways that complement the productive capability of the prevailing technology.

The absence of efforts by workers to use their skills to exercise control over their jobs enhances the ability of management to perform its productive roles of planning and coordinating the specialized division of labor on the shop floor. Unobstructed by job control on the shop floor, management can allocate workers to activities for which their skills are most appropriate and, indeed, can move particular workers from one activity to another in ways designed to develop their skills over time. By securing the cooperation of workers in the supply of effort at the various vertically related stages of the production process, management can coordinate the flow of work—or throughput—from one stage of the production process to the next. With unobstructed managerial coordination, work in progress does not lie idle, thus reducing the cost of capital tied up in inventories, a cost that would otherwise increase the firm's fixed capital costs. Moreover, confident that shop-floor workers will use their skills to create value rather than limit it, management is willing to rely on, and indeed develop, the skills of workers to aid in the shop-floor coordination of the flow of work.

Cooperative shop-floor relations, therefore, encourage the development of skills, often in relatively inexpensive ways, as well as the augmentation of the supply of effort. Management, however, must be not only willing but also able to provide workers with the employment stability, earnings increases, and improved work conditions that are the bases for cooperative relations. The stability of cooperative relations is vulnerable to those changes in the economic environment in which the firm operates but over which it can exercise little or no control.

When cyclical downturns reduce revenues, the managerial surplus shrinks, and a commitment to relatively high wage levels may make it difficult for management to meet its commitments to the firm's financiers. The higher the firm's fixed costs, the more vulnerable it is to the slump. In the absence of institutional arrangements that encourage managers, workers, and financiers to moderate their claims on the firm's current revenues, management may be confronted by challenges from workers and financiers that threaten managerial control. Despite the potential for both managers and workers to benefit from cooperative relations, therefore, macroeconomic instability as well as commitments to financiers may render management unable to make the long-term employment and pay commitments to workers that form the foundations for continued cooperation and the creation of value.

Also destabilizing of cooperative relations between managers and workers are innovative strategies of the firm's competitors. Faced by competitors who, through the development and utilization of their productive resources, succeed in selling higher quality products at lower cost, the firm's response can be either adaptive or innovative. At the shop-floor level, the adaptive response is the attempt to induce unremunerated effort from workers, a strategy that may well have the perverse effects on value creation outlined above as workers try to protect effort norms by restricting output.

Alternatively, if the firm can secure the necessary financial resources, it can pursue the innovative response of introducing effort-saving technology. If utilized sufficiently, the investments in technological change can permit a sharing-out of value gains without requiring more effort from workers. As depicted in Figure A.1, the effort-saving impact of technological change is measured by an increase in the production coefficient, α. If the firm introduces a new technology with a production coefficient that is greater than that of the technology it replaces, then more output can potentially be produced with the same effort. But whether or not the new technology will actually yield more value-created will depend both on the level of effort achieved on it and on the costs of introducing it relative to the effort level and costs that prevailed on the old technology.

Effort-Saving Technology

Recall that the value-created equation is $V = (p - gH)\alpha f(E) - F$. Let the production coefficient on the old technology be α_1. The value-created using this technology is described by the curve labeled $E_R G$ in Figure A.4. Now assume that the introduction of a new technology changes α and F but does not change p and gH. If the production coefficient on the new technology is greater than α_1—as will be the case whenever the new technology is effort saving—then the value-created curve using the new technology will be flatter than the curve $E_R G$ that is based on the old technology. Assume that the new technology is effort saving; then, if its fixed costs are less than the fixed costs (F_1) of the old technology, the new value-created curve will cut the effort axis below E_R and will lie wholly below the old value-created curve, $E_R G$. Given its low fixed costs and high production coefficient, for any level of effort, the new technology would yield more value-created than the old.

Assume, however, that the fixed costs of introducing the new, effort-saving technology are greater than F_1; then its value-created curve cuts the effort axis above E_R. The curves $E_S H$ and $E_T J$ in Figure A.4 describe the relation between value-created and effort when the firm adopts technologies with production coefficients α_2 and α_3, respectively. Both α_2 and α_3 are greater than α_1, and hence both the new technologies are effort-saving.

If, as depicted by $E_T J$, the fixed costs of the new technology are sufficiently greater than F_1, then the increased capital costs of the new technology can outweigh its effort-saving impact ($\alpha_3 - \alpha_1$) on value-created, even at E_M—

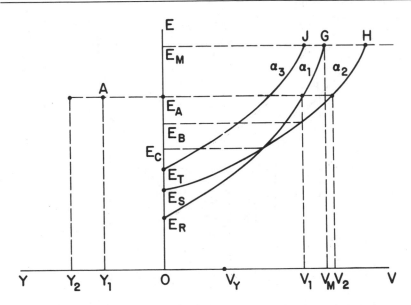

A.4 Effort, fixed costs, and effort-saving technological change.
E, productive effort; V, value-created; Y, firm's wage bill; α,
technological coefficient.

the maximum effort that workers can physically and mentally sustain per
unit of time. In this case, the new value-created curve lies wholly above the
old one. Despite the effort-saving nature of the technology, the high cost of
introducing α_3 into the workplace means that there is no feasible effort level
at which it yields more value-created than the old technology, α_1.

The most interesting, and perhaps most usual, case of technological
change is that described by $E_S H$ in Figure A.4. Although the fixed costs, F_2,
of the new technology are greater than F_1, value-created is greater at E_M
using α_2 rather than α_1. At levels of effort below E_C, the old technology
yields more value-created than the new technology. But at levels of effort
above E_C, the reverse is the case.

Assume, as depicted on the left-hand side of Figure A.4, that workers are
supplying E_A effort for Y_1 wages on the basis of the old technology, the
production coefficient of which is α_1. Given the value-created curve $E_R G$,
value-created is V_1. If $Y_1 = V_Y$, the managerial surplus equals $V_1 - V_Y$. The
maximum value-created attainable on this technology is V_M, at which point
effort is at E_M.

If, after introducing α_2 with its value-created curve $E_S H$, effort remains at
E_A and the wage bill at Y_1, value-created is V_2. The managerial surplus has
been increased by $V_2 - V_1$ without requiring workers to supply more effort

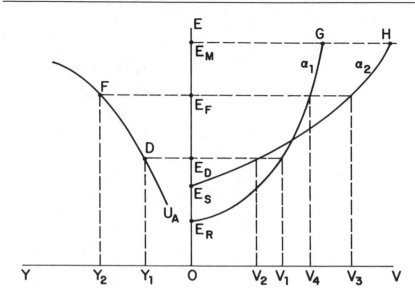

A.5 Customary effort norms and investment in technological change. E, productive effort; V, value-created; Y, firm's wage bill; α, technological coefficient.

or accept lower wages. Indeed, in Figure A.4, effort could fall to E_B or wages could increase to $Y_2 (= V_2 - V_1 + V_Y)$ without diminishing the managerial surplus compared with that achieved on the old technology. Given the relation between effort and wages on α_1, the effort-saving nature of the new technology and the costs of technological change make it possible to create value that can unequivocally make both management and workers better off. Effort-saving technological change forms the foundations for cooperative shop-floor relations in the value-creation process.

Note, however, that if the effort level had been below E_C on α_1, it would not have been worthwhile for management to introduce α_2 unless, in utilizing the new technology, it could have been sure of increasing effort or decreasing wages, or some combination of the two. If, using α_2, management seeks to restore its surplus by depressing wages, it will not induce value creation but will merely be redividing a smaller amount of value-created. Not only are high levels of effort critical for the creation of value, but adherence to *customary* levels of effort may make it impossible for an effort-saving technology to increase the value shares of both management and workers without requiring workers to supply more effort than they had supplied in the past.

Assume, for example, as depicted in Figure A.5, that the effort level on α_1 (the value-created curve of which is $E_R G$) is E_D, and that the wage bill is Y_1 and the managerial surplus is $V_1 - Y_1$. If, after introducing α_2 (which generates the value-created curve, E_SH), the effort level remains at E_D, then value-created will fall to V_2. Unless management can decrease the wage bill—a strategy that is certain to cause a confrontation with labor—the managerial surplus will decrease. If, however, management could convince workers to supply more effort for a higher wage, it is possible that both sides could be made better off. For example, if (as illustrated on the left-hand side of Figure A.5) workers could be convinced to supply E_F for Y_2, they could achieve the same level of utility, U_A, at point F as they did at point D. Value-created on the new technology would be increased to V_3. If $V_3 - Y_2$ is greater than $V_1 - Y_1$, management benefits from the introduction of α_2, and workers are no worse off than before. By paying workers somewhat more or having them supply somewhat less effort, the firm could redistribute some of the increase in the managerial surplus to workers, thereby making both management and workers better off.

Note that on the *old* technology the supply of E_F for Y_2 instead of E_D for Y_1 would have increased value-created from V_1 to V_4. Workers' utility is unchanged at point F compared with point D in Figure A.5. But if $V_4 - Y_2$ is less than $V_1 - Y_1$, then the managerial surplus on the old technology is less at E_F compared with E_D, and the extra value that could have been created by supplying the extra effort, $E_F - E_D$, would not have made both sides better off. Hence, even though the higher level of effort could have created a positive-sum outcome on the *new* technology with production coefficient α_2, workers' effort–earnings preferences would have discouraged management from trying to use wage incentives to elicit this effort on the old technology with its lower productive capability.

Therefore, when the customary effort level on the old technology is low, the problem that management faces in introducing α_2 is to convince workers that they will be better off supplying higher levels of effort in response to wage incentives. If workers do not believe that they will gain by responding to wage incentives subsequent to the technological change, the managerial surplus might be greater using α_1 than α_2. If so, management has no incentive to invest in the new technology, even though α_2 has the potential to make both management and workers better off at higher levels of effort. Customary effort norms, therefore, may be one source of what has been called the productive–technology dilemma.

But why might management have difficulty in securing the cooperation of workers in generating sufficient value-created to make it worthwhile to introduce a technological change that can make both sides better off? The answers are basically the same as those outlined in the previous discussion of effort bargaining on a given technology. Workers may believe that management is engaged in a strategy that will result in job loss or unremunerated effort. They may see the increase of earnings from Y_1 to Y_2 as a means of establishing high effort norms on the new technology that will subsequently remain in place as wages are reduced back toward Y_1. Workers will feel particularly vulnerable to a managerial strategy to extract unremunerated effort if changes in the nature of the skills inherent in the transition from α_1 to α_2 make existing workers more easily replaceable. Indeed, if management expects resistance from shop-floor workers to the implementation of technological change, it might very well choose new technologies that reduce its dependence on workers' skills that are costly to replicate; the choice of technology might represent a strategy to displace skilled workers.

Shop-Floor Control

In an adversarial industrial-relations environment, workers are not without their defenses, even in the absence of unions. When management exercises considerable social power over workers in extracting unremunerated effort, workers can turn to sabotage—the willful infliction of damage to processes and products—as a means to control the relation between effort and pay. Sabotage can result in work stoppages that reduce output, and hence revenues, per unit of time. It can also result in greater wastage of materials, in effect increasing H (the quantity of materials per unit of output). Insofar as sabotage causes permanent damage to the productive capabilities of plant and equipment, the firm will have to expend more on fixed costs to possess a given productive capability as captured by the production coefficient, α. The firm will be more vulnerable to shop-floor sabotage the more its productive capabilities are dependent on the skills and efforts of its shop-floor workers. The more expensive the physical technology and the more vulnerable its productive capabilities to sabotage, the greater the threat that such activity poses to value-created and the managerial surplus.

When a new technology is constantly breaking down and damage to equipment and materials is extraordinarily costly, management may suspect sabotage, but it may be difficult to detect. In the utilization of any given technology, it is difficult, if not impossible, for management to distinguish between the relative productive contributions of technology and effort. It is the workers themselves, not management, who are better positioned to judge how hard they are working. The problem of distinguishing between the productive contributions of technology and effort is particularly difficult on new technologies for which production standards have not been established through shop-floor practice. In response to managerial coercion to supply more effort, workers may sabotage the new technology, arguing in their own defense that it is the production engineers' overestimation of its productive potential that is causing breakdowns and damage.

The message to management is that, for the sake of avoiding the destruction of costly capital, supervisors would be well advised to slow the pace of work. In effect, workers are using their power to sabotage as a means of convincing managers that the true production coefficient of the new technology is lower than what the engineers think it is, and that it is useless to try to speed up the pace of work by replacing current workers.

In such a conflictual industrial-relations environment, management may take measures to eliminate its dependence on workers who have sought to use their skills to restrict output. In particular, management might invest in new technologies that deskill the contributions of shop-floor workers to the value-creation process, or it might introduce new hierarchical divisions of labor that vest certain key skills in managerial personnel rather than leaving them on the shop floor in the possession of workers. In adding to the firm's fixed costs, these investments in equipment and personnel may diminish the social power of labor, but they do not solve the economic problem facing the firm. Rather, the augmented fixed costs make the firm all the more dependent on eliciting high levels of effort from their workers. Faced by a deskilled, but alienated, work force, management must try to erect a new structure of cooperation on the shop floor.

In sum, cooperative relations between management and workers promote not only the greater utilization of an existing technology but also effort-saving technological change—a process that is essential for increasing the limits of value creation beyond the constraints posed by the mental and physical capabilities of workers. On the basis of cooperative shop-floor relations, effort-saving technology can potentially make both sides better off. With cooperative relations, moreover, management has an interest in developing shop-floor skills in ways that complement the productive capabilities of physical capital. In the presence of cooperative shop-floor relations, management's ability and incentive to invest in technological change—in both effort-saving machines and workers' skills—depend on the size of the current and expected managerial surpluses. Workers' incentives to supply sufficient effort to maintain or increase value-created on the new technology depend on their expectations concerning the impacts of technological change on the effort they will have to supply and the earnings they will get in return. Cooperative shop-floor relations generate a distribution of value-created that encourages the development and utilization of productive resources that permit the value to be created in the first place. Put another way, shop-floor value creation is the outcome of the dynamic interaction between relations and forces of production, with cooperative arrangements for the sharing-out of value-created providing the critical institutional foundations for generating value.

For workers who want employment stability, improved work conditions, and higher incomes, therefore, the prime industrial-relations issue should not be whether there will be an increase in the managerial surplus at any point in time but what management will do with the value-created under its control over time. Will management, by investing in new technology (including the appropriate retraining of existing workers), use the surplus to protect jobs, increase earnings, and create better work conditions? Or will it devote the surplus primarily to increasing managerial salaries and perquisites or to paying higher than normal rates of returns to financiers (a use of the managerial surplus that interests managers who have substantial shareholdings in the firm)?

Innovation and Adaptation

It is the firm's innovative investment strategy that can create the conditions for cumulative value creation. Just as cumulative value creation can be set in motion by an innovative strategy that gives the firm a competitive advantage, so too can it be brought to a halt by the more successful development and utilization of productive resources by the firm's competitors. As the firm loses market share, value-created is reduced. At the same time, however, the firm needs to devote more resources to finance the new investment strategy. To help augment the managerial surplus in a period of declining value-created, management is tempted to reduce labor's share of value-created while demanding that shop-floor workers supply more effort.

The more that workers perceive that management is actually using its control over the surplus to try to restore the firm's competitive advantage and recreate the conditions for employment stability, earnings increases, and better work conditions, the more likely will they be to continue to cooperate with management in creating value on the basis of a new investment strategy. The willingness of labor to cooperate will be strengthened all the more if management also sacrifices some of its personal share of value-created to help finance the new investments.

Management may, however, decide not to meet the competitive challenge but to live off the productive capability, embodied in the firm's fixed capital stock, that has been accumulated in the past. Rather than reduce its personal claims on value-created, management may attempt to enrich itself by diverting funds from the reinvestment process. At the same time, knowing that the firm is not making the investments that will, over the long run, enable it to compete with its competitors, management may try to increase the managerial surplus by laying off workers, while demanding wage reductions and more effort from those who remain. Once workers perceive that management is pursuing such an adaptive strategy—that it is taking the managerial surplus out of the enterprise rather than putting it back in—and that the firm can no longer offer the employment stability, wage levels, and work conditions that it had in the past, cooperative shop-floor relations will turn into conflict. As both management and workers engage in what Thorstein Veblen called "the conscientious withdrawal of efficiency," a process of cumulative value creation gives way to a process of cumulative value depletion.

Notes

Introduction: Organization, Technology, and Value Creation

1. Karl Marx and Friedrich Engels, *Communist Manifesto* (Washington Square Press, New York, 1964), p. 65.
2. Karl Marx, *Capital,* vol. 1 (Vintage, New York, 1977), p. 799.
3. Marx and Engels, *Communist Manifesto,* p. 116.
4. Joseph A. Schumpeter, *The Theory of Economic Development* (Oxford University Press, New York, 1961), p. 60n.
5. See the Appendix for the basic analytics of value creation in the presence of effort-saving technological change.
6. Alfred D. Chandler, Jr., *The Visible Hand: The Managerial Revolution in American Business* (Harvard University Press, Cambridge, Mass., 1977), pt. 3. For the analysis of how scale economies are achieved on the shop floor, see the Appendix.
7. See Alexander J. Field, "Modern Business Enterprise as a Capital-Saving Innovation," *Journal of Economic History* 47 (June 1987): 473–485.
8. Marx, *Capital,* chaps. 15, 25.
9. A portion of the work that refers explicitly to British or U.S. manufacturing workplaces includes E. J. Hobsbawm, *Labouring Men: Studies in the History of Labour,* esp. chap. 17, "Customs, Wages, and Workload in Nineteenth-century Industry," (Weidenfeld & Nicolson, London, 1968); Stephen Marglin, "What Do Bosses Do?: The Origins and Functions of Hierarchy in Capitalist Production," *Review of Radical Political Economics* 6 (Summer 1974): 33–60; Katherine Stone, "The Origins of Job Structures in the Steel Industry," *Review of Radical Political Economics* 6 (Summer 1974): 61–97; Harry Braverman, *Labor and Monopoly Capital: The Degradation of Work in the Twentieth Century* (Monthly Review, New York, 1974); Keith Burgess, *The Origins of British Industrial Relations* (Croom Helm, London, 1975); Herbert Gintis, "The Nature of the Labor Exchange and the Theory of Capitalist Production," *Review of Radical Political Economics* 8 (Summer 1976): 36–54; Andrew L. Friedman, *Industry and Labour: Class Struggle at Work and Monopoly Capitalism* (Macmillan, London,

1977); Raphael Samuel, "The Workshop of the World: Steam Power and Hand Technology in Mid-Victorian Britain," *History Workshop* 3 (1977): 6–72; Jill Rubery, "Structured Labour Markets, Worker Organisation, and Low Pay," *Cambridge Journal of Economics* 2 (March 1978): 17–36; Michael Burawoy, *Manufacturing Consent: Changes in the Labor Process under Monopoly Capitalism* (University of Chicago Press, Chicago, 1979); Richard Edwards, *Contested Terrain: The Transformation of the Workplace in the Twentieth Century* (Basic Books, New York, 1979); William Lazonick, "Industrial Relations and Technical Change: The Case of the Self-Acting Mule," *Cambridge Journal of Economics* 3 (September 1979): 231–262; Bernard Elbaum and Frank Wilkinson, "Industrial Relations and Uneven Development: A Comparative Study of the American and British Steel Industries," *Cambridge Journal of Economics* 3 (September 1979): 275–303; David Montgomery, *Workers' Control in America* (Cambridge University Press, New York, 1979); Andrew Zimbalist, ed., *Case Studies in the Labor Process* (Monthly Review, New York, 1979); Richard Hyman and Tony Elger, "Job Controls, the Employers Offensive, and Alternative Strategies," *Capital and Class* 15 (Autumn 1981): 115–149; David M. Gordon, Richard Edwards, and Michael Reich, *Segmented Work, Divided Workers: The Historical Transformation of Labor in the United States* (Cambridge University Press, New York, 1982); Stephen Wood, ed., *The Degradation of Work? Skill, Deskilling, and the Labour Process* (Hutchinson, London, 1982); Howard Gospel and Craig Littler, eds., *Managerial Strategies and Industrial Relations* (Heinemann, London, 1983); Richard Price, "The Labour Process and Labour History," *Social History* 8 (January 1983): 57–75; and the subsequent debate between Price and Patrick Joyce in *Social History* 9 (January 1984): 67–76 and 9 (May 1984): 217–231; Eric Hobsbawm, *Workers: Worlds of Labor* (Pantheon, New York, 1984); Michael Piore and Charles Sabel, *The Second Industrial Divide: Possibilities for Prosperity* (Basic Books, New York, 1984); Royden Harrison and Jonathan Zeitlin, eds., *Divisions of Labour: Skilled Workers and Technological Change in Nineteenth Century England* (Harvester Press, Sussex, 1985); David Noble, *Forces of Production: A Social History of Industrial Automation* (Knopf, New York, 1984); Martin Brown and Peter Phillips, "Craft Labor and Mechanization in Nineteenth-Century American Canning," *Journal of Economic History* 46 (September 1986): 743–756; Sonya O. Rose, "'Gender at Work': Sex, Class, and Industrial Capitalism," *History Workshop* 21 (Spring 1986): 113–131; Wayne Lewchuk, *American Technology and the British Vehicle Industry* (Cambridge University Press, Cambridge, 1987); Ruth Milkman, *Gender at Work: The Dynamics of Job Segregation by Sex during World War II* (University of Illinois Press, Urbana, 1987); David Montgomery, *The Fall of the House of Labor* (Cambridge University Press, New York, 1987); Nelson Lichtenstein and Stephen Meyer, eds., *On the Line: Essays in the History of Auto Work* (University of Illinois Press, Urbana, 1989). For recent surveys, see William Lazonick, "The Labour Process," in J. Eatwell, M. Milgate, and P. Newman, eds., *The New Palgrave* (Macmillan, London, 1987); Stephen Wood, "The Deskilling Debate, New Technology and Work Organization," *Acta Sociologica* 30 (1987): 3–24; Philip Scranton, "None-Too-Porous Boundaries: Labor History and the History of Technology," *Technology and Culture* 29 (October 1988): 722–743; John Foster, "Conflict at Work," *Social History* 14 (May 1989): 233–241.

10. For a critique of Braverman as "technological determinist," see William Lazonick, "Technological Change and the Control of Work: The Development of Capital–Labour Relations in U.S. Mass Production Industries," in Gospel and Littler, *Managerial Strategies*, and William Lazonick, "Klasserna i det kapitaliska företaget" [Class relations and the capitalist enterprise], translated into Swedish by Inger Humlesjö, *Häften för Kritiska Studier* 19 (1986): 49–78. For a critique of Montgomery's neglect of technology, see William Lazonick, "The Breaking of the American Working Class," *Reviews in American History* 17 (June 1989): 272–283.

11. Joseph Schumpeter, *Capitalism, Socialism, and Democracy* (Harper & Row, New York, 1950), p. 82.

12. Ibid., p. 44.

13. Marx, *Capital*, p. 492.

14. Ibid., pp. 645, 1019–38.

15. Marglin, "Bosses."

16. See Bernard Elbaum and William Lazonick, eds., *The Decline of the British Economy* (Clarendon Press, Oxford, 1986).

17. William Lazonick and William Mass, "The Performance of the British Cotton Industry, 1870–1913," *Research in Economic History* 9 (1984): 1–44.

18. Marx, *Capital*, p. 799.

19. Richard Herding, *Job Control and Union Structure* (Rotterdam University Press, Rotterdam, 1972); Thomas A. Kochan, Harry C. Katz, and Robert B. McKersie, *The Transformation of American Industrial Relations* (Basic Books, New York, 1986); Harry C. Katz, *Shifting Gears: Changing Labor Relations in the U.S. Automobile Industry* (MIT Press, Cambridge, Mass., 1987).

1. Theory and History in Marxian Economics

1. Karl Marx, *Capital*, vol. 1 (Vintage, New York, 1977), chaps. 1–6.

2. Ibid., p. 280.

3. Adam Smith, *An Inquiry into the Nature and Causes of the Wealth of Nations* (Modern Library, New York, 1937), p. 66.

4. Ibid., p. 259.

5. Marx, *Capital*, pp. 874–875.

6. Ibid., pt. 8.

7. William Lazonick, "Karl Marx and Enclosures in England," *Review of Radical Political Economics* 6 (Summer 1974): 1–32.

8. J. D. Chambers, "Enclosure and the Labour Supply in the Industrial Revolution," *Economic History Review,* 2nd ser., 5 (1952): 319–343; T. S. Ashton, *An Economic History of England: The 18th Century* (Methuen, London, 1961), pp. 39, 47; G. E. Mingay, *English Landed Society in the Eighteenth Century* (Routledge & Kegan Paul, London, 1963), pp. 98–99; R. W. Harris, *A Short History of 18th-Century England* (Mentor, New York, 1963), p. 24; W. H. Chaloner, "Preface" to A. Redford, *Labor Migration in England, 1800–1850,* 2nd Ed. (Manchester University Press, Manchester, 1964), p. vii; J. D. Chambers and G. E. Mingay, *The Agricultural Revolution, 1750–1880* (Batsford, London, 1966), pp. 90–98; David S. Landes, *The Unbound Prometheus: Technological Change and Industrial Development in Western Europe from 1750 to the Present* (Cambridge University Press, Cambridge, 1969), pp. 114–115; Phyllis Deane, "Great Britain," in C. Cipolla, ed., *The Fontana Economic History of Europe,* vol. 4, pt. 1 (Collins, London, 1973), pp. 191–192; Michael Turner, *Enclosures in Britain, 1750–1830* (Macmillan, London, 1984), pp. 67–80.

9. Landes, *Unbound Prometheus,* p. 115; my emphasis.

10. Marx, *Capital,* pp. 795–796.

11. Chambers, "Enclosure," p. 327; Ashton, *Economic History,* p. 39; Mingay, *English Landed Society,* p. 195; Chambers and Mingay, *Agricultural Revolution,* p. 90.

12. Chambers, "Enclosure," p. 327n.

13. E. P. Thompson, *The Making of the English Working Class* (Vintage, New York, 1963), p. 218.

14. Marx, *Capital,* p. 883.

15. Chambers, "Enclosure," pp. 325–332.

16. See Lazonick, "Karl Marx," p. 22; see also John Saville, "Primitive Accumulation and Early Industrialisation in Britain," in Ralph Miliband and John Saville, eds., *Socialist Register* (Merlin, London, 1969), pp. 261–262.

17. Chambers, "Enclosure," p. 338; Chambers and Mingay, *Agricultural Revolution,* pp. 92–93.

18. L. A. Clarkson, *Proto-Industrialization: The First Phase of Industrialization?* (Macmillan, London, 1985); David Levine, "Industrialization and the Proletarian Family in England," *Past and Present* 107 (1985): 168–203.

19. Marx, *Capital,* chaps. 14–15.
20. Ibid., p. 455.
21. Ibid., pp. 455, 456; my emphasis.
22. Raphael Samuel, "Workshop of the World: Steam Power and Hand Technology in Mid-Victorian Britain," *History Workshop* 3 (1977): 6–72.
23. Sidney Pollard, *The Genesis of Modern Management* (Penguin, Harmondsworth, 1968), chap. 2; J. G. Rule, *The Experience of Labour in Eighteenth-Century English Industry* (St. Martin's, New York, 1981); Maxine Berg, Pat Hudson, and Michael Sonenscher, eds., *Manufacture in Town and Country before the Factory* (Cambridge University Press, Cambridge, 1983); G. D. Ramsay, *The English Woolen Industry, 1500–1750* (Macmillan, London, 1984), chap. 3; Maxine Berg, *The Age of Manufactures, 1700–1820* (Fontana, London, 1985); Clarkson, *Proto-Industrialization;* David Landes, "What Do Bosses Really Do?" *Journal of Economic History* 46 (September 1986), pp. 585–593.
24. Thompson, *English Working Class,* chap. 9; Duncan Bythell, *The Sweated Trades* (St. Martin's, New York, 1978); James A. Schmiechen, *Sweated Industries and Sweated Labor* (University of Illinois Press, Urbana, 1984).
25. Pollard, *Genesis,* chap. 5; E. P. Thompson, "Time, Work-Discipline, and Industrial Capitalism," *Past and Present* 38 (1967): 56–97; Rule, *Experience of Labour.*
26. Marx, *Capital,* p. 927.
27. C. B. MacPherson, *The Political Theory of Possessive Individualism: Hobbes to Locke* (Clarendon Press, Oxford, 1962); Christopher Hill, "Pottage for Freeborn Englishmen: Attitudes to Wage Labour in the Sixteenth and Seventeenth Centuries," in C. H. Feinstein, ed., *Socialism, Capitalism, and Economic Growth* (Cambridge University Press, Cambridge, 1967).
28. Marx, *Capital,* p. 808n.
29. Pollard, *Genesis,* pp. 190–193.
30. Thompson, "Time."
31. Stephen Marglin, "What Do Bosses Do? The Origins and Functions of Hierarchy in Capitalist Production," *Review of Radical Political Economics* 6 (Summer 1974), pp. 45–51; Rule, *Experience of Labour;* Berg, *Age of Manufactures,* pp. 221–222, 308–310; Landes, "Bosses," p. 602.
32. Thompson, *English Working Class,* chap. 9; Duncan Bythell, *The Handloom Weavers* (Cambridge University Press, Cambridge, 1969).
33. Marx, *Capital,* p. 382.
34. Ibid., p. 549; Andrew Ure, *The Philosophy of Manufactures* (Knight, London, 1835), p. 15.
35. Marx, *Capital,* p. 489.

36. Ibid., p. 553.
37. Ibid., pp. 489–490.
38. Ibid., pp. 485, 489.
39. Ibid., p. 789.
40. Ure, *Philosophy,* pp. 23, 368.
41. William Lazonick, "Industrial Relations and Technical Change: The Case of the Self-Acting Mule," *Cambridge Journal of Economics* 3 (September 1979): 231–262; William Lazonick, "Production Relations, Labor Productivity, and Choice of Technique: British and U.S. Cotton Spinning," *Journal of Economic History* 41 (September 1981): 491–516.
42. Pollard, *Genesis,* pp. 51–66; Lazonick, "Industrial Relations," pp. 232–233.
43. Ure, *Philosophy,* p. 366, cited in Stephen Marglin, *Growth, Distribution, and Prices* (Harvard University Press, Cambridge, Mass., 1985), pp. 106–107, to explain wage stickiness.
44. Michael Anderson, "Sociological History: The Industrial Revolution and the Working-Class Family," *Social History* 3 (1976): 317–334.
45. E. J. Hobsbawm, *Labouring Men: Studies in the History of Labour* (Weidenfeld & Nicolson, London, 1968), p. 350.
46. Lazonick, "Industrial Relations."
47. Samuel, "Workshop"; Bernard Elbaum and Frank Wilkinson, "Industrial Relations and Uneven Development: A Comparative Study of the American and British Steel Industries," *Cambridge Journal of Economics* 3 (September 1979): 275–303; Charles More, *Skill and the English Working Class, 1870–1914* (Croom Helm, London, 1980); Robert Gray, *The Aristocracy of Labour, c. 1850–1914* (Macmillan, London, 1981); Stephen Wood, ed., *The Degradation of Work? Skill, Deskilling and the Labour Process* (Hutchinson, London, 1982); Hobsbawm, *Workers: Worlds of Labor* (Pantheon, New York, 1984), chaps. 11–14; Royden Harrison and Jonathan Zeitlin, eds., *Divisions of Labour: Skilled Workers and Technological Change in Nineteenth Century Britain* (Harvester, Brighton, 1985); see also Chapter 6.
48. Marx, *Capital,* p. 599; my emphasis.
49. Ibid., pp. 599–600.
50. Schmiechen, *Sweated Industries,* p. 25.
51. Marx, *Capital,* p. 601.
52. Ibid., p. 602.
53. Ibid., p. 601.
54. Ibid., p. 603; my emphasis.
55. Ibid., pp. 603–605.
56. Ibid., p. 603.
57. Schmiechen, *Sweated Industries,* p. 24.

58. Joan Thomas, "A History of the Leeds Clothing Industry," *Yorkshire Bulletin of Economic and Social Research*, Occasional Paper No. 1 (January 1955).
59. Schmiechen, *Sweated Industries*, p. 26.
60. Ibid., chap. 6.
61. Robert Davies, *Peacefully Working to Conquer the World* (Arno, New York, 1976); David Hounshell, *From the American System to Mass Production, 1800–1932* (Johns Hopkins University Press, Baltimore, 1984).
62. Marx, *Capital*, p. 589.
63. John Prest, *The Industrial Revolution in Coventry* (Oxford University Press, Oxford, 1960), pp. 95–99.
64. Ibid., pp. 79, 113–118.
65. Ibid., pp. 119ff.
66. Ibid., p. 132.
67. Marglin, "Bosses."
68. Marx, *Capital*, p. 275.
69. William Lazonick, "The Subjection of Labor to Capital: The Rise of the Capitalist System," *Review of Radical Political Economics* 8 (Summer 1978): 1–31.
70. Marx, *Capital*, p. 799.
71. See Jane Humphries, "Class Struggle and the Persistence of the Working Class Family," *Cambridge Journal of Economics* 1 (September 1977): 241–258.
72. Karl Marx, *Value, Price, and Profit* (International, New York, 1935), p. 61.
73. See Chapter 6, note 14.
74. Marx, *Capital*, p. 344.
75. Ibid., pp. 439, 453.
76. Ibid., p. 454.
77. Ibid., p. 439.
78. Ibid., p. 447.
79. Ibid., pp. 442–443, also p. 446.
80. Ibid., pp. 443, 445–446.
81. Ibid., pp. 443–444.
82. Ibid., p. 444.
83. Ibid., p. 442.
84. Ibid., p. 451.
85. Ibid., p. 450.
86. Ibid., p. 451; my emphasis.
87. Ibid., pp. 457–458; my emphasis.
88. Adam Smith, *An Inquiry into the Nature and Causes of the Wealth of Nations* (Modern Library, New York, 1937), bk. 1, chap. 1.
89. Marx, *Capital*, p. 458; my emphasis.

90. Ibid., p. 469.
91. See William Lazonick, "Technological Change and the Control of Work: The Development of Capital–Labor Relations in U.S. Mass Production Industries," in Howard Gospel and Craig Littler, eds., *Managerial Strategies and Industrial Relations* (Heinemann, London, 1983).
92. Marx, *Capital,* p. 483.
93. Ibid., pp. 460, 468n; Nathan Rosenberg, "Adam Smith on the Division of Labour: Two Views or One?" *Economica,* n.s., 32 (May 1965): 127–139; Marglin, "Bosses," pp. 36–38.
94. Marx, *Capital,* p. 490.
95. Ibid., pp. 535–536.
96. Ibid., p. 536n.
97. Ibid., pp. 536–538.
98. Ibid., pp. 492–508.
99. See the Appendix.
100. Marx, *Capital,* p. 699.
101. Ibid., pp. 695, 697.
102. Ibid., p. 697.
103. See Chapter 6.
104. Marx, *Capital,* pp. 697–698.
105. Ibid., p. 700.

2. From Surplus-Value to Value Creation

1. Joan Robinson, *Further Contributions to Modern Economics* (Basil Blackwell, Oxford, 1980), p. 202.
2. Thomas Kuhn, *The Structure of Scientific Revolutions,* 2nd Ed. (University of Chicago Press, Chicago, 1970).
3. Joseph Schumpeter, "Science and Ideology," *American Economic Review* 39 (March 1949): 345–359.
4. Frederick Engels, *The Condition of the Working Class in England* (Panther, London, 1949).
5. John Sherwood, "Engels, Marx, Malthus, and the Machine," *American Historical Review* 90 (October 1985): 837–865.
6. William Lazonick, "Industrial Relations and Technical Change: The Case of the Self-Acting Mule," *Cambridge Journal of Economics* 3 (September 1979): 231–262; Bernard Elbaum and William Lazonick, "An Institutional Perspective on British Decline," in Elbaum and Lazonick, eds., *The Decline of the British Economy* (Oxford University Press, Oxford, 1986).
7. E. J. Hobsbawm, *Labouring Men: Studies in the History of Labour* (Weidenfeld & Nicolson, London, 1968), p. 290.

8. William Lazonick, "The Cotton Industry," in Elbaum and Lazonick, *Decline;* William Lazonick, "Strategy, Structure, and Management Development in the United States and Britain," in Kesaji Kobayashi and Hidemasa Morikawa, eds., *Development of Managerial Enterprise* (University of Tokyo Press, Tokyo, 1986).

9. Lazonick, "Industrial Relations"; Donald MacKenzie, "Marx and the Machine," *Technology and Culture* 25 (July 1984): 473–502; Sherwood, "Marx."

10. Karl Marx, *Capital,* vol. 1 (Vintage, New York, 1977), pp. 777–779; my emphasis.

11. Ibid., pp. 777–780.

12. Elbaum and Lazonick, "Institutional Perspective."

13. Alfred D. Chandler, Jr., *The Visible Hand: The Managerial Revolution in American Business* (Harvard University Press, Cambridge, Mass., 1977).

14. Alfred D. Chandler, Jr., *Strategy and Structure: Chapters in the History of the American Industrial Enterprise* (MIT Press, Cambridge, Mass., 1962).

15. Marx, *Capital,* p. 90.

16. Ibid., pp. 90–91; my emphasis.

17. Alfred D. Chandler, Jr., "The Growth of the Transnational Industrial Firm in the United States and the United Kingdom: A Comparative Analysis," *Economic History Review,* 2nd ser., 33 (August 1980): 396–410; Elbaum and Lazonick, "Institutional Perspective"; Lazonick, "Strategy, Structure." For a related effort to extend the Chandlerian perspective to the comparative analysis of the management of labor, see Howard F. Gospel, "The Management of Labour: Great Britain, the U.S., and Japan," *Business History* 30 (January 1988): 104–115.

3. Minders, Piecers, and Self-Acting Mules

1. Karl Marx, *Capital,* vol. 1 (Vintage, New York, 1977), chap. 15.

2. Ibid., pp. 562–563.

3. Andrew Ure, *The Philosophy of Manufactures* (Knight, London, 1835), p. 23.

4. Ibid., p. 199.

5. E. C. Tufnell, *Character, Object and Effects of Trades' Unions* (Ridgway, London, 1834), pp. 108–109.

6. Andrew Ure, *The Cotton Manufacture of Great Britain,* vol. 2 (Knight, London, 1836), p. 176.

7. Ibid., p. 152.

8. W. H Chaloner, "Robert Owen, Peter Drinkwater and the Early Fac-

tory System in Manchester, 1788–1800," *Bulletin of the Rylands Library* 37 (September 1954): 78–102; Michael Edwards, *The Growth of the British Cotton Trade, 1780–1815* (Manchester University Press, Manchester, 1967); John Kennedy, "Observations on the Rise and Progress of the Cotton Trade in Great Britain," *Memoirs of the Literary and Philosophical Society of Manchester* 3 (1819): 115–137; John Kennedy, "A Brief Memoir of Samuel Crompton," *Memoirs of the Literary and Philosophical Society of Manchester* 5 (1831): 318–353; C. Lee, *A Cotton Enterprise, 1795–1840* (Manchester University Press, Manchester, 1972); George Unwin with Arthur Hulme and George Taylor, *Samuel Oldknow and the Arkwrights* (Manchester University Press, Manchester, 1968).

9. Kennedy, "Brief Memoir," p. 335.

10. Sidney Pollard, *The Genesis of Modern Management* (Penguin, Harmondsworth, 1968), pp. 51–66.

11. G. Daniels, "Cotton Trade during the Revolutionary and Napoleonic Wars," *Transactions of the Manchester Statistical Society* (1915–16), p. 59; Mary D. George, "The Combination Laws Re-Considered," *Economic Journal* (Economic History Supplement) 1 (May 1927): 214–228; Neil Smelser, *Social Change in the Industrial Revolution* (Chicago University Press, Chicago, 1959), pp. 318–320; Unwin et al., *Samuel Oldknow*, pp. 32–34.

12. Sidney Chapman, *The Lancashire Cotton Industry* (Manchester University Press, Manchester, 1904), chap. 9; J. Hammond and B. Hammond, *The Skilled Labourer, 1760–1832* (Longmans, Green, London, 1919), chap. 5; W. Jevons, "An Account of the Spinners' Strike at Ashton-under-Lyne in 1830," in National Association for the Promotion of Social Science, *Trades' Societies and Strikes* (Parker, London, 1860); R. Kirby and A. Musson, *The Voice of the People: John Doherty* (Manchester University Press, Manchester, 1975); J. Lowe, "An Account of the Strike in the Cotton Trade at Preston in 1853," in National Association for the Promotion of Social Science, *Trades' Societies;* Select Committee on Combinations of Workmen, "First Report," *Parliamentary Papers* VII (1837–38); Tufnell, *Character;* H. A. Turner, *Trade Union Growth, Structure and Policy* (Toronto University Press, Toronto, 1962), chaps. 1, 2.

13. Labour Statistics, *Returns of Wages Published between 1830 and 1886,* (HMSO, London, 1887), p. 5.

14. Edward Baines, *History of the Cotton Manufacture in Great Britain,* (Cass, London, 1966), pp. 212–213; C. Shaw, *Replies of Sir Charles Shaw to Lord Ashley, MP, Regarding the Education, and Moral and Physical Condition of the Labouring Class* (Ollivier, London, 1843), p. 23; Ure, *Philosophy,* pp. 267–268.

15. Chapman, *Lancashire,* pp. 54, 59; Hammond and Hammond, *Skilled Labourer,* p. 53; B. Hutchins, *Women in Modern Industry* (Bell, London, 1915), p. 55; Julia D. Mann, "The Textile Industry," in Charles Singer, ed., *History of Technology,* vol. 4 (Clarendon, Oxford, 1958), p. 288; Ivy Pinchbeck, *Women Workers in the Industrial Revolution, 1750–1850* (Routledge, London, 1930), p. 148; Smelser, *Social Change,* p. 204.

16. The number of counts is equal to the number of hanks per pound of yarn, where one hank equals 840 yards. Hence, one pound of no. 40 yarn contains $40 \times 840 = 33,600$ yards of yarn.

17. For a detailed but very readable account of the development of the mechanisms of the mule, see Harold Catling, *The Spinning Mule* (David & Charles, Newton Abbott, 1970).

18. Select Committee on Combinations of Workmen, "First Report," pp. 306–307.

19. J. Sutcliffe, *A Treatise on Canals and Reservoirs* (Hartley, Rochdale, 1816), p. 36.

20. Lee, *Cotton Enterprise,* p. 19.

21. Kirby and Musson, *Voice,* p. 142.

22. Select Committee on Combinations of Workmen, "First Report," pp. 15, 17, 37–38, 40, 56–57, 63, 131, 230, 259; Inspectors of Factories, "Reports for the half-year ending 31 December 1841," *Parliamentary Papers* XXIII (1842), p. 86.

23. Ure, *Philosophy,* p. 365.

24. Catling, *Spinning Mule,* p. 49.

25. Factory Inquiry Commission, "First Report of the Central Board, Evidence Taken by Cowell," *Parliamentary Papers* XX (1833), pp. 78–79; Pollard, *Genesis,* pp. 213–225.

26. Smelser, *Social Change,* p. 232; Turner, *Trade Union Growth,* p. 42.

27. Chapman, *Lancashire,* pp. 213–214.

28. Baines, *History,* pp. 206–207.

29. R. Hills, *Power in the Industrial Revolution* (Kelley, New York, 1970), pp. 126–127; James Montgomery, *The Theory and Practice of Cotton Spinning; or the Carding and Spinning Master's Assistant* (Niven, Glasgow, 1833), pp. 188–190; Ure, *Philosophy,* pp. 186–198.

30. Ure, *Philosophy,* pp. 366–368.

31. Montgomery, *Theory and Practice,* p. 196.

32. Ure, *Philosophy,* p. 368.

33. Stanley D. Chapman, "Fixed Capital Formation in the British Cotton Manufacturing Industry," in J. Higgins and S. Pollard, eds., *Aspects of Capital Investment in Great Britain, 1750–1850* (Methuen, London, 1971), p. 80; E. Leigh, *The Science of Modern Spinning* (Palmer & Howe, Manchester, 1873), p. 242; Richard Marsden, *Cotton Spinning: Its*

Development, Principles, and Practice (Bell, London, 1884), p. 275; Cotton Factory Times (hereafter CFT), 13 March 1885, 4 September 1885, 30 October 1885, 19 February 1886, 25 March 1887; G. N. von Tunzelmann, *Steam Power and British Industrialisation to 1860* (Clarendon, Oxford, 1978), pp. 187–194.

34. H. Rose, *Manual Labour Versus Brass and Iron* (Pratt, Manchester, 1825), p. 3; Baines, *History,* p. 208; Factory Inquiry Commisssion, "First Report," p. 37; H. Brown, *The Cotton Fields and Cotton Factories* (Darton & Clark, London, 1840), p. 5.

35. Factory Inquiry Commission, "First Report," pp. 28–29; CFT, 9 November 1888.

36. G. H. Wood, *The History of Wages in the English Cotton Trade during the Past Hundred Years* (Sherratt & Hughes, London, 1910), pp. 28–29.

37. Henry Ashworth, *An Inquiry into the Origins, Progress, and Results of the Strike of the Operative Cotton Spinners of Preston* (Harrison, Manchester, 1838), p. 9; James Leach, *Stubborn Facts from the Factory* (Ollivier, London, 1844), p. 31.

38. D. Chadwick, "On the Rate of Wages in Manchester and Salford, and the Manufacturing District of Lancashire, 1839–1859," *Journal of the Statistical Society of London* 23 (1860), pp. 23, 29.

39. Inspectors of Factories, "Reports 1841," pp. 85, 92.

40. Arthur Redford, *Manchester Merchants and Foreign Trade, 1794–1858* (Manchester University Press, Manchester, 1934), p. 239; G. Daniels, "The Cotton Trade at the Close of the Napoleonic War," *Transactions of the Manchester Statistical Society* (1917–18), app. 3.

41. G. Schulze-Gaevernitz, *The Cotton Trade in England and on the Continent* (Simpkin, Marshall, London, 1895), p. 96; Webb Trade-Union Collection, in The British Library of Economics and Political Science, London School of Economics, sec. A, vol. 34, pp. 428–429.

42. William Lazonick, "Conflict and Control in the Industrial Revolution: Social Relations in the British Cotton Factory," in R. Weible, O. Ford, and P. Marion, eds., *Essays from the Lowell Conference on Industrial History, 1980 and 1981* (Lowell Conference on Industrial History, Lowell, 1981).

43. Turner, *Trade Union Growth,* pp. 115–116; Ashworth, *Inquiry,* p. 9; G. D. H. Cole, *Attempts at General Union* (Macmillan, London, 1953), chap. 4; *Manchester and Salford Advertiser,* 8 April 1837, 1 October 1842.

44. Leach, *Stubborn Facts;* Inspectors of Factories, "Reports 1841," p. 93; Inspectors of Factories, "Reports for the half-year ending June 1842," *Parliamentary Papers* XXII (1843), p. 6; R. C. O. Matthews, *A Study in Trade-Cycle History* (Cambridge University Press, Cambridge, 1954), chap. 9.

45. For evidence from Italy that supports these arguments, see Francesca Bettio, *The Sexual Division of Labour: The Italian Case* (Clarendon, Oxford, 1988), p. 141.

46. Mary Freifeld, "Technological Change and the 'Self-Acting' Mule: A Study of Skill and the Sexual Division of Labour," *Social History* 11 (October 1986), p. 321.

47. Ibid., p. 338; my emphasis.

48. Ibid., pp. 333–336.

49. Ibid., p. 337.

50. Ibid., pp. 324–326.

51. Ibid., pp. 323–324.

52. Ibid., p. 337.

53. Ibid., p. 322n. See also Michael Savage, "Women and Work in the Lancashire Cotton Industry, 1890–1939," in J. A. Jowitt and A. J. McIvor, eds., *Employers and Labour in the English Textile Industries, 1850–1939* (Routledge, London, 1988), p. 221, where my argument concerning the relation between technical skill and craft control is also mistakenly interpreted to mean that "textile manufacturing required little skill."

54. Lazonick, "Industrial Relations," p. 257.

55. Turner, *Trade Union Growth*, p. 128.

56. Ibid., pp. 122–128; Webb Collection, sec. A, vol. 34, p. 52, and vol. 36, p. 2.

57. William Marcroft, *The Marcroft Family*, 2nd Ed. (Heywood, Manchester, 1889), pp. 105–106.

58. Turner, *Trade Union Growth*, p. 128.

59. British Association for the Advancement of Science, *On the Regulation of Wages by Means of Lists in the Cotton Industry* (Heywood, London, 1887), p. 7; Oldham Operative Cotton Spinners' Provincial Association, *A List of Thirty Questions with the Answers Given Thereto Relating to the System of Payment to Minders &c. for Work Performed* (Oldham, 1875), pp. 32–33, 53–54.

60. James Montgomery, *The Cotton Manufacture of the United States of America Contrasted and Compared with that of Great Britain* (Niven, Glasgow, 1840), pp. 76–77; Mosely Industrial Commission to the United States of America, *Report of the Delegates* (1902), p. 126.

61. CFT, 1 May 1885, 26 February 1886, 3 March 1894, 21 December 1894, 19 November 1897; J. Lomax, *Fine Cotton Spinning* (Emmott, Manchester, 1913), p. 116.

62. Catling, *Spinning Mule*, p. 149; CFT, 13 February 1885.

63. Catling, *Spinning Mule*, pp. 148–149.

64. E. Spencer, "Improvements in Cotton Spinning Machinery," *Proceedings of the Institution of Mechanical Engineers* (1880), pp. 502–505; Thomas Thornley, *The Self-Acting Mules* (Heywood, Manchester,

1894), pp. 34–35, 39, 61–62, 80; Catling, *Spinning Mule,* pp. 98–100.

65. Catling, *Spinning Mule,* pp. 98–100.
66. Ibid., pp. 75–84.
67. Ure, *Cotton Manufacture,* pp. 175–176; Spencer, "Improvements," pp. 500–502; Thornley, *Self-Acting Mules,* pp. 297–301; Catling, *Spinning Mule,* pp. 83–84.
68. Catling, *Spinning Mule,* pp. 83–84; Thornley, *Self-Acting Mules,* pp. 301–302.
69. Catling, *Spinning Mule,* pp. 109–110.
70. Thornley, *Self-Acting Mules,* pp. 40–41.
71. J. Montgomery, *The Carding and Spinning Master's Assistant; or the Theory and Practice of Cotton Spinning* (Niven, Glasgow, 1832), p. 223.
72. Ure, *Philosophy,* p. 290.
73. A. J. Taylor, "Concentration and Specialisation in the Lancashire Cotton Industry, 1825–1850," *Economic History Review,* 2nd ser., I (1949): 114–122; V. A. C. Gattrell, "Labour Power and the Size of Firms in Lancashire Cotton in the Second Quarter of the Nineteenth Century," *Economic History Review* 30 (February 1977): 95–139; Stuart Jones, "The Cotton Industry and Joint-Stock Banking in Manchester, 1825–1850," *Business History* 20 (July 1978): 165–185.
74. Montgomery, *Cotton Manufacture,* pp. 77–80; Evelyn Knowlton, *Pepperell's Progress: History of a Cotton Textile Company, 1844–1945* (Harvard University Press, Cambridge, Mass., 1948), pp. 66–67; Massachusetts Bureau of Statistics of Labor, *Eleventh Annual Report* (Boston, 1880), p. 7; Massachusetts Bureau of Statistics of Labor, *Thirteenth Annual Report* (Boston, 1882), p. 304; United States Congress, Senate, *Report of the Committee of the Senate Upon the Relation Between Labor and Capital,* S. Rept. 1262, I (1885), p. 631; Mosely, *Reports,* p. 125; T. M. Young, *The American Cotton Industry* (Manchester University Press, Manchester, 1902), pp. 15, 44; T. W. Uttley, *Cotton Spinning and Manufacturing in the United States of America* (Manchester University Press, Manchester, 1905), pp. 15, 32, 35, 38.
75. W. Fraser, "The Glasgow Cotton Spinners, 1837," in J. Butt and J. Ward, eds., *Scottish Themes* (Scottish Academic Press, Edinburgh, 1976); *Statement by the Proprietors of Cotton Works in Glasgow and Vicinity* (Curll, Glasgow, 1825); Factory Inquiry Commission, "Second Report of the Central Board, Scotland District," *Parliamentary Papers* XX (1833): 4–56; A. Graham, *The Impolicy of the Tax on Cotton Wool* (Associated Cotton Spinners, Glasgow, 1836), pp. 35–36; Select Committee on Combinations of Workmen, "First Report," pp. 1–221, 285–301.

76. Inspectors of Factories, Reports for the half-year ending 31 December 1838, *Parliamentary Papers* XIX (1839): 47–57; W. Marwick, *Economic Developments in Victorian Scotland* (Allen & Unwin, London, 1936), pp. 144–145, 182–184; Wood, *History of Wages*, pp. 98–103; Webb Collection, sec. A, vol. 34, pp. 381–413; A. J. Robertson, "The Decline of the Scottish Cotton Industry, 1860–1914," *Business History* 12 (July 1970): 116–128.

77. Webb Collection, sec. A, vol. 24, pp. 386, 428–429; Schulze-Gaevernitz, *Cotton Trade*, pp. 102–103.

78. Baines, *History*, p. 379; Select Committee on Combinations of Workmen, "First Report," p. 261.

79. Factory Inquiry Commission, "First Report," pp. 63–64; Factory Inquiry Commission, "Second Report of the Central Board, Lancashire District," *Parliamentary Papers* XXI (1833), pp. 36, 54.

80. A. Reach, *Manchester and the Textile Districts in 1849* (Helmshore, 1972), p. 14.

81. John Foster, *Class Struggle and the Industrial Revolution* (Methuen, London, 1974), p. 231; my emphasis.

82. Ibid., p. 234.

83. A. E. Musson, "Class Struggle and the Labour Aristocracy, 1830–60," *Social History* 1 (October 1976): 335–356.

84. Marx, *Capital*, p. 536.

85. Turner, *Trade Union Growth*, pp. 115–116, 137–138; Sidney Webb and Beatrice Webb, *Industrial Democracy* (Longmans, Green, London, 1919), p. 475; L. Tippett, *A Portrait of the Lancashire Textile Industry* (Oxford University Press, London, 1969), p. 105; Keith Burgess, *The Origins of British Industrial Relations: The Nineteenth Century Experience* (Croom Helm, London, 1975), chap. 4.

86. H. Ashworth, *The Preston Strike* (Simms, Manchester, 1854); S. Robinson, *Friendly Letters on the Recent Strikes from a Manufacturer to his own Workpeople* (Groombridge, London, 1854); Lowe, "Account"; H. I. Dutton and J. E. King, *Ten Percent and No Surrender* (Cambridge University Press, Cambridge, 1981); Committee on Trades' Societies, "Report," in National Association for the Promotion of Social Science, *Trades' Societies;* H. Fawcett, "Strikes: Their Tendencies and Remedies," *Westminster Review* 51 (July 1860): 1–12; Samuel Smiles, *Industrial Biography* (Ticknor and Field, Boston, 1864), p. 125; British Association for the Advancement of Science, *Regulation of Wages*, pp. 11–12; CFT, 4 May 1888, 26 October 1894; J. Jewkes and E. Gray, *Wages and Labour in the Lancashire Cotton Spinning Industry* (Manchester University Press, Manchester, 1935), chaps. 4–7; Wood, *History of Wages*, pp. 1–2; Tippett, *Portrait*, p. 102; M. Wiggins, "The Cotton Industry," in F. Gannett and

B. Catherwood, eds., *Industrial and Labour Relations in Great Britain* (King, London, 1939).

87. E. Shorrock, *Address Delivered in Darwen in September 1878, after the Riots at Darwen and Blackburn* (Stanford, London, 1881); S. Andrew, *Fifty Years' Cotton Trade* (Oldham, 1887), pp. 10–11.

88. R. Smith, "A History of the Lancashire Cotton Industry between the Years 1873 and 1896," Ph.D. diss., University of Birmingham, 1954, pp. 384–388; Andrew, *Fifty Years'*; *CFT*, 20 November 1885, 21 December 1888.

89. Oldham Master Cotton Spinners' Association, *Year Book* (Dornan, Oldham, 1910); Jewkes and Gray, *Wages and Labour*, pp. 74–75, 207; Wood, *History of Wages*, p. 54.

90. Webb Collection, sec. B, vol. 93, p. 8; British Association for the Advancement of Science, *Regulation of Wages*, p. 200; *CFT*, 6 November 1885.

91. Jewkes and Gray, *Wages and Labour*, p. 32.

92. Wood, *History of Wages*, p. 131.

93. Sidney Chapman, "Some Policies of the Cotton Spinners' Trade Unions," *Economic Journal* 10 (December 1900): 467–473; Webb Collection, sec. A, vol. 35, pp. 84–86.

94. E. Thorpe, "Industrial Relations and the Social Structure: A Case Study of Bolton Cotton Mule-Spinners, 1884–1910," M.Sc. thesis, University of Salford, 1969, p. 254; *Textile Mercury*, 26 April 1890; *CFT*, 20 July 1894, 19 August 1894, 7 May 1897; Alan Fowler, "Lancashire Cotton Trade Unionism in the Inter-War Years," in Jowitt and McIvor, *Employers and Labour*, p. 108.

95. *CFT*, 16 March 1888.

96. Board of Trade, *An Industrial Survey of the Lancashire Area* (HMSO, London, 1932); Jewkes and Gray, *Wages and Labour*, pp. 16, 201; Wood, *History of Wages*, p. 131.

97. *CFT*, 11 December 1891, 25 December 1891.

98. Smith, "History of the Lancashire Cotton Industry," p. 214; Jewkes and Gray, *Wages and Labour*, pp. 187–190.

99. Turner, *Trade Union Growth*, p. 142.

100. Board of Trade, "Return of Rates of Wages in the Principal Textile Trades of the United Kingdom," *Parliamentary Papers* LXX (1889): Appendix.

101. *CFT*, 12 November 1886, 19 November 1886, 3 December 1886, 31 December 1886, 11 June 1897.

102. *CFT*, 1 May 1885, 26 November 1885, 3 December 1886, 4 March 1887, 20 May 1904, 1 December 1911.

103. *CFT*, 17 April 1885.

104. *CFT*, 21 August 1885.

105. *CFT*, 22 January 1886.

106. *CFT*, 22 June 1888.

107. *CFT*, 13 November 1885, 11 March 1887.

108. Smith, "History of the Lancashire Cotton Industry," p. 301; Webb Collection, sec. A, vol. 36, p. 44.

109. Jewkes and Gray, *Wages and Labour,* pp. 165–171; Board of Trade, "Report by the Chief Labour Correspondent on the Strikes and Lock-Outs of 1894," *Parliamentary Papers* XCIII (1895), p. 318; *CFT,* 17 September 1897.

110. Thorpe, "Industrial Relations," Appendix, table 3.

111. Oldham Operative Cotton Spinners' Provincial Association, *Monthly Report,* May 1895, p. 165.

112. Jewkes and Gray, *Wages and Labour,* p. 169; *CFT,* 20 July 1894, 14 May 1897.

113. See the Board of Trade's annual reports on strikes and lockouts beginning with 1888; Joseph White, *The Limits of Trade Union Militancy: The Lancashire Textile Workers, 1910–1914* (Greenwood, Westport, 1978), pp. 204–209.

114. *CFT,* 7 May 1897; Jewkes and Gray, *Wages and Labour,* pp. 173–175.

115. For a comparison of mule spinning in New England and Lancashire, see Chapter 4.

116. W. Taggart, *Cotton Mill Management: A Practical Guide for Managers, Carders, and Overlookers* (Macmillan, London, 1923), pp. xix–xx.

4. More Than One Way to Spin a Mule

1. H. A. Turner, *Trade Union Growth, Structure and Policy* (University of Toronto Press, Toronto, 1962), pp. 137–138; Sidney Webb and Beatrice Webb, *Industrial Democracy* (Longmans, Green, London, 1919), p. 475; Board of Trade (Labour Department), *Trade Unions Report, 1905–1907* (London, 1919), p. xiv; L. H. Tippett, *A Portrait of the Lancashire Textile Industry* (Oxford University Press, London, 1969), pp. 102, 105; Henry Ashworth, *The Preston Strike* (Manchester, 1854); Committee on Trades' Societies, "Report," in National Association for the Promotion of Social Science, *Trades' Societies and Strikes* (London, 1860); J. Lowe, "An Account of the Cotton Trade at Preston in 1853," in National Association for the Promotion of Social Science, *Trades' Societies;* Henry Fawcett, "Strikes: Their Tendencies and Remedies," *Westminster Review* 51 (July 1860): 1–12; British Association for the Advancement of Science, *On the Regulation of Wages by Means of Lists in the Cotton Industry* (Manchester, 1887),

pp. 11–12; *Cotton Factory Times* (hereafter *CFT*), 4 May 1888, 26 October 1894; G. H. Wood, *The History of Wages in the English Cotton Trade during the Past Hundred Years* (Sherratt & Hughes, London, 1910); J. Jewkes and E. Gray, *Wages and Labour in the Lancashire Cotton Spinning Industry* (Manchester University Press, Manchester, 1935), chaps. 4–7.

2. See Chapter 3; also J. H. Porter, "Industrial Peace in the Cotton Trade, 1875–1913," *Yorkshire Bulletin of Economic and Social Research* 19 (May 1967): 49–61; British Association for the Advancement of Science, *Regulation of Wages,* pp. 19ff; Oldham Master Cotton Spinners' Association, *Yearbook* (Dornan, Oldham, 1910); Wood, *History of Wages,* pp. 52–55; James Winterbottom, "A Criticism of the Oldham and Bolton Lists of Earnings for Mule Spinning," *Journal of The British Association of Managers of Textile Works* 6 (1914–15); Roland Smith, "A History of the Lancashire Cotton Industry between the Years 1873 and 1896, Ph.D. diss., University of Birmingham, 1954, pp. 276–318; Charles Macara, *The New Industrial Era* (Sherratt & Hughes, Manchester, 1923), p. 322; W. M. Wiggins, "The Cotton Industry," in Frank E. Gannett and B. F. Catherwood, eds., *Industrial and Labour Relations in Great Britain* (King, London, 1939).

3. E. J. Hobsbawm, *Labouring Men: Studies in the History of Labour* (Weidenfeld & Nicolson, London, 1968), chap. 15.

4. Ellis Thorpe, "Industrial Relations and the Social Structure: A Case Study of Bolton Cotton Mule-Spinners, 1884–1910," M.Sc. thesis, University of Salford, 1969; *Textile Mercury,* 26 April 1890; *CFT,* 16 March 1988, 19 August 1894, 1 May 1897.

5. Philip T. Silvia, Jr., "The Position of Workers in a Textile Community: Fall River in the Early 1880s," *Labour History* 16 (Spring 1975): 230–248.

6. D. A. Farnie, *The English Cotton Industry and the World Market, 1815–1896* (Clarendon, Oxford, 1979), chap. 7; Sylvia Lintner, "A Social History of Fall River, 1859–1879," Ph.D. diss., Radcliffe College, 1945, pp. 26–28; H. Earl, comp., *Fall River and Its Manufactories,* 14th Ed. (Fall River, 1894), pp. 36–50.

7. Robert K. Lamb, "The Development of Entrepreneurship in Fall River, 1813–1859," Ph.D. diss., Harvard University, 1935, chap. 12, pp. 6–8; Massachusetts Bureau of Statistics of Labor (hereafter Mass. BSL), *Eleventh Annual Report* (Boston, 1880), pp. 6–9; Robert Howard, "Progress in the Textile Trades," in George McNeil, ed., *The Labor Movement: The Problem of Today* (Milwaukee, 1891), p. 215. More generally, see Isaac Cohen, "Workers' Control in the Cotton Industry: A Comparative Study of British and American Mule Spinning," *Labor History* 26 (Winter 1985): 53–85.

8. Peck and Earl, *Fall River*, p. 8; Lintner, "Social History," pp. 14–16; Mass. BSL, *Eleventh Report*, pp. 57–62; Mass. BSL, *Thirteenth Annual Report* (Boston, 1882), pp. 229ff; Howard, "Progress," pp. 217–219.

9. Lintner, "Social History," chap. 3; Philip T. Silvia, Jr., "The Spindle City: Labor Policy and Religion in Fall River, Massachusetts, 1870–1905," Ph.D. diss., Fordham University, 1973, chaps. 3–4; Howard, "Progress," pp. 219–233; Mass. BSL, *Eleventh Report*, pp. 30, 36–42, 53–63; Mass. BSL, *Thirteenth Report*, pp. 201–207.

10. Silvia, "Spindle City," pp. 109–110.

11. Howard, "Progress," pp. 233–234.

12. Silvia, "Spindle City," chap. 6; Lintner, "Social History," pp. 26–28.

13. Silvia, "Spindle City," chap. 9.

14. *Wade's Fibre and Fabric*, 22 September 1888, p. 243, 18 January 1889, p. 372.

15. Mosely Industrial Commission to the United States of America, October–December, 1902, *Report for the Delegates*, p. 126.

16. *CFT*, 13 February 1885; Harold Catling, *The Spinning Mule* (David & Charles, Newton Abbott, 1970), p. 116.

17. William Taggart, *Cotton Mill Management: A Practical Guide for Managers, Carders and Overlookers* (Macmillan, London, 1923), pp. 19–20.

18. *CFT*, 20 March 1885; Ministry of Labour and National Service, *The Cotton Spinning Industry*, Supplement, *Mule-Spinners' Wages* (HMSO, London, 1946), p. 9.

19. Jewkes and Gray, *Wages and Labour*, p. 16; Hobsbawm, *Labouring Men*, pp. 286–287.

20. *CFT*, 13 March 1885, 3 April 1885, 20 November 1885, 11 May 1888, 22 June 1888, 6 July 1888, 7 December 1888, 22 May 1891, 7 December 1894; "Trade Union Problems," *Journal of the National Federation of Textile Works Managers Associations* 5 (1925–26), pp. 36–37.

21. See, e.g., *CFT*, 2 March 1894, 13 November 1905.

22. See William Lazonick, "Industrial Relations and Technical Change: The Case of the Self-Acting Mule," *Cambridge Journal of Economics* 3 (September 1979), p. 255.

23. *CFT*, 4 December 1885: Smith, "Lancashire Cotton Industry," pp. 292–293; Jewkes and Gray, *Wages and Labour*, p. 205.

24. See, e.g., *CFT*, 25 December 1885, 23 December 1888, 4 January 1889, 9 January 1891, 1 January 1897; see also Porter, "Industrial Peace"; Smith, "Lancashire Cotton Industry," pp. 217ff, 394–395, 458–478; Joseph L. White, *The Limits of Trade Union Militancy: The Lancashire Textile Workers, 1910–1914* (Greenwood, Westport, 1978), pp. 212–215.

25. Amalgamated Association of Operative Cotton Spinners, *Annual Report for Year Ending December 31, 1888* (Manchester, 1889), p. 14.
26. Porter, "Industrial Peace," pp. 51, 53; Smith, "Lancashire Cotton Industry," pp. 458–578; Wiggins, "Cotton Industry," pp. 230–232; *CFT*, 22 January 1897.
27. Porter, "Industrial Peace," pp. 52–57; see also Roger F. Dyson, "The Development of Collective Bargaining in the Cotton Spinning Industry, 1893–1914," Ph.D. diss., University of Leeds, 1971; Smith, "Lancashire Cotton Industry," p. 459; *CFT*, 15 November 1889.
28. Mass. BSL, *Eleventh Report*, p. 7.
29. Lamb, "Entrepreneurship," chap. 15; Silvia, "Spindle City," pp. 180, 270; Mass. BSL, *Eleventh Report*, p. 54; Mass. BSL, *Thirteenth Report*, p. 304; U.S. Congress, Senate, *Report of the Committee of the Senate Upon the Relation between Labor and Capital*, S. Rept. 1262, 48th Cong., 2d sess., vol. 1, p. 631, vol. 3, p. 74; Annawan Manufacturing Co., Payroll Book, 7 January 1882, Manuscript Division, Baker Library, Harvard University, Boston, Mass.
30. *CFT*, 26 March 1886; Mosely, *Reports*, pp. 125–128; T. M. Young, *The American Cotton Industry* (Manchester University Press, Manchester, 1902), pp. 15–44; T. W. Uttley, *Cotton Spinning and Manufacturing in the United States of America* (Manchester University Press, Manchester, 1903), pp. 16, 32, 35, 38; Bolton and District Managers and Overlookers' Association, *Report of Delegates on American Tour* (Bolton, 1920), pp. 75–79.
31. Mosely, *Reports*, p. 126.
32. Amalgamated Association of Operative Cotton Spinners, *Annual Report,* 31 December 1903.
33. See Chapter 3.
34. I am grateful to Iain Murton of the University of Cambridge for personal communication on the mobility of mule spinners and other related issues; Uttley, *Cotton Spinning*, p. 27; Young, *American Cotton Industry*, p. 12; Bolton and District Managers and Overlookers' Association, *Report*, p. 80.
35. Silvia, "Spindle City," pp. 265–268; Lintner, "Social History," pp. 62, 119, 139; John A. Garraty, ed., *Labor and Capital in the Gilded Age* (Little, Brown, Boston, 1968), pp. 33–36.
36. *Fall River versus the Massachusetts Bureau of Statistics* (Fall River, 1882), p. 8.
37. *Textile Manufacturer,* 15 July 1884; New England Cotton Manufacturers Association (hereafter NECMA), *Transactions* 21 (1879): 40; *CFT*, 1 March 1886; Mosely, *Reports*, pp. 127–129; Uttley, *Cotton Spinning*, p. 13; Young, *American Cotton Industry*, p. 12; Melvin T. Copeland, *The Cotton Manufacturing Industry of the United States*

(Harvard University Press, Cambridge, Mass., 1921), p. 61; James Winterbottom, *Cotton Spinning, Calculations and Yarn Costs,* 2nd Ed. (Longmans, Green, London, 1921), p. 204.

38. William Mass, "The Adoption of the Automatic Loom," photocopy, Harvard University, April 1980; William Lazonick and William Mass, "The Performance of the British Cotton Industry, 1870–1913," *Research in Economic History* 9 (1984): 1–44; and Chapter 5.

39. Copeland, *Cotton Manufacturing,* p. 184; Silvia, "Spindle City," p. 603.

40. Derived from data in Stuart W. Cramer, *Useful Information for Cotton Manufacturers,* 2nd Ed. (Charlotte, N.C., 1904); Taggart, *Cotton Mill Management,* pp. 202–203.

41. Based on average hourly earnings in 1891 and 1897, the wages of a Massachusetts mule spinner were 32 percent and 44 percent greater, respectively, than those of an Oldham minder and 174 percent and 203 percent greater, respectively, than those of an Oldham big piecer. Mass. BSL, *Twenty-Seventh Report* (Boston, 1898), p. 6; Wood, *History of Wages,* p. 54.

42. Unit labor cost figures were derived from the sources cited in notes 39 and 40. For data on cotton prices by grade and staple length, see Winterbottom, *Cotton Spinning,* pp. 232ff.

43. See William Lazonick, "Factor Costs and the Diffusion of Ring Spinning in Britain prior to World War I," *Quarterly Journal of Economics* 96 (September 1981): 195–236; William Lazonick, "Industrial Organization and Technological Change: The Decline of the British Cotton Industry," *Business History Review* 57 (Summer 1983): 195–236; William Lazonick, "The Cotton Industry," in Bernard Elbaum and William Lazonick, eds., *The Decline of the British Economy* (Clarendon, Oxford, 1986).

44. Lintner, "Social History," p. 164; Lamb, "Entrepreneurship," chap. 15, p. 51; NECMA, *Transactions* 31 (1881): 21; NECMA, *Transactions* 34 (1883): 54; Mass. BSL, *Thirteenth Report,* pp. 313–314; Garraty, *Labor and Capital,* pp. 33–36; United States Industrial Commission, *Report on the Relations and Conditions of Capital and Labor* (Washington, 1901), pp. 344–348; Evelyn Knowlton, *Pepperell's Progress* (Harvard University Press, Cambridge, Mass., 1948), p. 171; Young, *American Cotton Industry,* p. 4; Silvia, "Spindle City," pp. 553–554.

45. See, e.g., *CFT,* 17 April 1885, 31 December 1886; Webb and Webb, *Industrial Democracy,* pp. 424–425.

46. While ignoring the relative magnitudes of unit cotton-cost differentials in two countries, Lars Sandberg and, following him, C. Knick Harley have argued that it was the higher unit labor-cost differentials of mule

yarn over ring yarn in the United States relative to that in Britain that accounts for the rapid diffusion of ring spinning in New England. Lars Sandberg, *Lancashire in Decline* (Ohio State University Press, Columbus, 1974), chap. 2; C. K. Harley, "Skilled Labour and the Choice of Technique in Edwardian Industry," *Explorations in Economic History* 11 (Summer 1974), p. 399. Sandberg, however, overestimated the unit labor cost on mules in both countries as well as output per spindle on ring-frames in the United States, and as a result overstated the relative unit labor cost advantage of rings in the United States. When correct data are used, we find that, while the labor-cost saving of ring over mules favored the introduction of ring in both the United States and Britain, it was an insignificant factor in accounting for the differences in the rate of diffusion of the newer technology. See Lazonick, "Factor Costs"; Lars Sandberg, "Remembrances of Things Past," *Quarterly Journal of Economics* 99 (May 1984): 387–392; William Lazonick, "Rings and Mules in Britain: Comment," *Quarterly Journal of Economics* 99 (May 1984): 393–398. See also the productivity data in William Whittam, *Report on England's Cotton Industry* (U.S. Government Printing Office, Washington, 1907), p. 19; Mason Machine Works, *Cotton Machinery* (Taunton, Mass., 1898), pp. 122–126; Mosely, *Reports,* pp. 129–130.

5. Spinning and Weaving to Industrial Decline

1. G. T. Jones, *Increasing Return* (Cambridge University Press, Cambridge, 1933), pp. 275–276.
2. R. Robson, *The Cotton Industry in Great Britain* (Macmillan, London, 1957), p. 345.
3. See William Lazonick, "The Cotton Industry," in Bernard Elbaum and William Lazonick, eds., *The Decline of the British Economy* (Clarendon, Oxford, 1986).
4. Donald McCloskey and Lars Sandberg, "From Damnation to Redemption: Judgments on the Late Victorian Entrepreneur," *Explorations in Economic History* 9 (Fall 1971), p. 102.
5. See the references in McCloskey and Sandberg, "From Damnation." See also Donald McCloskey, ed., *Essays on a Mature Economy: Britain after 1940* (Methuen, London, 1971). Subsequent contributions are McCloskey, *Economic Maturity and Entrepreneurial Decline: British Iron and Steel* (Harvard University Press, Cambridge, 1973); C. K. Harley, "Skilled Labour and the Choice of Technique in Edwardian Industry," *Explorations in Economic History* 11 (Summer 1974): 391–414; Lars Sandberg, *Lancashire in Decline* (Ohio State University Press, Columbus, 1974); W. Arthur Lewis, *Growth and Fluctuations,*

1870–1913 (Allen & Unwin, London, 1978); Charles Kindleberger, *Economic Response* (Harvard University Press, Cambridge, 1978); Peter Payne, "Industrial Entrepreneurship and Management in Great Britain," in Peter Mathias and M. M. Postan, eds., *The Cambridge Economic History of Europe*, vol. 7, pt. 1 (Cambridge University Press, Cambridge, 1978); Robert Allen, "International Competition in Iron and Steel, 1850–1913," *Journal of Economic History* 39 (December 1979): 911–937; William Lazonick, "Factor Costs and the Diffusion of Ring Spinning in Britain prior to World War I," *Quarterly Journal of Economics* 96 (February 1981): 89–109; William Lazonick, "Industrial Organization and Technological Change: The Decline of the British Cotton Industry," *Business History Review* 57 (Summer 1983): 195–236; Elbaum and Lazonick, *Decline*.

6. Lazonick, "Industrial Organization."
7. Jones, *Increasing Return*, pp. 116–117.
8. Ibid., p. 55.
9. Sandberg, *Lancashire*, chap. 5.
10. Jones, *Increasing Return*, p. 117.
11. Sandberg, *Lancashire*, p. 96.
12. Ibid., p. 221.
13. Lars Sandberg, "Entrepreneurship and Technological Change," in Roderick Floud and Donald McCloskey, eds., *The Economic History of Britain since 1700*, vol. 2, *1860 to the 1970s* (Cambridge University Press, Cambridge, 1981), p. 116; see also McCloskey and Sandberg, "From Damnation," p. 102. For the debates on technological choice and the performance of the British cotton textile industry, see William Mass and William Lazonick, "The British Cotton Industry and International Competitive Advantage: The State of the Debates," *Business History* 32 (October 1990), forthcoming.
14. Robson, *Cotton Industry*, p. 345.
15. A. Pearse, *The Cotton Industry of India* (International Federation of Master Cotton Spinners' and Manufacturers' Associations, Manchester, 1930).
16. Lars Sandberg, "Movements in the Quality of British Cotton Textile Exports, 1815–1913," *Journal of Economic History* 28 (March 1968), pp. 10–11.
17. G. Turnbull, *A History of the Calico Printing Industry of Great Britain* (Sherratt, Altrincham, U.K., 1951). It should be noted that rationalization and consolidation of the finishing section of the industry could very well have worked in the opposite direction: to raise finishing charges relative to cloth charges. Indeed, in the 1920s the monopolistic finishers were accused of doing just that. See ibid., p. 470; Freda Utley, *Lancashire and the Far East* (Allen & Unwin, London, 1931), p. 54.

18. R. Tyson, "The Cotton Industry," in Derek Aldcroft, ed., *The Development of British and Foreign Competition, 1875–1914* (Allen & Unwin, London, 1968).

19. A. J. Marrison, "Great Britain and Her Rivals in the Latin American Cotton Piece Goods Market, 1880–1914," in Barrie Ratcliffe, ed., *Great Britain and Her World, 1750–1914* (Manchester University Press, Manchester, 1975).

20. Ibid., p. 327.

21. Tyson, "Cotton Industry," p. 113; Blackburn Chamber of Commerce, *Report of the Mission to China of the Blackburn Chamber of Commerce, 1896–97* (North-East Lancashire Press, Blackburn, 1898); H. D. Fong, *Cotton Industry and Trade in China* (Nankai Institute of Economics, Tientsin, 1932).

22. William Mass, "Technological Change and Industrial Relations: The Diffusion of Automatic Weaving in Britain and the United States," Ph.D. diss., Boston College, 1984.

23. Lazonick, "Industrial Organization"; Lazonick, "Cotton Industry."

24. Percy Bean and S. Scarisbrick, *The Chemistry and Practice of Sizing,* 10th Ed. (Hutton, Hartley, Manchester, 1921), pp. 293–296; Henry Greenwood, *Handbook of Weaving and Manufacturing* (Pitman, London, 1926); M. T. Copeland, *The Cotton Manufacturing Industry of the United States* (Harvard University Press, Cambridge, Mass., 1912), p. 78.

25. H. Nisbet, *The History of Sizing* (Emmot, Manchester, 1912), pp. 2–4, 46–47; William Thomson, *The Sizing of Cotton Goods* (Palmer & Howe, Manchester, 1877), pp. 85, 90, 96, 112, 140; Thomas Thornley, *The Middle Processes of Cotton Mills* (Greenwood, London, 1923), pp. 308–309; Copeland, *Cotton Manufacturing,* pp. 77–78. Copeland argued that the natives of poor countries did not mind heavily sized cloth because they never washed their clothes. See also Bean and Scarisbrick, *Chemistry,* p. 6. The acceptability of such adulterated cloth, however, undoubtedly had more to do with low incomes than with low standards of cleanliness. It would be useful to calculate the cost saving that could be achieved by, say, 50 percent sizing with China clay, but I do not have information on the volume of yarn that 50 percent sizing would displace.

26. Bean and Scarisbrick, *Chemistry,* pp. 297–298, 329–330.

27. R. Robson, "Structure of the Cotton Industry: A Study in Specialization and Integration," Ph.D. diss., University of London, 1950, p. 190; Copeland, *Cotton Manufacturing,* pp. 365–370.

28. Copeland, *Cotton Manufacturing,* p. 368.

29. John Jewkes and Sylvia Jewkes, "A Hundred Years of Change in the Structure of the Cotton Industry," *Journal of Law and Economics* 9 (October 1966), p. 120.

30. Alfred Marshall, *Industry and Trade* (Macmillan, London, 1919), pp. 600–601.
31. John Jewkes, "The Localisation of the Cotton Industry," *Economic History* 2 (January 1930), pp. 92–93; D. A. Farnie, *The English Cotton and the World Market, 1815–1896* (Clarendon, Oxford, 1979), chaps. 2 and 8.
32. Lazonick, "Factor Costs," pp. 101–102.
33. Ibid., p. 106.
34. C. Brooks, *Cotton* (Spon & Chamberlain, New York, 1898), pp. 282–284; Copeland, *Cotton Manufacturing*, pp. 180–184.
35. Brooks, *Cotton*, p. 209.
36. See, for example, the innovation on the Lancashire loom of Thomas Pickles as reported in the *Cotton Factory Times* (hereafter *CFT*), 29 March 1904, 16 December 1906, 3 August 1906, 8 March 1907, 3 May 1907, 20 December 1907.
37. E. Hopwood, *The Lancashire Weavers' Story* (Amalgamated Weavers Association, Manchester, 1969), p. 36.
38. Roland Smith, "A History of the Lancashire Cotton Industry between the Years 1873 and 1896," Ph.D. diss., University of Birmingham, 1954, pp. 294ff, 545ff; Hopwood, *Lancashire*, p. 55; Farnie, *English Cotton*, p. 309; Andrew Bullen, "Pragmatism vs. Principle: Cotton Employers and the Origins of an Industrial Relations System," in J. A. Jowitt and A. J. McIvor, eds., *Employers and Labour in the English Textile Industries, 1850–1939* (Routledge, London, 1988).
39. Jones, *Increasing Return*, p. 277; Smith, "Lancashire Cotton Industry," p. 386; Hopwood, *Lancashire*, p. 188.
40. H. Clegg, A. Fox, and A. Thompson, *A History of British Trade Unions since 1889* (Clarendon, Oxford, 1964), pp. 117–119; Hopwood, *Lancashire*, chap. 17.
41. Great Britain, Board of Trade (Labour Department), *Trade Unions, Report, 1905–1907* (HMSO, London, 1909), p. xiv.
42. J. Hilton, *Are Trade Unions Obstructive?* (Gollancz, London, 1935); Geoffrey Brown, *Sabotage: A Study in Industrial Conflict* (Spokesman, Nottingham, 1977).
43. Sandberg, *Lancashire*, p. 96.
44. E. Phelps Brown and S. Handfield-Jones, "The Climateric of the 1890s: A Study in the Expanding Economy," *Oxford Economic Papers*, n.s., 4 (October 1952), pp. 297–298. My conclusion is based on a comparison of the Phelps Brown and Handfield-Jones figures with those in their cited source, Great Britain, Census Office, *Census of England and Wales 1911*, vol. 10, *Occupations and Industries*, pt. 1 (HMSO, London, 1914), p. 548.
45. Calculated from various Factory Inspectors' Reports (see note 46).
46. The number of operatives in 1911, 1912, and 1913 is estimated by

increasing the 1907 figures for spinning and weaving operatives by projected rates of increase in spindles and looms per operative (interpolated from the annual rate of increase 1904–1907) multiplied by the actual increase in spindles and looms from 1907 to 1911 and 1913, respectively. Throughout two half-timers are treated as one full-time operative. The resultant estimates for 1911 are consistent with the 1911 census figures (see Great Britain, Census Office, *Census 1911*, p. 548). Because the spinning and weaving sections of the industry developed almost as separate "industries" in Lancashire, it is useful to derive separate estimates of productivity change for spinning and weaving. For 1896, 1898, 1901, 1904, and 1907, the Factory Inspectors' Reports classified operatives as employed in the spinning or weaving sections of the industry. In the earlier reports, however, the number of operatives in spinning, weaving, and combined firms are given. To allocate the combined-firm operatives to the spinning and weaving sections for these years, it was assumed that combined firms are in the aggregate perfectly balanced between spinning and weaving—that is, that in the aggregate these firms spin just enough yarn to meet their weaving needs. The ratio of spindles to looms in combined firms is such as to support this assumption. The assumption that a perfect spindle : loom balance between specialized firms would be the same as within combined firms permits an estimate of the proportion of spindles in specialized spinning firms spinning yarn that is not woven (in Britain), and hence the proportions of spinning operatives in specialized firms who are not balanced with weaving operatives in specialized firms. An estimate of the ratio of "balanced" spinning and weaving operatives in all specialized firms can then be derived, and this ratio can then be applied to combined firms in order to allocate the combined-firm operatives to the spinning and weaving sections of the industry. Note that the annual percentages changes presented in Table 5.8 are compounded and are based on output averages of the years preceding, including, and following the initial and terminal dates. This averaging helps to adjust for cyclical fluctuations in output per worker. Over the typical four-year or five-year trade cycle, changes in output were much more pronounced than changes in operatives employed, the predominant practice being to work shorter hours rather than lay off workers. In the estimates of output per worker, all output data have been adjusted to the equivalent of a 56.5-hour workweek, which was the length of the workweek between 1874 and 1901.

47. Sandberg, "Movement"; Sandberg, *Lancashire*, p. 98.
48. Sandberg, *Lancashire*, p. 98.
49. 1913 is double weighted.
50. See for example J. Worrall, *The Cotton Spinners' and Manufacturers' Directory for Lancashire* (Oldham, Worrall, 1913).

51. Gary Saxonhouse and Gavin Wright, "New Evidence on the Stubborn English Mule and the Cotton Industry, 1878–1920," *Economic History Review,* 2nd ser., 37 (November 1984): 507–519.

52. William Lazonick, "Industrial Relations and Technical Change: The Case of the Self-Acting Mule," *Cambridge Journal of Economics* 3 (September 1979), pp. 236–237, 253–254.

53. *CFT,* 4 December 1885; Smith, "Lancashire Cotton Industry," pp. 392–393; John Jewkes and E. M. Gray, *Wages and Labour in the Lancashire Cotton Spinning Industry* (Manchester University Press, Manchester, 1935), p. 205.

54. See for example *CFT,* 14 February 1902.

55. Worrall, *Cotton,* p. 358; Jones, *Increasing Return,* p. 277; F. Jones, "The Cotton Spinning Industry in the Oldham District from 1896 to 1914," M.A. thesis, University of Manchester, 1959.

56. Jones, *Increasing Return,* p. 277.

57. G. H. Wood, *The History of Wages in the English Cotton Trade during the Past Hundred Years* (Sherratt & Hughes, Manchester, 1910), p. 145.

58. Ibid., pp. 143–146.

59. Based on returns in various Factory Inspectors' Reports (see note 46).

60. Wood, *History of Wages,* pp. 142–143; also E. M. Gray, "Wage-Rates and Earnings in Cotton Weaving," *Transactions of the Manchester Statistical Society* 10 (1938–1939): 62–76.

61. Hopwood, *Lancashire,* pp. 61–62.

62. Ibid., p. 61; Joseph White, *The Limits of Trade Union Militancy: The Lancashire Textile Workers, 1910–1914* (Greenwood, Westport, 1978), p. 102.

63. See, e.g., Oldham Operative Cotton Spinners' Provincial Association, *A List of Thirty Questions with the Answers Given Thereto Relating to the System of Payment to Minders etc. for Work Performed* (Oldham, 1875), p. 28.

64. Webb Trade-Union Collection, in the British Library of Economics and Political Science, London School of Economics, sec. B, vol. 95, item 5.

65. Hopwood, *Lancashire,* pp. 59–60.

66. These estimates are drawn from compensation announcements in the monthly reports of the Oldham Operative Cotton Spinners' Provincial Association from 1885 through 1913.

67. White, *Limits,* pp. 187–199.

68. Jones, "Cotton Spinning"; Lazonick, "Factor Costs," p. 96.

69. Calculations based on data in Jewkes and Gray, *Wages and Labour,* pp. 37, 117; and Lazonick, "Factor Costs," pp. 96–98, 107.

70. Calculations based on data in Mass, "Adoption"; and in Robson, *Cotton Industry,* p. 345.

71. F. Merttens, "Productivity, Protection and Integration of Industry,"

Transactions of the Manchester Statistical Society, 1903–1904, p. 12; Charles Macara, *The New Industrial Era,* 2nd ed. (Sherratt & Hughes, Manchester, 1923), p. 332; G. Armitage, *The Problem of the Cotton Trade* (reprinted from the *Manchester Guardian,* January 1929), p. 20.

72. CFT, 14 February 1902; *Journal of the British Association of Managers of Textile Works* (Lancashire Section) 5 (1913–14), pp. 10ff; *Journal of the National Association of Textile Works Managers' Associations* 4 (1924–25): 15–16; Jewkes and Gray, *Wages and Labour,* p. 172.

73. William Lazonick, "Production Relation, Labor Productivity, and Choice of Technique: British and U.S. Cotton Spinning," *Journal of Economic History* 41 (September 1981): 491–516.

74. J. Porter, "Industrial Peace in the Cotton Trade, 1875–1913," *Yorkshire Bulletin of Economic and Social Research* 19 (May 1967): 49–61; White, *Limits.*

75. For example, in 1901, the workweek was reduced by less than 2 percent, not by 3 percent as claimed in Sandberg, *Lancashire,* p. 97. Jewkes and Gray have indicated an increase in hourly wage rates from 1906 to 1913 of only 1.6 percent, not 6 percent as Sandberg asserted. Jewkes and Gray, *Wages and Labour,* p. 198.

76. Calculated from James Winterbottom, *Cotton Spinning Calculations and Yarn Costs* (Longmans, Green, London, 1921), p. 259; and Jewkes and Gray, *Wages and Labour,* p. 211.

77. In Sandberg's words: "1912–1914 was certainly a better period than was 1884–1886. Thus, if Jones' index is used for the 1885–1914 period a couple of percentage points should probably be subtracted from the index of real cost in 1914." Sandberg, *Lancashire,* p. 104.

78. See for example, G. Harcourt, *Some Cambridge Controversies in the Theory of Capital* (Cambridge University Press, Cambridge, 1970); Stephen Nicholas, "Total Factor Productivity Growth and the Revision of Post-1870 British Economic History," *Economic History Review,* 2nd ser., 35 (February 1982): 83–98.

79. According to Phelps Brown and Handfield-Jones, the cost of manufacturing equipment rose by 17 percent between 1885 and 1912. Phelps Brown and Handfield-Jones, "Climacteric," p. 305; also cited in Sandberg, *Lancashire,* p. 107. If this cost inflation was true of spinning and weaving equipment, book values would have tended to fall below replacement values.

80. Utley, *Lancashire,* pp. 26–27; also G. W. Daniels and John Jewkes, "The Post-War Depression in the Lancashire Cotton Industry," *Journal of the Royal Statistical Society* 91 (1928): 153–192.

81. Robson, *Cotton Industry,* pp. 340, 355–356.

82. Great Britain, Ministry of Production, *Report of the Cotton Textile*

Mission to the U.S.A. (HMSO, London, 1944); L. Rostas, "Productivity of Labour in the Cotton Industry," *Economic Journal* 55 (June–September 1945: 192–205; Productivity Team Report, *Cotton Spinning* (Anglo-American Council on Productivity, London, 1950); Productivity Team Report, *Cotton Weaving* (Anglo-American Council on Productivity, London, 1950); D. C. Shaw, "Productivity in the Cotton Spinning Industry," *Manchester School* 18 (January 1950): 14–30; Marvin Frankel, *British and American Manufacturing Productivity* (University of Illinois Bulletin Series No. 81, 1957).

83. Lazonick, "Industrial Organization."
84. Lazonick, "Cotton Industry."
85. W. Morton and H. Greg, "The Cotton Textile Industry in the U.S.A.," *Journal of the Textile Institute* 17 (October 1926): 147–152; A. Pearse, "Efforts to Rationalize the Cotton Industry of the U.S.A.," *Transactions of the Manchester Statistical Society* (1928–1929): 77–92.
86. Lazonick, "Cotton Industry."
87. Lazonick, "Industrial Organization."

6. The Persistence of Craft Control

1. R. C. O. Matthews, C. H. Feinstein, and J. C. Odling-Smee, *British Economic Growth, 1856–1973* (Stanford University Press, Stanford, 1982), p. 435. See also S. B. Saul, "The Export Economy, 1870–1914," *Yorkshire Bulletin of Economic and Social Research* 17 (1965), p. 12.
2. Angus Maddison, *Phases of Capitalist Development* (Oxford University Press, New York, 1982), p. 98.
3. Ibid., pp. 252–254; Matthews et al., *British Economic Growth*, p. 435.
4. This thesis is developed in Alfred D. Chandler, Jr., *Scale and Scope: The Dynamics of Industrial Capitalism* (Harvard University Press, Cambridge, Mass., 1990). See also William Lazonick, *Business Organization and the Myth of the Market Economy* (Cambridge University Press, Cambridge, 1991); and Chapters 7 and 9. For comparative data on mechanization, administrative overhead, and labor productivity in U.S. and British manufacturing in the first half of this century, see Seymour Melman, *Dynamic Factors in Industrial Productivity* (John Wiley & Sons, New York, 1956).
5. William Lazonick, "The Cotton Industry," in Bernard Elbaum and William Lazonick, eds., *The Decline of the British Economy* (Clarendon Press, Oxford, 1986). See also William Mass and William Lazonick, "The British Cotton Industry and International Competitive Advantage: The State of the Debates," *Business History* 32 (October

1990), forthcoming; Organization for Economic Cooperation and Development, *Modern Cotton Industry—A Capital-Intensive Industry* (OECD, Paris, 1965).

6. Edward Lorenz and Frank Wilkinson, "The Shipbuilding Industry, 1880–1965," in Elbaum and Lazonick, *Decline;* James McGoldrick, "Industrial Relations and the Division of Labour in the Shipbuilding Industry since the War," *British Journal of Industrial Relations* 21 (July 1983): 197–220.

7. G. C. Allen, *The British Disease* (Institute of Economic Affairs, London, 1976); Philip Bassett, *Strike Free: New Industrial Relations in Britain* (Macmillan, London, 1986), chap. 2.

8. Besides the contents of the preceding three chapters, the following summary draws on Bernard Elbaum and Frank Wilkinson, "Industrial Relations and Uneven Development: A Comparative Study of the American and British Steel Industries," *Cambridge Journal of Economics* 3 (September 1979): 275–303; Sidney Pollard and Paul Robertson, *The British Shipbuilding Industry, 1870–1914* (Harvard University Press, Cambridge, Mass., 1979); Keith Burgess, *The Origins of British Industrial Relations: The Nineteenth Century Experience* (Croom Helm, London, 1975); Charles More, *Skill and the English Working Class, 1870–1914* (Croom Helm, London, 1980); Royden Harrison and Jonathan Zeitlin, eds., *Divisions of Labour: Skilled Workers and Technological Change in Nineteenth Century Britain* (Harvester Press, Sussex, 1985).

9. See Chandler, *Scale and Scope,* pt. 3.

10. Burgess, *Origins,* pp. 23–24.

11. Elbaum and Wilkinson, "Industrial Relations," p. 285.

12. See Chapter 3; Burgess, *Origins,* chap. 1.

13. See, for example, Michael Huberman, "Industrial Relations and Productivity in Lancashire: Evidence from M'Connel and Kennedy, 1810–1840," photocopy, Trent University, 1989.

14. Henry Pelling, *A History of British Trade Unionism,* 3rd Ed. (Penguin, Harmondsworth, 1976), chap. 4; E. H. Hunt, *British Labour History, 1815–1914* (Humanities Press, Atlantic Highlands, N.J., 1981), chap. 8.

15. J. H. Porter, "Wage Bargaining under Conciliation Agreements, 1860–1914," *Economic History Review* 23 (December 1970): 460–475.

16. H. A. Clegg, Alan Fox, and A. F. Thompson, *A History of British Trade Unions since 1889,* vol. 1, *1889–1910* (Clarendon Press, Oxford, 1964), pp. 21–24.

17. Ibid., pp. 11–12; Burgess, *Origins;* Keith McLelland and Alastair Reid, "Wood, Iron and Steel: Technology, Labour, and Trade Union

Organisation in the Shipbuilding Industry, 1840–1914," in Harrison and Zeitlin, *Divisions of Labour*.

18. Quoted in Pelling, *History*, p. 112; see also Geoff Brown, *Sabotage: A Study in Industrial Conflict* (Spokesman Books, Nottingham, 1977), p. 121.

19. E. J. Hobsbawm, *Labouring Men: Studies in the History of Labour* (Weidenfeld & Nicolson, London, 1964), chap. 10.

20. See Chapters 4 and 5.

21. See, for example, Charles Macara, *The New Industrial Era,* 2nd Ed. (Sherratt & Hughes, Manchester, 1923). On the FMCSA formation and strategy as reactions to the union movement, see Arthur McIvor, "Cotton Employers' Organisations and Labour Relations, 1890–1939," in J. A. Jowitt and A. J. McIvor, eds., *Employers and Labour in the English Textile Industries, 1850–1939* (Routledge, London, 1988).

22. Lazonick, "Cotton Industry," pp. 28–30.

23. Bernard Elbaum, "The Steel Industry before World War I," in Elbaum and Lazonick, *Decline,* p. 51; Saul, "Export Economy," p. 13.

24. Elbaum, "Steel Industry," p. 58.

25. Steven Tolliday, "Steel and Rationalisation Policies, 1918–1950," in Elbaum and Lazonick, *Decline.*

26. Frank Wilkinson, "Collective Bargaining in the Steel Industry in the 1920s," in Asa Briggs and John Saville, eds., *Essays in Labour History, 1918–1939* (Croom Helm, London, 1977); Judith Eisenberg Vichniac, "Union Organization in the French and British Iron and Steel Industries in the Late Nineteenth Century," *Political Power and Social Theory 6* (1987), pp. 326–327.

27. Wilkinson, "Collective Bargaining," pp. 106–107; Elbaum and Wilkinson, "Industrial Relations," pp. 288–292; Vichniac, "Union Organization," pp. 328–331.

28. Wilkinson, "Collective Bargaining," p. 107.

29. Elbaum, "Steel Industry," pp. 69–70.

30. Burgess, *Origins,* chap. 1.

31. See Huberman, "Industrial Relations."

32. See Burgess, *Origins,* pp. 8, 18–19. Burgess argued that employers preferred systematic overtime because they "could not afford to keep expensive machinery idle." But in recessions, when systematic overtime became an industrial-relations issue, machine utilization was in any case constrained by depressed demand.

33. Compare, for example, John Jewkes and Sylvia Jewkes, "A Hundred Years of Change in the Structure of the Cotton Industry," *Journal of Law and Economics* 9 (October 1966): 115–134, with S. B. Saul, "The Mechanical Engineering Industries in Britain, 1860–1914," in Barry

Supple, ed., *Essays in British Business History* (Clarendon Press, Oxford, 1977).

34. G. D. H. Cole, "Some Notes on British Trade Unionism in the Third Quarter of the Nineteenth Century," in E. M. Carus-Wilson, ed., *Essays in Economic History,* vol. 3 (Arnold, London, 1962).

35. Burgess, *Origins,* p. 38.

36. Ibid., pp. 39, 45, 53.

37. M. and J. B. Jefferys, "The Wages, Hours, and Trade Customs of the Skilled Engineer in 1861," *Economic History Review* 17 (1947), p. 39.

38. Richard Hyman, "Class Struggle and the Trade Union Movement," in David Coates, Gordon Johnston, and Ray Bush, *A Socialist Anatomy of Britain* (Polity Press, London, 1985), p. 105.

39. S. B. Saul, "The American Impact on British Industry, 1895–1914," *Business History* 3 (December 1960): 19–38.

40. Jonathan Zeitlin, "The Labour Strategies of British Engineering Employers, 1890–1922," in Howard F. Gospel and Craig R. Littler, eds., *Managerial Strategies and Industrial Relations* (Heinemann, London, 1983), p. 33.

41. Ibid., p. 30.

42. Ibid., pp. 34–35.

43. Ibid., p. 34.

44. Ibid., p. 35. See also Alan McKinlay and Jonathan Zeitlin, "The Meanings of Managerial Prerogative: Industrial Relations and the Organisation of Work in British Engineering, 1880–1939," *Business History* 31 (April 1989): 32–47.

45. Wayne Lewchuk, *American Technology and the British Vehicle Industry* (Cambridge University Press, Cambridge, 1987), p. 74. See also, Zeitlin, "Labour Strategies," p. 39; James Hinton, *The First Shop Stewards' Movement* (Allen & Unwin, London, 1973), p. 129.

46. Hinton, *First,* pp. 79–80.

47. Ibid., p. 80.

48. Joseph Melling, "Employers, Industrial Welfare, and the Struggle for Work-Place Control in British Industry, 1880–1920," in Gospel and Littler, *Managerial Strategies,* pp. 71–72. On the roles of supervisors, see also Joseph Melling, " 'Non-Commissioned Officers': British Employers and Their Supervisory Workers, 1880–1920," *Social History* 5 (May 1980): 183–221; Keith Burgess, "Authority Relations and the Division of Labour in British Industry, with Special Reference to Clydeside, c. 1860–1930," *Social History* 11 (May 1986): 211–233.

49. Zeitlin, "Labour Strategies," p. 44.

50. Ibid., p. 47.

51. Ibid.

52. Lewchuk, *American Technology*, p. 109.
53. Ibid., chap. 9; Steven Tolliday, "High Tide and After: Coventry Engineering Workers and Shopfloor Bargaining, 1945–80," in Bill Lancaster and Tony Mason, eds., *Life and Labour in a Twentieth Century City: The Experience of Coventry* (Cyfield Press, Coventry, 1986); Steven Tolliday, "Government, Employers and Shop Floor Organisation in the British Motor Industry, 1939–69," in Steven Tolliday and Jonathan Zeitlin, eds., *Shop Floor Bargaining and the State: Historical and Comparative Perspectives* (Cambridge University Press, Cambridge, 1985). See also Jonathan Zeitlin, "The Emergence of Shop Steward Organization and Job Control in the British Car Industry: A Review Essay," *History Workshop* 10 (Autumn 1980): 119–137; Dave Lyddon, "Workplace Organization in the British Car Industry. A Critique of Jonathan Zeitlin," *History Workshop* 15 (Spring 1983): 131–140; Jonathan Zeitlin, "Workplace Militancy: A Rejoinder," *History Workshop* 16 (Autumn 1983): 131–136. On the quantitative importance of the "new" industries to the growth of the British economy from the 1920s to the 1970s, see Matthews et al., *British Economic Growth*, pp. 239–241, 257. In 1924, electrical engineering and vehicles together accounted for about 10 percent of value-added in British manufacturing; in 1937, 15 percent; in 1951, 16 percent; and in 1964, 20 percent. Ibid., p. 239.
54. Lewchuk, *American Technology*, chap. 8; Steven Tolliday, "Enterprise Management and the Control of Labor: Collective Bargaining and Labor Management in Ford Motor Company (Britain)," paper presented to the conference on New Directions in Business History: Industrial Performance and Enterprise, University of California, Santa Cruz, April 29–May 1, 1988.
55. Lewchuk, *American Technology*, p. 185.
56. Ibid., p. 94; Michael Jolly, "The British Motor Industry and the Labour Market during the Inter-War Period," Ph.D. diss., University of Toronto, 1988, p. 102.
57. Wayne Lewchuk, "Fordism and the British Motor Car Employers, 1896–1932," in Gospel and Littler, *Managerial Strategies;* Lewchuk, *American Technology*, chap. 8; Zeitlin, "Labour Strategies," pp. 39–40.
58. Lewchuk, *American Technology*, p. 142.
59. J. F. B. Goodman and T. G. Whittingham, *Shop Stewards in British Industry* (McGraw-Hill, Maidenhead, U.K., 1969), pp. 34–35; Lewchuk, *American Technology*, pp. 188–190; Lyddon, "Workplace Organization," pp. 131–132.
60. John Purcell and Keith Sisson, "Strategies and Practice in the Manage-

ment of Industrial Relations," in George Sayers Bain, ed., *Industrial Relations in Britain* (Basil Blackwell, Oxford, 1983), p. 101; Eric Batstone, *Working Order: Workplace Industrial Relations over Two Decades* (Basil Blackwell, Oxford, 1984), p. 99.

61. See William Brown, "A Consideration of Custom and Practice," *British Journal of Industrial Relations* 10 (March 1972), p. 62.

62. H. A. Turner, G. Clack, and B. Roberts, *Labour Relations in the Motor Industry* (Allen & Unwin, London, 1967), p. 214. See also Garfield Clack, *Industrial Relations in a British Car Factory* (Cambridge University Press, Cambridge, 1967). Clack says that "the shop steward organisation . . . aimed, ultimately, to keep men at work and to control—even discipline—union members. The senior shop stewards were involved in the enforcement of collective agreements, and concerned with the implementation (even planning) and co-ordination of many everyday details of production—such as the transfers of men around the factory, the scheduling of overtime or short-time working, and the recruitment and training of labour." Ibid., pp. 97–98.

63. Michael Terry, "Shop Steward Development and Managerial Strategies," in Bain, *Industrial Relations;* Batstone, *Working Order,* pp. 79–82.

64. On wage-drift, see, for example, A. I. Marsh and E. E. Coker, "Shop Steward Organization in the Engineering Industry," *British Journal of Industrial Relations* 1 (June 1963): 176–189. On the extent of the erosion of British profits relative to other advanced capitalist economies, see Philip Armstrong and Andrew Glyn, "Accumulation, Profits, State Spending: Data for Advanced Capitalist Countries, 1952–1983," unpublished data, Oxford Institute of Economics and Statistics, July 1986, p. 55.

65. Cited in Keith Sisson and William Brown, "Industrial Relations in the Private Sector: Donovan Re-visited," in Bain, *Industrial Relations,* p. 139.

66. Terry, "Shop Steward," p. 72.

67. Ibid.

68. John Child and Bruce Partridge, *Lost Managers: Supervisors in Industry and Society* (Cambridge University Press, Cambridge, 1982), p. 11.

69. Ibid.

70. William Lazonick, "Strategy, Structure, and Management Development in the United States and Britain," in Kesaji Kobayashi and Hidemasa Morikawa, eds., *Development of Managerial Enterprise* (University of Tokyo Press, Tokyo, 1986); Chris Smith, *Technical Workers: Class, Labour, and Trade Unionism* (Macmillan, London, 1987).

71. Geoffrey Crockett and Peter Elias, "British Managers: A Study of Their Education, Training, Mobility, and Earnings," *British Journal of Industrial Relations* 22 (March 1984): 34–46.

72. Batstone, *Working Order*, p. 183. See also Michael Terry, "The Inevitable Growth of Informality," *British Journal of Industrial Relations* 15 (March 1977): 76–90.

73. Batstone, *Working Order*, pp. 160–164; Lewchuk, *American Technology*, pp. 203–214. See also Tom Donnelly and David Thoms, "Trade Unions, Management and the Search for Production in the Coventry Motor Car Industry, 1939–75," *Business History* 31 (April 1988): 98–113.

74. R. McKersie, L. Hunter, and W. Sengenberger, *Productivity Bargaining: The American and British Experience* (U.S. Government Printing Office, Washington, D.C., January 1972), p. 4.

75. Sisson and Brown, "Industrial Relations," p. 148; McKersie, Hunter, and Sengenberger, *Productivity*, p. 9; Batstone, *Working Order*, pp. 157–159.

76. Batstone, *Working Order*, p. 177; Arthur Francis, Mandy Snell, Paul Willman, and Graham Winch, "Management, Industrial Relations and New Technology for the BL Metro," photocopy, Department of Social and Economic Studies, Imperial College, November 1982, pp. 3–5.

77. Paul William and Graham Winch, *Innovation and Management Control* (Cambridge University Press, Cambridge, 1985); Michael Edwardes, *Back from the Brink* (Pan Books, London, 1984); Lewchuk, *American Technology*, pp. 218–219. On the emerging conflicts over shop-floor control in the 1970s, see Richard Hyman and Tony Elger, "Job Controls, the Employers Offensive, and Alternative Strategies," *Capital and Class* 15 (Autumn 1981): 115–149.

78. John MacInnes, *Thatcherism at Work* (Open University Press, Milton Keynes, 1987), p. 66.

79. Armstrong and Glyn, "Accumulation," p. 31; Bassett, *Strike Free*, pp. 15–16.

80. Armstrong and Glyn, "Accumulation," p. 36; MacInnes, *Thatcherism*, p. 87; Bassett, *Strike Free*, pp. 7–9; Nicholas Oulton, "Plant Closures and the Productivity 'Miracle' in Manufacturing," *National Institute Economic Review* 121 (August 1987): 53–59.

81. MacInnes, *Thatcherism*, p. 100; see also Michael Terry, "How Do We Know If Shop Stewards Are Getting Weaker?" *British Journal of Industrial Relations* 24 (July 1986): 169–179; Frank H. Longstreth, "From Corporatism to Dualism? Thatcherism and the Climacteric of British Trade Unions in the 1980s," *Political Studies* 36 (September 1988): 413–432.

82. P. K. Edwards and Keith Sisson, "Industrial Relations in the UK: Change in the 1980s," an ESRC Research Briefing, Industrial Relations Research Unit, University of Warwick, 1989, summary page.

83. Ibid., p. 4.

84. Ibid., p. 3.

7. Managerial Capitalism and Economies of Speed

1. Simon Kuznets, *Economic Growth of Nations: Total Output and Production Structure* (Harvard University Press, Cambridge, Mass., 1971), pp. 316–317.

2. Angus Maddison, *Phases of Capitalist Development* (Oxford University Press, New York, 1982), pp. 45, 60.

3. R. C. O. Matthews, C. H. Feinstein, and J. C. Odling-Smee, *British Economic Growth, 1856–1973* (Stanford University Press, Stanford, 1982), pp. 240–241.

4. Bernard Elbaum and William Lazonick, eds., *The Decline of the British Economy* (Clarendon Press, Oxford, 1986).

5. Karl Marx, *Capital,* vol. 1 (Vintage, New York, 1977), p. 799.

6. For the definition of the managerial surplus and the analysis of this positive-sum situation, see the Appendix.

7. H. J. Habbakuk, *American and British Technology in the Nineteenth Century* (Cambridge University Press, Cambridge, 1962); Peter Temin, ed., *New Economic History* (Penguin, Harmondsworth, 1968); S. B. Saul, ed., *Technological Change: The United States and Britain in the Nineteenth Century* (Methuen, London, 1970).

8. Merritt Roe Smith, *Harpers Ferry Armory and the New Technology* (Cornell University Press, Ithaca, 1977); David Hounshell, *From the American System to Mass Production, 1800–1932* (Johns Hopkins University Press, Baltimore, Md., 1984), chap. 1; Nathan Rosenberg, *Perspectives on Technology* (Cambridge University Press, Cambridge, 1976), chaps. 1, 2.

9. Gary Kulik, "Pawtucket Village and the Strike of 1824: The Origins of Class Consciousness in Rhode Island," *Radical History Review* 17 (Spring 1978): 5–38; Jonathan Prude, *The Coming of Industrial Order: Town and Factory Life in Rural Massachusetts, 1810–1860* (Cambridge University Press, Cambridge, 1983); Barbara M. Tucker, *Samuel Slater and the Origins of the American Textile Industry* (Cornell University Press, Ithaca, N.Y., 1984).

10. Caroline Ware, *The Early New England Cotton Manufacture* (Russell & Russell, New York, 1931); Steve Dunwell, *Run of the Mill* (Godine, Boston, 1978), chaps. 1, 2; Thomas Dublin, *Women at Work: The*

Transformation of Work and Community at Lowell, Massachusetts, 1826–1860 (Columbia University Press, New York, 1979); William Lazonick and Thomas Brush, "The 'Horndal Effect' in Early U.S. Manufacturing," *Explorations in Economic History* 22 (February 1985): 53–96.

11. See Dunwell, *Run of the Mill,* chap. 2; Harry C. Dinmore, "Proprietors of Locks and Canals: The Founding of Lowell," in Arthur L. Eno, ed., *Cotton Was King* (New Hampshire Publishing, Somersworth, N.H., 1976), chap. 6.

12. Lazonick and Brush, "Horndal Effect," pp. 61–62, 74–82.

13. See Chapter 4.

14. William Mass, "Developing and Utilizing Technological Leadership: Industrial Research, Vertical Integration, and Business Strategy at the Draper Company, 1860–1930," *Business and Economic History,* n.s., 18 (1989): 129–139.

15. Nathan Rosenberg, *Inside the Black Box: Technology and Economics* (Cambridge University Press, Cambridge, 1982), chap. 3; Thomas Hughes, "The Order of the Technological World," in A. Rupert Hall and Norman Smith, eds., *History of Technology,* vol. 5 (Mansell, London, 1980).

16. Rosenberg, *Perspectives,* p. 24.

17. Hounshell, *American System.*

18. See Chapter 6.

19. David Montgomery, *The Fall of the House of Labor* (Cambridge University Press, Cambridge, 1987), p. 13; see also ibid., pp. 56, 179.

20. John Buttrick, "The Inside Contract System," *Journal of Economic History* 12 (September 1952): 205–221; Daniel Nelson, *Managers and Workers: Origins of the New Factory System in the United States* (University of Wisconsin Press, Madison, 1975), chap. 3; David Montgomery, *Workers' Control in America* (Cambridge University Press, Cambridge, 1979), chap. 1; Montgomery, *House of Labor,* chap. 1; Dan Clawson, *Bureaucracy and the Labor Process* (Monthly Review Press, New York, 1980), chap. 3.

21. Montgomery, *House of Labor,* pp. 9–13.

22. Daniel Nelson, *Frederick W. Taylor and the Rise of Scientific Management* (University of Wisconsin Press, Madison, 1980), p. 37.

23. Frederick Taylor, *The Principles of Scientific Management* (Norton, New York, 1967); Nelson, *Taylor.*

24. Quoted in Montgomery, *House of Labor,* pp. 253, 258.

25. Taylor, *Principles,* pp. 48–49.

26. Ibid., pp. 50–52.

27. See the Appendix for a formal analysis.

28. United States Bureau of the Census, *Historical Statistics of the United States, Colonial Times to 1970* (U.S. Government Printing Office, Washington, D.C., 1976), p. 177.

29. Ibid., p. 178.

30. Harold Livesay, *Andrew Carnegie and the Rise of Big Business* (Little, Brown, Boston, 1975), pp. 138–139; Montgomery, *House of Labor*, p. 16.

31. Quoted in David Brody, *Steelworkers in America* (Harvard University Press, Cambridge, Mass., 1960), pp. 53–54.

32. Montgomery, *House of Labor*, pp. 269–275.

33. See Nelson, *Taylor*.

34. Ibid., chap. 6.

35. Montgomery, *House of Labor*, p. 225.

36. Ibid., p. 215; see also ibid., pp. 41, 233–234, 323.

37. Ibid., p. 32.

38. Alfred D. Chandler, Jr., *Strategy and Structure: Chapters in the History of the American Industrial Enterprise* (MIT Press, Cambridge, Mass., 1962); Alfred D. Chandler, Jr., *The Visible Hand: The Managerial Revolution in American Business* (Harvard University Press, Cambridge, Mass., 1977); Leonard Reich, *The Making of American Industrial Research* (Cambridge University Press, Cambridge, 1985); David C. Mowery, "Industrial Research, 1900–1950," in Elbaum and Lazonick, *Decline;* David Hounshell and John K. Smith, *Science and Corporate Strategy: Du Pont R&D, 1902–1980* (Cambridge University Press, Cambridge, 1988).

39. U.S. Bureau of the Census, *Historical Statistics*, pp. 140, 142.

40. Seymour Melman, "The Rise of Administrative Overhead in the Manufacturing Industries of the United States, 1899–1947," *Oxford Economic Papers* 3 (1951), p. 66.

41. David Noble, *America by Design: Science, Technology, and the Rise of Corporate Capitalism* (Oxford University Press, New York, 1977).

42. U.S. Bureau of the Census, *Historical Statistics*, p. 386.

43. Edwin T. Layton, *The Revolt of the Engineers: Social Responsibility and the American Engineering Profession* (Johns Hopkins University Press, Baltimore, Md., 1986), p. 3.

44. Anglo-American Council on Productivity, *Education for Management* (Anglo-American Council on Productivity, London, 1951), pp. 48–51; Norman C. Hunt, *University Education for Business in the U.S.A.*, Management Education Series No. 1 (European Productivity Agency, Organization for European Economic Cooperation, Paris, 1953), p. 11.

45. William Lazonick, "The Integration of U.S. Higher Education into Agricultural Production," photocopy, Harvard University, 1977.

46. Noble, *America by Design*.

47. William Lazonick, "Strategy, Structure, and Management Development in the United States and Britain," in Kesaji Kobayashi and Hidemasa Morikawa, eds., *Development of Managerial Enterprise* (University of Tokyo Press, Tokyo, 1986).

48. "The Nine Hundred," *Fortune* 46 (November 1952): 132–135, 232, 234–236; Mabel Newcomer, *The Big Business Executive* (Columbia University Press, New York, 1955); W. Lloyd Warner and James C. Abegglen, *Occupational Mobility in American Business and Industry* (University of Minnesota Press, Minneapolis, 1955); Suzanne Keller, *The Social Origins and Career Lines of Three Generations of American Business Leaders* (Arno, New York, 1980).

49. Chandler, *Strategy and Structure;* Lazonick, "Strategy, Structure."

50. Mike Davis, "The Stopwatch and the Wooden Shoe: Scientific Management and the Industrial Workers of the World," *Radical America* 9 (January-February 1975): 69–95; Geoff Brown, *Sabotage: A Study in Industrial Conflict* (Spokesman Books, Nottingham, 1977), chap. 3.

51. Thorstein Veblen, *The Engineers and the Price System* (Huebsch, New York, 1921).

52. See Michael Nuwer, "From Batch to Flow: Production Technology and Work-Force Skills in the Steel Industry, 1880–1920," *Technology and Culture* 29 (October 1988): 808–838.

53. Nelson Lichtenstein, "Auto Worker Militancy and the Structure of Factory Life, 1937–1955," *Journal of American History* 65 (September 1980): pp. 336–337.

54. See Martin Brown and Michael Nuwer, "Strategic Jobs and Wage Structure in the Steel Industry: 1910–1930," *Industrial Relations* 26 (Fall 1987): 253–266, for an analysis of the role of "strategic" semi-skilled workers.

55. Stanley Mathewson, *Restriction of Output among Unorganized Workers* (Viking, New York, 1931), pp. 125–126; partially quoted in Montgomery, *Workers' Control,* p. 44.

56. Davis, "Stopwatch."

57. Marx, *Capital,* pp. 697–698.

58. Sumner Slichter, *The Turnover of Factory Labor* (Appleton, New York, 1919), p. 350.

59. Nelson, *Managers and Workers,* p. 78.

60. U.S. Bureau of the Census, *Historical Statistics,* pp. 142–143.

61. Horace Arnold, "Ford Methods and Ford Shops," *Engineering Magazine* 48 (1914), p. 349, quoted in Wayne Lewchuk, *American Technology and the British Vehicle Industry* (Cambridge University Press, Cambridge, 1987), p. 62.

62. John Commons, "Introduction," in Commons, ed., *Trade Unionism and Labor Problems,* 2nd Ed. (Ginn, Boston, 1921), pp. 6–7.

63. William Lazonick, "Technological Change and the Control of Work: The Development of Capital–Labour Relations in U.S. Manufacturing Industry," in Howard Gospel and Craig Littler, eds., *Managerial Strategies and Industrial Relations* (Heinemann, London, 1983).

64. Slichter, *Turnover*, p. 131.

65. Lewchuk, *American Technology*, p. 46.

66. Stephen Meyer III, *The Five-Dollar Day: Labor, Management and Social Control in the Ford Motor Company, 1908–1921* (State University of New York Press, Albany, 1981), pp. 91–92.

67. Quoted in Keith Sward, *The Legend of Henry Ford* (Rinehart & Company, New York, 1948), p. 56.

68. Meyer, *Five-Dollar Day*, p. 119.

69. Ibid., chap. 5.

70. Ibid., pp. 101–102.

71. Ibid., p. 112.

72. Daniel M. G. Raff, *Buying the Peace: Wage Determination Theory, Mass Production, and the Five-Dollar Day at Ford* (forthcoming); see also Daniel M. G. Raff, "Wage Determination and the Five-Dollar Day at Ford," *Journal of Economic History* 48 (June 1988): 387–407.

73. Raff, *Buying*; Lewchuk, *American Technology*, pp. 45, 51.

74. Sward, *Legend*, p. 78.

75. Hounshell, *American System*, chap. 7; Alfred D. Chandler, Jr., *Giant Enterprise: Ford, General Motors, and the Automobile Industry* (Harcourt, Brace, & World, New York, 1964).

76. Chandler, *Giant Enterprise*, p. 3.

77. Richard Tedlow, *New and Improved: The Story of Mass Marketing in America* (Basic Books, New York, 1990), chap. 3.

78. Chandler, *Giant Enterprise*, pp. 194–195. The best account of Ford's labor relations remains Sward, *Legend*, pt. 3.

79. Arthur J. Kuhn, *GM Passes Ford, 1918–38: Designing the General Motors Performance-Control System* (Pennsylvania State University Press, University Park, 1986); Tedlow, *New and Improved*, chap. 3.

80. Sward, *Legend*, chap. 14; Kuhn, *GM*.

81. Hounshell, *American System*, chap. 7.

82. See the list in Chandler, *Visible Hand*, Appendix A.

83. U.S. Bureau of the Census, *Historical Statistics*, p. 667.

84. Ibid., p. 683.

85. Ibid., pp. 137, 684–685.

86. Ibid., p. 162.

87. Spurgeon Bell, *Productivity, Wages and National Income* (The Brookings Institution, Washington, D.C., 1940), p. 28; see also Maurice Leven, Harold G. Moulton, and Clark Warburton, *America's Capacity to Consume* (The Brookings Institution, Washington, D.C., 1934).

88. Bell, *Productivity,* p. 29.
89. George H. Soule, *Prosperity Decade: From War to Depression, 1917–1929* (Rinehart, New York, 1947).
90. Bell, *Productivity,* p. 95; Frank Stricker, "Affluence for Whom?—Another Look at Prosperity and the Working Classes in the 1920s," *Labor History* 21 (Winter 1983): 5–33.
91. Mathewson, *Restriction of Output.*
92. See the Appendix.
93. Sanford Jacoby, *Employing Bureaucracy: Managers, Unions, and the Transformation of Work in American Industry, 1900–1945* (Columbia University Press, New York, 1985), chaps. 4, 5.
94. Sumner Slichter, "The Current Labor Policies of American Industry," *Quarterly Journal of Economics* 43 (May 1929), p. 395.
95. U.S. Bureau of the Census, *Historical Statistics,* pp. 178–179.
96. Slichter, "Current Labor Policies," p. 395.
97. Jacoby, *Employing Bureaucracy,* chaps. 4, 5.
98. Quoted in David Brody, *Steelworkers in America* (Harvard University Press, Cambridge, Mass., 1960), p. 228. See Howard Gitelman, "Welfare Capitalism Reconsidered," photocopy, Adelphi University, July 1989; see also Stuart D. Brandes, *American Welfare Capitalism, 1880–1940* (University of Chicago Press, Chicago, 1976).
99. Quoted in Katherine Stone, "The Origins of Job Structures in the Steel Industry," *Review of Radical Political Economics* 6 (Summer 1974), p. 78; Brody, *Steelworkers,* p. 228, quotes a truncated and somewhat different version of Gary's statement.
100. Nelson, *Managers and Workers,* chap. 3.
101. Ibid., p. 44.
102. Slichter, *Turnover,* chap. 12; F. H. Colvin, *Labor Turnover, Loyalty and Output* (McGraw-Hill, New York, 1919), chap. 7; B. Emmet, "Labor Turnover and Employment Policies of a Large Motor Vehicle Manufacturing Establishment," *Monthly Labor Review* 7 (October 1918): 837–854.
103. Jacoby, *Employing Bureaucracy,* p. 137; see also Henry Eilbert, "The Development of Personnel Management in the United States," *Business History Review* 33 (August 1959): 345–364.
104. Jacoby, *Employing Bureaucracy,* p. 233.
105. Ibid., chap. 5.
106. Ibid., p. 233.
107. Ibid., p. 194.
108. Ibid., pp. 186–187.
109. See Daniel Nelson, "The Company Union Movement, 1900–1937: A Reexamination," *Business History Review* 56 (Autumn 1982): 335–357.
110. Ibid., p. 211.

111. Ibid., p. 205.

112. Ibid., pp. 214, 223.

113. William Preston, Jr., *Aliens and Dissenters: Federal Suppression of Radicals, 1903–1933* (Harper Torchbooks, New York, 1963).

114. Montgomery, *House of Labor*, pp. 374–375.

115. Preston, *Aliens and Dissenters*, chaps. 4–8; James R. Green, *The World of the Worker: Labor in Twentieth-Century America* (Hill and Wang, New York, 1980), chap. 4; Roger B. Keeran, "Communist Influence in the Automobile Industry, 1920–1933: Paving the Way for an Industrial Union," *Labor History* 20 (Spring 1979): 189–225.

116. Montgomery, *House of Labor*, pp. 433–434.

117. Irving Bernstein, *The Lean Years: A History of the American Worker, 1920–1933* (Penguin, Baltimore, 1960), pp. 146–151.

118. Ibid., p. 74. For example, on autos, Joyce Shaw Peterson, *American Automobile Workers, 1900–1933* (State University of New York Press, Albany, 1987), chap. 7; on rubber, see Daniel Nelson, *American Rubber Workers and Organized Labor, 1900–1941* (Princeton University Press, Princeton, N.J., 1988), chaps. 2–4.

119. William R. Leiserson, "The Worker's Reaction to Scientific Management," in E. E. Hunt, ed., *Scientific Management since Taylor* (McGraw-Hill, New York, 1924); Jean T. McKelvey, *AFL Attitudes Towards Production, 1900–1932* (Cornell University Press, Ithaca, 1952); Milton Nadworny, *Scientific Management and the Unions, 1900–1932* (Harvard University Press, Cambridge, Mass., 1955), chaps. 7, 8.

120. Sanford Jacoby, "Union-Management Cooperation in the United States: Lessons from the 1920s," *Industrial and Labor Relations Review* 37 (October 1983): 18–33; Montgomery, *House of Labor*, pp. 422–424.

121. U.S. Bureau of the Census, *Historical Statistics*, p. 178.

122. Ibid., p. 179.

123. W. A. Berridge, "Labour Turnover in American Factories," *Monthly Labor Review* 29 (July 1929): 62–65; Slichter, "Current Labor Policies," pp. 429–431; U.S. Bureau of the Census, *Historical Statistics*, p. 182; Jacoby, *Employing Bureaucracy*, p. 171; Arthur M. Ross, "Do We Have a New Industrial Feudalism?" *American Economic Review* 48 (December 1958), pp. 906–912.

8. Perspectives on the Twenties

1. William Lazonick, "Technological Change and the Control of Work: The Development of Capital-Labour Relations in U.S. Manufacturing

Industry," in Howard Gospel and Craig Littler, eds., *Managerial Strategies and Industrial Relations* (Heinemann, London, 1983).

2. Sanford Jacoby, *Employing Bureaucracy: Managers, Unions, and the Transformation of Work in American Industry, 1900–1945* (Columbia University Press, New York, 1985), pp. 167–174.

3. Stanley Lebergott, *Manpower in Economic Growth: The American Experience since 1800* (McGraw-Hill, New York, 1964), pp. 512–513.

4. Christina Romer, "New Estimates of Prewar Gross National Product and Unemployment," *Journal of Economic History* 46 (June 1986), p. 343.

5. Paul Douglas, *Real Wages in the United States, 1890–1926* (Houghton, Boston, 1930), p. 445; Jacoby, *Employing Bureaucracy*, p. 168; Irving Bernstein, *The Lean Years: A History of the American Worker, 1920–1933* (Penguin, Baltimore, 1960), p. 59; Sumner Slichter, "Current Labor Policies of American Industry," *Quarterly Journal of Economics* 43 (May 1929), p. 429.

6. See Jacoby, *Employing Bureaucracy*, pp. 168–171, for a brief, but incomplete, review.

7. U.S. Bureau of the Census, *Historical Statistics of the United States: Colonial Times to 1970* (U.S. Government Printing Office, Washington, D.C., 1976), p. 668; see also Jacoby, *Employing Bureaucracy*, pp. 168–169.

8. Jacoby, *Employing Bureaucracy*, p. 169.

9. Bernstein, *Lean Years*, p. 60.

10. Paul Baran and Paul Sweezy, *Monopoly Capital: An Essay on the American Economic and Social Order* (Monthly Review Press, New York, 1966), p. 237.

11. U.S. Bureau of the Census, *Historical Statistics*, p. 668.

12. Ibid., pp. 676, 679.

13. See Chapter 6.

14. U.S. Bureau of the Census, *Historical Statistics*, p. 105.

15. David Montgomery, *The Fall of the House of Labor* (Cambridge University Press, Cambridge, 1987), p. 462.

16. Gavin Wright, *Old South, New South: Revolutions in the Southern Economy since the Civil War* (Basic Books, New York, 1986), p. 201; on the black migration, see Florette Henri, *Black Migration: Movement North, 1900–1920* (Anchor, Garden City, N.Y., 1976).

17. See Jacoby, *Employing Bureaucracy*. On a comparison of long-term employment in the early 1890s and late 1970s, see Susan B. Carter, "The Changing Importance of Lifetime Jobs, 1892–1978," *Industrial Relations* 27 (Fall 1988): 287–330.

18. See Chapter 7, note 24.

19. Jacoby, *Employing Bureaucracy,* p. 2.
20. Slichter, "Current Labor Policies," pp. 396–397; emphasis in original.
21. Ibid., p. 397; see also Sumner Slichter, "The Secret of High Wages," *The New Republic* 54 (28 March 1928): 183–185.
22. Slichter, "Current Labor Policies," p. 398.
23. Ibid., pp. 405–410.
24. Ibid., pp. 411–414.
25. Ibid., p. 414.
26. Ibid., p. 420.
27. Jacoby, *Employing Bureaucracy,* pp. 173–174.
28. Ibid., p. 174.
29. Ibid., p. 204.
30. Ibid.
31. Ibid., p. 205.
32. Ibid., pp. 163–164.
33. Ibid., p. 164.
34. Ibid., p. 173.
35. National Industrial Conference Board, *Collective Bargaining through Employee Representation* (National Industrial Conference Board, New York, 1933), p. 54.
36. Alfred D. Chandler, Jr., *Strategy and Structure: Chapters in the History of the American Industrial Enterprise* (MIT Press, Cambridge, Mass., 1962), chap. 3.
37. Alfred P. Sloan, Jr., *My Years with General Motors* (Anchor Books, Garden City, N.Y., 1963), p. 459.
38. Jacoby, *Employing Bureaucracy,* p. 195.
39. Mortier W. La Fever, "Workers, Machinery, and Production in the Automobile Industry," *Monthly Labor Review* 19 (October 1924), p. 23.
40. Jacoby, *Employing Bureaucracy,* p. 193.
41. Ibid., pp. 202–203.
42. U.S. Bureau of the Census, *Historical Statistics,* p. 142.
43. Jacoby, *Employing Bureaucracy,* p. 205.
44. Ibid., p. 9.
45. Personal communication from Sanford Jacoby.
46. Wright, *Old South, New South,* p. 137.
47. Ibid., p. 201.
48. Stephen Jay Kennedy, *Profits and Losses in Textiles: Cotton Textile Financing since the War* (Harper, New York, 1936), p. 251.
49. Slichter, "Current Labor Policies," p. 424.
50. Ibid., p. 431.
51. Ibid., p. 425.
52. Ibid., p. 426; my emphasis.

53. Alfred Marshall, *Principles of Economics,* 9th (variorum) Ed., vol. 1 (Macmillan, London, 1961), p. 233.

54. Ibid., p. 233n. See Karl Marx, *Capital,* vol. 1 (Vintage, New York, 1977), pp. 744–745, for an early critique of Nassau Senior's theory of abstinence.

55. William Lazonick, "Financial Commitment and Economic Performance: Ownership and Control in the American Industrial Corporation," *Business and Economic History,* 2nd ser., 17 (1988): 115–128.

56. Slichter, "Current Labor Policies," p. 430.

57. Ibid., pp. 430–431.

9. The Challenge of Flexible Mass Production

1. It should also be noted that from 1913 to 1929, Japan's share of world manufacturing exports increased from 2.5 to 4.1 percent, mainly as a result of capturing textile markets from Britain. See Chapter 5. For shares of manufacturing exports, see R. C. O. Matthews, C. H. Feinstein, and J. C. Odling-Smee, *British Economic Growth, 1856–1973* (Cambridge University Press, Cambridge, 1982), p. 435. For unemployment rates, see U.S. Bureau of the Census, *Historical Statistics of the United States from Colonial Times to 1970* (U.S. Government Printing Office, Washington, D.C., 1976), p. 126; S. Howson, "Slump and Unemployment," in Roderick Floud and Donald McCloskey, eds., *The Economic History of Britain since 1700,* vol. 2 (Cambridge University Press, Cambridge, 1981), p. 266 and references therein.

2. See Paul Baran and Paul Sweezy, *Monopoly Capital: An Essay on the American Economic and Social Order* (Monthly Review Press, New York, 1966), chap. 8; Robert Aaron Gordon, *Economic Instability and Growth: The American Record* (Harper & Row, New York, 1974), chaps. 2, 3; Lester V. Chandler, *America's Greatest Depression, 1929–1941* (Harper & Row, New York, 1970), pp. 23, 36 for evidence on reduced capital utilization and employment in the most concentrated industrial sectors.

3. David Brody, *Workers in Industrial America* (Oxford University Press, New York, 1980), p. 73; Emma Rothschild, *Paradise Lost: The Decline of the Auto-Industrial Age* (Vintage, New York, 1974), p. 36.

4. Chandler, *America's Greatest Depression,* p. 36.

5. Irving Bernstein, *The Turbulent Years: A History of the American Worker, 1933–1941* (Houghton Mifflin, Boston, 1970), chaps. 10, 11.

6. Brody, *Workers,* chap. 3.

7. Howell John Harris, *The Right to Manage: Industrial Relations Policies of American Business in the 1940s* (University of Wisconsin Press, Madison, 1982); Nelson Lichtenstein, *Labor's War at Home:*

The CIO in World War II (Cambridge University Press, Cambridge, 1982).

8. Frederick H. Harbison and Robert Dubin, *Patterns of Union–Management Relations* (Science Research Associates, Chicago, 1947), p. 50.

9. Quoted in David Gartman, *Auto Slavery: The Labor Process in the American Automobile Industry, 1897–1950* (Rutgers University Press, New Brunswick, N.J., 1986), p. 278.

10. Harry C. Katz, *Shifting Gears: Changing Labor Relations in the U.S. Automobile Industry* (MIT Press, Cambridge, Mass., 1985), p. 15.

11. Arthur M. Ross, "The General Motors Wage Agreement of 1948," *Review of Economics and Statistics* 31 (February 1949): 1–7; Frederick H. Harbison, "The General Motors-United Auto Workers Agreement of 1950," *Journal of Political Economy* 58 (October 1950): 397–411. See also Nelson Lichtenstein, "UAW Bargaining Strategy and Shop-Floor Conflict: 1946–1970," *Industrial Relations* 24 (Fall 1985): 360–381; Steve Jefferys, *Management and Managed: Fifty Years of Crisis at Chrysler* (Cambridge University Press, Cambridge, 1986).

12. Clinton S. Golden and Harold J. Ruttenberg, *The Dynamics of Industrial Democracy* (Harper, New York, 1941), chap. 5.

13. Ibid., p. 120.

14. Ibid., p. 121.

15. Brody, *Workers*, p. 77.

16. See Frederick H. Harbison, *The Seniority Principle in Union–Management Relations* (Industrial Relations Section, Princeton University, Princeton, N.J., 1939); see also Frederick H. Harbison, *Seniority Policies and Procedures as Developed through Collective Bargaining* (Industrial Relations Section, Princeton University, Princeton, N.J., 1939); Ronald W. Schatz, *The Electrical Workers: The History of Labor at General Electric and Westinghouse, 1923–60* (University of Illinois Press, Urbana, 1985), chap. 5.

17. William B. Gould IV, *Japan's Reshaping of American Labor Law* (MIT Press, Cambridge, Mass., 1984), chap. 5. On the problems of continuity of employment as well as job assignment that female blue-collar workers faced in the automobile and electrical manufacturing industries, see Ruth Milkman, *Gender at Work: The Dynamics of Job Segregation by Sex during World War II* (University of Illinois Press, Urbana, 1987).

18. Sumner Slichter, James J. Healy, and E. Robert Livernash, *The Impact of Collective Bargaining on Management* (Brookings Institution, Washington, D.C., 1960), p. 561.

19. Helen Baker and John M. True, *The Operation of Job Evaluation Plans* (Industrial Relations Section, Princeton University, Princeton, N.J.,

1947), chap. 7; see also Charles W. Lytle, "Job Evaluation—A Phase of Job Control," *Personnel* 16 (May 1940): 192–197.

20. Vincent D. Sweeney, *United Steelworkers of America: Twenty Years Later* (United Steelworkers of America, 1956), chap. 22; Baker and True, *Operation,* p. 83.

21. Frederick H. Harbison, "Seniority in Mass-Production Industries," *Journal of Political Economy* 48 (December 1940), p. 859; see also Helen Baker, *Company Plans for Employee Promotions* (Industrial Relations Section, Princeton University, Princeton, N.J., 1939), pp. 28, 34; Harbison and Dubin, *Patterns,* pp. 76–77; Brody, *Workers,* pp. 178–179.

22. Slichter, Healy, and Livernash, *Impact,* pp. 106–107; see also Morris Stone, *Labor–Management Contracts at Work* (Harper, New York, 1961), chap. 3; Richard Herding, *Job Control and Union Structure* (Rotterdam University Press, Rotterdam, 1972); Kazuo Koike, *Understanding Industrial Relations in Modern Japan* (St. Martin's, New York, 1988), chap. 3.

23. Michael J. Piore, "American Labor and the Industrial Crisis," *Challenge* 25 (March–April 1982): 5–11; Michael J. Piore and Charles F. Sabel, *The Second Industrial Divide: Possibilities for Prosperity* (Basic Books, New York, 1984), pp. 113–115; Herding, *Job Control;* Katz, *Shifting Gears,* pp. 40–44; Thomas A. Kochan, Harry C. Katz, and Robert B. McKersie, *The Transformation of American Industrial Relations* (Basic Books, New York, 1986), pp. 28–29, 88–89; Steven Tolliday and Jonathan Zeitlin, "Shop Floor Bargaining, Contract Unionism, and Job Control: An Anglo-American Comparison," in Nelson Lichtenstein and Stephen Meyer, eds., *On the Line: Essays in the History of Auto Work* (University of Illinois Press, Urbana, 1989).

24. On shop-floor conflict in the automobile industry, see Nelson Lichtenstein, "Conflict over Workers' Control: The Automobile Industry in World War II," in Michael H. Frisch and Daniel J. Walkowitz, eds., *Working-Class America: Essays on Labor, Community, and American Society* (University of Illinois Press, Urbana, 1983).

25. Nelson Lichtenstein, " 'The Man in the Middle': A Social History of Automobile Industry Foremen," in Lichtenstein and Meyer, *On the Line,* pp. 166–172; Charles P. Larrowe, "A Meteor on the Industrial Relations Horizon: The Foreman's Association of America," *Labor History* 2 (Fall 1961), p. 260.

26. Larrowe, "Meteor"; Lichtenstein, "Man in the Middle"; see also Herbert B. Northrup, "The Foreman's Association of America," *Harvard Business Review* 23 (Winter 1944–45): 187–202; Fritz J. Roethlisberger, "The Foreman: Master and Victim of Doubletalk," *Harvard Business Review* 23 (Spring 1945): 283–298; Donald E. Wray, "Marginal

Men of Industry: The Foremen," *American Journal of Sociology* 54 (January 1949): 298–301; James W. Driscoll, Daniel J. Carroll, Jr., and Timothy A. Sprecher, "The First-Level Supervisor: Still the Man in the Middle," *Sloan Management Review* 19 (Winter 1978): 25–38.

27. Philip Armstrong and Andrew Glyn, "Accumulation, Profits, and State Spending: Data for Advanced Capitalist Countries, 1952–1983," photocopy, Oxford Institute of Economics and Statistics, July 1986.

28. Alfred D. Chandler, Jr., *The Visible Hand: The Managerial Revolution in American Business* (Harvard University Press, Cambridge, Mass., 1977); Alfred D. Chandler, Jr., *Scale and Scope: The Dynamics of Industrial Capitalism* (Harvard University Press, Cambridge, Mass., 1990).

29. Armstrong and Glyn, "Accumulation," pp. 28, 35.

30. See David M. Gordon, "Capital vs. Labor," in Maurice Zeitlin, ed., *American Society, Inc.* (Markham, Chicago, 1977); Thomas E. Weisskopf, David M. Gordon, and Samuel Bowles, "Hearts and Minds: A Social Model of U.S. Productivity Growth," *Brookings Papers on Economic Activity* 2 (1983): 381–450.

31. U.S. Department of Health, Education, and Welfare, *Work in America* (MIT Press, Cambridge, Mass., 1972), chaps. 1 and 2.

32. For the concepts of exit and voice, see Albert O. Hirschman, *Exit, Voice, and Loyalty: Responses to Decline of Firms, Organizations, and States* (Harvard University Press, Cambridge, Mass., 1970).

33. Bill Watson, "Counter-Planning on the Shop Floor," *Radical America* 5 (May–June 1971): 77–85.

34. Armstrong and Glyn, "Accumulation," p. 36; U.S. Bureau of the Census, *Historical Statistics of the United States, Colonial Times to 1970* (U.S. Government Printing Office, 1976), pp. 162–163.

35. See James Crotty and Leonard Rapping, "The 1975 Report of the President's Council of Economic Advisers: A Radical Critique," *American Economic Review* 65 (December 1975): 791–811.

36. *Business Week,* 27 April 1974, p. 108.

37. See Elton Mayo, *The Human Problems of an Industrial Civilization* (Viking, New York, 1960); Fritz J. Roethlisberger and William Dickson, *Management and the Worker* (Harvard University Press, Cambridge, Mass., 1939); Richard E. Walton, "How to Counter Alienation in the Plant," *Harvard Business Review* 50 (November–December 1972): 70–81.

38. Irving Bluestone, "How Quality-of-Worklife Projects Work for the United Auto Workers," *Monthly Labor Review* (Conference Papers), July 1980, p. 40; see also Richard E. Walton, "Work Innovations in the United States," *Harvard Business Review* 57 (July–August 1979): 97.

39. Bluestone, "Quality-of-Worklife," p. 41.

40. Kochan, Katz, and McKersie, *Transformation,* p. 150. On the failure to transform the organization of work in the 1970s, see Richard E. Walton, "The Diffusion of New Work Structures: Explaining Why Success Didn't Take," *Organizational Dynamics* 3 (Winter 1975): 3–22; Andrew Zimbalist, "The Limits of Work Humanization," *Review of Radical Political Economics* 7 (Summer 1975): 50–59; Stephen A. Marglin, "Catching Flies with Honey: An Inquiry Into Management Initiatives to Humanize Work," *Economic Analysis and Workers' Management* 13 (1979): 473–488.

41. Richard E. Walton, "From Control to Commitment: Transforming Work Force Management in the United States," in Kim B. Clark, Robert H. Hayes, and Christopher Lorenz, eds., *The Uneasy Alliance: Managing the Productivity–Technology Dilemma* (Harvard Business School Press, Boston, 1985), p. 257.

42. Lichtenstein, "Man in the Middle," p. 166.

43. Robert H. Guest, "Quality of Work Life—Learning from Tarrytown," *Harvard Business Review* 57 (July–August 1979): 76–87.

44. Barry Bluestone and Bennett Harrison, *The Deindustrialization of America* (Basic Books, New York, 1982), p. 35.

45. Ibid., chaps. 2, 6; Kochan, Katz, and McKersie, *Transformation,* pp. 47–75.

46. See Bennett Harrison and Barry Bluestone, *The Great U-Turn: Corporate Restructuring and the Polarizing of America* (Basic Books, New York, 1988), chap. 2.

47. See Bruce R. Scott, "National Strategies: Key to International Competition," in Bruce R. Scott and George C. Lodge, eds., *U.S. Competitiveness in the World Economy* (Harvard Business School Press, Boston, 1985); Stephen S. Cohen and John Zysman, *Manufacturing Matters: The Myth of the Post-Industrial Economy* (Basic Books, New York, 1987), pp. 69–75.

48. Cohen and Zysman, *Manufacturing,* p. 70.

49. Ibid., p. 75.

50. Ibid., p. 11.

51. Alan Altshuler, Martin Anderson, Daniel Jones, Daniel Roos, and James Womack, *The Future of the Automobile* (MIT Press, Cambridge, Mass., 1986) p. 24.

52. See the discussion in William J. Abernathy, Kim B. Clark, and Alan M. Kantrow, *Industrial Renaissance: Producing a Competitive Future for America* (Basic Books, New York, 1983), pp. 58–59.

53. See the data presented in ibid., p. 60; and the discussion in Robert E. Cole and Tazio Yakushiji, eds., *The American and Japanese Auto Industries in Transition* (Center for Japanese Studies, University of Michigan, Ann Arbor, 1984), pp. 124–126.

54. Cole and Yakushiji, *Auto Industries,* pp. 119–128; Abernathy, Clark, and Kantrow, *Industrial Renaissance,* p. 61.
55. For a comparative analysis of the interaction of organization and technology, see William Lazonick, *Business Organization and the Myth of the Market Economy* (Cambridge University Press, New York, 1991), chap. 2.
56. The following account of Japanese shop-floor practices draws heavily on Michael Cusumano, *The Japanese Automobile Industry* (Harvard University Press, Cambridge, Mass., 1985). Cusumano's analysis is based on the experiences of Toyota and Nissan, but its implications for the role of shop-floor relations in value creation are generally applicable to dominant mass producers in Japan. See also Taiichi Ohno, "How the Toyota Production System Was Created," *Japanese Economic Studies* 10 (Summer 1982): 83–101; and the series of articles by Yasuhiro Monden, "What Makes the Toyota Production System Really Tick?" *Industrial Engineering* 13 (January 1981): 36–46; "Adaptable Kanban System Helps Toyota Maintain Just-in-Time Production," *Industrial Engineering* 13 (May 1981): 29–46; and "How Toyota Shortened Supply Lot Production Time, Waiting Time, and Conveyance Time," *Industrial Engineering* 13 (September 1981): 22–30; Gary Jacobson and John Hillkirk, *Xerox: American Samurai* (Collier Books, New York, 1986), chap. 7.
57. Cusumano, *Japanese Automobile,* pp. 285–287.
58. For the importance and meaning of economies of scope, see Chandler, *Scale and Scope;* Lazonick, *Business Organization,* chap. 1. See also David Teece, "Economies of Scope and the Scope of the Enterprise," *Journal of Economic Behavior and Organization* 1 (September 1980): 223–248.
59. Cusumano, *Japanese Automobile,* pp. 265–266.
60. Ibid., pp. 276, 305–307, 327–328.
61. Ibid., pp. 265, 293, 328.
62. Ibid., pp. 320–321.
63. Ibid., p. 333.
64. See the Appendix for the theoretical rationale for this argument. On the "productivity–technology dilemma," see Clark, Hayes, and Lorenz, *Uneasy Alliance.*
65. Harley Shaiken, Stephen Herzenberg, and Sarah Kuhn, "The Work Process Under More Flexible Production," *Industrial Relations* 25 (Spring 1986): 167–183; see also Harley Shaiken, *Work Transformed: Automation and Labor in the Computer Age* (Holt, Rinehart & Winston, New York, 1984).
66. See David F. Noble, "Social Choice in Machine Design: The Case of Automatically Controlled Machine Tools," in Andrew S. Zimbalist,

ed., *Case Studies on the Labor Process* (Monthly Review Press, New York, 1979). David F. Noble, *Forces of Production: A Social History of Industrial Automation* (Knopf, New York, 1984).

67. Piore and Sabel *Second Industrial Divide,* chaps. 2, 10, 11; see also Charles Sabel and Jonathan Zeitlin, "Historical Alternatives to Mass Production: Politics, Markets, and Technology in Nineteenth-Century Industrialization," *Past and Present* 108 (August 1985): 133–176.

68. Alfred D. Chandler, Jr., *Strategy and Structure: Chapters in the History of the American Industrial Enterprise* (MIT Press, Cambridge, Mass., 1962).

69. See William Lazonick, "Strategy, Structure, and Management Development in the United States and Britain," in Kesaji Kobayashi and Hidemasa Morikawa, eds., *Development of Managerial Enterprise* (University of Tokyo Press, Tokyo, 1986); Lazonick, *Business Organization,* chap. 2.

70. Cusumano, *Japanese Automobile,* p. 265.

71. See Chapter 7, note 55.

72. Armand V. Feigenbaum, "Total Quality Control," *Harvard Business Review* 34 (November–December 1956): 98; emphasis in original.

73. Ibid.; see also Cusumano, *Japanese Automobile,* pp. 324–325.

74. Cusumano, *Japanese Automobile,* p. 331.

75. For a more general comparison of organizational integration and segmentation in Britain, the United States, and Japan, see Lazonick, *Business Organization,* chap. 2.

76. David F. Noble, *America By Design: Science, Technology, and the Rise of Corporate Capitalism* (Oxford University Press, New York, 1977); Lazonick, "Strategy, Structure"; Shin'ichi Yonekawa, "University Graduates in Japanese Enterprises before the Second World War," *Business History* 26 (July 1984): 193–218; E. Daito, "Recruitment and Training of Middle Managers in Japan, 1900–1930," in Kobayashi and Morikawa, *Development of Managerial Enterprise.*

77. Compare Daito, "Recruitment," and Lazonick, "Strategy, Structure"; see also J. Hirschmeier and T. Yui, *The Development of Japanese Business,* 2nd Ed. (Allen & Unwin, London, 1981), pp. 205–207.

78. Daito, "Recruitment," p. 174; Koike, *Understanding,* chap. 4. On foremen in the United States, see note 26.

79. Andrew Gordon, *The Evolution of Labor Relations in Japan: Heavy Industry, 1853–1955* (Harvard University Press, Cambridge, Mass., 1985), pts. 2, 3; Solomon Levine, *Industrial Relations in Postwar Japan* (University of Illinois Press, Urbana, 1958), chap. 3; Reiko Okayama, "Japanese Employer Policy: The Heavy Engineering Industry, 1900–1930," in Howard Gospel and Craig Littler, eds., *Managerial Strategies and Industrial Relations* (Heinemann, London, 1983);

Robert Evans, Jr., "Evolution of the Japanese System of Employer–Employee Relations, 1868–1945," *Business History Review* 44 (Spring 1970): 110–125.

80. Gordon, *Evolution,* p. 24.
81. Ibid., p. 25; see also ibid., pp. 33–35.
82. Okayama, "Japanese Employer," pp. 162–163; Levine, *Industrial Relations,* pp. 61–62; Kenji Okuda, "Managerial Evolution in Japan," *Management Japan* 5 (Summer 1972): 16–23.
83. Levine, *Industrial Relations,* pp. 62–64. See also Sheldon Garon, *The State and Labor in Modern Japan* (University of California Press, Berkeley, 1987).
84. Evans, "Evolution," pp. 116–118; Okayama, "Japanese Employer," pp. 160–161; Gordon, *Evolution,* pp. 36–59.
85. Okayama, "Japanese Employer," p. 169.
86. Ibid., p. 164.
87. Ronald Dore, *British Factory–Japanese Factory: The Origins of Diversity in Industrial Relations* (University of California Press, Berkeley, 1973), p. 387.
88. Gordon, *Evolution,* pt. 3.
89. Ibid., p. 330; see also Joe Moore, *Japanese Workers and the Struggle for Power, 1945–1947* (University of Wisconsin Press, Madison, 1983).
90. Gordon, *Evolution,* p. 343.
91. Ibid., chap. 10; Cusumano, *Japanese Automobile,* chap. 3; Michael Halberstam, *The Reckoning* (Morrow, New York, 1986), pt. 3.
92. See Ronald Dore, *Taking Japan Seriously: A Confucian Perspective on Leading Economic Issues* (Stanford University Press, Stanford, 1987), pp. 70–72.
93. Gould, *Japan's Reshaping;* Robert E. Cole, *Japanese Blue Collar* (University of California Press, Berkeley, 1971); Kazuo Koike, "Human Resource Development and Labor–Management Relations," in Kozo Yamamura and Yasukichi Yasuba, eds., *The Political Economy of Japan,* vol. 1, *The Domestic Transformation* (Stanford University Press, Stanford, 1987); Koike, *Understanding,* chap. 4.
94. Wickham Skinner, "The Taming of Lions: How Manufacturing Leadership Evolved, 1780–1984," in Clark, Hayes, and Lorenz, *Uneasy Alliance,* p. 63.
95. Kochan, Katz, and McKersie, *Transformation;* D. Quinn Mills and Janice McCormick, *Industrial Relations in Transition* (John Wiley & Sons, New York, 1985), chaps. 1, 12; Walton, "From Control."
96. See Richard Florida, Martin Kenney, and Andrew Mair, "The Transplant Phenomenon: Japanese Automobile Manufacturers in the United States," Carnegie Mellon School of Urban and Public Affairs Working Paper 88–29, May 1988.

97. See Shaiken, *Work Transformed;* Donald M. Wells, *Empty Promises: Quality of Working Life Programs and the Labor Movement* (Monthly Review Press, New York, 1987); Mike Parker and Jane Slaughter, *Choosing Sides: Unions and the Team Concept* (South End Press, Boston, 1988); John P. Hoerr, *And the Wolf Finally Came: The Decline of the American Steel Industry* (University of Pittsburgh Press, Pittsburgh, 1988). See also Vicki Smith, "Self-Management as Self-Exploitation," *Socialist Review* 18 (October–December 1988):171–177. From a somewhat different perspective, see Shoshana Zuboff, *In the Age of the Smart Machine: The Future of Work and Power* (Basic Books, New York, 1988), pt. 2.

10. Organization and Technology in Capitalist Development

1. See Alfred Marshall, *Principles of Economics,* 9th (variorum) Ed., vol. 1, *Text* (Macmillan, London, 1961), bk. 4.

2. On the role of the Japanese state, see Chalmers Johnson, *MITI and the Japanese Miracle* (Stanford University Press, Stanford, 1982); Thomas K. McCraw, ed., *America versus Japan* (Harvard Business School Press, Boston, 1986). For an important case study, see Marie Anchordoguy, *Computers, Inc.: Japan's Challenge to IBM* (Harvard University Press, Cambridge, Mass., 1989).

3. For an elaboration, see William Lazonick, *Business Organization and the Myth of the Market Economy* (Cambridge University Press, Cambridge, 1991). For references to the "commitment" literature, see D. E. Guest, "Human Resource Management and Industrial Relations," *Journal of Management Studies* 24 (May 1987): 503–521.

4. In the neoclassical theory of the firm, the problem of fixed costs is eliminated by assuming that the firm instantaneously sells its profit-maximizing level of output—that is, that attaining a market share that brings down unit costs is not a fundamental business problem. In my view, the transformation of fixed costs into low unit costs is *the* fundamental challenge facing a business. For an elaboration, see Lazonick, *Business Organization.*

5. Lazonick, *Business Organization,* chap. 1.

6. See Kazuo Koike, "Human Resource Development and Labor–Management Relations," in Kozo Yamamura and Yasukichi Yasuba, eds., *The Political Economy of Japan,* vol. 1, *The Domestic Transformation* (Stanford University Press, Stanford, 1987); Kazuo Koike, *Understanding Industrial Relations in Modern Japan* (St. Martin's, New York, 1988), chap. 7; James C. Abegglen and George Stalk, Jr., *Kaisha, The Japanese Corporation* (Basic Books, New York, 1985). For a contrast between British and Japanese unions and industrial rela-

tions, see Ronard Dore, *British Factory–Japanese Factory: The Origins of Diversity in Industrial Relations* (University of California Press, Berkeley, 1973), chaps. 4–7.

7. See Koike, *Understanding,* chap. 4. On "organizational learning" more generally, see Ken-ichi Imai, Ikujiro Nonaka, and Horotaka Takeuchi, "Managing the New Product Development Process: How Japanese Companies Learn and Unlearn," in Kim B. Clark, Robert H. Hayes, and Christopher Lorenz, eds., *The Uneasy Alliance: Managing the Productivity–Technology Dilemma* (Harvard Business School Press, Boston, 1985).

8. Dore, *British Factory,* chap. 6; Abegglen and Stalk, *Kaisha,* pp. 195–198.

9. P. Sheard, "Auto Production Systems in Japan," *Papers of the Japanese Study Centre* (Monash, Australia) 8 (November 1983): 1–79; Ronald Dore, *Flexible Rigidities: Industrial Policy and Structural Adjustment in the Japanese Economy, 1970–1980* (Stanford University Press, Stanford, 1986), pt. 3; Michael Best, *The New Competition* (Polity Press, Cambridge, 1990), chap. 5; Michael J. Smitka, "Competitive Ties: Subcontracting in the Japanese Automobile Industry," *Business and Economic History,* 2nd ser., 19 (1990), forthcoming.

10. On the labor-force participation of Japanese women, see Linda N. Edwards, "Equal Employment Opportunity in Japan: A View from the West," *Industrial and Labor Relations Review* 41 (January 1988): 240–250. On the historical impact of family structure on the participation of men and women in the paid labor force, see Jane Humphries, "Class Struggle and the Persistence of the Working-Class Family," *Cambridge Journal of Economics* 1 September 1977): 241–258.

11. Andrew Ure, *The Philosophy of Manufactures* (Knight, London, 1835), p. 366.

12. See Claudia Goldin, "Monitoring Costs and Occupational Segregation by Sex: A Historical Analysis," *Journal of Labor Economics* 4 (January 1986): 1–27; Ruth Milkman, *Gender at Work: The Dynamics of Job Segregation by Sex during World War II* (University of Illinois Press, Urbana, 1987).

13. Milkman, *Gender.*

14. See Martin Bronfenbrenner and Yasukichi Yasuba, "Economic Welfare," in Yamamura and Yasuba, *Political Economy of Japan,* pp. 125–126. On the historical exploitation of Japanese women in industry, see E. Patricia Tsurumi, "Female Textile Workers and the Failure of Early Trade Unionism in Japan," *History Workshop* 18 (August 1984): 3–27.

15. Kathy Cannings and William Lazonick, "Equal Employment Opportu-

nity and the 'Managerial Woman' in Japan," *Barnard College Department of Economics Working Paper Series,* 90-3 (October 1989).

16. See Michael R. Reich, Yasuo Endo, and C. Peter Timmer, "Agriculture: The Political Economy of Structural Change," in McCraw, *America versus Japan;* Thomas K. McCraw and Patricia O'Brien, "Production and Distribution: Competition Policy and Industry Structure," in McCraw, *America versus Japan.* See also Koiji Taira, "Japan's Low Unemployment: Economic Miracle or Statistical Artifact?" *Monthly Labor Review* 106 (July 1983): 3–10.

17. Albert O. Hirschman, *Exit, Voice, and Loyalty: Responses to Decline of Firms, Organizations, and States* (Harvard University Press, Cambridge, Mass., 1970). For an application of the Hirschman framework to the "loyalty" of North American managers, see Kathy Cannings, "An Exit-Voice Model of Managerial Attachment," *Journal of Economic Behavior and Organization* 12 (July 1989): 107–129.

18. See Chapter 7, note 62.

19. Thomas E. Weisskopf, David M. Gordon, and Samuel Bowles, "Hearts and Minds: A Social Model of U.S. Productivity Growth," *Brookings Papers on Economic Activity* 2 (1983): 381–450; Juliet B. Schor, "Employment Rents and the Incidence of Strikes," *Review of Economics and Statistics* 69 (November 1987): 584–592; Juliet B. Schor, "Does Work Intensity Respond to Macroeconomic Variables: Evidence from British Manufacturing, 1970–1986," Harvard Institute of Economic Research Discussion Paper No. 1379, April 1988.

20. Michael Edwardes, *Back from the Brink* (Pan, London, 1983), pp. 216–217.

21. George A. Akerlof and Janet L. Yellen, eds., *Efficiency Wage Models of the Labor Market* (Cambridge University Press, New York, 1986); Lawrence F. Katz, "Efficiency Wage Theories: A Partial Evaluation," in Stanley Fischer, ed., *NBER Macroeconomics Annual 1986* (MIT Press, Cambridge, Mass., 1986).

22. The term *shirking* implies that the worker is supplying less effort than he or she had contracted to perform—a form of "cheating." See for example George A. Akerlof and Janet L. Yellen, "Introduction," in Akerlof and Yellen, *Efficiency Wage,* pp. 4–5. Employers may be prone to view restriction of output as "cheating," but workers will tend to view it as their prime means of *setting* output norms. Indeed, in contrast to employers' use of the term *shirking,* workers refer to the intentional slowdowns of the pace of work as "working to rule."

23. See Carl Shapiro and Joseph E. Stiglitz, "Equilibrium Unemployment as a Worker Discipline Device," in Akerlof and Yellen, *Efficiency Wage.*

24. For the radical perspective, see Samuel Bowles, "The Production Pro-

cess in a Competitive Economy: Walrasian, Neo-Hobbesian, and Marxian Models," *American Economic Review* 75 (March 1985): 16–36, and the references therein. For a useful attempt to question the mainstream assumptions for understanding a particularly important case, see Daniel M. G. Raff and Lawrence H. Summers, "Did Henry Ford Pay Efficiency Wages?" *Journal of Labor Economics* 5 (4, pt. 2) (October 1987): S57–S86.

25. On Marx, see Chapter 1. For modern Marxist orthodoxy on the capitalist use of technology to extract unremunerated effort from workers, see Harry Braverman, *Labor and Monopoly Capital: The Degradation of Work in the Twentieth Century* (Monthly Review Press, New York, 1974). More tentative are Samuel Bowles's remarks that capitalists may adopt "machine-paced production as a means of increasing the intensity of labor. In this case, costs may be lowered not only by producing more with the same inputs, but by extracting more of one of the inputs—labor—for the same price, and thus lowering the unit cost of labor." Bowles added that "machine-paced production may of course also be efficient," but he did not explicitly mention "effort-saving" as the characteristic of technological change that creates the possibility for total unit costs to fall even though workers earn higher wages and supply less effort than before the change in technology. Bowles, "Production Process," pp. 27–28.

26. For a more complete analysis of business organization, innovation, and competitive advantage, see Lazonick, *Business Organization*.

27. Joseph A. Schumpeter, *Capitalism, Socialism, and Democracy* (Harper & Row, New York, 1950), p. 106.

28. Martin Weitzman, *The Share Economy: Conquering Stagflation* (Harvard University Press, Cambridge, Mass., 1984).

29. Ibid., pp. 4–6.

30. Ibid., p. 146.

31. Ibid., p. 10.

32. Ibid., p. 11.

33. Alfred D. Chandler, Jr., *The Visible Hand: The Managerial Revolution in American Business* (Harvard University Press, Cambridge, Mass., 1977); Alfred D. Chandler, Jr., *Scale and Scope: The Dynamics of Industrial Capitalism* (Harvard University Press, Cambridge, Mass., 1990); Lazonick, *Business Organization*; Best, *New Competition*.

34. Weitzman, *Share Economy*, pp. 119–120.

35. Ibid., p. 108.

36. Ibid., pp. 74–76. Weitzman argued that "there is no evidence . . . that the prewar Japanese labor market was fundamentally different from other labor markets throughout the capitalist world. It has been well documented that lifetime employment, the bonus system, and the spe-

cial treatment of workers barely existed before the end of the war. Japan may have provided fertile soil, but the plant was not yet growing. Only in the postwar years, perhaps building on certain prewar tendencies and traditions, does the unique Japanese labor market system begin to emerge as a significantly distinct pattern." Ibid., pp. 75–76. I beg to differ. As argued in Chapter 9, the most innovative and substantial Japanese firms did accord many male blue-collar workers "special treatment" before World War II because of the need to develop and utilize their industrial skills. Key workers had "de facto" permanent employment before the war, even though enterprise unions had not yet arisen to institutionalize this long-term attachment and regularize the payment of group bonuses.

37. Robert B. Reich, *The Next American Frontier* (Penguin, New York, 1983); Michael J. Piore and Charles F. Sabel, *The Second Industrial Divide: Possibilities for Prosperity* (Basic Books, New York, 1984); Stephen S. Cohen and John Zysman, *Manufacturing Matters: The Myth of the Post-Industrial Economy* (Basic Books, New York, 1987); Ronald Dore, *Taking Japan Seriously: A Confucian Perspective on Leading Economic Issues* (Stanford University Press, Stanford, 1987); Charles C. Heckscher, *The New Unionism: Employee Involvement in the Changing Corporation* (Basic Books, New York, 1988). See also Beat Hotz-Hart, "Comparative Research and New Technology: Modernization in Three Industrial Relations Systems," in Richard Hyman and Wolfgang Streeck, eds., *New Technology and Industrial Relations* (Basil Blackwell, Oxford, 1988).

38. Some authors, most notably Michael Piore, Charles Sabel, and Jonathan Zeitlin, argued that, by creating the possibility for small-batch production, flexible technology had created a new role for small enterprise and a reassertion of control over the production process by the skilled worker within advanced capitalist economies. See Piore and Sabel, *Second Industrial Divide;* Charles Sabel and Jonathan Zeitlin, "Historical Alternatives to Mass Production: Politics, Markets, and Technology in Nineteenth-Century Industrialization," *Past and Present* 108 (August 1985): 133–176. On Japan, see David Friedman, "Beyond the Age of Ford: The Strategic Basis of Japanese Success in Automobiles," in John Zysman and Laura Tyson, eds., *American Industry in International Competition* (Cornell University Press, Ithaca, N.Y., 1983); David Friedman, *The Misunderstood Miracle: Industrial Development and Political Change in Japan* (Cornell University Press, Ithaca, N.Y., 1988). Slighted in the "flexible specialization" arguments is the role of planned coordination in creating the organizational structures, bound together by organizational commitments, within which so-called flexible specialists can develop and utilize their productive re-

sources. Over time, as the Japanese have shown, these integrated organizations, their specialist firms tightly linked to an already dominant mass producer through organizational commitments, have been able to capture world markets through what I have called "flexible mass production," including the use of skilled workers in combination with flexible machinery to generate economies of both scale and scope on the shop floor. See Chapter 9. For the tendency of "flexible specialization" to degenerate into "market flexibility" in Britain, see Richard Hyman, "Flexible Specialization: Miracle or Myth?" in Hyman and Streeck, *New Technology*. Stephen Cohen and John Zysman's distinction between dynamic and static flexibility appears to be similar to my distinction between organizational flexibility and market flexibility. See Cohen and Zysman, *Manufacturing Matters*, pp. 131–134.

39. Dore, *Taking Japan;* Dore, *Flexible Rigidities*.
40. Dore, *Flexible Rigidities*, p. 6.
41. Clark, Hayes, and Lorenz, *Uneasy Alliance*.
42. See William Lazonick, "Financial Commitment and Economic Performance: Ownership and Control in the American Industrial Corporation," *Business and Economic History*, 2nd ser. 17 (1988): 115–128; William Lazonick, "Controlling the Market for Corporate Control: The Historical Significance of Managerial Capitalism," paper presented to the Third International Joseph A. Schumpeter Society Conference, Airlie, Va., June 3–5, 1990.
43. Samuel Bowles and Herbert Gintis, *Schooling in Capitalist America* (Basic Books, New York, 1976).
44. See William Julius Wilson, *The Truly Disadvantaged: The Inner City, the Underclass, and Public Policy* (University of Chicago Press, Chicago, 1987); Louis Ferleger, "Explaining Away Black Poverty: The Structural Determinants of Black Employment," in Richard Goldstein and Stephen M. Sacks, eds., *Applied Poverty Research: Who Benefits?* (Rowan & Allenheld, New York, 1983).
45. On U.S. indebtedness to Japan, see Daniel Burstein, *Yen!: Japan's New Financial Empire and Its Threat to America* (Simon & Schuster, New York, 1988).

Index